TRIBUTES OF THE AMERICAN ACADEMY

COMMEMORATIVE
TRIBUTES
OF THE AMERICAN
ACADEMY OF ARTS
AND LETTERS
1905-1941

Essay Index Reprint Series

BOOKS FOR LIBRARIES PRESS
FREEPORT, NEW YORK

LIBRARY OF CONGRESS CATALOG CARD NUMBER:
68-20286
PRINTED IN THE UNITED STATES OF AMERICA

THE COMMEMORATIVE TRIBUTES IN THIS

VOLUME HAVE BEEN REPRINTED FROM

THE ORIGINAL PAMPHLETS ISSUED AT IN-

TERVALS DURING THE YEARS 1905-1941

LIST OF THE TRIBUTES

1905-1912

CHARLES FOLLEN McKIM

CHARLES ELIOT NORTON

JOHN QUINCY ADAMS WARD

THOMAS BAILEY ALDRICH

JOSEPH JEFFERSON

BY WILLIAM MILLIGAN SLOANE

THE KEENEST enjoyment of a finer mind is in whatever makes the absent and unreal present and apparent. This emotion is basic to all the fine arts without exception, for it gives almost unhampered play to the imagination, to the representative faculties, which embody without the limit and clog of matter that subtle essence which in successive stages of social development is felt to be beautiful. Poetry, painting, and sculpture, the imitative arts, do this manifestly; less patently, but even more poignantly, do likewise music and architecture. Whatever the inner structure of the music, the resultant voice of its production arouses emotions which in their very vagueness are universal and to the initiated almost articulate, which entrance because they summon thoughts and visions from sources never before tapped and often unsuspected to exist. Architecture, aside from the categorical imperative of utility to which it is subject, presents to the eye, as music to the ear, intricate combinations that likewise afford a unitary resultant free from the trammels of imitation, which abstractedly and vaguely lures the mind into a sense of proportion and sublimity that awakens spiritual aspiration.

These familiar and generally accepted views are recalled

I

to connect the commemoration of Charles Follen McKim with those of the founders who preceded him in their passage to the beyond. It is noteworthy as an aid to memory that our great composer and our great architect were in recollection left to us and to posterity as comrades in time and activity, the one with world renown for his appeal to humanity through the trained ear, the other with similar fame through his command of the trained eye. Both have been honored in other lands than this, their local fame has been carried to the stars by appreciative fellow-laborers and by a national public. What posterity may decide we know not, but the test of genius is as fully in the inspiration and stimulus given to the present age as it is in the instruction and the plaudits of succeeding ones. In this respect McKim stands forth a preëminent figure. His life began in a heroic epoch of tumult and national reform, and ended in an age of struggle for emancipation from materialism and its complementary tension of nervous exaltation. Throughout he stood apart, a citizen of the nation and of the world, detached from the popular movement, as had been his ancestry, but keenly observant of the slowly forming aspiration of society toward permanence of institutions and the equilibrium of mind and matter, of soul and body, of social and personal balance. Historically minded in the highest degree, he marked the moment of his nation's birth, the stock of which it was a mighty bough, the forms in which its already ancient civilization had then expressed itself. He felt intense interest in the divagations of national taste, in the evidences of contrition for structural faults in politics and art, in the eclecticism which was proof of a search for garments that would fit, in the freaks of selection or abortion which were misnamed pure American, in the totality of effort, conscious or unconscious, for a place in the procession of nations and ages. In short he was a profound student, a shrewd observer, a man of meditation and philosophy before he became the poetic creator which he finally was. This was the spiritual and intellectual training which drew upon him the attention of his fellows, of his own people, of craftsmen and artists beyond the sea. The sincerity and vigor of his art made him the prophet of a school, much, there is reason to believe, against his will. But the greatness which was his own having once been recognized and leadership having been thrust upon him, he did not shrink from the responsibility. During his ripest years he was hospitable to collaboration, receptive to all assistance from the ancillary arts, catholic in association and taste. Commanding his clients, personal, corporate, or national, he dominated them and their commissions by force of character and the array of proof. It was thus that he made the capital city of his country one focus of his ellipse, her metropolis the other. For both the lines of architectural development in present and future work were convincingly set forth by weighty argument. And for one generation at least the public taste was directed toward the beginnings of national architecture in those modifications of Georgian and classical style which seemed to him in further evolution likely to furnish the perfect garb for the faith and ambition of his land, the solid substance of the vision vouchsafed to a people who had asserted partnership in the affairs of the world. For politics, for commerce, and for the fine arts he left symbolic structures: the War College, the Pennsylvania station, the Morgan library, all of which exhibit complicated unity, sensibility in structure, refinement in decoration, and adequacy in mass. These alone would suffice as permanent foundation for his fame as a creative artist. Space forbids the enumeration of his works in other fields of human life; they are quite as illustrious each in its own way—his homes for the club, the family, the church.

THE WARY writer does not venture in these days to give any positive definition of beauty. Men do many, many things in play solely because they choose to do them. In pleasing themselves they give permanent delight to many others. The elect few or many have the instinct of these, but the multitude yearns to have the matter set forth in syllogism. The average taste is not the best, somehow; the average man desires to know both why he should admire the compositions of MacDowell and the buildings of McKim. He ought to be told, he ought to hear, how the born artist or poet is further trained, to what point this training is general, where it becomes individual, and finally the secret mystery of personal liberty, the emancipation at last from tradition, rule, maxim; the portal through which genius alone may enter and bring forth for common use that which is fine and is art, the fine arts of music or architecture, of sculpture, painting, or poetry, all of which lift us into the realm of imagination. This is the work of the critic. Put flatly, it is his business to point out alike the faults and beauties of each. Long since in the fine arts, as in every other sphere of human activity, authority reigned supreme, and within the memory of man it was discarded. The critic dare no longer deal in positive standards: high and low alike flout them. He can appeal to the indefinite and negative, the cautious groping of superior minds, to the enthusiasms of one generation, to the reactions of the next.

This was the sense in which Charles Eliot Norton was preëminently a critic. In every fiber of his being he was sensitive and alive. Like McKim, he was of reforming stock, he of the English Puritan type, the other of the Scotch; both rebels born, against complacency and sham, both intense, impatient, fecund. The one was a devotee of fine art in literature, just as the other was in architecture. Norton from the beginning exhibited in his attitude the furthest degree of revolt from spiritual and intellectual authority. His Unitarian ancestry made him an ultra protester, his fine education made him exquisite in taste, his strength as a reasoner made him both a cautious and somewhat precious writer as well as a caustic and convincing critic. Nothing argues higher training in a fertile mind than the capacity for substitution and for the transubstantiation of itself. This Norton could do. He was a man of the Renaissance projected into the nineteenth century, an Italian in subtlety, a Briton of the Preraphaelite type, an American in his innate contempt for medievalism. His profession was the research and the instruction of history as revealed in the long, unsophisticated record of the human soul manifesting itself through art. Since art is the untrammeled play of the spirit, men have evolved what pleased them for the time in ornament, in drawing, in form generally, and in color. The record of the fine arts, pure or applied, is therefore truer and more legible than any other. What Norton taught about this was fascinating, his transmutation of himself at every epoch was alchemy. He was Hellenist in the Greek air when he breathed it; his Italian was impeccable; his Dante scholarship not only rich, but supreme; he was so Victorian that Ruskin and Carlyle were under his spell, and so American that he was a motive power in the Boston school of letters at its apogee. This must not be mistaken for versatility. On the contrary, the basic concept of a Puritan soul is immediacy, and to every exhibit of the man-power in action he was subtly sensitive and sensible. It was the comprehensiveness of the scholar. What he had not, and what he disdained, was spiritual feeling; for those who groped after the unknown he was intolerant; for the exercise of finite powers the finite world was quite a sufficient field, and in that field the relation of man to his environment was to him more important than the learning of theology, with which he was saturated as a boy, and against which in manhood he rebelled with the distaste of satiety. They say there are only three metropolitan cities, London, Paris, and New York, since the inhabitant of any one will gladly abuse and join in abuse of his own, so secure is he in its supremacy that he fears no attack on it, and refuses to assume the defensive. Norton was in this very high sense a patriot: as a fellow-member wrote of him recently, he became so convinced of his country's place in history that to correct its bumptiousness, prune its exuberance, and train its powers was to him a cheerful duty. Its art and its literature expressed to him the degrees of his people's civilization: to direct, to warn, to stimulate, he understood to be imperative on all who had the trained gift, and sloth in that regard he detested. He was almost an academy in himself, authoritative and fearless, a man of the academic type.

I N MARKED contrast to him was our great sculptor John Quincy Adams Ward. Put to the categorical question, he would probably have admitted the value of all the esthetic disciplines—those of the amateur, the philosopher, and the critic; he would have admitted also the existence and the validity of rules and axioms. But neither the rule nor the trained beholder was his first concern. Each instance presented to him a separate and absorbing problem, to be solved only by the communings of the individual artist with that particular task. The rule was well as far as it goes, but the test of the rule is the exception. Hence the interest of Ward's work in its varied, widely varied aspects.

Educated in American studios, unfamiliar in early life with great original creations of any epoch, he studied casts or pictures, read descriptions, and worked as opportunity came. As a craftsman he secured a manual training so fine that it gave restraint to his exuberant fancy. So far as he can be identified with a school he was a Hellenist and classical. To subjective, suggestive, impressionist sculpture he was utterly strange. In the pediment of the Stock Exchange in New York his genius reached its climax. He could not bear the restraint of low relief, scarcely of high, and those virile figures, each a superb American type, stand out full in the round with only a suggestion of attachment to the architecture which they adorn. His work is objective to the highest degree, and stands in close relation not only to the trained but to the average beholder by the conviction of reality which it enforces on the human eye.

Ward thoroughly understood the American public, and to that public he addressed himself, and was understood. Some of his ideas were no doubt alien to those generally cherished by the members of his guild, and it remains so far true that in the heroic and monumental he was not always at his best, so instinctive was his feeling for measure and proportion; but in what was purely statuesque, in breadth and scale, in the realization of his vision, he could and did accomplish what few have done, and was thus defiant of criticism. His knowledge and his sympathy were comprehensive, and his gift of expression was uncommon. A true democrat, he was not indifferent to the noisy, insistent self-assertion of mediocrity, for he knew its power in forming public opinion. Hence he never permitted himself to be silenced by its wearisome iteration. To it he often addressed himself with trenchant language, and as a rule came off triumphant against the cuckoo throng. There was nothing of what is styled in art the precious about his temperament or his work.

T HE MAN whose name is next on our honor-roll was neither an interpreter of national aspiration, nor a stern judge of taste and manners, nor yet a prophet with a message to the Philistine. His was the joy of holding up the mirror to three stages in a national evolution.

Our distinctively American literature dates from 1830. For the most part the books published this side the sea had been cheap reprints of foreign writings. The few native writers of importance unconsciously found inspiration in the European volumes which were their intellectual nourishment. But two generations of republican-democrats had now produced a third, which was the offspring of American tradition and education. Insensibly the literary and artistic output was more and more expressive of the environment in which it was engendered, and, the process once begun, the American quality grew more and more intense, until even British models were utterly neglected. There is of course a common and enduring element in all literature, especially in poetry, but the fine essence becomes in time peculiarly national, even local, and sometimes parochial. The doorstep poet is often preëminent-

ly the more extensive in his art because so intensive and penetrating in that mystery of vision and insight which creates
not alone verse or rhythm or cadence or musical regularity;
but recreates, represents, and gives definition to what was,
but is not, to what is imagined, but not yet found. Born in this
transition, and nurtured in the new American life, Aldrich
became the bond of union between the three cohorts of
American writers—those of the early nineteenth century,
those of the later generation, which again were finding inspiration amid novel conditions subsequent to the Civil War,
and the very last, which discovers a people imperious in temper, interested in itself as never before, and aware of a nationality that embraces the breeding-stocks of every race and
clime. To the soul of this new people, to its abode, to its mus-
ing, to its energizing, present and coming interpreters must
direct their attention and find for it some voice.

Throughout the long career of his authorship Aldrich was
an attentive listener to the men, a careful observer of the
nature, among whom and amid which he found himself. His
theme was neither one nor the other, but the interrelations
of both, the man personally and socially both in his home and
in his habitat. At twenty he published a fugitive piece of
verse which was so appreciated that he was encouraged to
further literary effort, and for half a century his pen was busy.
Throughout that long period he was the exemplification of
the artist in literature. The writing impulse was intermittent:
his genius was not in perpetual bloom, his fruitage was irreg-
ular. But from first to last he was intimate with his own production, which, though never academic, was alert against
crudity, and careful in workmanship; he was himself a stern
critic of what he made public. The sense of spontaneity which
his readers felt was due to his art. In long parturition he
matured his thought, and found the intimate connection
between conception in idea and the expression of it in verbal
signs which alone gives reality through sight and hearing.
Born in New Hampshire and by the accident of his father's

8

business demands a Louisianian in childhood, it was New York which made him an elect journalist, an author of promise. Boston summoned him, and his powers ripened in New England, whence he sprang. Conscientious in his study of contemporary literature, he was sensitive also to European movements. Hence his work as a whole possesses much variety in its essential unity, and is marked by the charm and grace of wide experience. There is little that is polemic in it, and most of it bears the stamp of Arcadian lightness. There were times when he ate his bread in tears, but his inborn joyousness consigned the influences of trial for the most part to oblivion. His drama is never tragic, because melancholy of the sort that grips was not natural, and, when insistent, was due to causes which could be and were dismissed by force of will. Nor is either his poetry or his prose stamped with the hall-mark of passion. Prosperity was essentially and peculiarly his blessing, and the permanent elements of his genius exhibit the temporary emergence of American letters into the blithe upper air from out the storm-and-stress period in which they began, and again from beneath the desperate urgency in which they struck the war-note during the struggle of the Civil War.

UPON THE question whether the true actor is or is not the creator of his part there will be long discussion in the future as in the past. But in any case the actor who loses himself in his part is lost indeed, for he is no longer the master of that by which he creates, to wit: his gesture, his speech, and his costume. On the contrary, he has become their slave, and is the creature, not the creator. Into this pit Joseph Jefferson, third and greatest of his name, fourth of his stock likewise to be a player, never fell. His personality was so genial, his soul so kind and appreciative, his quality so sensitive, his humor so good, and his heart so true, that to outward and surface seeming his heredity blended completely with his environment, and the beholder felt as if the actor and the character

portrayed were one. But those who were favored with his intimacy knew quite to the contrary. Within that capacious brow
and in the convolutions of that spacious brain was a mind of
grasp and penetration, its own severest critic, sternest judge,
and fairest jury. His great rôles were neither the imaginings
of the author nor his own. From the powers of the playwright,
the manager, and the interpreter was made a careful selection for securing the resultant which we all saw and at which
we all wondered. The performances, moreover, were not
iterations or repetitions: each stood out by itself, marked by
little whimsical touches of genius which made every presentation of the dramatic tale a new experience to the playgoer.
To have seen Jefferson once in a part was the sure induce-
ment to seeing him again and again and again in the same
part. Autopsies and the use of the knife do not reveal genius,
nor does wordy analysis. To be great in any line requires a
great man. To this the actor is no exception. Our greatest
American actors have been great men off the stage as well as
on it, fit for any Olympian circle. Jefferson could be judged
by his intimacies and by his avocation of painting almost as
well as by the art in which he was so grand a master. He was
a worthy comrade in conversation with statesmen, with writers, with creative minds of every kind, thoroughly versed in
the ways of men throughout the past and at the present hour.
His amusements were varied, and among other recreations
was that of outdoor sport: his prowess as an angler admitted
him to high circles of the gentle art, and there his lighter
gifts found the freest play. But his painting was almost a passion, and while he remained an amateur to the end, there was
depth and breadth in his composition, a revel of color in his
spaces, and great suggestiveness in the moods of nature as he
sought to present them. Solitude in the forest, careless ease
in the use of brush and pigment, a temperament disposed to
gentle melancholy, given these, and you have the design and
purpose together with the handicraft of the actor-painter.
His life was opulent in friends and in worldly success; his

hand was open to relieve the embarrassments of his fellows; the reservoir of his gladness to lend a hand was overflowing.

Of the five men thus briefly and inadequately commemorated, all belong to the eight selected by the original seven as coadjutors. But the fifteen were equals in power on their respective fields of activity, and the men of our list were peers and compeers of their contemporaries. Widely different in vocation, they were strangely alike in the Americanism which alone can and does give quality to our Academy, which seeks to associate men eminent not in one, but in all of the fine arts.

AUGUSTUS SAINT-GAUDENS
EDMUND CLARENCE STEDMAN
SAMUEL LANGHORNE CLEMENS
JOHN HAY
EDWARD MacDOWELL

BY BRANDER MATTHEWS

THREESCORE YEARS ago and more Emerson declared that in this country literature suffered from a lack of companionship. "If something like the union of like-minded men were attempted, as formerly at Will's or Button's coffee-houses, or in the back room of the bookseller's shop, where scholars might meet scholars without passing the picket and guard-post of etiquette, it would add happy hours to the year." What Emerson asserted of literature was equally true of the other arts which adorn life. Perhaps we may go further and say that if it is wholesome for the practitioners of any single craft to get together and thus to create an atmosphere of common endeavor, it is beneficial also for men of varied interests to be drawn closer for that unconscious stimulus which one art may exert upon another. The poet may thus borrow color from his commerce with the painter, and the historian may find his imagination stirred by association with the sculptor.

> All arts are one,—all branches on one tree,—
> All fingers, as it were, upon one hand.

The necessity for that union of like-minded men which Emerson wished for was felt by many of us; and in time it led to the organization of the National Institute of Arts and Letters, wherein every one of the arts was fully represented. The Institute was established in 1898; and year by year its membership was enlarged until in time it enrolled almost every one of the leaders in their several callings. Then in 1904, in order to give greater definiteness to its work of protecting and furthering literature and the other arts, the Institute believed itself strong enough at last to found the American Academy of Arts and Letters. It confided the election of the later associates to a chosen seven of its own members, whose right there was none to dispute,—William Dean Howells, Augustus Saint-Gaudens, Edmund Clarence Stedman, John La Farge, Samuel Langhorne Clemens, John Hay, and Edward MacDowell,—a seven-branched candlestick on the altar of art.

These seven accepted the duty of adding to themselves eight others, and to these fifteen was intrusted the further obligation of extending their numbers to twenty. Then this first score, thus cautiously selected, slowly expanded our membership to half a hundred, which is to be the limit for the present. It was upon the first seven that lay the major part of the responsibility; and if this American Academy is to endure, if it is to accomplish its honorable purpose, and if it is to become a power for good in the land, we shall stand eternally indebted to the seven men who bore the burden and heat of the day and who laid the solid foundation for the future.

It was Joseph de Maistre who once declared that "the fatherland—*la patrie*—is an association on the same soil of the living and the dead, with those who are yet to be born." We hold that every man should be loyal to his fatherland; and by this word we do not mean merely so much of the earth's surface arbitrarily set off by political boundaries; we have in mind ever the men who have made our country worth living in and worth dying for. We mean also and always the lofty traditions they have transmitted to us, the high ideals they cherished, and the noble examples they have bequeathed.

This American Academy of Arts and Letters is already an association of the living and the dead; and we have a firm hope that it will abide to be an association with those yet to be born. Of the seven men to whom the task of its organization was intrusted only six years ago, six have already left us. They died full of years and also full of honors, for they had survived long enough to win wide recognition for their services to their fellow-countrymen and to the world outside our borders.

As we draw nearer to the end of the journey of life, we find that every milestone is a tombstone, with a friend buried beneath it. One by one they have left us; we are the lonelier for their departure, as we are also the richer for what they did and for what they were. We may have recognized their worth while they were still with us, and yet a false shame may have prevented the adequate expression of our appreciation. Now they are gone, and it is too late for them to learn the high esteem in which we held them and to savor the grateful incense of our praise. None the less is it now our duty to express this esteem, to voice this approbation, and to declare our ample regard for their achievements. Here we can take pattern by the French, who preserve the classical standard of propriety. For more than two centuries and a half it has been the honored custom of the French Academy to require that every man elected to its membership shall pronounce the eulogy of the deceased member to whose seat he has succeeded. Perhaps in the future this worthy tradition may establish itself in the American Academy of Arts and Letters.

To-day, however, it is my solemn task to commemorate five of the seven founders of this Academy. Their fame is secure. To them it matters little what may now be said in praise of them or of their achievements; and it is not for their sake, but for ours, that we pay them this tribute. They were chiefs in their several callings, Saint-Gaudens the sculptor and MacDowell the musician, Stedman the poet-critic and Mark Twain the humorist-moralist, John Hay the historian, who was also a statesman. They were all my friends, and on me is laid the sad duty of tendering to them our last greeting.

SAINT-GAUDENS, like so many Americans, came of commingled stocks. He was at once French and Irish, and perhaps he drew from ancestors so dissimilar some part of his varied endowment. He acquired at first the delicate craft of the cameo-cutter; and it may be that he owed to this early training the exquisite quality of his later portraits in low relief. Then he underwent a strenuous apprenticeship as a sculptor. He was able to achieve the union of strength and refinement. There is a stark virility in his single figures, standing or seated, and a masculine vigor in his mounted men. He was an insatiable artist, resolutely grappling with technical problems and untiring in seeking a fit solution. He was not easily satisfied with what he had wrought, being ever hungry for an intangible perfection. Sir Joshua Reynolds, having in mind his own art of the portrait-painter, so closely akin to that of the sculptor, once asserted that a man could put into a face only what he had in himself. And this test Saint-Gaudens withstood triumphantly, for the faces he modeled have power and beauty and grace.

EDMUND CLARENCE STEDMAN

STEDMAN was a poet who was prevented by adverse circumstances from giving his whole heart to poesy. In the battle-years of half a century ago he served for a season as a war-correspondent, and for the rest of his life he bore himself valiantly on the firing-line of another battle-field, where the fighting was as fierce, even though the weapons were bloodless. He allowed himself to be tempted from poetry to prose, and the larger part of the scant leisure he could snatch from the turmoil of the market he surrendered to literary criticism. He devoted loyal and laborious years to the evaluation of contemporary poets, his masters and his rivals. This criticism was the more intimate, the more searching, the more inspiring, because he was himself a poet with an instinctive understanding of the aims of the lyric artist and of the secrets of the art. To poetry, which he worshipped, he could give only the remnants of his busy life; and it is a marvel that he was able to achieve what he did. He hung an ode upon Hawthorne, like Orlando in the Forest of Arden; and he evoked the quaint figure of Pan in Wall Street, piping like Orpheus to charm the strange beasts which roam at large through that disenchanted thoroughfare. If we apply to him the loftiest standard, as he would have wished us to do, he may not have been a great poet; but he was a true poet, with a true poet's directness of vision and certainty of touch.

MARK TWAIN—for it is idle to give him any other name than that which he had made for himself—grew up in the Middle West, settling at last in the East while he was yet young. With his own eyes he saw many aspects of American life, and what he had seen he recorded with unforgettable felicity. He had a sturdy simplicity of phrase. Abundant humor was his as well as abundant good humor. From faithful transcripts of travel and adventure he turned in time to story-telling, to a fiction as faithful and as immitigably veracious as his earlier descriptions of things actually seen by himself. With the advancing years he ripened and mellowed;

and the melancholy which sustained the fun of Cervantes and Molière and Swift was his also. He revealed the same piercing insight into the weakness of human nature which they possessed. A master of narrative, he was also a master of style; and underlying his stories there was a deep feeling for the meaning of life. A great humorist he was, beyond all question, controlling the springs of laughter; but he was also a profound moralist, with a scorching contempt for many of the meannesses of our common humanity.

JOHN HAY led a career of unusual variety, and revealed a versatility characteristic of America. He began as the secretary of Lincoln. Then he went abroad to fill a minor post in the diplomatic service. He returned to write a graphic description of Spain and to labor awhile on a newspaper. He dropped into poetry, and composed a group of Pike County Ballads, vigorous in episode, picturesque in character, and racy in vernacular terseness. Then, like the earlier American historians Parkman and Motley, he adventured himself in fiction; and his story, anonymous as it was, met with a wider approval than theirs. But he devoted the full strength of his maturity to the life of the great chief he had served in his youth, to the history of the American who had made history. Finally he came back to the service of the nation and took charge of our foreign affairs at a critical moment. By a striking coincidence, the author of the life of him who had saved this country from disunion was able himself to preserve from dismemberment an ancient Oriental empire.

MACDOWELL was the youngest of the seven founders of this American Academy, and he was also the youngest to die, untimely taken off before his work was done and perhaps even before his genius had achieved its fullest expansion. He was the foremost of American composers, with a fragrant originality of his own. He was also the first to win wide recognition abroad. His compositions had marked individuality; they were modern and yet classic. His music was poetry, for he had the vision and the faculty divine. He had the sensitiveness of the poet, and the poet's delicacy of perception as well; and he possessed also the structural simplicity which we discover in the masterpieces of the major poets. The true lyrist's integrity of workmanship he had in addition, doing nothing in haste or at random, and holding himself always to the severest standard of artistic perfection. Although he had early reaped the reward of his work, and although success had come to him, he was not led astray by it. He went on his lonely way uncontaminated by applause, as though he had taken to heart the wise saying of Confucius which bids us "rate the task above the prize."

Such they were, the five men of varied achievement whom it is my privilege to commemorate to-day. They aspired each in his own way to an Attic excellence, and they left us examples of Attic urbanity. The Athenians, so Dionysius of Halicarnassus declared, "made gentle the life of the world." And this praise might be bestowed also on these five Americans. They differed widely in their accomplishments and in their aims, but they had the grace of urbanity. And they had in common one other characteristic: they had all of them the full flavor of the soil of their nativity; they were intensely American. Perhaps their careers were most of them possible only in this New World, cut off from ancient Europe by the wide leagues of the Western ocean. They were American in nothing more than in their avoidance of overt eccentricity and in their desire to be judged by standards not local, but cosmopolitan and universal. Stedman once told me that he had prepared his volume on the Victorian poets so that he might feel free afterward to write his book on the American poets; and MacDowell refused to allow his works to be performed in a concert of exclusively American music, insisting that it had to hold its own without any adventitious support of patriotic prejudice in favor of a native composer.

Washington Irving was the earliest of our men of letters to win acceptance abroad, and he explained modestly that some part of the welcome he received from our kin across the sea was due to the surprise of the British at discovering an American with a quill in his hand instead of a feather in his hair. It is always difficult for Europeans to perceive that although we may be a young nation, our artists have had as many forebears as those of any other stock. We are the legitimate inheritors of the best of the past; and to be ourselves, to be intensely American, we do not need to assert any violent and freakish originality. We are the heirs of the ages; and we have all the mighty men of old as our artistic ancestors. Sometimes the kinship with the foreigner is very close; it is scarcely too much to say that Rousseau was a collaborator of the writer of the Declaration of Independence and that Montesquieu was one of the authors of the Constitution.

These five Americans, the sculptor, the musician, and the three authors, were glad to continue the transmitted traditions of their several arts and to labor in honorable rivalry with their fellow-craftsmen in other lands. And yet, although they might profit by all that had been wrought by those who had gone before both here and abroad, they were rooted in the land of their birth. They proved by their works that the arts can flourish here in our own new country; and they themselves were "new births of our new soil."

RICHARD WATSON GILDER
JOEL CHANDLER HARRIS
EDWARD EVERETT HALE
CARL SCHURZ
WINSLOW HOMER

BY HAMILTON W. MABIE

O F THE five members of the Academy whom it is my privilege to commemorate, four, showed how local is the maxim of the specialists that a man can do only one thing well, and reinforced the ancient opinion that talent of a high order is a force that can be applied successfully along several lines of aptitude and interest. Richard Watson Gilder was a poet, an editor, and a man of those affairs which concern the common welfare; and in each of these capacities his work was memorable. His formal education did not go beyond the old-fashioned seminary, but his vital education was a by-product of all his activities. The bugle sounded in his youth, but there were more commanding calls for him. Journalism afforded him a brief apprenticeship in preparation for the editorial direction of *Hours at Home,* of *Scribner's Monthly,* and finally of the *Century Magazine,* a connection of life-long duration and of effective service to the rising art and widening literature of the country. His nature was quick to respond to the unspoken appeal of neglected children and to the evil conditions of over-crowded tenements; he was a citizen whose ideals sent him into most laborious and painstaking work, and inspired him with the vision of a city that should be clean, wholesome, and beautiful. Organized decency and organized art found in him an apostle whose gifts of mind and of character made him a leader; while the activity of his hands and the deep stirrings of his heart enriched his poetry and gave it a fine sincerity, a moving sense of brotherhood with

RICHARD WATSON GILDER

men in their various fortunes. The slender volumes of verse
in which his life and art find record have been gathered into
a single book of lyrics; for he was a song-writer after the older
English fashion. His sensitive imagination; his delicate touch,
invigorated by conviction and thought; his artistic temperament, enamoured of the beautiful and drawn to new and
freer poetic forms, gave his verse vitality and charm, half-
pathetic and half-prophetic of the better fortunes of the race
to come.

"BORN AND bred in a brier-patch" in middle Georgia, like
Brer Rabbit, it was the good fortune of Joel Chandler
Harris to play in the fields he was to describe, to live with
the characters whose local traits piqued the curiosity of the
world, and to overhear a new kind of fairy-tale, the romance
of which lay in natural cunning, in a humor abounding,
spontaneous, and original, and in a philosophy so domestic
and familiar that it became an informal wisdom of life. His
path to his vocation, as in the case of many another man of
original gift, made credible the homely adage that might have
come from his own cornfields—the longest way round is the
shortest way there. He set type, read law, became an editor
of a leading Southern journal, and wrote books as original in
substance, quaint in style, and rich in human interest as the
countryside of which they form an authentic and enduring
record. Uncle Remus is one of the real figures in American
literature. He is a raconteur of legends which are as classic in
their way and place as the *Arabian Nights*. These tales, full
of appeal to the imagination of children and to the memory
of their elders, preserve the humor and wisdom of a vanished social condition; and Uncle Remus emerging from the
romanticism and tragedy of the ante-bellum period and the
cheap exaggeration of the minstrel-show that followed the
war, attains the dignity of the protagonist of a vanished type
—the plantation negro. In apparent unconsciousness, Uncle
Remus shows us the reaction of slavery on the slave: his

easy, care-free attitude; his humorous philosophy born of helplessness; his kindliness; his homely sagacity of the cabin and the cotton-field; his shrewd observation of the people he served, and his keen thrusts at their foibles and weaknesses; his sense of the mystery of the animal world, and his primitive relation with it; the pathos of the struggle of the weak against the strong; and the never-failing spirit of mischievous fun in which the powerful and alert are outwitted and disarmed. Uncle Remus, Daddy Jake, Brer Rabbit, and Tiddy will be *ex-officio* members of the folklore societies for all time to come; but they belong to literature, and their creator to the group of those Americans who have made original contributions to literature.

THE RANGE of social and climatic conditions in this country could hardly be more strikingly brought out than in the contrast between Joel Chandler Harris, the faithful recorder of a cross-section of Georgia life, and Edward Everett Hale, the New Englander who became neighbor to the whole country. The stamp of New England education was on Dr. Hale from the beginning. He came of a family notable for intelligence and individuality of character; he was born in Boston; he was prepared for college in the Latin School; he was graduated from Harvard; he studied theology and entered the Unitarian ministry. During a long life of varied and tireless activities his home was in Roxbury. He was predestined to be an editor, and knew how to set type almost as soon as his head was level with the case. He loved history, and wrote it as a journalist writes of the events of the day. He was a story-teller by nature, and wrote tales as if he were writing history. He had something of Defoe's gift of giving fiction the simple and convincing detail of fact. He was never an exact writer; but he had a genius for getting at the truth. He was neither emotional nor dramatic; but his heart was in his work of whatever kind, and he was a rare preacher of the gospel of helpfulness. His aim was practical, he was never a student of style, his strength lay in invention rather than in imagination; but it was his good fortune to write a short story so close to the facts of human nature that it almost defies the endeavor to class it with fiction. *The Man Without a Country* has the pathos of a tragedy of personal life, staged so simply that it escapes all suggestion of artifice, and, unless duly authenticated as fiction, it will some day be read as history. A citizen of one of the centers of light and leading in the New World, Dr. Hale was brother to all men; in the informal, unconventional society of America he accepted the ultimate inferences of democracy not with the timidity of the man of academic training, but with the joyful courage of a serene faith in the spiritual worth of humanity. He organized helpfulness as if it were the chief business of mankind, wrote its legends and text-books, and spoke and acted as if society were a league of men and women bent on helping instead of preying upon one another. He had the saving common sense, the habit of industry, and the illuminating humor of one to whom men as men were dear and companionable.

THE CONTRIBUTIONS of Germany to thought and life in this country were less evident in the early stages of our history than those of England, Holland, and France; but since the awakening of American intelligence to its intellectual isolation in the decade between 1820 and 1830, German philosophy, poetry, and music have formed probably the most powerful single stream of influence that has come to us from Europe. Quite as important has been the addition to our population of a host of men and women of German blood and education, and foremost among American citizens of German breeding was Carl Schurz. He was a student in the University of Bonn when his love of liberty took him into the ranks of the revolutionists in 1848. He came to this country in 1852, and was admitted to the bar; but he was irresistibly swept into the anti-slavery movement, and so into the field of political action. He was a convincing and lucid speaker, and his advocacy was an effective reinforcement of the anti-slavery party. When the great debate ended and the war began, he served with credit as an officer in the field. After a successful career as a journalist, he entered the United States Senate, where his trained intelligence and power of statement gave him both popular reputation and legislative influence; while his political idealism and independence made him the advocate of reform in the civil service and in party organization, of sound money, of tariff for revenue only, and of the Independent movement, which has raised the standards of public service and political action in this country.

Mr. Schurz's work as a writer was marked by candor, intelligence, and distinction of tone and manner. His *Life of Henry Clay* lacked the intimacy with local conditions which a man born on the soil of which Clay was so characteristic a product would have given it; but it has genuine historical value and marked narrative interest. He was at variance with Lincoln on important points of policy during the war, and was not slow to express his dissent; but his monograph, written in later years and from riper knowledge, is an interpretation of Lincoln's character and career of permanent value. His most important contribution to literature is his *Reminiscences, 1829-1863,* written after his retirement from political and editorial activity, a memorable addition to the small group of American biographies which have the double value of historical record and personal narrative. The story of Mr. Schurz's life is an adventure of the spirit, told with clearness, vigor, and a strong infusion of personal quality. He was by training and breadth of interest a man of cosmopolitan temper; but he was an American in his devotion to popular government and his ardent service of what may be called applied freedom.

WINSLOW HOMER

Winslow Homer was a great personal force poured into a single channel. He was a painter by instinct and by intention. He was born in Boston in 1836, and spent his boyhood in Cambridge, which was then a New England village with open spaces ample for the out-of-door activities of a vigorous boy. Unusual skill as a draftsman gave him pleasure and training in childhood, and at the age of nineteen he was doing the artistic work of a lithographer's office. Two years later he was making illustrations; and in 1859 he had his own studio in New York, worked in the night class of the Academy of Design, and learned from Rondel how to set his palette and handle his brushes. His chance for original work came with the Army of the Potomac in 1865; and the series of pictures which he put on canvas, including *Prisoners from the Front,* made a deep impression by their vigorous technic and unaffected human feeling. From this direct dealing with the facts of life, Homer's work gained its distinctive note in American painting. He was an authentic and authoritative recorder of three or four phases of American life; daringly intimate, sincere, and frank. Largely self-educated, and unaffected by European associations, he was a painter of the New World whose clear vision made him an uncompromising truth-teller, and whose powerful imagination and vigorous technic emphasized his rugged strength. His studies of army life, of the massive ocean front of Maine, of Adirondack scenery, of men of elemental occupation and vigor,—sailors, soldiers, farmers, teamsters, negroes,—showed uncompromising fidelity to the fact vitally presented. He was an open-air, out-of-door painter of real men in primitive occupations and experiences; but his range was neither narrow nor one-sided. His later work was dramatic, powerful, at times almost brutal; but in earlier life he painted landscapes of idyllic and shimmering charm, combining at times the most vivid realism with the subtle skill that records the stir of the wind and the translucence of diffused sunlight.

No American painter has surpassed him in the ease with

which he lifts great waves and sends them crashing against the rocks with a force that fills the imagination with a deafening roar. Vigorous composition, bold use of color, passion for the elemental struggles of strong men, nature in moments of intense action, lay well within Homer's art; and to him was given the power to paint "the surge and thunder of the Odyssey." His nature was in the tone of his art: he was fearless, independent, unconventional, and loyal.

HORACE HOWARD FURNESS
HENRY CHARLES LEA
DONALD GRANT MITCHELL
DANIEL COIT GILMAN

BY ARTHUR TWINING HADLEY

Forty-one years ago Horace Howard Furness published his variorum edition of *Romeo and Juliet*. Within the compass of a single volume he brought together the materials and results of Shakespearean scholarship which the reader had hitherto been forced to seek in many books and many places. No such work had been done in England for half a century; no such work had ever been done in the United States.

What first impressed the critics was the comprehensiveness and thoroughness of the collection. It included whatever was worth including; it reproduced with accuracy whatever it quoted. But as time went on and as similar editions of other plays followed, the essential importance of Furness's own contributions came more and more into the foreground. His selection and quotation were marked by the spirit of the scholar. His own comment, brief as it often was, had, beside the merit of scholarship, the added charm of literary form.

On both shores of the Atlantic it was recognized that we had here a man who understood Shakespeare and could help to the world's understanding of him, a man of letters in his own right. And the world's chief regret about this edition now is that the span of human life was too short for even Furness's amazing industry to cover quite half of the field which he had chosen.

It has been the misfortune of Shakespearean critics in general that they have allowed themselves to be surrounded and befogged by the cloud of controversy; and too often this cloud has thickened as years went on until little was left of the original illumination except angry flashes of lightning. With Furness it was otherwise. Although he was bred to the law, or perhaps because he was bred to the law, he learned that the ideas which he had to convey would be most fully accepted if he kept clear of unnecessary argument or quarrel. As a consequence, each decade saw him more admired and loved by his fellow-workers, more serene in temper, and more charming in courtesy. The wine of his nature was of that full-flavored kind which is mellowed rather than soured with age. For it was not by his writings alone that he elucidated the spirit of Shakespeare. He did it yet more fully in his life and in his person. I knew no greater pleasure than that of listening to Furness as he read with whole-hearted enthusiasm and occasional quaint comment some familiar play whose text took new life through his voice. For he had lived with the great dramatist until Shakespeare's spirit had become his; and if, as we hope, he is gone where he may hold personal converse with the immortals of three hundred years ago, the Raleighs and the Bacons and the Jonsons will welcome him as one of their number. For to that society did he already belong while yet he was here with us.

I T IS but a short time since Dr. Furness was himself called upon to deliver a commemorative address in honor of a fellow-member of our body, Henry Charles Lea. I cannot

forbear making a brief quotation from what was then said of
one friend by another who was so soon to follow in his foot-
steps:

"A man's light [as Jeremy Taylor says] burns awhile and then
turns blue and faint, and he goes to converse with spirits: then he
hands his taper to another." But where shall we find him who is
worthy to accept Lea's taper? Of him who shall venture to hold it,
it will crave wary walking to keep its flame as pure and bright as
when it illumined the pages beneath Lea's own hand.

And warily must a man walk, as critics have often found
to their cost, who will try to estimate Lea's work in its full
profundity. If I had to pick out his salient characteristic, I
should say that it was honesty; strict, uncompromising devotion to truth. He had two sides to his public life, the practical
and the scholarly; yet in each of them the same fundamental
characteristics were manifest. As a practical man of affairs he
stood for honest government; as a scholar and writer he stood
for honest treatment of history.

Those of us who have ever tried to write history, even on
a small scale, know how hard this is. It is so easy to generalize
on inadequate evidence, and so vastly laborious to hunt down
facts which may in the end run counter to our own prepos-
sessions, that most men, especially if they have the gift of
literary style, incline toward the smoother path. This temptation must have been particularly subtle in the case of Lea.
For he did not approach the *History of the Inquisition,* or the
various other topics of medieval and modern jurisprudence
which he treated, in the spirit of a mere chronicler. It was for
principles, not for facts, that he cared. The instinct of generalization was strong within him. The ethical element was
ever before his mind. Yet with all these excuses for preferring
what is commonly called the philosophic treatment of his subject, he kept himself to the strictly historic one. Lea showed
us how history ought to be written, and he showed us the
resolution with which a true man of letters can resist the
temptation to write it otherwise.

We can well close this tribute with the words of Mr. James Bryce, himself a shining example of the combination of honest citizenship and honest scholarship: "I may sum up the impression which Mr. Lea's intellectual character and attitude leave upon his readers, and left most of all upon those who knew him personally, by saying that he loved truth with a whole-hearted devotion."

B RED, like Furness, to the law, Donald Grant Mitchell found the attractions of literature stronger than those of forensic ambition. While Furness was frequenting the society of Elizabethan days, Mitchell, in his own quaint and quiet way, was preparing himself for the companionship of choice souls of another type. I doubt not that he has already received a warm welcome from the congenial spirits of Izaak Walton and Dr. Thomas Browne and our own Washington Irving; and has compared notes with Horace and Pliny about Sabine farms or Tuscan villas. For his was essentially the field of the contemplative essay, the dream or reverie, in which the autobiographical form adds charm to the style and felicity to the thought.

If he passed from the speculative to the practical side of life, it was to touch with deft hand upon the joys and cares of the country gentleman. Of this good old English type Mitchell was himself a superb representative; handsome in person, genial in manner, unfailing in kindness of heart. Living on a hillside farm just outside of the city, but during his lifetime untouched by the city's expansion,—"My Farm of Edgewood," of which he wrote so delightfully,—the view from his window over the spires of the town to the woods and the sea beyond them was symbolical of his whole outlook on life.

In the last public address which he delivered Mitchell summarized in characteristic fashion his attitude toward certain present-day educational movements:

There are oldish people astir, gone-by products of these mills of

28

learning—who will watch anxiously lest harm be done to apostles of the old humanities. You may apotheosize the Faradays and Danas and the Edisons and Huxleys, and we will fling our caps in the air. But we shall ask that you spare us our Plato, our Homer, our Vergil, our Dante, and perhaps our "chattering" Aristotle and scoffing Carlyle. Truth, however and wherever won, without nervous expression to spread and plant it, is helpless—a bird without wings! And there are beliefs tenderly cherished—and I call the spires of nineteen centuries to witness—which do not rest on the lens or the scalpel.

It was fortunate for American education that it numbered among its leaders men who took the same large view of life that Mitchell did. And of such men none was more eminent for his catholicity of understanding than Daniel Coit Gilman. Well might he have said, with the Roman of old, *Homo sum, humani nihil a me alienum puto.* His literary activity indicates his breadth of interest. In his work on Monroe he is a historian; in his life of Dana he is a biographer; in his two books on education he appears as an essayist and a critic.

There was but one thing which Gilman demanded of a subject, and that was that it should be interesting. Dullness, whenever and wherever found, was an unpardonable fault; persistent and confirmed dullness was the sin against the Holy Ghost which could not be forgiven. This demand was what most frequently brought Gilman into conflict with the conservatives in educational matters. As far as mere pedagogic theory was concerned, he was by no means so radical as Eliot or White. For classical study, if classical study could be made stimulating, he had the strongest sympathy; to a well-ordered curriculum, if it could enlist the active interest of the students, he gave appreciation and approval. But the college curriculum as Gilman generally found it was not made interesting. Language was taught mechanically; psychology and metaphysics were handled according to the dictates of the Scotch school, that apotheosis of dullness; history and science were either learned by rote or not learned at all. No wonder that his earlier years at Yale and at California were spent in waging conflicts not always successful against those who loved the dry bones of routine or inefficiency.

At Johns Hopkins he was given a freer hand, and was able to collect about him as the nucleus of a new university men who were animated by intellectual interest of a type akin to Gilman's own. They cared enough about their several subjects to make researches. They were animated by Gilman's example and precept to give the benefit of their researches to the world of science and letters. Students were not numerous, appliances were not adequate; but Gilman had created, as Socrates in his day had created, a phrontistery, a thinking-shop, of a kind America has probably never seen before or since.

No man's total contribution to science or letters is measured by his own published work. The best service which he renders is generally found in the stimulus which he gives to others about him and after him. He who approves what is vital and rejects what is sterile, who encourages the men of talent and genius and protects them against the tyranny of routine, is the man whose labor counts for most in the end. Measured in this fashion, Gilman's work stands out in its true proportions as a contribution to the arts and letters of the country and the world.

> Thus thought on thought is piled, till some vast mass
> Is loosened, and the nations echo round.

THOMAS WENTWORTH HIGGINSON
JULIA WARD HOWE
FRANCIS MARION CRAWFORD
WILLIAM VAUGHN MOODY

BY BLISS PERRY

COMPARED with the men treasured in Thomas Wentworth Higginson's inexhaustible memories, he himself belonged to the "second growth" of our literature, but he had sprung tall and straight and graciously from the as yet unexhausted New England soil. In the attics of old houses in Salem there may still be seen wide boards of clear, straight-grained pine, toned to a mellow violin coloring by the stray shafts of sunlight. Colonel Higginson's prose had that same flawless texture, the same heritage and tinge of sunshine. His style matured very early. It was already perfected when he wrote the gay, supple, singing *Charge with Prince Rupert*. It is as difficult to date one of his essays by the test of its style as it is to date one of Aldrich's songs or Longfellow's sonnets. He did not have the fortune, like his friend Mrs. Howe, to win fame by one ecstatic lyric, or, like Watson and Ellery Channing, to be remembered by one famous line. Yet there is quality throughout Higginson's prose and his slender pages of verse, and there is rich variety.

It would be hard to find in American literature any nature essays which surpass his *Water-Lilies*, *Foot-Paths*, and *A Summer Afternoon;* or an ethical essay more tonic than *Saints and Their Bodies*. We have had no biographical essay more wholly admirable than the *Theodore Parker*, and certainly none more delightful than the *John Holmes;* while a more clever controversial essay than *Ought Women to Learn the Alphabet* has not been written since the alphabet came into general use. Higginson coasted by the shores of Romance in *Malbone* and *The Monarch of Dreams*. He tested repeatedly his gifts as a biographer. In *Army Life in a Black Regiment* we touch autobiography. The book demanded tact and humor, a sense of human and historical values, and a professional pride in which the colonel of the First South Carolina Volunteers was never wanting. I remember that upon one of the last occasions when he attended a meeting of the Massachusetts Historical Society a paper was read demonstrating the ignorance and illiteracy of the negroes of the South Atlantic States, who, we were assured, could scarcely speak or even understand English. The veteran colonel of the First South Carolina rose very unsteadily to his feet and made this perfect reply: "My men could understand *me* when I gave the word 'Forward!' "

To praise Higginson's *Cheerful Yesterdays* is to praise him, so perfectly was it a part of him; not the mere inevitable and conscious betrayal of the personality of an author, but the unconditional surrender of it to the minds and hearts of his friends. In other words, Mr. Higginson was one of those fortunate writers who could transfer to his pages the whole of his personal character. You can no more subtract from his books his idealism, his consistent courage, his erect Americanism, than you can subtract Sir Philip Sidney's knightly qualities from his essay on the nature of poetry.

Higginson loved children and all innocent things. He was chivalrous not merely toward women, which is easy, but toward "woman," which is somewhat more difficult. His wit had always a touch of tartness for the American *parvenu,* for he had lived long in Newport and was a good field naturalist. His satire also amused itself with the Englishmen who could not understand what our Civil War was fought for. But in general Higginson's list of antipathies was not much longer than such a list should be. Surrounded all his life by reformers, he had, like Emerson, a shrewd, detached sense of the eccentricities of reformers. He wrote an amusing essay about it. He used to bare his noble gray head whenever he entered a polling-booth, but he never took off his hat to any mere vulgar political or literary majority. To the very end he remained what Europeans call an "1848" man; he carried that old idealism serenely through the demoralized American epoch of the eighties and nineties into the new idealistic current of to-day. It is no wonder that he was idolized by the young.

Yet his good fortune lay not merely in this identification of his character with his work as a man of letters. He was also fortunate in settling upon a form of literature precisely adapted to the instincts of his mind. He was a born essayist and autobiographer. Too versatile a workman, and too dependent upon his pen for bread, to confine himself to his true genre, he still kept returning to it, like the homing bee. The flexibility of the essay form, its venturesomeness, its perpetual sally and retreat, tempted his happy audacity. But beneath the wit and grace and fire of his phrases there is the fine conservatism of the scholar, the inimitable touch of the writer whose taste has been trained by the classics. His essays on *An Old Latin Text-Book* and *Sunshine and Petrarch* reveal the natural bookman. That style of his, as light and flexible as a rod of split bamboo, is the style of many of the immortal classics and humanists; and it holds when the bigger and coarser styles warp and weaken.

No contemporary of any writer can solve what Higginson once called "the equation of fame." That equation contains too many unknown quantities. Lamb's *Essay on Roast Pig*, which has simply a good deal of Charles Lamb in it, is now as sure of immortality, as far as we can see, as Gibbon's *Decline and Fall of the Roman Empire*. At least we can say, here are a dozen volumes into which Thomas Wentworth Higginson has put a great deal of himself, clear-grained, seasoned, sun-bathed stuff. They will outlast our day and many days.

M RS. JULIA WARD HOWE, the first woman to be honored by an election to the American Academy of Arts and Letters, was, like her friend Colonel Higginson, a representative of the best stock of Colonial America. Like him she lived to a great age, and received with unfeigned pleasure the homage of the third generation of writing men and writing women. Her first books and her earliest literary friendships date from that quaint New York of the forties, the Washington Irving period as it was about to vanish. Thenceforward her home was in Boston. Her marriage to Dr. Howe and her quick responsiveness to ethical impulses brought her into intimate relations with that restless, aspiring movement of reform which characterized New England for a score of years before and after the Civil War. Mrs. Howe flung herself with girlish enthusiasm into a dozen "causes," the education of the blind, the relief of the poor, the Americanization of foreigners, the liberalizing of religion, the emancipation of women, the movement for international peace. She was tireless, witty, undismayed, gifted with an amazing bodily endurance and a flashing radiance of spirit. She wrote essays, verses, sermons, and a play, but her fame as a writer rests almost wholly upon her *Battle Hymn of the Republic*. The poem was scribbled hastily in the gray dawn after a sound night's sleep. It was composed, like many of the songs of Burns, to a well-known tune. It interpreted, as no other lyric of the war quite succeeded in interpreting, the mystical glory of sacrifice for freedom. Soldiers sang it in camp; women read it with tears; children repeated it in school, vaguely but truly perceiving in it, as thirty years before their fathers had perceived in Webster's *Reply to Hayne,* the idea of union made "simple, sensuous, passionate." No American poem has had a more dramatic and intense life in the quick-breathing imagination of men.

Mrs. Howe lived for half a century after her famous lyric was written, but the aureole of that one achievement rested over her until the end. She was a notable figure at public gatherings, and her commemorative verses on various centenary occasions were received with delight. She prepared a poem for the first meeting of the American Academy of Arts and Letters at Washington, in December, 1909. She was then eighty, and to the very close, in her public appearances, she preserved the clear, telling voice, the wit, the indomitable energy, of youth. A very human woman, a very feminine and wise woman, Mrs. Howe had a place all her own in the affectionate admiration of her contemporaries.

Francis Marion Crawford, cosmopolite and story-teller, became a singularly successful professional soldier in that regiment of literature, "the strangest in her Majesty's service," in which Mrs. Howe, his kinswoman, had served as a brilliant volunteer. Crawford's youth was passed mainly in Italy, in that American colony whose pioneer period has been sketched by Mr. Henry James in his life of W. W. Story. But he also studied at Trinity College, Cambridge, and at Heidelberg, and, like Mr. Kipling, he had edited a newspaper in India before he became a special student of Sanskrit at Harvard in 1881.

It was in the following year that his uncle, Samuel G. Ward, knowing the rich fund of experience which lay in the young man's mind, awaiting some magical evocation, half persuaded and half forced Crawford to write that most purely fascinating of all his books, *Mr. Isaacs*. The exotic qualities of a fertile and somewhat mystical imagination were restrained even in that first book by a skilful sense of what could be spun in a yarn rather than adumbrated in a poem. Novel after novel followed in a stream uninterrupted until the author's death—novels written with a rapidity which rivaled that of Walter Scott, even as they almost seemed to rival Scott's popularity. A workman as intelligent as he was facile, Crawford set forth his theory of the novel in the phrase, "It is a pocket stage." He illustrated his theory by brilliant dialogue and moving action and in sketching his varied backgrounds of southern European life. Himself, and in a double sense, an adopted child of Rome, Italy had few secrets that were hidden from Crawford's view. He wrote comprehensive books on Rome and Venice in a style happily blended of the anti-

35

quarian and the sentimental traveler. It may be surmised that Thomas Carlyle, if he could have had the pleasure of reading Crawford's tales, might have found that long row of delightful and often powerful stories deficient in a "message," and indeed it is difficult to affirm that they contained any doctrine except the enchanting one that this world is full of a number of things. But no reader of Crawford cared, such was the glamour of his inventiveness, the fidelity with which he reproduced the tone and spirit of picturesque Europe.

Crawford was personally but slightly known to his fellow-workers in the craft of literature; but the most casual meeting with him revealed a certain sailor-like quality of frankness and directness which gave charm to his person and to his conversation. He will no doubt remain a representative figure of literary cosmopolitanism. In the new alignments caused by the strong currents of contemporary change he may well prove greater or less than we think him now; but it will be long before we shall find a more adept guardian of Aladdin's lamp.

IN THE death of William Vaughn Moody the Academy has lost a poet of rich endowment and great distinction. Like Colonel Higginson, Mrs. Howe, and Mr. Crawford, he had the cosmopolitan temper, and he was haunted by the beauty of Greek literature. Unlike them, he was perplexed by our modern world, and was never fully at home in it. Perhaps this is only saying that he was a poet. As a Harvard undergraduate, Moody revealed a mind of uncommon richness and complexity of pattern; but even at forty he had not wholly succeeded in bringing that mind into lucid order, into a steady grasp of structural design. A lover of Milton, Shelley, and Euripides, he was enraptured of beautiful words. His lyrics sing in burdened, thrush-like cadences which are too heavy with thought, too deeply drenched with passionate feeling; the wet boughs of his fragrant verse bend low, blinding the eyes of his readers. But more than once, as in the masterly

Ode in Time of Hesitation, in *Gloucester Moors,* and in some of the songs in his dramas, feeling and form were wrought into consummate perfection of expression. Here were "thoughts that voluntary moved harmonious numbers."

Moody's incompleted trilogy, *The Fire-Bringer, The Masque of Judgment,* and *The Death of Eve,* contains memorable passages, but the key to his cosmologies and mythologies is hard to find, and perhaps—perhaps there was none. One of his prose plays, *The Great Divide,* had notable success upon the boards, but at the time of his death he seems to have abandoned the ambitions of a playwright. Never quite at ease in our contemporary America; teaching literature with abundant scholarship, but with no love for his profession; writing poetic dramas which few persons read; dear beyond most men to his friends, but shy and wilful; splendidly courageous in hazarding every sacrifice in the service of poetry, William Vaughn Moody lost much that other men of letters care for, but he won, who shall say how much more, in inner power and in creative mastery over the forms of his art. His friend Mr. Percy Mackaye has nobly written his eulogy in *Uriel;* and surely it is in verse only, and not in prose, that we should fitly record the passing of this strong, perturbed spirit. He chose high and hard paths, but paths which were surely leading to serenity of vision, as they had already led him into the secret places of beauty and close to the passionate and troubled heart of the sons of Eve.

JOHN LA FARGE
EDWIN AUSTIN ABBEY
FRANCIS DAVIS MILLET

BY THOMAS HASTINGS

WHILE HERE assembled, let us pay tribute to the distinguished services of three members of this Academy who have recently been taken from us: John La Farge, Edwin Austin Abbey, and Francis Davis Millet. As they lived in their work, they are still alive in the influence their untiring endeavors have produced upon modern art. They have helped to quicken within us our sense of beauty, and to aid us to understand better its uplifting and refining influences. Such lives largely contribute to the happiness of their fellow-men. Those of us who enjoyed personal intercourse with them must realize how they themselves found happiness in their work; they were happy temperamentally, and so imparted happiness to others. There was another inherent quality of character of which they all had full measure—that enthusiasm which made all intercourse with them interesting and stimulating. It was the enthusiasm of the real artist, the enthusiasm which stimulates the creative faculties and intuitively quickens the insight and understanding. When we find the experience and knowledge which come with age stimulated by an enthusiasm which does not grow old under these conditions, men have retarded their declining years and have often produced their best work late in life. The flowing stream never becomes stagnant. While a man's interest in the opportunities of life continues, the possibilities of productiveness are unlimited. We may think that by observation we have learned what to expect of one another, but if we still have enthusiasm, we need know no limitations in what we may expect of ourselves. The loss of enthusiasm is the end of the artist's career.

JOHN LA FARGE

JOHN LA FARGE was a young old man. He was born in New York in March, 1835. His father was a Frenchman, an officer in the navy, who, in 1806, took part in an expedition to Santo Domingo, where he married the daughter of a planter who is said to have had some skill as a miniature-painter. John La Farge married Margaret M. Perry, the granddaughter of Commodore O. H. Perry. In his early life La Farge undertook the study of law; but, always attracted to art, it was not long before he devoted himself wholly to the study of painting. At that time, while in Newport, he studied under William Morris Hunt. The charm of some of his early landscapes, painted there and while he was studying with Couture in Paris, is well remembered by those of us who have seen them at our current exhibitions.

It was in the early seventies that he first began experimenting in glass that afterward resulted in his ingenious and well-known new methods of construction and use of materials, with their accompanying brilliancy of color. His work in this direction made a remarkable impression upon American glass. Through all the years of glass-working he continued to paint, producing many important decorations, more especially in some of our churches. An event in his life was when H. H. Richardson commissioned him to decorate Trinity Church in Boston. Later, his work appeared in the Church of the Ascension, the Church of the Paulist Fathers, the Brick Church, and the St. Thomas's Church that was destroyed by fire.

In 1886, La Farge went to Japan with his friend Mr. Henry Adams, and afterward to the South Sea Islands. His correspondence, which later appeared in the *Century Magazine,* established him in the minds of the public as a writer of unusual natural ability. In his later work as a literary man he showed an unusual degree of versatility and flexibility of mind. For those of us who know well the extent and unusual quality and merits of the man's talents, it is futile at this time to comment further upon his undertakings, his drawings, his water-colors, his paintings, his glass, or his writings, or to attempt to enumerate the many honors he received during his long and successful life—honors not only from his own country, but from France, England, and Germany. Had we time, we would rather dwell upon him as our friend and fellow-Academician, a remarkable character, an artist-philosopher. Those of us who knew him would agree, I believe, that, when all else had been said, to know him and to talk with him was to find La Farge at his best. He was indeed an artist in conversation, a man of ideas, with as brilliant a coloring in his personality as in his painting. His talk, drawn from his broad experience, was always full of suggestion, delightful in anecdote and incident, with a profound sense of humor, and a literary quality of great refinement unusual even in written form.

FROM THE time of Benjamin West until John S. Sargent, there has always been a considerable number of self-expatriated American artists who have given renown to American art in Europe. Edwin Austin Abbey was unquestionably one of the most illustrious of this number. He was born in Philadelphia, April 1, 1852, a grandson of Roswell Abbey, a prosperous merchant, who was also an inventor of type-foundry appliances and a man of decided artistic temperament. He was the son of William Maxwell Abbey, who was likewise a Philadelphia merchant, and something of an amateur artist.

In 1866, when only fourteen years of age, Abbey published his first drawings in Oliver Optic's paper, *Our Boys and Girls*. During the early years of his life he was a student in the Philadelphia Academy of Fine Arts. Coming to New York at the age of twenty, he quickly developed, and was soon after employed by *Harper's Magazine*. Here he acquired a remarkable facility as a draftsman in black and white. His distinguished work as an illustrator gave him at an unusually early age a wide and popular reputation. Even at this time

Old-World legends had a potent influence upon his character and the general direction of his work. In his portrayal of old songs and ballads, as well as in his illustrations of historic characters, he seemed to bring to life and to make real the finest fancies of English literature. *She Stoops to Conquer, The Deserted Village,* Herrick's poems, and Shakespeare's plays, were brought into a new light by the facile pen of the young artist. It was perhaps this special interest in English literature that, in 1883, influenced him to make his residence in England.

At frequent intervals his work, more especially his drawings, pastels, and water-colors, has been shown both here and abroad at the exhibitions of the numerous societies to which he belonged. It always attracted the admiration of a large and appreciative audience. It was not until 1895, through the influence of Charles F. McKim, that he was commissioned to paint his first important decoration, the well-known series of panels, *The Holy Grail,* for the Boston Public Library, which, with Sargent's notable decorations in the same building, have become renowned as perhaps the most remarkable mural decorations ever painted by American artists. Not only did he show in this comparatively new undertaking his great ability as a painter, but he fulfilled to the utmost what his earlier work had promised—a studious conscientiousness in all matters of detail, with a remarkable capacity for research into the costumes and customs of past ages.

In 1890 he married Gertrude Mead of New York, and for many years they lived in Fairford, Gloucestershire, England, surrounded by a most artistic atmosphere.

In 1901 he was commissioned by King Edward VII to paint for Buckingham Palace the official picture of the coronation. From that time the greater part of his life was devoted to painting, his last and most recent work being three important decorative panels for the State House at Harrisburg, in his native State. Unfortunately, he did not live to see this work completed.

41

In this country many honors and university degrees were conferred upon him, and he was the recipient of many foreign decorations, and in 1898 he was made a Royal Academician. His last year was the sixtieth of his life, and judging from the progressive excellence of his work and the vitality and enthusiasm of the man, there was every promise of even greater and finer results if he had lived longer to reap more fully the benefits of experience and his constant and untiring habits of work.

AN UNPARALLELED event in the history of navigation was the foundering of the great steamship *Titanic*. Francis Davis Millet was one of her passengers. In mid-ocean, under a starlit sky, which had dissolved the darkness of the night, he must have seen the last of this world. Amid the confusion and débris of the sinking ship, he could see only an unbroken horizon over the waters of the Atlantic, a circle on the earth's surface, emblem of eternal life. Thinking more of the safety of others than of himself, our friend was taken from us in the fullness of his power. I know of no other American artist who has served such high and varied purposes with such unselfish devotion to the interests of American art, and with such an untiring capacity for work, unhesitatingly sacrificing his time for the good of others. Indeed, he was so public-spirited that I have often thought he gave himself so freely that his unselfishness seriously interfered with his own private interests in life.

Though gentle and unassuming, he was a leader of men, an educator of men. He would have succeeded in whatever he might have undertaken. He had a singular gift for making friends. To know him was to love him. He had a remarkable fund of interesting information on the widest variety of subjects.

We were members together of the National Fine Arts Commission in Washington, where I learned to know what a delightful privilege it was to work with him. Intellectually he was somewhat inclined to wander, being often drawn into other channels than art.

He was born at Mattapoisett, Massachusetts, in November, 1846. He was the youngest man of sixty-six I have ever known. During the Civil War he was a drummer in the 50th Massachusetts Regiment. In 1869 he was graduated from Harvard, later associating himself with Boston journalism, and devoting what spare time he could find to the study of art. It was not long before he went to Europe and entered as a student in the Royal Academy of Antwerp, where he made great progress and showed much promise. He then traveled widely, returning to Boston to assist La Farge in his work in Trinity Church.

For his brilliant services as correspondent for the New York and London papers in the Russo-Turkish War, and for bravery on the battle-field, he was decorated by the czar. Later he was sent as a war correspondent to the Philippines. He was chairman of the Advisory Committee of the National Museum, a member of the Municipal Art Commission of New York, a trustee of the Metropolitan Museum of Art, secretary of the American Federation of Arts, and member of the National Fine Arts Commission. He had recently been appointed the executive officer of the United American Academy and the American School of Classical Studies at Rome, and was returning on the *Titanic* after visiting Rome in the interest of this institution. It seemed a fitting place for him, with his unusual ability for organization.

In 1879 he married Elizabeth Greeley Merrill. While their home was in Broadway, Worcestershire, England, his life in recent years was spent mostly between Washington, New York, and Rome. With all this time given to traveling and public affairs, it seems almost incredible that he could have produced so much in painting, which was the actual means of his livelihood. He had traveled extensively all over the world, and spoke nearly all of the principal languages of Europe.

In 1891 he made a canoe trip the full length of the Danube for Harper Brothers, who published his book entitled *The Danube from the Black Forest to the Black Sea*. About the same time appeared his collection of short stories and his translation of Tolstoi's *Sebastopol*.

In recent years he devoted a great deal of time to decorations. The historical paintings in the capitol at St. Paul, the decorations in the custom-house at Baltimore, and a historical decoration in the court-house at Newark, New Jersey, are among his most important later works.

Few men enjoyed life as he did, and few men gave more enjoyment to others. He will be missed, and no one man can be found to fill his place—alas, so many places!

Millet was a strong, intelligent man of character, with a sweetness and simplicity almost childlike. His nature was joyous, which attracted men to him, and always assured him their collaboration in whatever work he undertook.

1908

BRONSON HOWARD
BY AUGUSTUS THOMAS

BRONSON HOWARD died in August of 1908 in his sixty-sixth year. He was at that time, and had been for thirty years, the foremost dramatist of America. He was a vice-president of the National Institute of Arts and Letters, which he helped to organize, and he was a member of this Academy.

He was the son of a prominent merchant of Detroit, and the great grandson of an English ensign who fought under General Wolfe at the capture of Quebec and who in later manhood died in the sight of George Washington, whom he followed at Monmouth. Behind that Revolutionary soldier the family traced itself directly to the Howards of Norfolk, premier dukes of England.

At the usual age Bronson Howard prepared for admission to Yale University, but, owing to a serious trouble with his eyes, did not enter. As a later writer has said of himself, he was forced to choose between journalism and an education. He turned his attention to humorous writing for the Detroit *Free Press*.

In 1865 he came to New York City to work as a reporter on the *Tribune* under the direction of Horace Greeley. Mr. Howard was then twenty-three years old. He worked for the *Tribune* and later for the *Evening Post*. On these two papers, before he left them to embark altogether upon play-writing as his profession, he labored seven years, the historic time of service that Jacob agreed upon with Laban.

Between the years 1870 and 1899 he was the author of seventeen plays, the greater part of which were successful. In a profession that has no curriculum but sympathetic living and understanding, and no diploma but the smiles and tears of his fellow-men, he won a first distinction.

Very soon after he began to write for the stage his accurate observation, his fine apprehension of motive, his delicate measurement of effect, his truthful transcription and vivid presentation of life, placed him in a class by himself among American playwrights. In an epoch of hurried and commercial and very conventional production his careful, lifelike, and unhackneyed offerings were in the main artistic masterpieces, valuable not only for the refreshing qualities that they served to the public of that time, but as examples of considered workmanship, and as models to men already in his profession and to those preparing to join it. This is especially true of the work of his matured and ripened years. His painstaking amounted almost to genius, and its effect upon a play was a finish less enamel than it was bloom. The body of the play was solid, too. It gave an impression of life. The happenings seemed not only true, but intimate and inevitable. The people were like ourselves; like us not only in their better and heroic moments, when we hoped they were our very kindred, but like us in their shortcomings, their failings, and their meannesses, when we knew they were.

The blue pencil of the city editor had taught Bronson Howard the unpardonableness of being dull. He had learned our general incapacity for sustained attention, our thirst for variety, our delight in surprise, our readiness to laugh, and our blindness to the ambush of the pathetic. He knew that skilful counterpoint was the way to keep us rocking and susceptible, and he could sit at his table and dramatize not only the people of his play, but those dim gatherings beyond the barrier of the footlights that should lean and listen, gasp and inhale and laugh, frown and be tender, weep and clap hands, like reflected moods invoked in a magic, but shadowed, mirror.

The older theater-goers will remember with respect and affection his great successes, *The Banker's Daughter* and

Young Mrs. Winthrop, Shenandoah and *The Henrietta;*
and while his reputation will probably rest upon these four
fine plays, his other work was of wide range and high merit.

Mr. Brander Matthews, the writer most qualified by acquaintance with the man and his epoch and with the theater
to write of them all, has called our attention to the fact that
Bronson Howard's career as a dramatist covered the transition period of the modern drama, when it was changing from
the platform stage to the picture-frame stage; that period that
was dismissing "the rhetorical emphasis, confidential solilo-
quies to the audience, and frequent change of scene in the
course of an act." And almost as though he were being guided
by the wisdom of Polonius on fashions, he was

> . . . not the first by whom the new is tried,
> Nor yet the last to lay the old aside.

He moved with his time, and so discreetly that men working
under the tacit acceptance of his leadership suffered neither
martyrdom nor neglect.

His associates were the leading managers and the foremost
actors of the time. His material circumstances changed from
the embarrassing lack of an overcoat during his reportorial
adventure in New York to a life of comfort and the means
to make an endowment to the American Dramatists' Club,
with substantial bequests in other directions.

The Dramatists' Club was an outgrowth of the unusual
modesty that was a Bronson Howard characteristic. He had
had some success in England, and our insular brethren there
insisted on regarding him not only as an American playwright of prominence, but as the only one existing. With the
avowed purpose to answer and inform and correct this attitude, he got together in 1890 fifty men in America who had
professionally produced their plays. A society was formed
that still exists, and includes in its membership the principal
dramatists of the United States. Mr. Howard was its first
president, and held that office until his death. He left to the

society his dramatic library, one of the largest in the country, and also left a fund to maintain and to increase it. He so arranged his affairs that upon the death of Mrs. Howard a sustaining endowment came to the society itself, together with the valuable rights to his plays.

But if Bronson Howard had never written a play or delivered a lecture upon that art, or established and endowed a society of dramatists, he would still be a notable figure in the history of the drama in America, as it was owing to his initiative and persistence, his advocacy and persuasion, that dramatic compositions finally obtained proper protection under the United States copyright law, and in the various States similar protection under the common law for plays that had not been copyrighted. This achievement was the work of many years, embracing repeated trips to Washington, many appearances and contests before committees, and volumes of correspondence with authors, journalists, attorneys, and legislators. This monument to the man is the finer from the fact that for many years before its accomplishment he personally had virtually retired from the field.

To commemorate only this professional side of his life, however, would be to neglect the larger and the finer part of the man. Play-writing seemed rather the avocation of a full and broad and deep and vibrant soul, the *chief* expression of which was life itself. His understanding was so complete, his sympathy so general, his patience so detached and yet so fraternal, his justice of such even balance, his humor so lubricant and healing, that any business he might have chosen would have seemed an equal abdication of his larger rights. He looked like a successful general who had quit the arts of war to practise medicine. He smiled like a righteous judge who hesitated to convict because he understood the promising humanity of the offense. He listened like a father who had been a playmate, and all who knew him remember, and many have commented in some fashion upon, his singularly blue eyes, and the steadiness of their gaze, encouraging,

48

not disconcerting, and which seemed not to pierce, but to infiltrate. He was an adequate and noticeable factor of any assembly, the most delightful associate in the ideal companionship of two, and perfectly sufficient to himself in the longest hours of self-chosen solitude.

I remember visiting him for two or three short consultations during a winter in the middle nineties, when it was his daily custom to leave New York in the morning with his lunch in a paper, and spend the day in a little, eight-by-ten-foot wooden cabin built in the corner of the back yard of a cottage he had owned at New Rochelle. The furniture of this cabin was two wooden chairs, a deal table, a little cannon stove, a coal-hod, and a brierwood pipe. He found there the isolation and the quiet that his work required, and traveled in a virtually empty train both ways, as the commuting tide was opposite to his direction at this hour. This was at the period of his greatest artistic and financial success. His home in New York at that time was a comfortable, but unpretentious, apartment in a quarter not fashionable. Both the apartment and the cabin could be closed and left at the shortest notice, and their owner was free to follow where his whim invited. He knew that real happiness did not attach to things, and Fortune in her most enticing moods could deceive him no more than she had frightened him with her frowns. We must record him a man equipped with the emotional power of an artist, the generosity of a cavalier, and the temperance of a gentleman.

JOHN BIGELOW
BY WILLIAM MILLIGAN SLOANE

THE MAN of letters in public life practises a fine art second to no other. It is useless to analyze the causes which lead members of the Academy to choose their colleagues, for the finer senses are elusive in their action. But in the case of John Bigelow there was no mystery. He was not only a distinguished writer: he was also a famous publicist, statesman, and diplomat, with a genius alike for leadership and coöperation. In every impulse and instinct he was a colleague: when others faltered about the place of our organization in American life he was secure in his judgment, placing time, energy, and money at the service of this Academy. His convictions as to the work it had to do and his unshaken faith that in time its place would be established in American life were a source of inspiration to us all.

This was due to the fullest knowledge of men and their institutions in all lands, and to his comparative study of life in America with that elsewhere. He was born at Malden on the Hudson River in 1817 and died at ninety-four. For him there was neither youth nor old age, but a beautiful childhood and adolescence until he was graduated at eighteen from Union College, when he seems to have entered instantly on a maturity which lasted without withering for over seventy-five years. And such years!—the years during which his own and every other civilized land was totally reconstructed. He studied law, was admitted to the bar, and built up a handsome practice. But his heart was not absorbed in his profession, because he was a born publicist and pamphleteer. His fixed purpose was to earn a competence so that he might as early as possible become a public servant. This he accomplished by the time he was fifty; but long before that he began to write, and was a welcome contributor to no fewer than seven newspapers and periodicals. Of one, the *Plebeian,* he became the literary editor.

It was about 1838 that the magnet of this metropolis drew him from Hudson, the local capital, to New York. At once he became a member of an association, known as The Column, composed of brilliant young lawyers, taking themselves most seriously, which was in itself an embryo Academy. Their purpose was to broaden their culture and magnify their influence by the force of organization. Sooner or later they all became members of the Century Association, and the two venerable survivors, Parke Godwin and John Bigelow, while the latter was president of that famous guild, placed their emblem, a handsome column surmounted by the lamp of learning, in the keeping of the Association. Their notable careers were measurably due to their reactions upon each other, and this was one of the facts which influenced John Bigelow in his devotion to the National Institute with its Senate, the Academy.

Having found his powers and solidified his convictions, he entered the field of national politics as an ardent Free-Soil Democrat. So skilful and convincing was his polemic in favor of Van Buren that William Cullen Bryant secured him as a partner in the ownership and as a co-editor of the *Evening Post.* The struggle to prevent the extension of slavery into the Territories was regarded by that paper as most important, and to this the new editor particularly devoted himself. In journalism he had the "heavy fist" of stern conviction; but simultaneously, until he sold his shares to Parke Godwin in 1861 and withdrew, he was busy with literary work. He traveled in Jamaica, Haiti, and Europe, writing almost continuously social and political studies of the lands he visited, all of which were printed. Some were collected into book form. For long years he continued his contributions to the press, and to the end of his life he was as famous a pamphleteer as any man employing the English language.

It was in 1845 that his public service began. For three years he was an inspector of New York prisons, and it was by his measures that Sing Sing penitentiary became the model prison it once was. This was the moment when Tilden was beginning his political career as assemblyman. Three years older than Bigelow, he was not yet a Free-Soiler. But the two young statesmen of similar faith formed about this time an acquaintance, which, considerably later, ripened into a friendship extremely important in molding the character of both. Tilden was a distant and reticent man, with a comparatively small circle of friends, even of acquaintances; but he knew how to bind a select few both to his person and his interests. Almost the last act of John Bigelow was to reject with scorn the proffer of Congress for a Tilden bust to be placed in the Capitol at Washington. He thought his friend worthy of a monumental statue. It was he who remedied the results of Tilden's defective will, which was likely, as an invalid document, to thwart every desire of the would-be testator. By his influence the city of New York secured the great Tilden Foundation for a public library; and, as far as word or deed could accomplish it, the memory of Tilden was impressed on posterity as a man of feeling, of power, and of rectitude. Such loyalty was characteristic of John Bigelow; it was that quality in him which gave us the Bryant monument in Bryant Park.

His public life was destined to shine with great luster. In 1861 he was sent as consul to Paris, when the admirable Dayton was head of the legation. The barriers between consular and diplomatic service were not then so high as to-day, and in 1864, when Dayton died, Bigelow was put in charge of the office. So admirable had been his foreign career that he was speedily made envoy and minister, a position he held until 1867. These seven years in Paris at least parallel, if they do not surpass, in service rendered any similar period in the career of an American diplomat. By an important volume written in French and published in 1864 he set the situation of his country clearly before the Frenchmen of the Empire, then as always dumbly hostile to America. The Napoleonic government had connived with secret agents to permit the escape from French harbors of four armed and iron-clad cruisers. Bigelow not merely discovered and collected the necessary evidence, but so presented it to the French Government as to prevent the escape of a single ship. When we recall what happened in the case of the *Alabama* and the *Georgia,* built in England, we may estimate what his work as a diplomat meant during and after the war. His, too, were the negotiations, backed by a stalwart administration in Washington, which compelled Napoleon III to abandon the dream of his uncle that a great Latin empire should embrace the Gulf of Mexico. It was in Paris, too, that he obtained and published to the world the original and complete manuscript of Franklin's *Autobiography,* so shamefully mutilated by a grandson under the guise of editing.

The influences of European life on John Bigelow were culturally very profound; he returned to its various countries again and again after his public service was completed. It would be difficult to recall a great name of his epoch with whose possessor he was unacquainted; with most of the highly eminent he was at times in personal touch; with Gladstone he waged a bitter controversy in America's behalf. There is a type of American, largely represented over the seas, who beholds and admires Europe only to weaken his loyalty and make him apologize for his origin. Of such was not Bigelow. He was a severe critic of his country, as he was of himself, but the intrinsic truth and power of the American system was a part of his gospel, a faith from which he never wavered; his highest aim was to illuminate it by comparative study. At the time of his death it was recalled that he had lived under every President of the country except Washington, and was even a contemporary of Napoleon. His mental range was as extensive as his life and experience of living;

but everything focused in a land which was his as it belonged to few others: his family had been on the soil since 1642.

His passion for liberty made him a strong individualist. He was in economics the most extreme free-trader of his day. Socially he was exquisitely considerate of others, but his time was the capital of which his Creator had made him the steward, and his style of life was delightfully original. At a festival in the house of his birth a loyal son once put in use the pulpit and pews from the old Malden Presbyterian Church, of which his grandsire had been an elder and upon which his famous father had sat as a child; but spiritually John Bigelow was a rebel against the historic faith of his sires. While in the island of St. Thomas when he was about forty years of age a Swedish gentleman had drawn his attention to the work of Emanuel Swedenborg as an interpreter of the Bible, the literary supremacy of which volume then as ever fascinated Bigelow, though some of the contents were to him, literally construed, a hard saying. He was attracted by the doctrine of the Stockholm philosopher as to "correspondences" between nature and spirit, and was until his sixtieth year or longer a devoted and critical student of that type of theosophy. Later his ardor was somewhat diminished, and he told me, as doubtless others, when he was far advanced in the eighties, that he could not consider himself a regular member of the sect with which he had long identified himself. Yet he had found and stored deep in his mind the "arcana cœlestia," and never lost the serene optimism or the implicit trust of a childlike faith. As few others, he was a spiritually minded man.

Besides his fugitive writings, there are nineteen titles to John Bigelow's credit in the history of American letters. Most of these represent substantial books, in the biographies of Tilden, Bryant, and Franklin, as well as in his own recollections, two and three volumes. In all those thousands of pages there is not a careless word or thought. He was a conscientious writer, with a clear, vivid, trenchant style, and he expounded the truth without fear as it was given to him. To such as he was the world gives its confidence and imposes on them great trusts. He was, of course, connected with the leading historical societies, those of the nation and his native State among the number; he sat on the managing boards of the Public Library and the Metropolitan Museum; he was a member of the Municipal Art Commission, and president of the Century Association. Such were his known activities, but there was the commanded reticence between his two hands in the matter of private beneficence; not even his nearest and dearest were in that secret of the Lord, which is with them that fear Him.

A philosopher in thought, a citizen in action, a paragon in domestic life, he reaped in full measure where he had sown. Thinkers, statesmen, and a circle of worth-while friends respected and loved him. His person was always attractive and to the end he wisely cultivated the style of dress in which he was most at ease, that of his fifties and sixties. As ever-advancing age bestowed its abundant bounties upon him, he became the first citizen of New York, in a measure, of the nation, and was on all occasions unfailingly recognized as such by those present. His features were boldly cut, generous but firm in line and dimension. His eyes were brilliant even in his latest years, and with his strong frame, his pleasant address, and self-respecting dignity there was something leonine in his personality. His humor was a never-failing buckler against an adversary's darts or his own petulance, an affliction carefully concealed if he had it. His wit was spontaneous, genial, and of his soul's very essence. For rising men and writers struggling with the adverse conditions of the hour he had a wealth of sympathy. His advice and suggestions were never perfunctory, and his sagacity generally indicated the tactics of practical common sense suited to each one of the many who consulted him. He was an asset of the greatest importance to this Academy, and his memory will abide in its history and traditions.

1913

GEORGE BROWNE POST
BY THOMAS HASTINGS

GEORGE BROWNE POST, the son of Joel B. and Abbey M. Post, was born in New York City, December 15, 1837. His career was most intimately associated for almost sixty years with the architectural development of this metropolis. In order to provide for the rapid increase of population during this time, there was an unparalleled growth in building. An endless variety of new problems had to be solved in order to meet the vast diversity and multiplicity of demands. Not only was the city reaching out along new avenues and over new areas of what were once fertile pasture-lands, but, alas! for want of legislative restraint, and not for want of space, one city was actually being builded over another, several times in height, reaching into the clouds, like so many Towers of Babel, scattered about in a confusion of styles. During this period Mr. Post was perhaps the most active and successful architect in finding a solution which would best meet the constructive difficulties of the modern tall building, involving the engineer's method of skeleton framework construction, accompanied by the development and general use of the passenger-elevator.

When designing the old Produce Exchange, one of our notable buildings, he employed for the first time, in the inner court of this building, iron columns and beams to support several stories of floors and walls. This was one of the first contributions to the evolution of the modern steel-frame building.

There were no traditions in the history of the art which would seem to suggest the solution of this problem, and there was a real demand for originality to meet such a hopeless situation. It is difficult to realize to what an extent Mr. Post paved the way for others to follow. In the art of architecture more than in any other creative pursuit, perhaps, the general public ofttimes finds it difficult to discern the true author of what may be a very original conception. Lost in the many modifications and slight variations, the same idea is so often reproduced by others that it becomes commonplace. A conspicuous example might be cited in Michelangelo's dome of St. Peter's, one of the most original designs ever conceived by the genius of man. Its originality can be appreciated only when one realizes that other domes, such as the Val-de-Grâce, Les Invalides, Soufflot's Panthéon, or Wren's St. Paul's were all built at a later date, and that no dome of this character, with the pendentive and the drum, preceded this most original masterpiece of architecture.

Mr. Post was really doing pioneer work at a time when the educational advantages and the condition of American architecture were not to be compared with those of the present day. In his early life he served his country in the Civil War as aide on the staff of General Burnside, who commanded the Army of the Potomac in 1862, at the first battle of Fredericksburg. He was at one time colonel of the Twenty-third Regiment of the National Guard of New York.

Mr. Post was first educated as an engineer, being graduated from the scientific school of New York University in the class of 1858. What we now recognize as engineering, with the innovation of steel and railroad construction, is comparatively a modern science, which rapidly became differentiated from the art of architecture. At that time there was little design in construction. As Mr. Post saw rather the qualitative than the quantitative side of construction, he was attracted to architecture, and he studied for three years with Richard Morris Hunt. Perhaps his first conspicuous work was the old Chickering Hall, on lower Fifth Avenue, now destroyed. He was one of the principal architects who conceived and constructed the Columbian Exposition of Chicago. I might almost say, without further mention, that we need only to look about us to see his many works. As a man he was fearless and strong, with a true sense of proportion and justice. He had unusual executive and administrative ability, and notwithstanding his great enthusiasm and impulsive temperament, there were always a quiet restraint and dignity which made him one of the most representative men of his profession. He was frequently called upon by both federal and municipal governments to render public service, both because of his generous willingness to give his valuable time and because of his distinguished personality, which made its impression upon men. The long and eventful life of our friend and fellow-Academician was ended November 28, 1913.

1914

ALFRED THAYER MAHAN
BY WILLIAM M. SLOANE

Alfred Thayer Mahan died last year at the age of seventy-four. Deriving in family, training, and confession from the old New York, his ancestry was notable. He was born at West Point, where his father, a learned engineer of high repute, was then professor. His career from his student days at Columbia University and Annapolis onward to his fiftieth year was that of a faithful, painstaking officer and Christian gentleman of the Anglican mold. In 1883 he had published an admirable professional study entitled *The Gulf and Inland Waters,* and two years later he was made lecturer on naval history and strategy at the Naval War College in Newport. Upon his duties as teacher he entered with the fitness due to university education and professional discipline. Five years later was published *The Influence of Sea Power on History.* During the twenty-three years following he published no fewer than seventeen pieces of important historical work, short and long, making a total of nineteen titles to his credit.

His biographies of Farragut and Nelson, as well as the finely studied bit of autobiography entitled *From Sail to Steam,* are all works of the highest importance. They exhibit the mind and style of the author with great clarity, because none of them is abstract, metaphysical, or controversial. Furthermore, they display the man, as his mind worked without artificial stimulus and naturally expressed itself in language. There is the patient, unwearying search for truth, for he had trained himself in archival study and the comparative method in establishing facts; there is his characteristic insight and grasp of meaning, for he was essentially a moralist and inter-preter; there is his plain dealing and lucid style. While he was a man of letters, he held his constructive imagination in firm control, a hand-maiden and not a mistress. It was the affair of his readers to supply the element of fancy, if they chose to do so. To the landsman the ocean is a favorite field for the play of that faculty, and readers give it full scope under the stimulus of his suggestions.

It has been the function of certain American historians to exhibit to European peoples the hidden meanings of their past. Among them Admiral Mahan was easily a chief. Were we to reckon the greatness of historical work by its contem-porary influence, his would be a reputation to which in the long list of modern historians in all lands none can be exactly paralleled.

Behind the historian was the man, a devout and orthodox Christian, with a strain of mysticism, inquiring into the divine purposes as revealed in the course of human events. Among all forms of this transcendent power in action the sailor-historian magnified that exhibited by national effort on the high seas. His epochal work, for it was nothing less, is contained in his series of six volumes on Sea Power, em-bracing substantially the historical ages in their entirety. Every people and every age was carefully examined in its relative importance, and naturally the older lands, entering on the portentous struggle to maintain territories and pres-tige, were more profoundly interested than the newer, his own included.

While therefore it cannot be said that he failed to secure from Americans the due meed of honor, yet it was beyond the seas that he was revered and admired with a passionate inten-sity never fully apprehended in his own country. When in 1902 he was president of the American Historical Associa-tion, the theme of his presidential address was *Subordination in Historical Treatment,* and his exposition related his own method in emphasizing the central elements of his thought as a historian. So successful was he in his sea-power books that his message was a revelation to Europe generally and to Great Britain particularly. Within a single year both Oxford and Cambridge bestowed upon him their highest honors. The advocates of the Greater England and the Three-Power Standard found in him their prophet and in his studies their justification. As the volumes appeared, they were, in whole or in part, translated into the leading European languages, and carefully edited excerpts were the textbooks for naval expansion. That the ocean, so far from being the barrier it had been considered, was in reality the great highway, the all-uniting menstruum of isolation, burst as a fact upon the consciousness of Europe like a convulsion of nature.

To be sure, the stress of expansion was already powerful in international politics, and the European world was beginning to groan in spirit over problems entailed by material prosperity and the growth of population. The forces of nature were being harnessed for the multiplication indefinitely of human industry and the inflation of wealth. Statesmen were sorely in need of pretexts for armament, and they seized for a corner-stone of their policy upon the fact ruthlessly exposed by the American historian that Nelson, rather than Wellington, had worn away to innocuous and tenuous inefficiency the portentous power of Napoleon. The ears which heard alike in England and Germany were only too receptive, the grasp of national understandings only too swift, and the subsequent activities only too mischievous. But we must not fall into the baneful fallacy of sequence as proving cause and effect. Secular history is not the record of human utopias, and what it reveals is not the dealings of regenerate mankind. Unvarnished truth is the characteristic of Mahan's pages, the truth fairly stated and philosophically considered; for him it was no counsel of perfection; it was an exhibition of how unstable is the equilibrium in the nice balance of political powers. His work, dispassionately considered, has neither charm nor seduction; in a high degree it is a caution against danger, a warning against false interpellations of facts. That self-seekers should abuse it is, alas, the way of the world.

Speaking from frequent contact with Admiral Mahan throughout many years of pleasant acquaintance, the writer must enter a protest against the charge that he was at any time, in conversation or in his writings, an apostle of war. So far from that, he was preëminently an apostle of peace. It is a sacrilege to distort the general tendency of a life-work by false emphasis on particulars. He did not write primarily for others, because, great as he was in other respects, he was greatest as an American, and the lesson he taught was intended for American patriots. He advocated a powerful fleet and battle-ships of great size, but solely for the safety and dignity of the land which was dear to him and to protect against violence a pacific evolution of the civilization he believed to be the highest. Knowing the genius of peoples as few others did, he realized the passions, ambitions, and unprincipled purposes of contemporary nationalities, the shiftiness of policies, the flimsiness of alliances and treaties, the lust for glory, for wealth, and for power. He had marked how the embittered hates of one generation were swiftly transformed into the fawning flatterings of the next, and how readjustment of understandings occurs in the twinkling of an eye when common material advantage imperiously commands it. Fully aware of such appalling truths, and sensitive to his own convictions about sea power, he desired his country to be on its guard against empty protests of affection and shallow pretenses of aloofness.

It was good to know a man of such elevated character, to hear his fascinating talk, to enjoy his courtesy, and to delight the eyes with his fine appearance. Tall, slender, erect, with expressive blue eyes and a clear complexion, he was moderate and modest in his intercourse with men, though fearless and often unsparing in the defense of his principles. He was mindful of his duties great and small, meticulous in his attention to obligations he had accepted, and so in our company a genial, appreciative comrade. He shrank from all notoriety and self-display, and during his years of incumbency in the Institute and Academy there was never a time when he was conspicuous to the degree of his eminence in the great world. As the perspective of time lengthens, our devotion to his memory is likely to increase. The trusted adviser of the Government, he died in Washington with all his armor as a patriot on, with faculties keen and alert. The awful convulsions of the hour had justified his interpretations of sea power, but I have heard that they had likewise filled him with consternation lest as a result, deferred perhaps, yet probable, the political map of America might eventually be as completely remade as that of Europe.

JOHN MUIR

BY ROBERT UNDERWOOD JOHNSON

SOMETIME, in the evolution of America, we shall throw off the two shackles that retard our progress as an artistic nation—philistinism and commercialism—and advance with freedom toward the love of beauty as a principle. Then it will not be enough that one shall love merely one kind of beauty, each worker his own art, or that art shall be separated from life as something too precious for use: men will search for beauty as scientists search for truth, knowing that while truth can make one free, it is beauty of some sort, as addressed to the eye, the ear, the mind, or the moral sense, that alone can give permanent happiness. When that apocalyptic day shall come, the world will look back to the time we live in and remember the voice of one crying in the wilderness and bless the memory of John Muir. To some beauty seems only an accident of creation: to Muir it was the very smile of God. He sang the glory of nature like another psalmist, and, as a true artist, was unashamed of his emotions.

An instance of this is told of him as he stood with an

acquaintance at one of the great view-points of the Yosemite Valley, and, filled with wonder and devotion, wept. His companion, more stolid than most, could not understand his feeling, and was so thoughtless as to say so.

"Mon," said Muir, with the Scotch dialect into which he often lapsed, "can ye see unmoved the glory of the Almighty?"

"Oh, it's very fine," was the reply, "but I do not wear my heart upon my sleeve."

"Ah, my dear mon," said Muir, "in the face of such a scene as this it's no time to be thinkin' o' where ye wear your heart."

No astronomer was ever more devout. The love of nature was his religion, but it was not without a personal God, whom he thought as great in the decoration of a flower as in the launching of a glacier. The old Scotch training persisted through all his studies of causation, and the key-note of his philosophy was intelligent and benevolent design. His wonder grew with his wisdom. Writing for the first time to a young friend, he expressed the hope that she would "find that going to the mountains is going home and that Christ's Sermon on the Mount is on every mount."

It was late in May, 1889, that I first met him. I had gone to San Francisco to organize the series of papers afterward published in the *Century Magazine* under the title of *The Gold-hunters of California,* and promptly upon my arrival he came to see me. It was at the Palace Hotel in San Francisco. I was dressing for dinner, and was obliged to ask him to come up to my room. He was a long time in doing so, and I feared he had lost his way. I can remember as if it were yesterday hearing him call down the corridor: "Johnson, Johnson! where are you? I can't get the hang of these artificial cañons," and before he had made any of the conventional greetings and inquiries, he added, "Up in the Sierra, all along the gorges, the glaciers have put up natural sign-posts, and you can't miss your way; but here there's nothing to tell you where to go."

With all his Scotch wit and his democratic feeling, Muir bore himself with dignity in every company. He readily adjusted himself to any environment. In the high Sierra he was indeed a voice crying in the wilderness; moreover, he looked like John the Baptist as portrayed in bronze by Donatello and others of the Renaissance sculptors, spare of frame, hardy, keen of eye and visage, and, on the march, eager of movement. It was difficult for an untrained walker to keep up with him as he leaped from rock to rock as surely as a mountain goat or skimmed the surface of the ground, a trick of easy locomotion learned from the Indians. If he ever became tired, nobody knew it, and yet, though he delighted in badinage at the expense of the "tender-foot," he was as sympathetic as a mother. I remember a scramble we had in the upper Tuolumne Cañon which afforded him great fun at my expense. The detritus of the wall of the gorge lay in a confused mass of rocks varying in size from a market-basket to a dwelling-house, the interstices overgrown with a most deceptive shrub, the soft leaves of which concealed its iron trunk and branches. Across such a Dantean formation Muir went with certainty and alertness, while I fell and floundered like a bad swimmer, so that he had to give me many a helpful hand and cheering word, and when at last I was obliged to rest, Muir, before going on for an hour's exploration, sought out for me one of the most beautiful spots I had ever seen, where the rushing river, striking pot-holes in its granite bed, was thrown up into water-wheels twenty feet high. When we returned to camp he showered me with little attentions and tucked me into my blankets with the tenderness that he gave to children and animals.

Another Scotch trait was his surface antipathies. He did not hate anything, not even his antagonists, the tree vandals, but spoke of them pitifully as "misguided worldlings;" yet he had a wholesome contempt for the contemptible. His growl —he never had a bark—was worse than his bite. His pity was often expressed for the blindness of those who, through unenlightened selfishness, chose the lower utility of nature in place of the higher.

Many have praised the pleasures of solitude; few have known them as Muir knew them, roaming the high Sierra week after week with only bread and tea and sometimes berries for his subsistence, which he would have said were a satisfactory substitute for the "locusts and wild honey" of his prototype. His trips to Alaska were even more solitary, and we should say forbidding, but not he; for no weather, no condition of wildness, no absence of animal life could make him lonely. He was a pioneer of nature, but also a pioneer of truth, and he needed no comrade. Many will recall his thrilling adventure of the Muir Glacier, told in his story entitled *Stickeen,* named for his companion, the missionary's dog. I heard him tell it a dozen times, how the explorer and the little mongrel were caught on a peninsula of the glacier, and how they escaped. It is one of the finest studies of dogliness in all literature, and, told in Muir's whimsical way, betrayed unconsciously the tenderness of his heart. Though never lonely, he was not at all a professional recluse: he loved companions and craved good talk, and was glad to have others with him on his tramps; but it was rare to find congenial friends who cared for the adventures in which he reveled. He was hungry for sympathy and found it in the visitors whom he piloted about and above the Yosemite Valley—Emerson, Sir Joseph Hooker, Torrey, and many others of an older day or of late years, including Presidents Roosevelt and Taft.

Muir was clever at story-telling and put into it both wit and sympathy, never failing to give, as a background, more delightful information about the mountains than a professor of geology would put into a chapter. With his one good eye—for the sight of the other had been impaired in his college days in Wisconsin by the stroke of a needle—he saw every scene in detail and in mass. This his conversation visualized until his imagination kindled the imagination of his hearer.

Adventures are to the adventurous. Muir, never reckless, was fortunate in seeing Nature in many a wonderful mood and aspect. Who that has read them can forget his descriptions of the wind-storm in the Yuba, which he outrode in a tree-top, or of the avalanche in the Yosemite, or of the spring floods pouring in hundreds of streams over the rim of the valley? And what unrecorded adventures he must have had as pioneer of peak and glacier in his study of the animal and vegetable life of the Sierra! Did any observer ever come nearer than he to recording the soul of nature? If "good-will makes intelligence," as Emerson avers, Muir's love of his mountains amounted to divination. What others learned laboriously, he seemed to reach by instinct, and yet he was painstaking in the extreme and jealous of the correctness of both his facts and his conclusions, defending them as a beast defends her young. In the Arctic, in the great forests of Asia, on the Amazon, and in Africa at seventy-three, wherever he was, he incurred peril not for "the game," but for some great emprise of science.

But Muir's public services were not merely scientific and literary. His countrymen owe him gratitude as the pioneer of our system of national parks. Before 1889 we had only one of any importance, the Yellowstone. Out of the fight which he led for the better care of the Yosemite by the State of California grew the demand for the extension of the system. To this many persons and organizations contributed, but Muir's writings and enthusiasm were the chief forces that inspired the movement. All the other torches were lighted from his. His disinterestedness was too obvious not to be recognized even by opponents. To a friend who, in 1906, made an inquiry about a mine in California he wrote: "I don't know anything at all about the ―― mine or any other. Nor do I know any mine-owners. All this $ geology is out of my line." It was in his name that the appeal was made for the creation of the Yosemite National Park in 1890, and for six years he was the leader of the movement for the retrocession by California of the Valley reservation, to be merged in the surrounding park, a result which, by the timely aid of Edward H. Harriman, was accomplished in 1905.

In 1896-97, when the Forestry Commission of the National Academy of Sciences, under the chairmanship of Professor Charles S. Sargent of Harvard, was making investigations to determine what further reservations ought to be made in the form of national parks, Muir accompanied it over much of its route through the Far West and the Northwest and gave it his assistance and counsel. March 27, 1899, he wrote: "I've spent most of the winter on forest protection; at least I've done little besides writing about it." From its inception to its lamentable success in December, 1913, he fought every step of the scheme to grant to San Francisco for a water reservoir the famous Hetch Hetchy Valley, part of the Yosemite National Park, which, as I have said, had been created largely through his instrumentality. In the last stages of the campaign his time was almost exclusively occupied with this contest. He opposed the project as unnecessary, as objectionable intrinsically and as a dangerous precedent, and he was greatly cast down when it became a law. But he was also relieved. Writing to a friend, he said: "I'm glad the fight for the Tuolumne Yosemite is finished. It has lasted twelve years. Some compensating good must surely come from so great a loss. With the New Year comes new work. I am now writing on Alaska. A fine change from faithless politics to crystal ice and snow." It is also to his credit that he first made known to the world the wonder and glory of the Big Trees; those that have been rescued from the saw of the sordid lumbermen owe their salvation primarily to his voice.

Muir's death, on Christmas Eve of 1914, though it occurred at the ripe age of seventy-six, and though it closed a life of distinguished achievement, was yet untimely, for his work was by no means finished. For years I had been imploring him to devote himself to the completion of his record. The material of many contemplated volumes exists in his numerous note-books, and though, I believe, these notes are to a great degree written in extenso rather than scrappily, and thus contain much available literary treasure, yet where is the one that could give them the roundness of presentation and the charm of style which are found in Muir's best literary work? One always hesitates to use the word "great" of one who has just passed away, but I believe that history will give a very high place to the indomitable explorer who discovered the great glacier named for him, and whose life for eleven years in the high Sierra resulted in a body of writing of marked excellence, combining accurate and carefully co-ordinated scientific observation with poetic sensibility and expression. His chief books, *The Mountains of California, Our National Parks,* and *The Yosemite,* are both delightful and vivid, and should be made supplemental reading for schools. When he rhapsodizes it is because his subject calls for rhapsody, and not to cover up thinness of texture in his material. He is likely to remain the one historian of the Sierra, importing into his view the imagination of the poet and the reverence of the worshiper.

Muir was not without wide and affectionate regard in his own State, but California was too near to him to appreciate fully his greatness as a prophet or the service he did in trying to recall her to the gospel of beauty. She has, however, done him and herself honor in providing for a path on the high Sierra from the Yosemite to Mount Whitney to be called the John Muir Trail. William Kent, during Muir's life, paid him a rare tribute in giving to the nation a park of redwoods with the understanding that it should be named Muir Woods. But the nation owes him more. His work was not sectional but for the whole people, for he was the real father of the forest reservations of America. The National Government should create from the great wild Sierra Forest Reserve a national park to include the King's River Cañon, to be called by his name. This recognition would be, so to speak, an overt act, the naming of the Muir Glacier being automatic by his very discovery of it. It is most appropriate and fitting that a wild Sierra region should be named for him. There has been only one John Muir.

The best monument, however, would be a successful movement, even at this late day, to save the Hetch Hetchy Valley from appropriation for commercial purposes. His death was hastened by his grief at this unbelievable calamity, and I should be recreant to his memory if I did not call special attention to his crowning public service in endeavoring to prevent the disaster. The Government owes him penance at his tomb.

In conclusion, John Muir was not a "dreamer," but a practical man, a faithful citizen, a scientific observer, a writer of enduring power, with vision, poetry, courage in a contest, a heart of gold, and a spirit pure and fine.

1915

CHARLES FRANCIS ADAMS
BY WILLIAM M. SLOANE

CHARLES FRANCIS ADAMS, fourth in descent from President John Adams through President John Quincy Adams and a scarcely less famous sire of his own name, died in his eighty-first year, a young man to the end. He was soldier, financier, and historian, consumed by zeal in each of his successive vocations. Of our company he had been a member for ten years. Unanimously chosen as a representative historian, he was active in the enterprises of the Academy, making public appearances of dramatic power, and generous in his support of its undertakings. His personality was altogether sympathetic among us. The members of other bodies, personal friends of longer standing than most of us, have described him in their public tributes as brusque and positive, yet open-minded and receptive; as aristocrat by temper and democrat in conduct; as like an iconoclast and a conservative; in short, as the embodiment of paradox, physical and mental.

Doubtless, in one sphere of his activities and during the years of combat, he so appeared and so was. Much, too, depended on the temper of his associates, who all unconsciously may have presented a similar front to him. He was a doughty gladiator in the cause of righteousness, and had a heavy fist where dishonesty in affairs lurked behind fine phrases and shiny euphemisms. While in a high degree endowed with insight, while his vision of the goal was always clear, and while his reasoning processes made him in many instances prophetic, he was really a warrior; he loved the joy of battle even more than conquest. The weapons of his concrete knowledge and ruthless logic were not unfair and never foully wielded, but they were unsparing. With gallant, honest foes he was even chivalrous. It was not safe to menace him with precedent or the ethos of history or the lessons of experience. He was sure to have interpretations of his own which were alike novel and founded on unsuspected aspects of familiar facts. Authority was for him no thunderbolt, but rather a flickering, dancing will-o'-the-wisp.

This temper he manifested as an officer of the line in the Civil War, as a student and director of railways and systems of transportation, as an advocate of radical changes in the higher education given by American universities, and, what concerns us most as his colleagues of Institute and Academy, in his treatment of history as a human discipline.

Among us he was always suave and genial, as befitted a recognized personage. For many years of his later life his home was in Washington, and in the national society comprising men and women from all regions and of all ages he found a flattering recognition as a sage, which calmed his spirit and softened his manners. But in matters of history he was a knight-errant to the last. He regretted the discovery of America as having occurred a century too soon; he discredited the veracity of the enthroned divinities of history from Herodotus onward; the accepted view of Washington as a strategist of the first order he sedulously attacked. He was an advocate of states' rights and supported the project for a monument to Lee in the national capitol. His attitude as a historian was preëminently that of the doubter and the iconoclast. It has been said of Voltaire that he transformed the writing of history by the sheer force of doubt. In the present-day era of modern and radical reconstruction Mr. Adams made his many readers keen and alert, even if he could not always command conviction.

His complete works are embraced in eleven volumes. In a sense he was a writer of pamphlets and miscellanies, but from first to last there is a unity of style and purpose, whether the theme be ancient, modern, or contemporary, social, economic, or political. His style is rugged and polished by turns, but always a style—readable and reasoned. The contents are uneven in value, but everywhere you find something worth while. For him there was all around a turbulent, living, throbbing world, little concerned with academic standards of form and fashion, indifferent to culture, hard-fisted, and selfish. The morals of such a world were more gristle than bone, and needed hardening. And so he was a teacher of ethics, not of the chair and school, but of the lawgiver. He writes magisterially, he enforces judicially, and he flays like the judges in the gate.

That he wielded power as a historian is beyond all peradventure, but it was not because of his style. His title to a high place rests on his untiring industry as an investigator. For drudgery he had both capacity and respect, since without the ceaseless murmur of the treadmill no power can be generated. In biography he excelled; the lives of his father and of Richard Henry Dana are masterpieces of composition and vivid description. His lectures delivered at Oxford and published as the last volume of his series are a fine performance of daring, didactic controversy. While he had a certain British cast to his Americanism, he never forgot, and did not entirely forgive, the treatment to which his country was subjected by official and social England during the Civil War. It was bold, though not over-bold, within the threshold of their own house, to instruct, to warn, and to correct the descendants of the sires who had so wrought. The university, aware of his sincerity and impartial in its own judgments, bestowed on him its highest honor but one, the degree of doctor of letters.

The visit was particularly fruitful in that, like a mole, he burrowed among the tap-roots of historical knowledge, namely, the private papers put at his disposal by the families whose progenitors had made English and American history. Nothing daunted him, age had neither withered nor staled him, and the leads which he opened he and his highly prized friend, Mr. Worthington C. Ford, most industriously worked, bringing a wealth of rich ore to be assayed in America. He may be said to have retained undiminished energy to the end of his long and strenuous life. While his independence of character, his unflinching treatment of public questions, and his proud consciousness of inherited obligations forbade any close organic connection with party machinery, he was nevertheless a statesman, an elder counselor in politics. His advice, when sought, was freely given, and, when not sought, was proclaimed in such ways as to secure general attention from the intelligent public. Legislators were powerfully influenced by it.

He was therefore in some sense a maker of history as well as a writer of it. His nature was eminently social; he frequented private dinners and receptions and was always prominent; he talked abundantly and listened attentively. Again and again he declared that no platform was better than that of a great public banquet, and as an after-dinner speaker he made addresses which were always weighty with thought. His intimate friends were proud and happy in his society and confidences, for he was alike witty and humorous. Like the monk of medieval fable whose name was "Give," he found comrades entitled "It shall be given," and with all the gravity of his nature, the seriousness of his purpose, and the occasional frostiness of his address, he enjoyed life to the full as few have done. It is a pleasant duty to commemorate his work and his stimulus in this association.

FRANCIS HOPKINSON SMITH
BY AUGUSTUS THOMAS

THOUGHTFUL STUDENTS of men have sometimes agreed that the mission of man is expression; an expression directed by attempts to accommodate himself to the unyielding elements in his environment, and his achievements in adjusting the flexible elements to his own needs and vision. Francis Hopkinson Smith was notable for his success on both sides of this readjustment, and for his expression of the results as measured by his own emotional reactions. He was an artist, which is to say that he was observantly conscious of his own emotions and possessed a definite avenue and method for communicating them intelligibly to his fellow-men. He was always conscious of the law of gravitation, conscious of the plumb-line and the horizon, of the perpendicular and the level; always too sane for that tolerable degree of seeming madness to which genius is allied. But he had the permanent and fine sense of proportion that is the parent of talent. Concerning those merely apprehended and haunted heights which only music explores or the lyrical line reflects he was silent. But within the circumference of his vision he saw definitely, clearly, securely, and was alive with expression to his very finger-tips. With pencil and brush, with written and spoken word, he was truthful and persuasive, and had a degree of mastery that not only permitted but compelled him to be playful. He could ride any of his hobbies bareback; and if the Olympian hostler had parked Pegasus in his paddock, he would have been merciful to the creature but quite unafraid, and would have unremittingly made him earn his feed.

By profession he was a mechanical engineer. His avocations were drawing, painting, writing, speaking; in each he gained a notable eminence. Born in the city of Baltimore, his point of view, his mental attitude towards life, his courtly bearing were those of the Southerner as America understands the term. With the Southerner's traditions and training and with the principal facts from which a Southern deduction is made, women in his treatment were always objects of romance and to be protected. The casual Russian female traveler in the compartment of a Continental car was for him a Princess, and on no initiative of his could have been considered as an adventuress or vampire.

There is a legend, perhaps a record, in our war for independence to the effect that when Lord Howe reported to the British Admiralty that the Americans had fled up the Bronx River he received an order by return messenger to take a gunboat and pursue them. There was no wider difference between the physical fact and the British Ministry's apprehension than there was between the actual River Bronx and Hopkinson Smith's poetical and romantic description of it in his *Day at Laguerre's*. Commuters moving towards New York on the New Haven road, passing the cemetery at Woodlawn, look to their left on a little creek not wider than the suburban dining-rooms they have left and at one point on its further bank a collection of sheds, a broken grape-arbor, a dilapidated two-story building. This undesirable property, seen with Hopkinson Smith's ability to transmute the ordinary into the beautiful, became a sylvan stream across which the weary traveler halloed to a girl who pushed over with her small paddle-boat and carried him into the desirable Arcadia where he was to spend his summer day.

Some critics have found a test of a novelist's rank in the number of enduring portraits that he has contributed. It takes time to make these recognizable and quotable. But we can believe that Colonel Carter will pass into type and stencil as definite as Micawber.

On the platform as a reader Hopkinson Smith was effective, with resonant voice, clear diction, lively expression, and simple and eloquent gesture. As a speaker without a manuscript he was ready and forceful. He had opinions on most important subjects, and was sufficiently partisan to be effective.

Some English essayist, making a distinction between the climate of France and that of England, regarded the French weather as rather incidental to the landscape, but in England he said the weather always seemed to be sitting for its portrait. That writer had only a fraction of the perspective of Francis Hopkinson Smith, for whom the weather the world over seemed always ready for the painter. Every day had for him

its particular enveloping atmosphere. This was so fundamental a recognition that his portfolio was filled with large
water-color cartons of different shades. He looked at the day
and drew from this collection of pastel tints the paper that
was in harmony with the time, and painted on it the physical
scene that he had selected and to which transcription he lent
the beauty of his temperament. His most notable work as an
artist was in water-color. If he did not make a picture a day,
he at least started one and carried it far enough to make it
secure in his record during the season that he devoted to this
avocation. While his most notable work was in this medium,
the most effective things he did were charcoal illustrations
made with an architectural truth but without servility, and
executed with a courage that would have been primitive if
not so modified by the poetry in the man. Doré, in his illustrations of Jerrold's *Pilgrimage of London,* with the assistance of the wonderful engravers that made his India washes
eloquent, fell somewhat short of the convincing effect that
Hopkinson Smith got into his charcoal drawings and preserved through their process reproductions.

In his early youth he had been a clerk in an iron works.
After entering his profession of engineer he built the sea-
wall around Governor's Island, another at Tompkinsville,
Staten Island, the Race Rock Light House off New London,
and the foundation at Bedloe's Island for the Bartholdi Statue
of Liberty. The battles with tide and wind and storm he
records in his stories, perhaps unconscious that nature had
already incorporated them in his acquired character. His inherited temperament was predisposed to their acquisition. If
one had to symbolize him by some selection from the animal
kingdom the eagle would furnish the nearest type.

As an artist he received a bronze medal from the Buffalo
Exposition, a silver medal from the Charleston Exposition,
gold medals from the Philadelphia Art Club and the American Art Society. He wrote some five and twenty novels and
books of short stories, but more than any fame of these or

recognition of his work as an artist or his success as an engineer we are justified in believing that he would prefer to be remembered, if it were possible, for his personal and social qualities. Besides being an artist in the fields described he was an artist also of living.

He died on the seventh day of April, 1915. For nearly seven years after the psalmist's span and limit he had been in looks the kind of middle-aged person that every young athlete hopes to become. To know him was to believe in vikings, crusaders, and cavaliers. Any group into which he came felt an accession of vitality and a quickened circulation. The company he left is conscious of a bereaving loss.

THOMAS RAYNESFORD LOUNSBURY

BY BRANDER MATTHEWS

WHEN THE National Institute of Arts and Letters decided that the time was ripe for the founding of an American Academy of Arts and Letters, it selected seven of its members and empowered them to select eight others. Thomas Raynesford Lounsbury was one of the eight thus chosen, and he was therefore one of the first fifteen original members of the Academy. He was faithful in his attendance at our annual meetings, journeying to Washington, to Philadelphia, and to Chicago, and enriching our programs on two occasions by papers of characteristic interest.

He was born on the first of January, 1838, and he was graduated from Yale when he was twenty-one. He labored for a year or two on the American Cyclopedia, edited by Ripley and Dana. At the outbreak of the Civil War he enlisted in the 126th New York Volunteers, serving to the end. At Gettysburg his regiment was deployed down the slope of Cemetery Ridge, the men being so exhausted that they went to sleep, despite the noise of the terrific artillery duel which preceded Pickett's charge.

THOMAS RAYNESFORD LOUNSBURY

Shortly after the end of the war Lounsbury was called to an instructorship in the Sheffield Scientific School of Yale; and to the Sheffield School and to Yale he rendered devoted service for nearly forty years. He was made professor of English in 1871; and in 1906 he was regretfully allowed to retire into the innocuous desuetude of the emeritus professor. Always indefatigable in research and in the accumulation of information scientifically verified, he was regretfully hampered in the later years of his life by a failing of sight, which forced him to limit his hours of labor. Yet he retained to the end his cheery good humor and his keen interest in life. Although he was seventy-six when he came to the meeting in New York in November, 1914, he seemed to be as full of vitality as ever. He survived until the following spring, dying in April, 1915.

At the time of his lamented death the position held by Professor Lounsbury was without parallel. He was recognized as the chief of all the scholars who in Great Britain and in the United States had devoted themselves to what is known in university circles as "English," and he was the final survivor of those of this group of students who maintained a commanding place in the two halves of the subject, in the history of the English language and in the history of English literature in both its branches, British and American. No other English scholar on either side of the Atlantic could speak with equal authority about both the language and the literature.

His brief history of the English language is a little masterpiece of carefully controlled information and of marvelously lucid exposition; and he followed this with later discussions of usage, of pronunciation, of spelling, and of Americanisms and Briticisms. These several books were the result of widespread and incessant investigation; they were solidly rooted in knowledge; they were informed with wisdom; and they were illumined by both wit and humor. Never was there a student of linguistics less pedantic than Lounsbury, or more human in his understanding of the essential fact that speech is the possession of the people as a whole and not an appanage of the self-appointed grammarians. In all his discussions of the English language, its idioms and its orthography, Lounsbury was as independent and as individual as he was as a biographer. He was willing to stand up and be counted in the company of the much decried spelling reformers. He attacked the Tories who ventured to defend our complicated and chaotic spelling, employing all the weapons furnished him by his erudition and his wit. Ten years ago he was one of the organizers of the Simplified Spelling Board, and for several years he served as its president, lending to the cause the weight of his authority and of his character.

The same sanity and good humor, the same comprehensive thoroughness, the same untiring industry in getting at the exact facts, the same sagacity in interpreting these facts anew, characterized his many contributions to the history of English literature. He mastered his successive subjects with the meticulous accuracy of a conscientious man of science, and he presented the results of his labor to the reader with the skill of an accomplished man of letters. His own task was hard in order that our work might be easy. He began his career as a biographer with his cordial and delightful study of Fenimore Cooper. He erected an enduring monument in the three solid tomes of his Chaucer. He devoted several volumes to the vicissitudes of Shakespeare's fame. He narrated with a host of new facts the early years of Browning's poetic activity, and he left incomplete at his death his final study of the slow and steady rise of the reputation of Tennyson.

He left it incomplete only in so far as it was unfinished and in part unrevised. But it is not a fragment; it covers the ground thoroughly as far as he had carried his work. It is larger in scope than a mere biography of Tennyson. It is this first of all, of course, but it is also a searching analysis of the literary history of Great Britain in the third, fourth, and fifth decades of the last century, made possible at the cost of tremendous labor in examining the files of a host of dead-and-gone periodicals. The result of this indomitable research, carried on unflinchingly despite many disadvantages, is a masterly reconstruction of the circumstances of English literature in the thirty years during which Tennyson was gaining the unchallenged position he occupied in the final thirty years of his life.

Nowhere does the author allow himself to be choked by the dust of the back-numbers he disturbed from their silent sleep. Everywhere he retains control of his vast mass of material, and everywhere does he handle it with a fine artistic sense of its significance. Everywhere does he reveal his own fundamental characteristics, his fairness, his tolerance, his transparent honesty, his understanding of human nature, and his omnipresent sense of humor. He is never overcome by the burden of his material; he is never hurried, and he conducts his leisurely inquiry in accord with his large and liberal method. He knew that he had a long job to do, and he did it as he felt that it ought to be done. What is more, he did it once for all; and most unlikely is it that any later delvers into this period will be able to add anything significant, or will find any occasion to modify the judgments here expressed.

Nor is it likely that critics of another generation will be tempted to attack the main positions taken by Lounsbury in his earlier studies of Chaucer, of Shakespeare, of Browning, and of Fenimore Cooper. Whatever memorial he was about to build, Lounsbury always sank his foundations down to bed-rock.

His position among American scholars was lofty, and it will be long before his authority will be in any way diminished. In fact, one might well apply to him a remark he himself made about Tennyson: "Every great writer attains in time to a certain wealth of reputation, not indeed an unearned increment, but an amount of compound interest which has been accruing since the investment was first made."

JOHN WHITE ALEXANDER

BY EDWIN H. BLASHFIELD

I<small>N</small> J<small>OHN</small> W<small>HITE</small> A<small>LEXANDER</small> a frail body lodged a tireless, eager spirit—tireless and unquenched by illness to the very end, eager not only in search for beauty, but in service to his fellows. Among artists, some are recorders, some arrangers, some are creators, and some are dreamers of dreams.

Now and then comes a man who may belong to any one of these groups, but who adds to his artistic gift and his technical acquirement a capacity for communication of enthusiasm to others and an instinctive desire to stimulate, to push at the wheels wherever he sees that they turn slowly. Such a man soon becomes a leader. Toward leadership John Alexander gravitated instinctively, and in it he established himself solidly, using the experience of one official position to affirm that of another, touching the circle of the arts at many points in its circumference, and strengthening himself by every fresh touch. If a man is strong enough physically to withstand the demands of such arduous effort, he gains enormously in the power to synthetize that effort and to build up from one department to another.

Alexander was not strong enough, and he paid the physical penalty; but while his life lasted he never relaxed that effort, and he made it fruitful, feeding it always with persistent enthusiasm.

For an instance in this synthetizing of effort, he worked first as a member of the Metropolitan Museum's board at increasing and safeguarding that museum's treasures; next as a member of the School Art League he worked at the provision of intelligent appreciation of those treasures—appreciation planted in the minds of the children of the city to grow till it should reward the museum's effort with understanding adult and trained.

He talked to the children who flocked to see the painting and sculpture and the art objects of all kinds. And when the children went away, he followed them to their East Side clubs and schools and talked to them again, encouraging them to try experiments of their own in painting and modeling, and he stimulated them with prizes that adjudged and sometimes instituted. He loved his work among the children, and he told me, with a twinkle, and more than once, of how these very young people managed to fortify the doubtful experiment of a journey into art by the undoubted pleasure of at least beginning that journey on roller-skates. "Dozens of them," said he, "skate to their lecture." If he was busy with the children's welfare, the interests of his comrades of all ages busied him still more. He was a painter through and through; nevertheless, the sister arts of music and the drama claimed and obtained his time in one of his favorite fields of effort, the MacDowell Club.

To the plastic presentation of the drama, its costuming, lighting, and colors, he gave enthusiastic attention, aided almost always by Mrs. Alexander. It was an easy progression for him from his canvases to the moving-pictures of a pageant or a play, and his swift inventiveness enabled him to get through a prodigious amount of work in a short time, in such productions, for instance, as Miss Maude Adams's *Jeanne d'Arc* at the Harvard Stadium, or in the many series of tableaux which he arranged for charity. "If you have a frame and some gauze," said he to me, "you have no idea how much you can do in a moment with a few colored rags." I had an idea, for I had seen him juggle with them and had admired the effects which he produced so easily, for he seemed to take pains easily, and with a geniality which relieved his beneficiary from a sense of too great obligation. This graceful suavity was a potent factor in his helpfulness; but he was so smiling and kindly that I fear one did not always realize how much his ready service sometimes tired him.

During the last year of his life I saw him many times a week, and we often came home together from the Academy council or from other committee meetings.

Although, as I have said, his spirit was not tired, his body was. Again and again he rose from a sick-bed to preside upon a platform. His delicate features, which recalled some cavalier's portrait by Van Dyke, were at times during his last year almost transparent-looking. And yet he was so resilient, he so responded to the stimulus of work to do, he had recovered so many times from severe attacks, that his death, when it came, was not only a great shock, but was a surprise.

Critics, writers of books, will talk to us at length of his art; there is time to-day for only the briefest impression of it. One would say that a refinement rising to distinction was its most obvious quality. Pattern and lighting were what seemed to interest him most of all. Long, sweeping, curving lines he sought for or rather seemed to find without searching, and they gave a decorative character to all his portraits.

In his color restraint was a notable quality, a notable preservative, a notable insurance against either crudity or lushness, against vulgarity of any kind. Now and again he composed large and elaborated groups, as in his panels for the Carnegie Institute of Pittsburgh, which make up one of the most considerable extensive series of decorations ever painted. But he loved simplicity, and thought simply in his painting, and he seemed to like best and be happiest in his treatment of single figures. It was peculiarly in these that his sense of pattern and of line, of long, sweeping curves, never failed him.

He was very personal in lighting, which was simple and large, yet at the same time was often extremely picturesque in its arrangement. Its effect was not a little enhanced by his predisposition toward masses of reflected light, which he used with great skill.

Restraint reaching to sobriety marked most of his color. He liked to use a warm gray in wide planes, and then to strike into it one or two dominant spots of rich or brilliant colors. Just before his death he built a very large studio in the Catskills, and I believe that the trees and hills of his beloved

Onteora got into the color of his pictures and helped toward that predilection for a whole gamut of greens which one may easily note on the walls of his exhibitions—gray greens, blue greens, olive greens, yellow greens, greens of the color of thick glass. His pigment was brushed easily and flowingly. Sometimes he painted a whole portrait with what artists would call a "fat brush," but usually the color was thin, with occasional loaded passages, the canvas being sometimes hardly more than stained.

The sureness of his recording was remarkable, and its swiftness was phenomenal. This of course was an extraordinary insurance against any kind of heaviness in his color, since overpainting is one of the worst enemies to freshness of surface. His swiftness of recording must be emphasized again. I should hardly dare to say in how short a time he executed one or two portraits that hung upon the walls of his drawing-room, and which he called unfinished, though they were very satisfying, certainly, to me.

Much as I should like to linger over his painting, I cannot keep away from the subject of his eagerness to help other artists to find a gallery adequate to the housing of their painting. The search for a home for the National Academy of Design was the central preoccupation of the last years of his life. It was interesting, indeed, when he spoke upon any platform and any subject, to see how many angles of approach he could find to that *one* subject which was nearest his heart, the new gallery, which should some day house a dozen different societies of artists.

I have said that some artists are recorders, some creators, and some are dreamers of dreams. Recorder and creator he certainly was. While he was still a child he was for a while a little messenger-boy, and he never ceased to be a messenger, bringing stimulus of words and example, writing his name with Ben Adhem's as a lover of his fellow-men. And a dreamer he was of dreams—of a dream which we fully believe will come true, when New York will have a great gallery all its own, and which we may link in our thought with the memory of that brilliant artist and devoted president of the National Academy of Design, John White Alexander.

1916

HENRY JAMES
BY BLISS PERRY

ALTHOUGH Henry James wrote at one time acute studies of New England character, he was never, in his relations to that section, or, for that matter, to any locality save possibly London, anything more than a "visiting mind." His grandfather was an Irish merchant in Albany. His father was a philosopher and wit, a man of comfortable fortune, who lived at times in Newport, Concord, and Boston, but who was residing in New York when his son Henry was born in 1843. No child was ever made the subject of a more complete theory of deracination. Transplanted from city to city, from country to country, without a family or a voting-place, without college or church or creed or profession or responsibility of any kind save to his own exigent ideals of truth and beauty, Henry James came to be the very pattern of a cosmopolitan. Avoiding his native country for nearly thirty years and then returning for a few months to write some intricate pages about that *American Scene* which he understood far less truly than the average immigrant, at the beginning of the war he renounced his American citizenship and became a British subject in order to show his sympathy with the Empire. It was the sole evidence of political emotion in a lifetime of seventy-three years.

American writing men are justly proud, nevertheless, of this expatriated craftsman. The task of really understanding him has been left chiefly to clever women and to a few critics, but ever since *A Passionate Pilgrim* and *Roderick Hudson* appeared in 1875, it has been recognized that here was a master, in his own fashion. What that fashion is may now be known by any one who will take the pains to read the author's prefaces to the New York edition of his revised works. Never, not even in the Paris which James loved, has an artist put his intentions and his self-criticism more definitely upon paper. The secret of Henry James is told plainly enough here: a specially equipped intelligence, a freedom from normal responsibilities, a consuming desire to create beautiful things, and, as life unfolded its complexities and *nuances* before his vision, an increasing passion to seek the beauty which lies entangled and betrayed, a beauty often adumbrated rather than made plastic, stories that must be hinted at rather than told, raptures that exist for the initiated only.

No one who ever had the pleasure of hearing James discourse about the art of fiction can forget the absolute seriousness of his professional devotion; it was as though a shy celebrant were to turn and explain, with mystical intensity and a mystic's involution and reversal of all the values of vulgar speech, the ceremonial of some strange, high altar. His own power as a creative artist was not always commensurate with his intellectual endowment or with his desire after beauty, and his frank contempt for the masses of men made it difficult for him to write English. He preferred, like Browning, a dialect of his own, and he used it increasingly after he was fifty. It was a dialect capable of infinite gradations of tone, endless refinements of expression. In his threescore books there are delicious, poignant moments where the spirit of life itself flutters like a wild creature, half-caught, half-escaping. It is for the beauty and thrill of these moments that the pages of Henry James will continue to be cherished by a few thousand readers scattered throughout the Republic to which he was ever an alien.

He was elected a member of the Academy in 1905, and died in 1916.

JAMES WHITCOMB RILEY

BY HAMLIN GARLAND

ONE DAY in 1885, while calling upon my friend Charles E. Hurd, the Literary Editor of the Boston *Transcript*, I noticed upon his desk a curious little volume bound in parchment entitled *The Old Swimmin' Hole and 'Leven More Poems*, by Benjamin F. Johnson of Boone.

Hurd, observing my interest, handed the book to me, saying, "Here is a man you should be interested in. He comes from out your way."

This was my introduction to "The Hoosier Poet." I read in this booklet *When the Frost Is on the Punkin, My Fiddle*, and other of the pieces which later became familiar through Riley's readings on the platform, and I tasted in them a homely flavor which no other American poet had given me. I became almost at once an advocate of the man and the book. I wrote to the author and thereafter read every line of his writings so far as I could obtain them. I felt that in James Whitcomb Riley America had a writer who voiced as no one else had voiced the outlook of the Middle Western farmer.

Year by year Riley grew in reputation and appeal. He published *Afterwhiles, Pipes o' Pan*, and other volumes of mingled verse and prose, partly in the Hoosier vernacular, partly in an English which was touched with the same quaint, individual quality. The magazines soon began to publish his poems, but in truth his success did not come so much in print as through his own reading of his lines from the platform. He had in him something of the minstrel. He possessed notable power to charm and move an audience, and everywhere he spoke he left a throng of friends. To hear him read—or recite —*A Song of the Airly Days* was to be moved in a new and unforgettable way. His vibrant individual voice, his flexile lips, his droll glance, united to make him at once poet and comedian—comedian in the sense which makes for tears as well as for laughter.

Year by year his popularity increased, until his royalties surpassed those of even the greatest of American novelists. He appealed with singular power to the people of his own State, but he also appealed to the readers in Eastern States. He expressed something of the wistful sadness of the middle-aged man who is looking back on the sunlit streams of his boyhood, and he voiced also with notable fidelity the emotions of children in the wonder-world of the present. In all this work of the homely American Hoosier type his pen was adequate. He was recognized at last as the chief singer in the rural vernacular.

In 1892 I visited Riley at his native town of Greenfield, Indiana, and the town and country gave moving evidence of the wonder-working power of the poet. To my eyes it was the most unpromising field for art, especially for the art of verse. The landscape had no hills, no lakes, no streams of any movement or beauty. Ragged fence-rows, flat and dusty roads, fields of wheat alternating with clumps of trees—these were the features of a country which to me was utterly common-place—and yet from this dusty, drab, unpromising environment Riley had been able to draw the honey of woodland poesy, a sweet in which a native fragrance as of basswood and buckwheat bloom mingled with hints of an English meadow and the tang of a Canada thistle.

In person Riley was as markedly individual as his verse. He was short, square-shouldered, and very blond, with a head which he was accustomed to speak of as "of the tack-hammer variety." His smoothly shaven face was large and extremely expressive, the face of a great actor. Though grim in repose it lighted up with the merriest smiles as he read or as he uttered some quaint jest. His diction when he wished it to be so was admirably clear and precise, but he loved to drop into the speech and drawl of his Hoosier characters, and to me this was a never-failing delight. I have never met a man save Mark Twain who had the same amazing flow of quaint conceits. He spoke "copy" all the time.

In his own proper person he was wise rather than learned. His speech had the charm of the proverb, the sententiousness of the homespun philosopher. Once he said to me, "I don't take no credit fer my ignorance—jest born that-a-way." At another time he remarked with a touch of mysticism, "My work did itself. I'm only the willer bark through which the whistle comes."

His dialect verse is written in two ways, one in the fashion of the man of little schooling who is expressing himself on paper, and the other, as the same man (or his neighbor) might express in actual speech the feeling which impelled him to utterance. In each case the expression is indirect, for Americans of his type are careful not to "slop over," as they call it. As Riley himself says, "I never represent people as the scholar thinks they *ought* to think and feel,—I never try to edit nature. Nature is good enough fer God, it's good enough fer me."

As he drew towards old age his health failed and the quality of his work declined in value. He repeated himself as Bret Harte did, and when he tried imaginative or formal verse he often failed. His genius was for the homely, the quaint, the pathetic, and his best expression was the vernacular. It was in poems like *Nothin' at All to Say* and *Griggsby's Station* that he won his fame, and not in fanciful pieces like *The Flying Islands of the Night*. There are a hundred American poets who can write conventional sonnets, there are very few who can catch the charm that is in *Kingry's Mill* and *Down Around the River*.

Others get the phonetics of everyday speech, but Riley *thought* in dialect. Common speech is the bones of his verse. It cannot be translated. It is not, of course, actual speech, but it suggests it, epitomizes it. No one else has ever caught more deftly the lisp and stammer of childhood. Eugene Field wrote about children, Riley dramatized them. In all that he wrote he retained his individuality—even in his more conventional verse he was never without his own savor.

He taught us once again the fundamental truth which we were long in learning here in America, that there is a poetry of common things as well as of epic deeds. His immense success with the common, non-literary public is to be counted for him and not against him. Either consciously or unconsciously his verses were wrought for the family. He never forced the erotic note. Surrounded by Americans, he wrote for Americans. To me his restraint is a fine and true distinction.

His verse sprang from a certain era of Mid-western development. It is a humble crop gathered from the corners of rail fences, from the vines which clamber upon the porches of small villages, and from the weedy side-walks of quiet towns far from the great markets of the world. For the people who are his kindred Riley was a spokesman, and his verses will not die so long as those of us who came up through the same lanes and by-ways live in the golden memories of the "Airly Days." The poets of to-day are writing of a different America, varying their accent to meet the demands of their day, and this is their privilege and their duty, but in the midst of the tumult of "the New America" I take pleasure in paying tribute to a man who did so much to embody a world that is gone.

As he said of his brother, so I say of him:

> With a cheery word and a wave of the hand
> He has wandered into a foreign land—
> He is not dead, he is just away!

WILLIAM MERRITT CHASE
BY KENYON COX

IN THE death, on October 25, 1916, of William Merritt Chase, the American Academy of Arts and Letters lost a member who had been one of the foremost figures in American art for nearly forty years and a painter of international reputation for at least a quarter of a century. From the moment of his return to this country, in 1878, from his studies in Munich he became a leader of what was then the younger school, and during all succeeding changes he never lost his dominating position. As a teacher he probably exercised a wider influence on American painting than any other artist has ever done.

He painted a great variety of subjects, from the nude figure, through portrait, genre, and landscape, to still life; and in a variety of manners, now precise and minute and again broad and even summary, dark and bituminous in tone in his early work, later often cool and bright, more generally in an intermediate tone neither somber nor over-brilliant. But with all the appearance and the presence of versatility, there is yet a singular unity in all his work, and a perfectly definite point of view, which never changes.

He was entirely of his time, that latter third of the nineteenth century, which was essentially naturalistic in its aims, and he never attempted to paint anything more than can be seen with the bodily eye. After his first few costume pieces, he scarcely went so far as to arrange the things he would paint, but preferred to take what came as it came, knowing that wherever he might be, there could be no lack of good, paintable material all about him, and devoting his acute vision and his skilled hand to the registering of his discoveries of the world in which he lived.

Yet, naturalist as he was in his choice of materials, he entirely escaped that besetting danger of naturalism, the scientific temper. He was never among the strenuous investigators of form or light or color; he was essentially the painter, using so much of the attainments of his time as he could readily compel to his own end of facile production, but with no notion of sacrificing his art that his successors might benefit by the invention of new tools or the acquisition of greater knowledge. Possessed of great energy and bodily vigor, of a cool, if keen, vision and of extraordinary technical ability, unbiased

93

by theories and untroubled by emotion, never attempting more than he could do easily, however difficult the doing of it might be to others, he poured forth with a genial fecundity a long series of works, ever new, yet ever the same, demonstrations of his lively interest in the differing aspects of nature and of his even livelier joy in the exercise of his own powers. His message to the world was no other than that simple yet profound one which Stevenson expressed in his *Child's Garden of Verses:*

> The world is so full of a number of things,
> I am sure we should all be as happy as kings.

Few of us can have been happier than Chase himself, whose life was devoted to the continuously successful accomplishment of tasks in which he delighted.

Profoundly convinced of the truth that the business of a painter is to paint,—inclined, perhaps, to the more doubtful belief that the sole business of a painter is to paint,—the same qualities that made William M. Chase seem revolutionary and protestant in his youth, when painting was lingeringly academic, literary, and sentimental, made him a conservative in his age, when painting was trying to purge itself of its representative element and to transform itself into an art of pure expression. At both extremes his influence was a wholesome one. It was well for us in America, in his early time, to be taught that it is not enough to have feelings, ideas, and knowledge, that one must also learn one's trade. It is well for all the world to-day to be reminded that the art of painting exists, that it is by its nature an imitative art, and that just observation and beautiful workmanship must always have their place in it and will always retain their value.

As man, as artist, and as teacher he had lived his life, had done what he had to do and said what he had to say. We who knew him will miss the invigorating contact with his intensely vital personality, but a longer life would scarcely have added greatly to the sum of what he was. His place in American art is fixed, and as long and as widely as that art may interest mankind, so long and so widely will his name be remembered.

HAMILTON WRIGHT MABIE
BY HENRY VAN DYKE

A TRIBUTE TO the memory of Hamilton Wright Mabie must be full of deep and warm affection if it would express in any measure the thoughts and feelings of the many who knew him personally while he walked the paths of earth, —a serene, wise, and generous comrade in the crowded pilgrimage of American life.

He was a man with a genius for friendship and helpfulness. Religious by nature and holding to Christian faith and ideals with unalterable conviction, he had a simple, practical, beautiful, common-sense quality of manhood which kept him from ever becoming a bigot, a fanatic, or a sentimentalist. He understood human nature, with all its faults and twists, and he loved it notwithstanding all. Steering his own course with a steady hand, he wished not to judge or dominate other men, but only to help them to see the star by which he steered and to make its light useful to them for guidance. Those who came to him for counsel got it clean and straight, often with that touch of humor which was the salt of his discourse.

Those who disliked and scorned him as an "old fogy," and followed him with a strange malice of petty mockery, found him silent, tolerant, content to go forward with his own work for human progress, and ready to help them if they got into trouble. He was the most open-minded and kind-hearted of men. To his acquaintances and his thousands of auditors on his lecture-tours he was a voice of tranquil wisdom, genial wit, and serene inspiration. To his intimates he was an incomparable friend.

I came to know him well only after he had passed middle

life. But I am sure that the spirit which was in him then had animated him from the beginning, and continued to illuminate him to the end of his life. Mabie was not a man to falter or recant. He advanced. He fulfilled the aim of Wordsworth's "Happy Warrior," who

> When brought
> Among the tasks of real life hath wrought
> Upon the task that pleased his childish thought.

He was born at Cold Spring, N. Y., in 1846, and graduated from Williams College in 1867, and from the Columbia College Law School in 1869. But the practice of law as a profession did not attract or satisfy him. In 1879 he became an editorial writer for *The Christian Union,* a religious periodical of broadening scope and influence which developed, under the leadership of Lyman Abbott and Hamilton Mabie and an able staff, into the liberal, national, Christian weekly well-named *The Outlook.* Mabie's work on this paper was constant, devoted, happy, and full of quiet inspiration for clearer thinking and better living. Most of his articles, which must have numbered thousands during his service of thirty-seven years, were unsigned. But they bore the image and superscription of his strong character, fine intelligence, broad sympathies, and high standards, both in literature and in life.

They were not sermons. They were simple words of wisdom uttered in season. They were sometimes pungent,—for he had a vivid sense of righteousness,—but they were never malicious or strident. They were the counsels of a well-wisher. He hated evil, but when he struck at it he desired to help those whom it had deceived and enslaved. For the most part he wrote from the positive rather than from the negative side, preferring the praise of right to the condemnation of wrong. Something in his character permeated his style. A certain unpretending reasonableness, a tranquil assurance of the ultimate victory of light over darkness, an understanding sense of the perplexities and shadows which overcast our mortal life, gave to the words which he wrote from week to week a quiet power of penetration and persuasion. They entered myriads of homes and hearts for good. In this service to modern life through the editorial pages of *The Outlook* he continued steadily, gladly, faithfully, until his earthly work ended on New Year's Eve, 1916.

During this long period of professional labor as a writer for the press, he developed a national influence perhaps even wider as a public lecturer and an author.

No man in America was more welcome to an intelligent audience, for a lyceum lecture or a commencement address, than Hamilton Mabie. Here his personal qualities had full play, perhaps even more than in his writing. His radiant nature, his keen sense of humor, his ready and attractive manner of speech, his sympathy with all sorts and conditions of men and women, gave him quick and easy access to his listeners. They went with him because he appealed to them. He reached them because he took the trouble to open the doors.

The material of his lectures, as in the case of Emerson, was that which he afterwards used in his books. But when he was speaking it was put in a different form—more free, more colloquial, adapted to the occasion. Why should a speaker regard his audiences as cast-iron receptacles for a dose of doctrine? Mabie never did that. But he always had something to say that was serious, well-considered, worth thinking about. That was the reason why thoughtful people liked to hear him.

He was a popular lecturer in the best sense of the phrase. The demands upon his time and strength in this field were incessant. In addition he had the constant appeal of humane and hopeful causes looking to the betterment of social life,—like the Kindergarten Society of which he was for many years the president. To these calls he was always ready to respond. It was his self-forgetfulness in such work that exhausted his strength and brought on his final illness. He was a soldier on the firing-line of human progress. In that cause he was glad to give his life.

His books have deserved and had a wide reading and a high appreciation. They show the clear carefulness of his thinking, the depth of his love for nature and human nature, the excellence of his skill as a writer of pure and translucent English.

Nothing could be better for the purpose for which they were intended than the volumes in which he rendered, for the boys and girls of to-day, the great stories and legends of the past,—*Norse Stories from the Eddas, Myths Every Child Should Know, Heroes Every Child Should Know,* and so on.

But much more significant and original is the series of books in which he made his contribution to the art of essay-writing,—*My Study Fire, Under the Trees and Elsewhere, Short Studies in Literature.* These are rich in the fruits of observation in the home, the library, the great out-of-doors,—

> The harvest of a quiet eye
> That broods and sleeps on his own heart.

These volumes were followed by others in which he expressed his deepening thoughts on the unity and the beauty of life in brief essays on *Nature and Culture, Books and Culture, Work and Culture, The Life of the Spirit,* and *The Great Word,*—by which he means *Love,* not blind and selfish, but open-eyed, intelligent, generous,—the kind of love which made his home a refuge of peace, a spring of joy and strength.

It is a fine ideal which guides the course of all these essays, —an ideal of the coöperation of nature and books and work in the unfolding of personality. Culture, in that sense, was Mabie's conception of the best reward that life has to give. *Kultur,* in the German sense, machine-made and iron-bound, he despised and hated. For this and other reasons he was ardent for the cause of the free and civilized nations against Germany in the barbaric war which she forced upon the world in 1914.

But the bulk of his work lies back of this sharp and bitter crisis, in a period of general tranquillity, through which his

writing flows like a pure and fertilizing stream in a landscape.
He was an optimist, but not of the rose-water variety. He
knew that life involves painful effort, hard conflict. Nevertheless he believed that for those who will face the conflict
and make the effort, help and victory are sure. He was a
critic, delighting to read and comment upon the great books,
—Homer, the Greek Tragedies, the Mediæval Epics, Dante,
Shakespeare, Milton, and the more modern classics. But he
was not a technical and scholastic critic. He sought to catch
the spirit and meaning of the literature which he loved. His
work always reminds me of that passage in *The Pilgrim's
Progress* which describes the "House of the Interpreter."
The beauty of his comment on the classics is that it has a way
of being right about their real significance.

This is true of his most important critical work,—*William
Shakespeare, Poet, Dramatist, and Man*. On this volume he
spent long, loving, patient study and toil. The result was one
of the best, clearest, most readable and illuminating books in
Shakespearean literature. Its central thesis,—that Shakespeare's poetic genius, his gift of vision, passion, and imagination, was the spring of his dramatic power, and that therefore, despite our imperfect knowledge of his biography, we
may be sure of his greatness as a man,—is thoroughly sound.
It is set forth with admirable lucidity and abundant illustration.

There is one of Mabie's books which is less known than
others. It is called *A Child of Nature*. It represents his first
and only attempt, so far as I know, in the field of fiction. But
it is fiction of a peculiar type,—no plot, little dialogue, no
incidents except birth and death and the ordinary run of life
in the New England village where John Foster spent his
days. The theme of the book, developed with deep fidelity
and subtle beauty, is the growth of this quiet, simple, lonely
man's spirit in the fellowship of nature and of great books.
He dies silent and alone, never having learned to speak to
the world or even to his neighbors the wisdom which he has

garnered. But some brief daily record of his experiences, his thoughts, the light of life that has come to him, he has written down and leaves behind him. Then comes a young man of another type, Ralph Parkman, scholar, traveler, and author, to live in the old farmhouse. He finds the forgotten papers, and their sincerity and beauty take hold of him. He gives them the form and finish which they need, and sends them out to the world.

"It was a little book which finally went forth from the old house, but it was very deep and beautiful; like a quiet mountain pool, it was far from the dust and tumult of the highways, and there were images of stars in it. With the generosity of a fine spirit the younger man interpreted the life of the older man through the rich atmosphere of his own temperament, but there was nothing in the beautiful flowering and fruitage which the world received from his hand which was not potentially in the heart and mind of John Foster. The silent man had come to his own, for God had given him a voice. After the long silence of a lifetime he spoke in tones which vibrated and penetrated, not like great bells swung in unison in some high tower, but like dear familiar bells set in old sacred places, whose sweet notes are half-audible music and half-inaudible faith and prayer and worship."

With these words of his own I leave this brief, imperfect tribute to Hamilton Mabie as man and author. The value of his work is still living in the hearts of his hearers and readers whom it has enlightened and encouraged. It is worthy to be treasured. To me the memory of his friendship is more precious than words can tell. Twenty years ago I tried to express something of its meaning in a bit of verse dedicated to his comradeship:

> O who will walk a mile with me
>   Along life's merry way?
> A comrade blithe and full of glee,
> Who dares to laugh out loud and free,
> And let his frolic fancy play,

HAMILTON WRIGHT MABIE

Like a happy child, through the flowers gay
That fill the field and fringe the way
   Where he walks a mile with me.

And who will walk a mile with me
   Along life's weary way?
A friend whose heart has eyes to see
The stars shine out o'er the darkening lea,
And the quiet rest at the end o' the day,—
A friend who knows, and dares to say,
The brave, sweet words that cheer the way
   Where he walks a mile with me.

With such a comrade, such a friend,
I fain would walk till journeys end,
Through summer sunshine, winter rain,
And then?—Farewell, we shall meet again!

GEORGE LOCKHART RIVES

BY WILLIAM MILLIGAN SLOANE

M R. RIVES'S VOLUMES entitled *The United States and Mexico, 1821-1848,* constitute a history of events leading up to the war of 1848. Its publication revealed the author as a foremost American historian, and gave him a chair in the American Academy of Arts and Letters. To those unacquainted with his career the event was perhaps startling, but to his nearer circle and the more observant critics it was a foregone conclusion. His long, full, active life had been a preparation for exactly such a culmination. His was the well-known Virginia family which gave to the public service senator and diplomat, with a great engineer and authors of renown. He, however, descended on his mother's side from famous New York Colony stock, was born in New York City in 1849, and died there in 1917. Educated at Columbia, and in Cambridge, England, he was eminent both in scholarship and sport. His vocation was the law; being rather more devoted to jurisprudence than to practice at the bar, it was as a legal adviser and administrator that he early became a foremost citizen of the metropolis. He was Assistant Secretary of State to Mr. Bayard under Cleveland, president of the commission to revise the New York charter, Corporation Counsel, and a member of the Rapid Transit Commission. He was a director of four great financial corporations and president of the New York Hospital. But above all he was president of the Public Library and of the Trustees of his Alma Mater. From three leading universities he received the highest academic degree. He was the author of many papers and monographs, and of several volumes, local in interest, as well as of the more national work mentioned above. This recapitulation, together with the fact that in some circles he was virtually a social dictator by reason of his varied gifts, his recognized station, and his judicious pronouncements, are sufficient to explain his presence in our company, for membership in the Academy should indicate not only great achievement but personal qualities equally eminent.

His personality was very marked and in our day quite exceptional. Imposing in looks and figure he possessed in high degree the two un-American traits of reticence and tranquillity. *Saevis tranquillus in undis* might have been his motto. Indeed he was a man of the William of Nassau type, aware of his opportunities, silent when candor did not forbid. Sternly self-respecting, he took the responsibilities of his own opinions and was entirely fearless in action. In the sense of knowing and keeping company with the best in life and letters he was an aristocrat, his private library was one of the most select known to the present writer. Yet he was essentially democratic in the power of putting himself in every man's place and securing every man's point of view.

This was the secret of his enormous influence. His writing is thoroughly studied, its contents are carefully constructed, and his judgments are eminently fair. Identical qualities were exhibited in his life. The Public Library of New York literally enfolds the masses of the city in its "interpreter's" palace; Columbia University represents in almost exact proportion each single element in the total population of the metropolis. Both became under the Board over which he presided so democratically popular that their numerical enormity renders their vast resources scarcely as adequate as the pence in a palmer's scrip. But like the pilgrim they take little thought for the distant scene and march on in the present. For such a policy Mr. Rives felt and assumed his full share of obligation and was always at the post of duty.

While in a sense history was his avocation, yet in his devotion to "door-step" activities he was the outstanding example that service in the larger sphere is valuable in almost exact proportion to its perfection in its immediate surroundings.

1918

~~~~~~

HENRY ADAMS
BY PAUL ELMER MORE

By the death of Henry Adams, in March of 1918, in his eighty-first year, the Academy lost a member distinguished in many ways, a man who reveled in all the riddles of life and himself left for those curious in the natural history of the human soul a riddle not easily solved. In one respect he was American by every fiber of his being. Great-grandson of the second President of the United States, grandson of a later President, son of the Minister to the Court of St. James's during the trying years of the Civil War, reared in a tradition of almost chauvinistic patriotism, he might be regarded as an impersonation of that New Englandism which penetrated the bones and marrow of the national character. And he was, throughout life, acutely conscious of his inheritance.

Yet from another side he was conspicuously un-American; and of this, too, he was conscious, and never felt really at home in the land of his ancestors. It was a difference in mind, in thought, which, whatever else may be said, has not been "the master part of us," and which was so in Henry Adams. This is not to say that America is mentally sluggish, or has failed of large accomplishment in scholarship and invention and the arts; but that detached intellectuality which dissolves the substance of life into a question, that restless inquisitiveness which pierces all veils of custom and is only strengthened the more it is baffled, that outreaching of "the imperious lonely thinking power" which makes an imprisonment of its very freedom, the spirit, in a word, which Matthew Arnold described in his *Empedocles,*—these are distinctly not American, and they distinctly are what characterize Henry Adams.

The variety of his intellectual achievement is more remarkable than its magnitude. As a teacher of history at Harvard for seven years he was one of the pioneers of the seminary method of study. Besides other more or less notable works in this field he published a *History of Jefferson's and Madison's Administrations,* monumental in bulk, and almost unique in its combination of documentary research, philosophical reflection, and literary charm. He divulged a scientific theory of the periods of human growth and decline in history which is strikingly original and, it must be added, rather sad. For six years he edited the *North American Review,* then the most solid magazine of the country. He wrote two novels, one of which, *Democracy,* aroused a good deal of heated comment by its satirical picture of Washington political society. He composed verse, not much in quantity, but weighted with thought and emotion and technically more than respectable. His letters, printed since his death, show him to have been a master of the quaint and whimsical in this delicate *genre.* Above all he has left two books of extraordinary quality, his *Education* and his *Mont-Saint-Michel and Chartres,* one of which is like the portrait of a naked mind caught by some art of spiritual photography, the other of which has made the whole mental and emotional life of the twelfth century a vehicle for the same insatiate personality. This, however one may judge the individual works, is a record scarcely paralleled by the production of any other American author.

In the long run interest probably will center on the last two works, the *Education* and the *Mont-Saint-Michel.* By education Adams meant not at all the mere accumulation of knowledge, of which, nevertheless, he had abundance, but that insight into the nature of things which should enable a man to know what the world is and what he himself is, and so to adjust his life to the forces that play upon it. In that sense education came to our Academician slowly, if it came at all, and the pages of his autobiography are a continual, and sometimes a bitter, complaint over the fact that he, the heir of all the ages and of all the Adamses, should be held at bay by the baffling sphinx of existence. He set his intellect to work in the various fields of learning of which the century was so proud—history, science, politics, art, religion—seeking an answer to the question everywhere put to him: Why are you here, and who am I who set you here? Only at the end of his life did he read the riddle, and for those who read his books left another riddle to solve.

Standing before the great dynamo at the Paris Exposition, in 1900, he thought he saw in that wheel, revolving with such vertiginous speed, so terribly silent, so majestically regular in its motion, a symbol of the ruthless, impersonal force which science discovers at the center of the universe: "Among the thousand symbols of ultimate energy, the dynamo was not so human as some, but it was the most expressive." Then from this inhuman sign he turned, by a kind of revulsion of feeling, to what was most opposite to it in every respect. He wrote his book to show that the Virgin Mother of God, in whose honor the cathedral of Chartres had been raised and adorned, was the real object of worship in the Middle Ages just because she was the symbol and warrant of something inconsequent, whimsically merciful, contemptuous of law, human, feminine, in the governing of the world. That he should have turned from one to the other of these forces is not strange, but that he should have found it consonant to adore them together is a feat of audacious thinking, if not of education.

ANDREW DICKSON WHITE

BY NICHOLAS MURRAY BUTLER

ANDREW DICKSON WHITE touched American public life at many and important points. He won the title of Academician both by scholarship, by literary performance, and by public service. His life was a fortunate and a happy one.

He could take no credit for clambering out of poverty, since his parents were in comfortable circumstances. He began life without knowing either poverty or riches, but with a sound training at the academies of Cortland and Syracuse and at Yale College. European travel broadened and enriched his mind and laid the foundation for those educational and public interests that dominated his maturer years. On returning to the United States he hesitated a little, as others have done, between education and politics, and finally chose both. He justly considered institution-building as the highest form of public service, and to it he devoted a great part of his life activity. Cornell University is his monument and a dozen other undertakings have been helped by his hand and guided by his vision. His legislative service in the State of New York was rather significant than important, although it gave him a hold upon the working political forces of the State that he never lost. His foreign service was acceptable in high degree both to his own people and to the governments to which he was successively accredited. In Germany, in particular, he was heartily received, and in Germany among both scholars and public men he exercised a wide and strong personal influence.

From boyhood Dr. White had profound respect for literature and its makers, and his strong scholarly instinct carried him inevitably into the field of authorship. His bibliography is rich and long, but perhaps the two titles included in it that are most to be remembered are his *History of the Warfare of Science and Theology* and his *Autobiography*. The former is his chief contribution to history and its understanding, and its composition and completion occupied his mind for quite a quarter-century. His purpose in writing this book was, as he himself has declared, to strengthen not only science but religion. His purpose was to aid in freeing science from trammels which for centuries had been vexatious and cruel, and also to strengthen religion by enabling its teachers to see some of the evils in the past which, for the sake of their charge, they ought to guard against in the future.

ANDREW DICKSON WHITE

His *Autobiography* is a work of singular charm. It not only tells the story of an honorable and distinguished life, but it throws a flood of light upon personalities and happenings of the greatest interest to all mankind.

Dr. White was elected to the Academy on January 28, 1908, to fill Chair 32. He died full of years and of honors on November 4, 1918.

1919

THEODORE ROOSEVELT
BY BRANDER MATTHEWS

THIS IS NOT the place, nor am I the person, to attempt a survey of the career and of the characteristics of Theodore Roosevelt. He was a many-sided man, traveler and explorer, soldier and statesman, naturalist and man of letters. It was because he was a man of letters, a historian and a biographer, an orator and an essayist that he was elected to the American Academy of Arts and Letters; and at this memorial meeting it is only as a man of letters that he can be considered. This limitation has its advantages, because his prominence in public life has tended to obscure his eminence as a writer. Perhaps it is not too much to suggest that if he had not entered the arena of politics his high position as an author would have been more widely recognized.

His earliest ambition was to be a historian; and while he was yet an undergraduate in college he made ready to write the *History of the Naval War of 1812*. His treatment of this difficult subject was so disinterested and so devoid of partisanship that a few years later when a coöperative history of the British navy was undertaken in London, he was invited to deal with this period,—a testimony alike to the open-mindedness of the British editor and to the fair-mindedness of the American contributor.

After the writing of the *History of the Naval War of 1812*, Theodore Roosevelt began the toilsome researches needed for a history of *The Winning of the West*,—which may be regarded as a continuation of Parkman's monumental chronicle of the century-long struggle between England and France for the possession of North America. For Parkman he had always the deepest admiration; and he sought to give his own successive volumes the solid qualities he found in Parkman's, —scientific integrity, artistic proportion, and, above all, unflagging human interest.

Like Parkman, he spared no pains in preparation for his work. He familiarized himself with the topography; he studied the Indian and the frontiersman; he diligently sought out all possible sources of information, in print, in manuscript, and in oral tradition. Having mastered his materials he digested them; and then he told the story veraciously and vividly, making the dim figures of the past start to life and stand erect before the reader's eye, in their habit as they lived. Like Parkman again he was a severely self-trained scientific investigator, who was also a consummate artist in narrative, a born story-teller. If the historian is only an investigator, the result of his labors is likely to be a sandy desert,—"an arid region abounding in dates," as an old gibe put it aptly; and if he is only a story-teller, his work will lack validity and it will be doomed to speedy disintegration. Like Parkman, once more, he possessed the qualities which Macaulay demanded in the historian—"perspicuousness, conciseness, great diligence in examining authorities, great judgment in weighing testimony, and great impartiality in estimating characters." The four volumes of *The Winning of the West* are his most substantial contribution to our literature; and their solid merits were fitly acknowledged by his fellow-workers in this field when they elected him president of the American Historical Association.

He found time also to prepare a lively little volume on New York, his native city, for the series of *Historic Towns* edited by Freeman; and to record the raising and the services of the Rough Riders. He collaborated with Henry Cabot Lodge in a stirring and stimulating collection of *Hero Tales of American History*, told with simple sincerity to arouse in the youth of our country a keener interest in the outstanding men of the past who had helped to make the nation what it is at present.

The biographer is blood-brother to the historian; and Theodore Roosevelt contributed lives of *Gouverneur Morris* and *Thomas Benton* to the American Statesman Series. Later he wrote an acute and appreciative life of *Oliver Cromwell*. His own *Autobiography* is an invaluable self-revelation. Longfellow once said that "autobiography is what biography ought to be;" yet it may be admitted that Theodore Roosevelt's *Autobiography* is not all that his biography should be, since it was written too soon, while he was still in the thick of the strife, so that it was impossible for him to tell us many things we should have liked to hear.

He resembled the statesmen of Rome, who were expected to prove themselves orators as well as soldiers. As a public speaker he was simple and direct. He stood on his own feet; he did his own thinking; he uttered his sincere thought; and he was as clear as he was cogent. He was no sleek rhetorician, weaving frail felicities and indulging in weasel words. Nor did he ever descend to the use of drum-like phrases, loud-sounding, empty, and monotonous. He was no dreamy idealist with his head in the misty clouds and his feet slipping from under him. His idealism was practical, for it was based on the strenuous life and the square deal. He had the gift of the winged phrase, sharply pointed, and barbed to flesh itself in the memory. There was never any necessity for explanation or extenuation; and when he branded certain "malefactors of large wealth" as "undesirable citizens" we all knew what he meant, and not a few of us knew whom he meant.

Historian, biographer, and orator, he was also a writer of travels and a writer of letters. As an explorer he was ever alert, observant, vigilant. He had the kodak-eye of the born reporter. He saw things himself with a plumbing vision; and he had the skill needed to make us see them ourselves, eye to eye with him. He liked to speak of himself as a faunal naturalist; but the animal in which he was most interested was man. He loved nature in all its aspects, sea and plain and mountain; but he loved human nature even more. He had the keen perception and the abundant humor which enabled him to understand his fellow-man wherever he might meet him,—on the throne, amid all the trappings of empire, or in a tent of branches in the depths of a forest.

As a letter-writer, as an inditer of familiar missives to his multitude of friends, he bids fair to take his place among the masters in that apparently artless department of literature. His letters are the immediate expression of himself, spontaneous, genuine, and frank. "Whatever record leaps to life, he will not be shamed," as Tennyson said of Wellington. His correspondence was seemingly limitless, and only a little of it has yet been sifted for our enjoyment. Yet he might almost rest his claim to an abiding place in literature on the letters he wrote to his children, helpful yet full of the tenderest feeling. Even in his hastiest notes, dashed off or dictated in thin intervals between pressing decisions, he disclosed his command over the vocabulary of our stubborn tongue; he rarely failed to find at once the necessary noun and the illuminating adjective. In his ampler books he painted characters with a bold brush and an assured stroke; and in his letters he etched with a swift needle portraits as life-like.

Now and again in the leisure he made for himself by a wise and rigid economy of time, he relaxed from more arduous labors by writing essays and literary criticisms. His essays, all too few, are pungent with his personality; and his literary criticisms reveal his possession of the four qualities which we have a right to demand in those who judge books and authors —insight, equipment, sympathy, and disinterestedness. He loved books all his life long; he was an omnivorous reader, and, what is quite as significant, a persistent re-reader. He knew the masterpieces of literature and he appreciated them for the value they have for us now. He searched the annals of many peoples; and he also sought out the primitive tradition, the half-forgotten folk-lore, which is often a clue to racial characteristics. He preferred the literature which was closest to life; he joyed in the struggle of strong men; and he had likings akin to those of the little boy whose mother offered to read to him out of the Bible and who begged her to pick out "the fightingest parts."

At the same time he could deal lovingly with the unassertive poems which present the uneventful aspects of life and which mirror for us the placidity of the backwaters of existence. He had a delicate perception of literary merit; and he was never taken captive by the labored paragraphs of those who think they can live by style alone and who inlay verbal mosaics to deck precious coffers,—empty more often than not. His own style is firm and succulent. He had sat at the feet of the masters of English; and he had profited by the lesson to be learned from the French and the Greeks. He wrote well because he had absorbed good literature for the sheer delight he took in it; and this had nourished his vocabulary with strong words which he could bend to his bidding. But he was not bookish in his diction; and we never catch him questing recondite vocables. He never indulged in "fine writing," so-called, often only the written equivalent of "tall-talk." His style was masculine and vascular; and he was not afraid of vernacular directness. At his best he achieved the ideal—the speech of the people in the mouth of the scholar.

It is by the interpreting imagination, by the vision and the faculty divine, that an occasional address like Lincoln's at Gettysburg, or a casual magazine article, like Theodore Roosevelt's *Great Adventure*, transcends its immediate and temporary purpose and is lifted up to the serener heights of pure literature. There is a poetic elevation and a noble dignity in the opening paragraph of the *Great Adventure* which testify to its kinship with Lincoln's address, and there is a severe concision also, recalling the stately terseness of the Greek inscriptions.

Perhaps this tribute, brief and inadequate, may best be brought to an end by the quotation of this passage:

Only those are fit to live who do not fear to die, and none are fit to die who have shrunk from the joy of life and the duty of life. Both life and death are parts of the same Great Adventure. Never yet was worthy adventure worthily carried through by the man who put his personal safety first. Never yet was a country worth living in unless its sons and daughters were of that stern stuff which bade them die for it at need; and never yet was a country worth dying for unless its sons and daughters thought of life not as something concerned only with the selfish evanescence of the individual, but as a link in the great chain of creation and causation, so that each person is seen in his true relation as an essential part of the whole, whose life must be made to serve the larger and continuing life of the whole.

By his own life, by what he did, by what he said, and by what he wrote, Theodore Roosevelt proved that he was fit to live and that he was fit to die.

KENYON COX

BY EDWIN HOWLAND BLASHFIELD

Kᴇɴʏᴏɴ Cox passed from us at a moment when we specially needed him. In these strenuous days of world-wide disputation, such clarity of mental vision as his, accompanied by such a high order of mental endowment, is invaluable—in the arts as elsewhere, for in such a time the arts will be modified with all else. His perception was almost crystalline, enabling him to see straight through to the core of a puzzling question, and his honesty in stating what he saw was absolute. More than once in a committee of artists who had argued long over which of two lines of action was the better to pursue, Cox quietly remarked that it was impossible to arrive by either line, and convincingly showed why! Such a mentor and guide is at times invaluable among a class of men to whom impulsiveness is attributed as a part of their temperament.

Cox was a veritable bulwark of directness in art, of sanity, of culture. In his technique, as was natural to one to whom directness was a passion, he loved best, among media, the *point,* whether of pencil, crayon, or charcoal; but whenever he took up his palette, he thought first and last of the Venetians. The artists of the full sixteenth century were those with whom he liked to live in communion. Among colorists, Paul Veronese was his divinity—Veronese with his simple, clear statements. When it came to line he loved Michael Angelo. In composition he remembered Raphael, Paul Baudry, and his Parisian master Gérôme. He painted large mural panels, little *genre* panels, and many portraits. He was fond of ornament, and frequently gave landscape backgrounds to his figures; and he modeled at least one statue in heroic size for the New York Custom House.

Cox's literary talent and charm of style, as marked as his pictorial gift, his wide reading, his clear-sighted observation and his honesty combined to make him a most admirable and discriminating writer on painting and sculpture. He held high offices in many societies of artists, and might have held many more had his health permitted. His passing from among us cannot fail to be deplored by every one who has at heart the true interests of culture and of art in America.

HENRY MILLS ALDEN

BY ROBERT UNDERWOOD JOHNSON

HENRY MILLS ALDEN may be said to have had a dual literary personality. More than his distinguished editorship of a great magazine for half a century, he probably valued the expression of his intimate self which is found in his two philosophical excursions, *God in His World* and *A Study of Death.* Here was his ego, his individual creative contribution to the greatest problem of life,—permeated with a subtle mysticism which fascinates even when it baffles. The present writer remembers the deep impression made by the first volume, which was so widely discussed and respectfully considered in the critical comment of the early nineties on both sides of the Atlantic. At fifty-seven—he was born in 1836—Alden thus interrupted the editorial activities of a life devoted to the service of other writers, in order to leave these personal testaments of his own penetrating intellect in the field of speculation. Valuable as may be the work of an editor of Alden's high calling,—there are few such left on earth— there are times when he craves to produce work that stands alone and for himself. It is not enough that from the bank one should encourage and train others in swimming; he covets the plunge into the current, with its measurement of force against force and its thrilling and vital reactions. I remember that Richard Watson Gilder once said to me that he would rather write one good poem than edit a magazine for a year; so doubtless felt his colleague, Alden, Nestor though he was of American magazine editors.

But the historian of the period of our highest achievement in literature as related to the magazines may look at things otherwise. If he does his duty he can discover that the activity of American authorship from 1835 well into the nineties was due in large part to the high standards and the helpful sympathy that were established or promoted by such editors as Lowell, Higginson, and Aldrich in the *Atlantic,* Alden in *Harper's Magazine,* Holland and Gilder in the *Century,* and a few others. Of these Alden from the start had the largest parish, but all were alert, hospitable, well poised, and discriminating. The journalistic spirit with its special virtues and vices had not yet taken possession of the magazine field, and there was still an atmosphere of repose in American life. Alden never learned the meaning of those detestable words and unliterary qualities "punch" and "pep." He once said to me that he was proud to think of *Harper's* as the solidest magazine in the world. I am not sure that he did not say "heaviest." What he meant was the most substantial, and he must be credited with a great achievement in the large additions to the world's knowledge and entertainment which he conveyed to the three generations of his memorable career.

But his chief influence was upon the fiction of his time. To mention his name to a writer of novels or short stories of that day who had come in touch with him was to call forth grateful report of some incident of his discrimination and generous helpfulness—some discernment of talent in the rough, some divination of a richer vein from indications slightly regarded by the author himself, some clarifying stroke of imagination, some quizzical linking-up of the affair in hand with the literary past. In those days the editor was not a mere shoveler into the hopper of the product of well-known writers, an agent of the counting-house "to haunt, to startle and waylay" the public; he was the friend and counselor and confidential critic of all, ready to give the author reasons for the faith or doubt that was in him, with the chief purpose of making the most of the talent that came before him, and with pride and happiness in the discovery of new writers. For this high function Alden was equipped with a rare sense of proportion, with sane literary and moral standards, and a poise against which the fads and eccentricities of his time made no impression. The literature of revolt, with its barking note of self-consciousness, did not disturb his mastiff-like serenity. The principles of intellectual art were his refuge and joy, and in his last days his sense of humor kept him clear of *vers libre*, so largely compounded of threadbare fancies, small analogies, and ugly suggestion, set to corduroy movements.

Alden's influence lay in the pervasiveness of his humane, frank, sweet, wholesome, unselfish nature. Much as he did for the art of writing in America, the dominant impression he makes upon us by his career is of a noble spirit profoundly touched by the sacredness of life.

Alden was elected to the Academy in 1910, and died in 1919.

JULIAN ALDEN WEIR

BY EDWIN HOWLAND BLASHFIELD

BY HIS COMRADES of the studios Julian Alden Weir was admired for his brilliant talent, esteemed for his character, and beloved for his personality.

His character, indeed, was to catch immediately the imagination of the young, of those who were his contemporaries in Paris. To the American students of the early seventies his name was already notable. The Americans of the Rive Gauche surrounded him, and the men, too, of the Rive Droite, of Montmartre, learned to think of him as of one who had "arrived" *d'emblée,* in the opinion of his French comrades, as the friend of Bastien and other protagonists of the advanced movement of the day, and they knew him personally as the bluff, genial, handsome athlete who later was perpetuated in the bronze of Olin Warner's beautiful bust. He was not only a hard worker at his easel but an active participant in every kind of jollity, quite ready also to bite his thumb at either Montague or Capulet if he thought them untrue to the principles of their art.

For Weir was essentially an artist. Like Thayer, he never for a moment compounded with his principle, but, unlike Thayer, he now and then compounded with his own opinion, or at any rate was baffled by it momentarily. He was elusive and sometimes unequal; today you would find him painting with profoundest subtility and convictions, and tomorrow trying an experiment which perhaps surprised his admirers, and which, once proven unsatisfactory, he abandoned the day after tomorrow without regret.

High distinctions always accompanied his hours of best inspiration and never entirely failed him. The fugitive and almost impossible delicacy of flowers he fixed as few have been able to do, and his mastery of white, that basic and most noble pigment, was rare and was shown with extraordinary skill and feeling throughout all his work. Whether you agreed with him, as you usually did, or disagreed, you felt the sincerity of his work; for he did not play to the gallery or think about making his spectators "sit up."

Although very simple and direct of speech, he was widely as well as deeply cultured in art, and was a critic who could back up in discussion his natural *flair* in the discovery of interesting work by other men.

He painted portraits, figures, and flowers; and he passed through a phase which testified to the fascination which New York after twilight offers in its piled-up lighted windows of business buildings. But often he turned and returned to landscape, for he was emphatically one of those people of Browning's *Artemis,* who "love green haunts and loneliness," and was always ready for deep woods and for fishermen's camps.

In the various and sometimes varying artistic camps, too, he was honored. He was one of "The Ten" whose talent has given so much impulse to the healthier side of so-called "advanced work," and he was also a beloved president of the Academy of Design, resigning the office only when fatigue and illness compelled him to do so.

He was born August 30, 1852, and was elected a member of the Academy November 18, 1915. He died December 8, 1919. His name will be remembered with pride and affection by his fellows of the Academy and by a host of artist comrades.

HORATIO PARKER

BY GEORGE WHITEFIELD CHADWICK

HORATIO PARKER, composer, conductor, organist and teacher, inherited from both parents an uncommonly retentive and alert mind and an artistic temperament; from his mother, also musical talent, or at least musical taste. His father was a well-known architect. Several large edifices in

Boston and other cities of New England are specimens of his work. He was for some time superintendent of construction of the Boston Post Office and other public buildings in Massachusetts, and was a man of wide and varied knowledge.

Parker's mother, daughter of a Baptist minister, was a woman of great refinement and cultivation. An excellent Latin and Greek scholar, she had also considerable facility as a writer of English verse. To the care of four children she added the duties of organist in the village church at Auburndale, and gave music lessons besides.

Undoubtedly Parker owed to her, who was his first teacher, the love of good music which became the passion of his life. As a boy he gave little indication of this. The woods of Auburndale and the Charles River (near which he lived) occupied much more of his attention than his piano practice. At fourteen he could hardly play a simple scale on the piano, but shortly after that his soul awakened to the beauty of music, especially of harmony, for which his latent talent developed with great rapidity. At sixteen he became organist of a small Episcopal church in Dedham, Massachusetts, and at once began to compose hymn tunes, anthems, and services for the choir. For the next two years he had lessons in pianoforte and harmony with various Boston teachers and made great progress.

At eighteen his ambition reached out toward orchestral composition. In this he was probably stimulated by the recent success of John K. Paine's two symphonies and of other American composers. It was at this time that my acquaintance with him began. He had already acquired remarkable facility in harmony and modulation, to which was added a very fertile vein of lyric melody, and both his melodies and harmonies had a distinct and individual character of their own, which may be detected in his later and more mature compositions. It was easy to predict even then that this combination of qualities would carry him far.

As my pupil he was far from docile. In fact, he was impatient of the restrictions of musical form and rather rebellious of the discipline of counterpoint and fugues. But he was very industrious and did his work faithfully and well. His lessons usually ended with his swallowing his medicine, but with many a wry grimace. It was quite natural that before long our relation should develop from that of teacher and pupil into a warm and sincere friendship, as it ever afterward remained.

It was during this period that he wrote the beautiful *Twenty-third Psalm* for women's voices and organ, revised and published some years after with harp and violin obligato. In 1882, he went to Munich and entered the Royal Music School, in Rheinberger's class, both in organ playing and in composition.

Rheinberger, although a composer of operas, orchestral works and of much romantic and beautiful chamber and choral music, was, as a teacher, conservative, almost to the verge of pedantry. Under his rigorous discipline Parker acquired that mastery of contrapuntal choral writing which so distinguished his later work.

While in school he wrote several works for orchestra and chamber music which were performed at school concerts. At his graduation in 1885 a cantata for chorus, solos, and orchestra, called *King Trojan,* was performed under his own direction. Although this work showed some of the naïve qualities of youth and inexperience, its spirit was so fresh and spontaneous, and its construction and instrumentation so sure and authoritative, that it must be considered a remarkable effort for a young student of twenty-two. It was afterward performed at the Worcester Festival and in several other places.

He returned to America in 1885, and for the next seven years lived in New York. He took charge of the music department of the Cathedral School at Garden City and was afterward appointed as instructor at the National Conservatory, at the same time fulfilling his duties as organist at St. Andrews Church and later at Holy Trinity. Much of his church and organ music dates from this period, although he also wrote some secular choral works and piano music.

In 1891, during a period of serious ill health and of poignant domestic grief, he began the composition of *Hora Novissima*. He had made a beginning on another mediæval Latin hymn, *Vita nostra plena bellis*, but abandoned it on account of the monotony and inflexibility of the rhythm. The great hymn of Bernard, which is the foundation of several of our best-loved modern hymns of the church, was in the same collection of poetry. Probably encouraged by his mother, who made the translation for him, he set to work on the *Hora Novissima*. It was finished in 1892 and sent in for the prize offered by the National Conservatory for a work for chorus and orchestra. It did not receive the prize, which was awarded to him for a much less important though charming work called *The Dream King and His Love*.

Hora Novissima was performed for the first time by the Church Choral Society of New York on May 2, 1892, at the Church of Zion and St. Timothy, under his own direction. It was immediately recognized as an important work of permanent value. Performances in Boston by the Handel and Haydn Society in February, 1894, and at the Springfield Festival of the same year were succeeded by many others in different cities of the country, and eventually in England, where it has been performed more than twenty times. The solid musical worth of *Hora Novissima*, its skillful and impressive choral writing, the poetic beauty of the solos, and the varied and colorful instrumentation, endear it to musicians, while its lofty spiritual atmosphere, its fervent religious expression, although tinged with a romantic mysticism, make a strong appeal to the general music public.

In 1893 Parker was called to Boston to assume the position of organist and choirmaster at Trinity Church. The close proximity of his old home, the congenial companionship of his old friends, the active musical life in Boston, his growing reputation, all stimulated him to further effort. In December,

1893, he wrote his ballad for baritone and orchestra, *Cahal Mor of the Wine-red Hand*. This strange and remarkable poem by James Clarence Mangan made a strong appeal to his imagination, and he produced a score that in dramatic power, poetic suggestion and vivid orchestral coloring has seldom been surpassed in this form by any American composer.

When, in 1894, the department of music at Yale University was reorganized as a completely equipped school of theoretical and applied music, he was appointed as its head, receiving at the same time the honorary degree of M. A. He was at first rather reluctant to accept this position, involving as it did the necessity of lecturing on Musical History and Aesthetics, of which he had never made any special study. But this deficiency was very soon made up, and his general lectures soon became an important as well as popular part of the curriculum. He organized and conducted a symphony orchestra, which became an indispensable laboratory of the department, since it furnished the necessary experience for composers, conductors, singers, and players who were studying in the school. During his administration the great organ in Woolsey Hall was built, to be succeeded after some years by a still mightier instrument. He also lived to see his department housed in a beautiful and fully equipped building of its own through the munificence of Mrs. F. S. Coolidge, herself a cultivated musician and the daughter of a Yale graduate.

Of Professor Parker as a teacher, others may speak with more authority than I. From his comprehensive knowledge of the classics as well as his sympathy with modern developments, his profound knowledge of, and masterly command of counterpoint and form, his genius for tone-painting with the orchestra, strikingly demonstrated in his operas, he was eminently fitted to be a guide and leader of young composers. He gave them his unstinted interest in the classroom and out, and some of them have risen to very honorable positions. He was succeeded by one of them as Dean of the Music School at Yale, and many there are to call him blessed.

In 1897 he wrote his oratorio of *St. Christopher*. The poem of this work was written by his mother and was a labor of love. Working side by side, the poem and music grew at the same time. He introduced into this work two Latin hymns, one of which, *Jam sol recedit,* is an unsurpassed masterpiece of choral writing for unaccompanied voices. *St. Christopher* was first performed by the Oratorio Society of New York under Walter Damrosch in 1898, shortly afterward at the Springfield Festival, and in 1902 at both the Norwich and Bristol Festivals in England. It has never achieved the great popularity of *Hora Novissima,* but is still in the repertoire of choral societies.

In 1899 he was invited to England to conduct *Hora Novissima* at the Three Choir Festival at Worcester. Both he and his work were welcomed with such enthusiasm that he was invited to contribute a new work to the Hereford Festival of the next year. Here the Wanderer's Psalm (the 107th, called the *Cantus Peregrinus*) was produced. In the same year *Hora Novissima* was performed at Chester. This was followed by the *Star Song,* a poem by Henry Bernard Carpenter, for the Norwich Festival in 1902 (for this piece he had already received the Paderewski prize), and *St. Christopher* at Bristol. The same year he received the degree of Mus. Doc. from Cambridge University. If we consider the conservatism of English musical taste, especially in cathedral towns, we must admit that this is rather a remarkable record for a young American in his thirties. The prophet is not without honor in England, at any rate.

For the Bicentennial of Yale University in 1902 he composed a Greek ode for male chorus and orchestra — the *Hymnos Andron*—a piece of singular power and beauty. He returned from England in order to conduct it at the Bicentennial exercises.

In 1911 he won the prize offered by the Metropolitan Opera Company for the best grand opera written in English and composed by an American, which was his opera *Mona,* the libretto by Brian Hooker. In 1914 he won a similar prize offered by the Women's Federated Musical Clubs with his opera *Fairyland,* the libretto by the same poet.

This is not the proper time or occasion for a critical estimate of his two operas. He had little sympathy for the conventions and the artificialities of the stage, and perhaps he was lacking in what the Germans call *theater blut.* This, combined with inexperience in composing for the stage and plots which made little appeal to the average theatre-goer, militated against the popular success of these works, but they proved his complete mastery of modern harmony and modern orchestration, and both of them were awarded valuable prizes. In the case of *Mona* it was the unanimous opinion of the judges that no other award was possible.

In his morality play, *The Dream of Mary,* which he wrote in collaboration with John Jay Chapman, he returned to simple form of expression appropriate to such an art form. The characters narrate the story as well as sing; the audience takes part as in the Greek chorus, assisted by the choral forces on the stage. The atmosphere of the work is profoundly devout and religious.

Another work in which he collaborated with Mr. Chapman is a masque or serenata called *Cupid and Psyche*—a delightful composition in which, with very simple means, he has reflected the spirit of the Italian Renaissance. It was performed at Yale University in 1915.

In his last work, the music to the commemorative poem by Brian Hooker, in memory of the Yale men who gave their lives to their country in the late war, Parker has written his own Requiem. To this noble poem he has given a very impressive setting, elegiac in spirit but with some thrilling dramatic touches, as for instance at the words "One shall have sweet sleep"—the trumpet is heard in the distance sounding taps. It is an heroic tribute to heroic men, some of whom were his own students.

After he went to Yale he developed a decided literary ability. To a close and discriminating observation he added an individuality of expression, illuminated by gleams of pungent humor which caused him to be sought after as a speaker and contributor to various periodicals. His essay on contemporary music, delivered before the American Academy of Arts and Letters, is a good example of his ability in this direction. The individuality of his style was no less evident in his literary work than in his music.

He was fond of making paradoxical observations, sometimes rather difficult for less subtle minds to follow. Of a certain piece for organ and orchestra he said, "That has no business to sound so well." This was really a retroverted compliment to the composer for making a successful mixture of organ and orchestral tone, a problem which requires an expert musical chemist. Berlioz said that the orchestra was king and the organ pope, and when they came together there was usually a clash.

As a musician, Parker's instrument was the organ. His master, Rheinberger, admired his playing and delegated him to play the solo part at the first performance of his concerto in F major. He continued his duties as organist at Trinity Church in Boston for six years after he went to New Haven, making the journey each week for the purpose. While making no pretensions as an organ virtuoso he often gave recitals, and in 1903 performed his organ concerto, then new, with the Chicago Symphony Orchestra, and shortly afterwards with the Boston Symphony Orchestra in Boston. This work, noble and dignified in character, is an important addition to the rather meagre repertory of compositions for organ and orchestra. He held an organ position in New York until a few years before his death, and conducted two singing societies in Philadelphia at the same time.

With his masterly command of orchestral resources it seems strange that he should have composed so little for the orchestra alone. He was often urged to do so, and he would not have lacked a hearing. The symphony orchestras of

America and probably of England were open to him, but he felt that he needed words as a vehicle and poetry for his inspiration, and in writing for voices he was in his element. His most important composition for orchestra alone is the *Northern Ballad,* first performed by the Boston Symphony Orchestra, and afterwards in Chicago and other places.

He wrote with great facility, and his industry was prodigious. With all his varied activities as teacher, conductor, and organist, he kept steadily at composition, and in the summertime he allowed nothing—even his favorite golf or his bicycle—to interfere with it.

As a congenial companion, a loyal comrade, and a steadfast friend, Parker has left a blessed memory. His conversation, punctuated with keen wit, was stimulating, and not of the prima donna variety. Devoted as he was to his own art, he found time to be interested in politics, in literature, and in other arts. His mind was stored with a variety of information, and his memory was as remarkable for facts as it was for music.

His judgment was sound, and based on a comprehensive knowledge of the musical art. While his musical creed was founded on beauty of design, melodic breadth, and logical structure, he was interested in all modern developments in harmony and instrumentation. He had a singularly open mind in regard to modern compositions, and often expressed himself enthusiastically about some of the most "advanced" of them. Often he would say, "That is not as bad as it sounds." But with pretense or shams of any kind he had no patience, and he was quick to detect them in some of the modern fads of polyharmony and polycacophony.

He was fond of outdoor life, and an ardent devotee of golf and the bicycle. Many of his summers were spent in the vicinity of Tegernsee in the Tyrol, where he tramped in the mountains and rode his bicycle as a relaxation from his work. His amiability and cheerfulness never forsook him, even during the painful attacks of rheumatism from which he suffered all his life.

With the remarkable success of *Hora Novissima*, both in America and in England, it was natural that his anthems, services and hymns for the church should have achieved great popularity. He was easily the most distinguished musician in the American church, and it was perhaps inevitable that he should be classed as an ecclesiastic composer. But he was not a mystic or an ascetic; he was a simple, devout Christian gentleman who loved his church and all her offices, and he gave the best that was in him to her service. In the very last year of his life he gave valuable assistance to the commission on the revision of the hymnal.

But many pages of his music, from *Cahal Mor* throughout his orchestral works and operas, show that his real place is among the romanticists, and it is a high one. He was an honor to the name of American musician, and he commanded respect for it not only in his own country, but abroad.

1921

BARRETT WENDELL
BY JAMES FORD RHODES

BARRETT WENDELL died in his sixty-sixth year (February 8, 1921)—too soon for an American scholar to pass away. "A good book is the precious life-blood of a master spirit," declared Milton, and so must be regarded Wendell's *The Traditions of European Literature*, published in the autumn of 1920, only a few months before his death. In it is shown an acquaintance with classic writings and, what is more wonderful, a knowledge of the traditions of the Middle Ages. The book ends with Dante, and it was Wendell's intention to bring his treatise through modern times. Would not his treatment of Shakespeare have been interesting, who, so Wendell wrote, "created a greater number and variety of living characters than any other writer in modern literature;" and with the universality of his taste our critic would have pointed out that our Mark Twain had created for us in Huckleberry Finn the Don Quixote of American life, a character that might rival in some degree the portraits which Shakespeare drew in his comedies.

Wendell read histories, which "make men wise." He wrote, "For narrative skill and sustained interest, Herodotus remains enduringly excellent; for thoughtful and animated statement of contemporary fact, no writer has excelled Thucydides." As every one knows his Herodotus and Thucydides, one is led to accept Wendell's characterization of our American historians. He spoke of Bancroft's "diffuse floridity" of style, of Motley's "sincerely partisan temper." He said that Prescott combined "substantial truth with literary spirit." Parkman had "full sympathy for both sides, untiring industry in the accumulation of material," judicial good sense, and a style that finally became "a model of sound prose."

So much for Wendell, the scholar. He wrote many books, and no one will be censured who deems *The France of To-day* the best, as it is the most celebrated. He was the first lecturer on the Hyde Foundation at the Sorbonne and other French universities, and the scholar, as we see him in *The Traditions* and in the *Literary History of America,* then became a keen observer, as was de Tocqueville during his brief visit to the United States. Entering the best society, assisted in the way that only a woman can by his devoted wife, he has given a picture of French society that is original and that has commended itself to all sympathizing Americans. It is needless to say that the French look upon the book as a model of clear thinking and thorough comprehension. He tackled indirectly the question that has puzzled many, why, if "French women are among the best creatures a good God ever made, should they not appear so in French literature?" The answer was given in the words of Maupassant, *"l'honnête femme n'a pas de roman."*

American literature numbers among her worthies James Russell Lowell, and an article on him as a teacher came from Wendell's pen in *Scribner's Magazine* (November, 1891) shortly after Lowell's death. Wendell knew whereof he wrote. A lecture of Charles Eliot Norton had excited in him the desire, while an undergraduate at Harvard, to become a member of Lowell's Dante class, and to the scholar and observer was joined the listener who would learn the method of teaching from him who proved an exemplar. He said to Lowell, "You are the most inspiring teacher I ever had." Lowell "knew literature and knew the world;" and so did Barrett Wendell.

ABBOTT HANDERSON THAYER

BY EDWIN HOWLAND BLASHFIELD

ABBOTT HANDERSON THAYER became a member of the Academy October 20, 1909, and died May 29, 1921. He was born in Boston on the 12th of August, 1849, and became a pupil of Gérôme and Lehmann at the School of Fine Arts in Paris. His art was dedicated almost entirely to the dignity and loveliness of womanhood and to the charm of childhood, and it is marked throughout by thought, refinement, distinction, and spirituality. His achievement is in the purest field of art, and his earnest and deep-set eyes sought and found the elements that lie at the very root of beauty. In his pursuit of nobility of form he avoided the characterlessness which comes from too great generalization; his vision was set not only upon a type but upon an individual of the type. Adolescence appealed to him intensely, and as chosen models he reared up around his own fireside a brood of angels to whose humanity he fitted wings, just as did the masters of the quattrocento. These figures sit in his pilastered and pedimented frames, and look out at us, now sturdy, now ethereal, and are perhaps what we remember best among his presentations.

Together with austerity in his feeling went the freedom of a very personal technique. He was willing to experiment in every direction, eschewing the study of nothing save what approached vulgarity. His color, which was often, indeed most often, beautiful, corresponded to his temperament, but was controlled also by an observation so curious, so nature-loving, that he gave virtually ten years of his life to a minute investigation of the handiwork of the Great Master in birds and beasts and fishes. Some of this observation he gave out in his works of research which he called *Studies of Protective Coloration in Animals,* and it enabled him also to offer valuable service during the late World War. By laying before the naval experts of the Allies his miniature demonstrations in pigment, clay, and cardboard of the vanishing properties of colors, he contributed materially to the success of camouflage.

In figure painting as well as in landscape the beauty which appealed to him most surely was that of loftiness and grandeur; yet this note of austerity did not exclude tenderness. He was above affectation in the arts, and saw beyond the ephemeral. In his admiration of the old masters he often mentioned Tintoretto to me as a favorite, perhaps as *the* artist of his predilection; but he remained modern in the true sense of the word, and faithful to himself.

Like all whose aim is set high, he was not always equal, and some variation in his success must be attributed to his frequent experimentation; but one felt that his work was invariably on the highest plane. His noble and solid canvases hold the wall with authority; in many cases by their character as well as by their subject they seem real "enthronements" of loveliness. Certainly he was an artist through and through, one of whom America may be lastingly proud.

1922

THOMAS NELSON PAGE
BY ROBERT UNDERWOOD JOHNSON

O NE DAY IN 1881 there came to the editorial office of
Scribner's Monthly, afterward the Century Magazine,
the manuscript of a story destined to be of large significance
in American fiction. It was a tale of Virginia during the Civil
War and was entitled "Marse Chan," and it was signed by
a name not known to the editorial staff, that of Thomas Nelson Page. The editor-in-chief, Richard Watson Gilder, being
then in Europe, as a matter of routine it was first submitted
to the "reader," Mrs. Sophie Bledsoe Herrick, who (so to
speak) "discovered" it and passed it on to the present writer
with a warm recommendation that it be accepted. It proved
to be a story of such obvious merits that it fell into the class
of manuscript that, in the lingo of the editorial office, "accepts
itself." It had but one fault of importance, that of redun-
dancy, the action being retarded by a surplusage of interesting
detail. This is a fault not only far from infrequent in young
writers but fortunately one easy to remedy. With the consent
of the author, excision was made of this digressive material—
perhaps a third of the original manuscript—and I believe that
none of the omitted portions was restored in the publication
in book form of this and other stories by the same author.
The narrative is wholly cast in negro dialect, which at that
time was much in favor. The magazine had already on its accepted list a number of admirable examples of such stories
by well-known writers and the obligation of precedence, and
not a lack of appreciation of the tale itself, was the occasion
of the delay of its publication for nearly three years.

When it did appear, in the Century for April, 1884, "Marse

Chan" made a sensation. It was not only interesting in itself, as a well-told narrative, but it was typical of what may be called the "Southern literary invasion" which came in the twenty-five years that followed the Civil War. The Southern writer of that period did not study life analytically but was content to report it objectively. Cable was perhaps the only one whose method was conspicuously dramatic. "Marse Chan" and Page's later stories had the Southern literary trait of straight-forward, felicitous narrative style, the somewhat leisurely current sweeping into a swifter climax. He may be considered as standing at the head of this group in pathos, humor and a convincing truthfulness. The local color of much American fiction has been challenged—often from a too matter-of-fact point of view—but no one has ever detected a forced or false note in the work of Thomas Nelson Page. This first story is among the foremost in the list of the best American short stories produced during the post-bellum renaissance, and among the most notable episodes in fiction is that of the duel between Marse Chan and the father of the girl he loved, Colonel Chamberlain. It closes thus:

"Den I heerd Mr. Gordon say, 'Gent'mens, is yo' ready?' and bofe of 'em sez 'Ready,' jes' so. An' he sez, 'Fire, one two' —an' ez he said 'one' old Cun'l Chahmb'lin raised he pistil an' shot right at Marse Chan. De ball went thoo his hat. I seen he hat sort o' settle on he head ez de bullit hit it; and *he* jes' tilted he pistil up in de a'r an' shot *bang*; an' ez de pistil went *bang* he sez to Cun'l Chahmb'lin, 'I mek yo' a present to yo' fam'ly, seh'!'"

"Marse Chan" is typical of Page's works in two respects. First, in dealing with sectional prejudices, it has that fine quality, whether of a gentleman or an author, a generous candor, and, next, it has a tenderness that in the writer's attitude toward women amounts to chivalry. Page was not ashamed to portray love as a principle rather than a passion, and his sincerity enabled him to escape sentimentality. He made the most of the background of the Civil War and in a dignified way presented the devotion and sacrifice of the South without bitterness or vaunting. This was seen particularly in his second story of note, "Meh Lady," the motive of which, the reconciliation of prejudiced foes, the present writer had the good fortune to suggest to him. His treatment of sectional questions is unexceptionable, despite the fact that his local traditions were sunned and watered in a soil of two centuries. He is the adequate exponent of Virginia aristocracy turned democrat. The hero of his youth was Robert E. Lee, to whom he paid the tribute of an admirable biography, and his ancestors of the Revolutionary period always seemed to be speaking through him.

This is not the place for a critical estimate of Page's numerous books. They have homogeneity rather than diversity, but they never fail of ease or charm of atmosphere, and while they make no presumption to profundity, they show no "variableness or shadow of turning" from the truth either of history or of human nature. They are indispensable to the understanding of the character of Virginia, which, with certain quite attractive traits of provinciality, is perhaps the most American State in the Union.

In 1913 Page was designated Ambassador to Italy. His service covered the entire period of the Great War and terminated with his resignation in the spring of 1919. As his successor, it may be presumed that the present writer would be familiar with the character and scope of that service; but the usefulness of diplomats is not recorded in embassy records and, if it were, those that come after are too busy making the history of the day to occupy themselves with even the immediate past. They must be content to await the years to come, when it may be proper to make public the confidential records of the Department of State and their own private journals. But no one who knew Page's temperament and intelligence and his ardent love of Italy could doubt that his official function—most delicate and important in the trying times of war—was loyally and amply fulfilled. His volume *"Italy and*

the World War," published in 1920, is not concerned, even
by inference, with his own influence upon events, but is an
astonishing *tour de force* of narrative,—comprehensive, temperate, judicial, well-balanced, with flashes of special illumination, and, throughout, presenting the much-misunderstood
attitudes and actions of Italy, first toward the Allies, and later
as one of them. His spirit is that of a champion who comes to
the rescue of one who is maligned and neglected. In every
chapter he not only indicates the streams of influence contributing to Italy's always important and often decisive action
in the War, but also lets us see the deep currents of patriotism
and pride which carried her past and under inconceivable
obstacles. One must be deficient either in intelligence or in
heart who could rise from a perusal of this volume without a
conviction of the heroism and nobility and the indispensable
force of Italy's participation in the War.

Thomas Nelson Page was born in Hanover County, Virginia, April 23, 1853, and died at the old homestead November 1, 1922. His boyhood and youth were spent in Virginia
and his mature life largely in Washington, with summer so-
journs in York Harbor, Maine. He was one of the charter
members of the National Institute of Arts and Letters and
one of the group of twenty elected to the Academy immediately after the completion of the first quota of thirty. He was
a man of warm affections warmly reciprocated, of rigid conscientiousness, of inclusive sympathies, of reasoned convictions, at once a man of the world and of the study. He had, in
the best sense of the word, a sweet nature and was lovable,
loyal and courageous. Though by nature of a gentle lassitude,
as shown by his conversation and his gait, he was capable of
indignation and resentful protest against wrong. He spoke
boldly for the rights of authors and lashed the pretentious-
ness and triviality of certain social classes, and he would have
given his life for the land which he faithfully served in Rome,
or for the land to which he was accredited and which he loved
second only to his own. When the private records of his career

shall see the light we may be sure that they will only accentuate what we now know of this charming author, good citizen, faithful ambassador and admirable man.

ELIHU VEDDER
BY JOHN C. VAN DYKE

VEDDER has written his own story in his *Digressions of V* and happily forestalled his obituarist. It is impossible to be funereal in reading that story for it is full of humor, gaiety, and caprice. It wanders, rambles, digresses delightfully, and breaks off just when you expect him to say something serious about Rome and Raphael and academic drawing. He omits —how much he omits!—about his art. But then we have the art itself to supplement the *Digressions*. If it were not so, if we held by the story alone, we might receive an inadequate impression of the man. He smiles all through the book, but he smiles not at all in his art. The characters in his pictures are as world-worn as the Sibyls and Prophets on the Sistine ceiling, as sorrow-laden as Rossetti's Blessed Damozel, as Burne-Jones's Angel of the Annunciation.

Does that mean that Vedder was another Thomas Hood— smiling without but within consumed by sadness? By no means. He was one man socially and another man artistically. In dealing with the world he preferred to use the social convention. Everyone, at his club, liked his good humor, his appropriate stories, his unique personality. But painting a picture was another matter. That called for serious, sober reflection. He shut the door, took counsel of the Muses, the Fates, the Sibyls, and let slip his romantic imagination. One gets from the *Digressions* little idea of this except as, now and then, he drops a casual remark that suggests what went on behind the door. He was poetic and romantic from his boyhood. When, as a student in Sherburne, he went sketching he "sought for lofty granite peaks catching the last rays of the sun, for hills convent-crowned or castles on abrupt cliffs frowning down on peaceful abbeys below." He tells us: "I was always looking for things with a tinge of romance in them," and "I had been reading Tennyson and my mind was full of the gleaming Excalibur." And still further on: "I always try to embody my moods in some picture."

This paper trail of quotations leads straight to Vedder's studio and suggests the young artist and his early art. Some of us are not so young that we cannot remember the talk that went the rounds concerning Vedder's Lair of the Sea Serpent, his Questioner of the Sphinx, and his Lost Mind. They had a weird imagination, a touch of the uncanny, that caught the public fancy. Even down into the early eighties there was discussion and explanation of those pictures. Who and what was the personified Lost Mind? What was the Questioner asking the Sphinx? Was the Sea Serpent really painted from a large eel? Vedder says they were all done out of his head— his poetic, romantic head. It cannot be doubted. As a young man he was influenced by Doré's work and his pictures of the Roc's Egg and the Fisherman and the Genii bear witness to it. His imagination at this time was the most attractive quality of his art. That it was more literary than artistic did not matter. The public loved it, praised Vedder, and hailed him as a genius. "I was proud while this first glimmer of Fame lasted. It soon wore off and I have never been proud since." He was to reach higher than serpents and sphinxes, though the swirl of the one and the mystery of the other were to remain with his art to the end.

This was about 1864 and Vedder was twenty-eight. He was born in Varick Street, New York, in 1836. He was not a Yankee, as is often supposed, but a Dutchman of the Dutch. His boyhood was passed in New York. At seven he was taken to Cuba, then to Schenectady, and so backward and forward several times. His early education must have been limited. As a boy he had the humor for drawing and he was encouraged in this by his mother who wished him to be an artist.

His first start was in an architect's office, and after that he studied for some time with T. H. Matteson of Sherburne. At twenty he went to Paris and was in the Atelier Picot for eight months. That seems to have been the extent of his professional training. The rest he got by study of the masters. After Paris he went to Rome and Florence, staying in the latter city four years, meeting many persons of the Landor-Browning set and encountering various art influences. He speaks of talks with Inchbold about the art of the Pre-Raphaelites, thinks had he been born in England he might have been one of the P.R.B. The romance, the sentiment, the melancholy of the Pre-Raphaelites quite caught his fancy. And then he came back to New York and found the Civil War and hard times. He took a room in Beekman Street, and, quite unknown, started the struggle for recognition, now such a familiar part of artist-biography. It was then and there that he painted the Lair of the Sea Serpent, the Lost Mind, the Questioner of the Sphinx. These pictures shown at the exhibitions of the National Academy of Design soon brought him into notice and placed him above want, though he records that the Sea Serpent picture—the most effective of the three—was sold for the modest sum of $300.

In 1865, with the Civil War at an end—Vedder had tried to enlist but was rejected because of a defective arm—he started again for Paris. He stayed there (with trips to Brittany and England) for a year, and then went to Rome where he remained for the rest of his life, barring return visits to America, and a latter-day residence at Capri. Rome seemed to appeal to him, to be his proper environment, and to furnish him suggestion and even inspiration. It was the city of romance, the Popes had lent it authority and the painters austerity, and Vedder was still devoted to such things. He was also reaching out towards the mysterious. "It delights me to tamper and potter with the unknowable." He had been much impressed by the drawings of William Blake and now in Rome he must have been mightily moved by the ceiling of

Michelangelo. He does not say so in his book and there is nothing in his art that can be pointed out as directly emanating from Michelangelo, and yet there is the same feeling of mystery and weirdness in the drawings for Omar Khayyam as in the Sistine ceiling.

The Rubáiyát drawings will probably always be considered Vedder's masterpiece. The poetry of Omar, as paraphrased by FitzGerald, was particularly appealing to him. It had to do with "the unknowable," it was a study in the mysteries, and it had a swing of sound that seemed to translate itself into a swirl of line. It fitted Vedder to a nicety and yet taxed his ingenuity to the utmost. The Rubáiyát was lofty poetry and the illustrator had to hitch his wagon to a star. But who shall now say which flew at the greater height— Omar or Vedder? How well the illustrator met and supplemented the poet! His work was well thought, well wrought, and well brought. It was magnificent. And if today there is no disposition to question the comparative worth of poem and illustration it is due perhaps to the fact that the two blend together and cannot be thought of as things apart. Vedder may have come to some fame through Omar's poetry, but it can be said also that Vedder gave a new lease of life to the Rubáiyát.

At any rate, in these drawings he showed the stuff that was in him. His early work carried almost wholly by its literary or illustrative subject and its sense of the uncanny or the supernatural. The decorative in line or color or composition is not very apparent in the Lost Mind, the Roc's Egg and the Questioner of the Sphinx. But the decorative in the Omar drawings is most marked. Each sheet is arranged as a Japanese would arrange flowers in a vase; the figures are swung into place with beautiful outlines; the borders supplement and complement with profound grace. How rhythmical the network of lines that run and interplay throughout the pattern!

The drawings were done on grey paper with black and

white crayons. How decorative they are, with not a touch of color in them, and yet with the suggestion of color all through them. One wonders where Vedder got all this profound artistic knowledge. How did he learn to draw and model so well? How did he learn to see things all of a piece, do them all of a piece, hold a whole series together as a piece? He was contemporary with La Farge, Inness, Homer Martin, Winslow Homer. Practically speaking, all of them were self-made and self-taught. They eked out their meagre technical training by study of the great masters, but their principal reliance was upon themselves. Vedder was fortunate in being in Rome, in contact with great art, but when all is said and done the fact remains that his art is overwhelmingly Vedderesque—the expression of his own individuality. The Vedder of the Omar drawings is the Vedder of the Lair of the Sea Serpent, only he had arrived at maturity in the Omar and to his early imagination he now brought a very high artistic quality. The two together place him on a pedestal, in his own peculiar niche, and from that lofty place he will not be dislodged.

I cannot speak of Vedder as a friend or companion because I knew him only as a casual acquaintance. Once or twice I met him in Rome, but we got no further than passing the time of day. Every one spoke highly of him, loved his frank genial personality, and to this day men continue to talk about him at his club and elsewhere; but I never was so fortunate as to be in his charmed circle. Nor can I speak about him as an Academician. He was elected a member of the Academy in 1908 but during his fifteen years of membership he lived in Italy and took no active part in the proceedings of the body. Still it was a satisfaction to know that his name was on the rolls. He was an honor to the Academy, for he has always been an outstanding figure in American art. There is no reason why his success should not be our pride.

WILLIAM ROSCOE THAYER

BY JAMES FORD RHODES

AN ENGLISHMAN who was Professor at Harvard and with whom I assisted at many funerals always had the same word to pronounce over the dead body, "*his* work is done." He could not have said that of William R. Thayer who passed away before he had reached the age of 65; and many of his years were those of inability to produce the work which he had at heart. In the centenary of Francis Parkman we have heard much of his heroic writing under great physical drawbacks, and our minds have reverted to William H. Prescott, who produced his many volumes under greatly impaired eyesight. Thayer's trouble was of the nervous system. Between *The Dawn of Italian Independence,* which was published in 1893, and *The Life and Times of Cavour,* published in 1911, he had an attack of nervous prostration which unfitted him for work on Italy for a number of years. He could not walk from his house to Harvard Square, a distance of less than half a mile, without being perturbed at some trifling affair which, when he was well, would have been looked upon as utterly commonplace. When his devoted wife went upon some errand, he would give her twenty minutes and, were she not back within the appointed time, he would have a nervous attack. He could not pursue his chosen work on the Risorgimento without such mental suffering as compelled him to desist. Therefore Thayer must be joined to Parkman and Prescott as another whose work was performed under physical limitations.

If one were asked about Thayer in 1911 one would say that, in addition to his labors as editor of the "Harvard Graduates' Magazine," he represented Italy in Cambridge, Massachusetts, that had been noted for her Italian scholars and lovers of Dante. His chosen theme was the Risorgimento,—the resurrection of Italy from the depths, until she became united and her capital was Rome. When the *Life and Times of Cavour* appeared, it was at first regarded as merely a step in the story of Italy; but it was only a little while before it came to be looked upon as a great story of a great man. Have you read Thayer's new book? was the common inquiry. He characterized Italy enthusiastically as "that Enchanted Land whose beauty is inexhaustible and whose boundless interests touch men and women who perceive the deepest concerns of the human soul." Cavour, with Lincoln and Bismarck, was regarded by him as one of the three great men of his time. But is the work impartial? asked one of the critics. "Absolutely judicial," was the reply of an admiring lawyer.

Of course *Cavour* was not "absolutely judicial," but when Thayer quit the high ground of impartiality he was almost always entrancing. His tendency to speak of matters of which his mind was full and on which he had decided ideas, but which perhaps had naught to do with the thread of his narrative, sometimes got him into trouble, but his friends know that his dicta came from no prejudice but from rare and complete intelligence.

We all looked upon Thayer as a radical, so were somewhat surprised that he took the conservative and opportunist Cavour instead of Garibaldi or Mazzini for his hero in the story of Italy's independence. As an English critic of the book remarked, Cavour admitted that "anyone who had done the things he had done for anything less than the cause he was championing would have been a rogue." Nevertheless Thayer in his preface spoke of the "brilliant volumes" of Trevelyan on Garibaldi. Thayer and Trevelyan were an example of a literary friendship of a high order. One was devoted to Cavour, the other to Garibaldi, yet during their writing they exchanged manuscripts. They also criticized each other's work in print. When Trevelyan came to this country during the Great War, Thayer was foremost in entertaining him and was a powerful influence in inducing the Tavern Club to give him the high compliment of a dinner.

Thayer's successful *Life and Times of Cavour* was made

more so by his knowledge of European affairs. As one reads the story, one is amazed at his varied information and the charm he has thrown upon the setting of his subject. He exhibits himself as the gentleman who has been much in Italy and has lost no opportunity of familiarizing himself with the friends and contemporaries of Cavour.

Having made the literary conquest of Italy he thought that he ought to use his talent in a study of his own country, and, an opportunity having been given him to write the life of John Hay, he counseled with me in regard to it. I advised him to stick to Italy, on which he was the greatest authority writing in English. He said he could not go on from where he left off in 1861. Up to that time he had a hero in Cavour who, in spite of doing things Thayer could not admire, nevertheless brought his great aim to pass. Subsequent to Cavour, Italy fell into the hands of designing politicians, who, as politicians are apt to be the world over, were unscrupulous and sometimes corrupt. Hay appealed to him as being a high-toned man in politics and therefore desirable to write about. In this study he grasped in his quest the original materials in manuscript, and showed historic qualities not dimmed by his work on Italy. His two chapters entitled "Letters to Henry Adams" are a marvel and exhibit Hay at his best. Adams was Hay's warmest friend, whom he at times addressed as "My cherished Livy;" and the letters themselves are an intimate story. In his search for material Thayer pulled all strings, social as well as scholastic, and the result is a life-like biography, from which even those who knew Hay well can learn much, through an author who never enjoyed a rare personal acquaintance.

After the *Hay* came the *Roosevelt*. Roosevelt died in January, 1919, and the book of 454 pages was written between that date and August of the same year. It was a wonderful piece of work to do in so brief a period. Thayer knew Roosevelt well, and this helped him much in the personal touches. The book is of great value in the glimpses one gets of Roosevelt, who spoke to Thayer with the utmost confidence. While engaged on this work he was attacked with impaired eyesight, so that he could not read the proof or correct some errors of detail into which he fell.

Thayer was also a stylist of no mean order, which is the reason his books were in such demand. I wondered where he got that virile expression until chance put a volume into my hands which he published in 1890. In this volume he printed what he considered the best plays of Marlowe, Ben Jonson, Beaumont and Fletcher, and Webster. He wrote a preface to them which may fitly be compared to James R. Lowell's lectures on the English Dramatists, and Thayer joins with Lowell in giving Webster a high rank. It is often said that had not the others been dominated by Shakespeare they would have achieved great literary fame. "Unsurpassed in the history of literature," wrote Thayer, "and equalled only once in Greece, the great poets of the Age of Elizabeth took all human nature" for their province. "From Marlowe to Webster is less than thirty years, less than an average lifetime; yet within that brief period the Elizabethan drama blossomed and withered." These citations will give an idea of the illuminating preface, which tells where Thayer got his virile style. The English critics find fault with his use of colloquialisms, that sometimes even degenerated into slang, and they do not see the strength beyond that. According to my idea they are right when they criticize Thayer for his colloquialisms, which he thought gave pungency to the written word, but if you eliminate the colloquialisms, what strength and fluency are still left! His splendid style came from communion with Shakespeare and the contemporary dramatists, and I could sympathize with his lament that, owing to his failing eyesight, he could not read them himself.

I am proud of my friendship with Thayer. He was a many-sided man, and to those whom he liked he was a true friend. I cannot fail to remember his characterization of the different men who walked the stage. He was a brilliant biographer, a good historian, and a learned man.

BASIL LANNEAU GILDERSLEEVE
BY PAUL SHOREY

GILDERSLEEVE began, as Oliver Wendell Holmes would have us all begin, by choosing his ancestry wisely. He was of good Anglo-American stock, tempered by enough of French blood to leaven the heavy Anglo-Saxon or Germanic paste. Nor, to take the second topic of Greek panegyric and of Taine's philosophy of literature, was the environment unfavorable. To a Matthew Arnold, a small Southern city of the 1830s would seem provincially far, indeed, from the centre. But if the Old South had little systematic and critical scholarship, it had in spots a very genuine personal culture of an old-fashioned type. Of no spot was this more conspicuously true than of Charleston, as those who cannot pursue their researches further may learn in Professor Trent's *Life of Simms,* where we get a glimpse of the "gentlemen and scholars" with whom young Gildersleeve, just returned from Göttingen with a German degree, foregathered in Russell's bookshop on King's Street.

To have been born in that little Charleston, son of a father who preached the gospel and edited religious newspapers, can be regarded by no sane American critic as a "handicap" in the long race of the distinguished career that was to follow. Provinciality and narrowness, if such they were, could be shed as the life moved on to widening and ever wider circles of experience and influence. But the foundations of character and intelligence remained fixed. Like the spirit of a youth that means to be of note, Gildersleeve began betimes. He was a precocious boy, and legends are told of his translating Anacreon at the age of 14, and of the extent of his undergraduate reading in French and Italian. He was graduated from Princeton at the age of 18, and he received his doctor's degree from Göttingen with a dissertation *de Porphyrii studiis Homericis.*

This, too, was a favorable conjunction. The examples of Hamilton, Jay, Jefferson and others of the elder statesmen show that the old-fashioned American college could train men. But to come to it too old, or to linger in it too long would produce the type which the Greeks satirize as "the late learner." Escaping from it at the age of 18, Gildersleeve used it for what it was—a preparatory school—and found his ideals of scholarship under the very different teaching of what his idealizing memory styles "the serene wisdom of Boeckh, the vehement affluence of Karl Friedrich Hermann, the rapt vision of Welcker, the inspired swing of Ritschl."

The young graduates of the old American college—the Lanes, the Childs, the Whitneys, the Gildersleeves, the Goodwins—were naturally much more impressionable by German scholarship than the more sophisticated products of the new American universities who made the German pilgrimage from 1880 to 1914. And the Germany which they knew and fondly remembered all their lives was the good old kindly *gemütlich* Germany, to which the group of Americans that celebrated the sixtieth anniversary of Gildersleeve's Göttingen degree in 1913 looked back for the last time, perhaps with some illusions, but which we cannot be mistaken in thinking was something different from the *schneidig* Germany of the Pickelhaube and of industrial and imperialistic expansion.

To Gildersleeve the scholarship and the life of that older Germany were a revelation and an inspiration of which he always treasured the grateful memory and about which he overflowed in anecdote and reminiscence to congenial auditors. The division of the records of the mind brought by the great war was to him, as to many other American scholars, an irreparable tragedy that in his less cheerful moods darkened his later years. He could not agree with his German friends, and he would not vilipend the culture to which he owed so much.

It would be a mistake, however, to suppose that Gildersleeve belonged to that too common type of American students who were overwhelmed and dominated by the erudition of the Germans. His keen intelligence, the range of his reading, and above all his growing superiority in accurate knowledge of the Greek language preserved him from that. Popular American usage calls any scholarship German that is minute, erudite and highly specialized. In this sense, Gildersleeve, when he pleased, was a scholar of the German type. He continued to read widely in the new German philology, followed it with friendly but penetrating and critical comment in the pages of *Brief Mention* and satirized its excesses and vagaries with dazzling wit in his second Presidential address before the American Philological Association.* But he never succumbed to the weakness of its more recent developments, the pyramiding of hypotheses and the supporting of conjectures by misconstruing Greek. He knew Greek too well for that.

The first three years after Gildersleeve's return to America were spent in study, writing, and tutoring, I learn from the memorial notice published in the American Journal of Philology, January 1924, by his colleague, Professor C. W. E. Miller. They were, Professor Miller tells us, "years of bitter waiting. Gradually despairing of a classical career, the young doctor was launching out into literary life when, in the autumn of 1856, he was elected Professor of Greek in the University of Virginia."

At the University of Virginia he spent twenty years—for many men a lifetime, of teaching, but for him only the preparation for the more conspicuous career which opened when he was called to organize the department of Greek in the newly established Johns Hopkins University in 1876.

*Oscillations and Nutations of Philological Studies. Johns Hopkins University Circulars. No. 150, March 1901.

In his first Presidential address before the American Philological Association in 1878 he describes himself as one of those "who, for a large segment of their intellectual existence, were cut off not only from contact with those who were pursuing the same line of study and pressing forward toward the same ideals, but cut off from new books, new journals, every sign of life from without, now by the pillar of fire which is called war, now by the pillar of cloud which is called poverty." But the final effect of such temporary limitation depends upon the man. It was by "intensive" reading of the Greek texts in these years, as he himself elsewhere hints, that he acquired the sure feeling for the language that gave him confidence to conduct the first graduate Greek seminar which this country had known, and four years later to found and edit the first American Journal of Philology.

It was in these years, also, during his tenure of the additional Chair of Latin, 1861-1867, that he prepared what remains the most readable and stimulating and perhaps the best of Latin grammars. To this period likewise belong most of the papers republished in *Essays and Studies* (1890), and originally contributed to the *Southern Review*. Among these the essays on Lucian, Apollonius of Tyana and the Emperor Julian are still readable and instructive, though Gildersleeve's mature judgment found defects in them, due to his lack of access to libraries, and would probably have softened the harshness of some of his estimates of pagan criticism of life in Lucian and of pagan virtue in Marcus Aurelius.

The pleas for the classics and the papers on education included in the same volume leave little for later American scholars to say on these topics, though they must continue to make reply to the twentieth century counterparts of one "Jacob Biglow, M.D., Boston, 1867," who assailed the classics with "a vivacious ignorance" which Gildersleeve rebuked more in sorrow than in anger. In re-reading these papers I am even more impressed by the writer's good sense than by the wit and imagination of which his pupils and admirers think first.

If I may supplement the inadequacy of this sketch by generalization about Gildersleeve's life, it seems to sum itself in the statement that he was first a typical Southern gentleman, then a great American—a great American scholar—and lastly, by virtue of diversity of opportunity and the fortunate prolongation of the powers of maturity into extreme old age, an inspiring example of continuous development and growth beyond the years in which we ordinarily look for growth.

He was a typical Southern gentleman. It is pleasant to recall this at a time when so much of the wit, the literary smartness, and the exuberant comminatory vocabulary of the self-appointed guides of the undergraduate intelligentsia, is devoted to the sneering disparagement of all things American, the minimization of American scholarship, the lampooning of the narrow pioneer and provincial American culture, the denunciation of American puritanical morality, and more particularly to vilipending of the South, which by a curious revenge of the whirligig of time has remained or become a chief stronghold of the old-fashioned Americanism that is as a red rag to the bullies of a cosmopolitanized criticism.

But this is no place for the controversy which such fulminations are perhaps intended to provoke, and Gildersleeve himself has set us a better example in the mildness and sweet reasonableness, under far greater stress of temptation, of his own reply to similar taunts. "Southern men," he writes in *The Creed of the Old South*, "were proud of being gentlemen, although they have been told in every conceivable tone that it was a foolish pride." "But the very pride," he gently replies, "played its part in making us what we were proud of being, and whether descendants of the aforesaid deboshed younger sons of decayed gentry, of simple English yeomen, of plain Scotch Presbyterians, and sturdy stock of Huguenots of various ranks of life, we all held the same standard."

I have neither the knowledge nor the pen to portray the old-fashioned type of Southern gentlemen whom I divined beneath the more sophisticated Gildersleeve of the maturity

BASIL LANNEAU GILDERSLEEVE

that I knew. As Mark Twain once said, the native novelist is
the only expert authority in such matters. I could only touch
on a few suggestive traits—the delicate sensitiveness of honor
which felt a stain like a wound; the framework of dignity and
courtesy encompassing all the wit and colloquial ease of his
conversation; the reticence, which was not secretiveness,
about the deeper things; the unfailing and delightful gallan-
try which no refined woman ever misunderstood or feared.
One little endearing touch is perhaps not too trivial for mention. In some of our later conversations I noticed, or fancied
that I noticed, what I had never observed before—an occasional recurrence or recrudescence of a recognizable Southern accent. Perhaps it was the call of the motherland as he
drew nearer home.

I do not know how far he enlarged the bounds of the perhaps slightly "fundamental" theology and philosophy of life
that were his from his father and the environment of his boyhood, and of which one may fancy we discern the surviving
traces in the harshness of his early judgment of pagan moralities and pagan ersatz-makeshifts for religion in the articles on
Lucian, Marcus Aurelius, and Apollonius of Tyana in *Essays
and Studies.*

But my guess is that his development in this respect was
the gradual and painless ripening and growth of a larger
tolerance, and if in the process he experienced any of those
spiritual crises described by Mr. Gosse's *Father and Son* and
in so many Victorian autobiographies, he consumed his own
smoke. In any case he retained a working faith in stabilized
ideals and standards of conduct and thought, and he was
never allured or besotted by philosophies whose pragmatic result is that one thing is as true as another, that beauty is only
the expressiveness of the ugly, and that there exists no practical criterion of choice between what are euphemistically
styled the many group moralities of the many kinds and
classes of men. But though in all fundamentals what the
latest emancipated criticism would stigmatize as a provincial

and puritanical American moralist, in the minor aesthetics and conduct of life he was anything but a puritan, as those who have sat at meat with him and enjoyed still more the after feast of reason and flow of soul happily remember.

We distinguished perhaps somewhat fancifully the original type of the Southern gentleman from the mature American in Gildersleeve. All such classificatory divisions put asunder what God and nature have joined together, but this one points, however arbitrarily, to one or two things it is needful to get said. The first is that Gildersleeve felt no incompatibility between loyalty to his most sacred memories and the larger American patriotism which the irresistible course of history and the beautiful necessity to which Emerson chants a characteristic hymn have happily made possible and imperative for us all. There was no room for rancor in his spirit and all his utterances on that unhappy but happily cemented division were informed not only with tact but with a depth and nobility of feeling that touched the hearts as well as commanded the assent of the most impassioned partisans of either part.

And the second point is, that by the maturing experience of the long years, by varied travel and study and intercourse with the scholars of all nations, and it may be by the opportunities of his life work in the earliest of American universities and in the mediating city Baltimore, Gildersleeve developed into what it is pleasant to believe is the ideal type of the cultured and scholarly American. While never compromising his fundamental Americanism, he became in all good and desirable senses of the word more truly a cosmopolitan, more truly a citizen of the entire intellectual world, than often happens with European scholars, or is ever possible for those Americans who forget that the true citizen of the world must be at home in his own country too, and that "that man's the best cosmopolite who loves his native country best." We like to think that in the measure of their lesser capacities this is characteristic of other American scholars who, remaining unspoiled Americans, love the great tradition of English literature and politics, cherish grateful memories of formative study in Germany, and have taught themselves to appreciate and in some slight degree to emulate something of the superior lucidity, delicacy, penetration, and refinement of French intelligence and taste. Whatever the deficiencies of our positive achievements, the best type of American scholar combines these four loves, loyalties, and admirations in a measure possible to no other cosmopolite.

To follow out these thoughts and try to trace in Gildersleeve's work the currents of the German, French, and English affluents of the broad and deep stream of his culture would be the task of a critical study of his scholarship for which this is not the place. Gildersleeve regarded the technical study of syntax as a means to the end of a finer literary expression. In his hands it became that—for to a sufficiently delicate appreciation there is no absolute demarcation between syntax, idiom, and artistic phrasing, between the vesture or rather the body of the thought and the thought itself. And Gildersleeve combined in rare, perhaps unique, degree the power of penetrating logical analysis with the sentiveness of the born literary critic to shades of meaning and beauty of expression.

Indeed, he sometimes said that his own native bent was to literature rather than to mere scholarship, and he half regretted that he was deflected from the orbit by the weightier or heavier attractions of teaching and investigation. He was not mistaken in this self-estimate. The natural gifts of an endowment for literature were his in rich measure—the prodigious verbal memory that enabled him to amuse himself with *tours de force* of vocabulary twenty years beyond the age at which Emerson's memory for words failed him, the facility of associations that manifested itself in the unexpected juxtapositions, the picturesque yet pertinent imagery and the unfailing flow of ideas that made notable his conversation, his letters, and the slightest product of his pen. His use of these gifts did more to humanize American classical scholarship than a score of explicit pleas and conventional dissertations on the soulfulness of the Greek genius could have done. For he touched nothing that he did not electrify as well as adorn, and the deadest subject lived by the indescribable relish and tang imparted to it by his wit, his metaphor, his power of incisive, pregnant, antithetic, and memorable statement.

The number of things that his discursive facility of association brought to the surface of his unpremeditated talk was as marvelous as is the wealth of matter in the apparent incoherence of the form in his *Atlantic Monthly* papers on a *Southerner in the Peloponnesian War* and *My Sixty Days in Greece.* We cannot regret that he did not always tame this luxuriance of nature with the pruning hook of Horace and Boileau, though we commend that more prudent course to some of his students and imitators. His nonchalance in this respect exposed him to the snipings of minor critics, and few things piqued him more than the Saturday Reviewer's pronouncement on the ground of a single gypsy phrase in his *Pindar,* "a symphony in God and blood," that his style was atrocious. Nothing could be more unfair.

But literature, like the law, is a jealous mistress, and Gildersleeve's work in this kind remained a by-product of a life absorbed in teaching, editing, and investigation. It is not for this reason insignificant. The *Essays and Studies* have been widely read by scholars at least, and are still good reading. The Introduction to the *Pindar* contains several brilliant and memorable pages. His Presidential Addresses to the American Philological Association blend wit and definitive good sense in a fashion of which he only had the secret. *Hellas and Hesperia* is a delightful example of the mellow discursiveness of a full and richly stored mind. The *Index Scoliodromicus* or criss-cross index to the non-syntactical miscellanies dispersed through the *Brief Mentions* of forty years will guide the literary epicure to many a tit-bit. *The Creed of the Old South* is an American classic, and has recently been reprinted as such in Mr. Christopher Morley's collection of modern essays.

I shall not attempt by the method of Taine to explain Gildersleeve's literary output as an inevitable product of the man, the environment, and the epoch; nor make those spectroscopic analyses of his style in which with the aid of Dionysius of Halicarnassus his own measurements of the diction of Plato and Pindar and the Attic orators vied with the invisible gratings for which the Johns Hopkins department of Physics was famed.

But there is one fancy of my own which it would be interesting to develop if time allowed. It is that the best guide to our conjectures of the kind of writer that Gildersleeve would have been if he had devoted himself unreservedly to letters would be a Plutarchian parallel between him, our foremost scholar, and our foremost man of letters, Lowell.

I would not push such a parallel to the point of a Fluellen parody; but the common traits of native endowment and acquired culture and style multiply when our attention is directed upon them. There is the irrepressible fertility in what matter-of-fact readers and pedestrian critics might deem imperfectly apposite ideas. There is the wit genuine and spontaneous but also sometimes curiously and eruditely elaborated with a recondite ingenuity that puzzles the reader and disconcerts the critic who does not recognize the sources. There is the inimitable gift for thinking in imagery which I should be prepared to maintain was rarely exercised by either at the expense of either logic or good taste, but which it must be admitted has sometimes misled imitators of Lowell and pupils of Gildersleeve who strive to bend the bow of Ulysses.

There are the many reminiscences in Gildersleeve's writings of the images, the quips, the turns of phrase, in Lowell's earlier essays, which singly trivial would collectively establish an "influence" in a doctoral dissertation.

There is the wealth of allusion to the two classical and the chief modern literatures which the culture of a long life of reading and study made natural to each but which offends as pedantry critics who date literature from the year 1911 (or is it 1908?) and who have ingeniously and ingenuously substituted lists of one another's names for the old-fashioned allusiveness to world literature whose decay Gildersleeve wittily deplored in one of his latest *Brief Mentions*. There is the occasional violation of academic and professional dignity by the very exuberance of these qualities which shocks finical critics, but which in fact both Lowell and Gildersleeve knew how to repress when their own canons of taste told them that it would be inopportune. There is little or nothing of it in Lowell's *Commemoration Address* or in the great speech on *Democracy*, very little in the papers which Gildersleeve contributed to the *Atlantic*, nothing at all in the noble and dignified *Creed of the Old South*.

I hope no surviving Southern Fire Eater will resent this comparison. Gildersleeve himself did not. For once when I suggested it and told him I was prepared to maintain it in true thesis fashion, he smiled and half assented.

He read the first *Biglow Papers* at Berlin in 1850. There was a time when they were of course estranged. But Lowell's magnificent *Palinode to Virginia* bridged the aloofness if some of the scars remained. And the fascinating story in the *Creed of the Old South* of their intercourse when Lowell lectured in Baltimore fills me with retrospective yearnings to have been an overhearer of the conversation of the two Americans to whom I owe most and whom in the domain of literature and scholarship I most admire.

To return to the life. During the fifty years of American classical scholarship for the history of which I may be permitted to refer to my sketch in the Transactions of the American Philological Association for 1919, the figure of Gildersleeve dominated throughout. At first he seemed to tower almost alone. His was the Greek "seminary," the one centre of research and critical study in the Greek language and literature. His students were in demand to fill the Greek chairs of every self-respecting college. His journal was the one publication to which ambitious young scholars looked. His *Pindar* was the best American edition of any Greek poet, his *Persius* and *Justin Martyr* were models of editing, their notes crammed with nuggets of erudition which he cached there. His applause was most prized, his censure most feared.

Honors came thick and fast, corresponding membership in foreign academies, honorary degrees from Oxford and Cambridge, and half a dozen of the leading American universities, including the University of Chicago, where he upset academic dignity by holding the audience that filled the tent of those days convulsed with laughter for an hour, election to the American Academy, recognition by European scholars, tributes of love and admiration from the growing body of his own students throughout the country, the rare compliment of a second election to the Presidency of the American Philological Association.

It was a long life, and happy "as for a man," in the qualification of Aristotle's Ethics. If the last years were not wholly free from suffering, Carlyle has warned us that the exit of every mortal is in a fiery chariot of pain. The years, of which the sensualist says, "I have no pleasure in them," were for Gildersleeve solaced by the loving tendance of a devoted family, and cheered at each recurring anniversary with testimonies of honor and affection from his university, his city, his colleagues and pupils throughout America, his friends and admirers throughout the world such as have fallen to the lot of no other scholar of our time. The infirmities of extreme age, the defect of hearing which forced him at last to give up teaching, the failing eyesight which deprived him of a scholar's chief consolations in retirement, he bore not only bravely and without complaint but cheerfully.

They did not affect the vigor and clearness of his intelligence, which he preserved by a mental gymnastic through the watches of sleepless nights that would have exhausted ordinary men in their prime, but did not weary that tireless mind. The friends who came to entertain his enforced idleness found him still the best of company, and were themselves entertained by his unfailing flow of wit, anecdote and reminiscence. And so he revealed aspects of character which those who had thought mainly of the brilliancy of his intellect might otherwise not have known, and crowned his life with the only guerdon of praise that remained for him to win. He showed us how the truly brave and great-souled man endures what must be and awaits the inevitable end.

And at the service held in his honor at Baltimore by the university of which he had so long been the pride, it was universally remarked that the speakers with unconcerted unanimity dwelt not so much on the wit, the brilliancy, the scholarship, which they took for granted, as on the moral qualities of the man, the teacher, the companion, the helper, the friend.

MAURICE FRANCIS EGAN
BY DAVID JAYNE HILL

CHAIR NO. 14 of the Academy, first occupied by Theodore Roosevelt, was left vacant for the second time on January fifteenth, 1924. On that day, after a long and desperate struggle for life against heavy odds, Maurice Francis Egan, scholar, poet, critic and diplomatist, to use his own expression, followed his predecessor and friend into "the other room."

To all who personally knew Dr. Egan there was a note of extreme pathos in the announcement of this event. They who had followed the course of his fatal malady months before had been prepared for this ending; and yet when it came, it fell like a blow, for there had been manifested in the life of this man a spirit of youth and courage that seemed to have baffled death.

In all that the expression implies, Maurice Egan was a

man of letters. He literally lived in literature. It was his inspiration, his solace, his amusement, his passion and his vocation. It directed and dominated his life, furnished the contacts with others that brought him friendship and distinction, and crowned his existence with honor and eminence.

There were three great traditions that entered into Maurice Egan's development: the tradition of the Gaelic race, the tradition of the Roman Catholic Church, and the tradition of American political freedom. As they were tempered and harmonized in the mind of this conscientious scholar and thinker, these three traditions constitute an incomparable trinity of potent yet well-balanced influences in the shaping of a human life. His lineage, his nature and his education aided in promoting their effect upon him, and enabled him to find in them a wealth of material for thought and expression.

Born in Philadelphia, on May 24, 1852, he inherited from his parents the sensibility and imagination of a race that is marked by strong individual qualities of personality and a remarkable self-expression. Even as a child, we learn from his account of his early life, he was an eager reader of many books, with a strong relish for something "with a fight in it." He found the New Testament "radiant with interest," and came to the conclusion that "nobody could tell a short story as well as our Lord Himself." One of his favorite characters was the Centurion,—"he seemed such a good soldier; and his plea, 'Lord, I am not worthy'," he says, "flashes across my mental vision every day of my life."

"The Life of Saint Rose of Lima" produced a quite different effect upon him. He cites the passage

So pure was the little Saint, even in her infancy, that when her uncle, who was her godfather, kissed her after her baptism, a rosy glow, a real blush of shame, overspread her countenance.

"In that book," he adds, "I read no more that day!"

Educated in La Salle College and Georgetown University,

from which he was graduated in 1875, Egan devoted his time chiefly to editorial work upon several periodicals published in the interest of the Catholic Church, until 1880, when he became professor of English Literature in the University of Notre Dame, whence he was called in 1895 to a similar chair in the Catholic University of America, at Washington, which he occupied with distinction for twelve years.

During this whole period he was prolific in both prose and verse, producing nearly a score of volumes on various subjects. To lucidity and precision his style adds charm—that indefinable glamour that only imagination tinged with emotion can give to the printed page. Accurate learning, patient exposition, penetrating wit and keen discrimination mark his writing. In all he wrote he revealed the hand of an artist, but his art was not mere spontaneous efflorescence. It issued in a style devoid of exaggeration, chastened by self-criticism, the result of conscientious workmanship that did not hesitate.

> To file off the mortal part
> Of thought with Attic art.

As a teacher of literary form, he considered versification a useful exercise for perfecting the art of expression. Its rigid laws of quantity, rhythm, rhyme and cadence,—against which *vers libre* rebels,—were to him, like the paradigms of the classic languages, an apparatus of discipline not to be lightly disregarded. Nor did he think them merely disciplinary. They were inherent canons of expression for the emotions, comparable to the laws of thought for the operation of intelligence; for as there is beauty in formal truth, there is also a kind of truth in formal beauty. No art can live, he thought, which does not recognize its own laws of life. To satisfy the most exacting of these laws, as he understood them, he would sometimes rewrite his sonnets forty or fifty times, in quest of perfection.

It was the love of letters that brought Theodore Roosevelt and Maurice Egan together and cemented between them an enduring friendship. There was in Egan nothing of the politician in the ordinary sense of the word. He was too broadly human to be a mere partisan. It was not the man of letters seeking office, but the President seeking to utilize the man of letters, that led to Professor Egan's appointment to the diplomatic service of the United States.

In the formidable catalogue of books read by President Roosevelt in the first two years of his Presidency, as recorded by him in a letter to Dr. Butler, and printed in Bishop's Life, —a list that might well cover the lifetime of an ordinary man, —we find, imbedded in a whole library of history, biography, adventure, romance, essays and drama, Dasent's translation of the *Sagas of Gisli and Burnt Njal*, Lady Gregory's and Miss Hull's *Cuchulain Saga*, together with the *Children of Lir*, the *Children of Tuirenn*, the *Tale of Deirdre*, etc.

In the last paragraph of the last complete book Dr. Egan published, referring to these Irish folk-tales, he modestly writes of this great book-lover:

Do you remember his *Dante in the Bowery*, and *The Ancient Irish Sagas?* He caught fire at the quotation from the "Lament of Deirdre;" and concluded at once that the Celts were the only people who, before Christianity invented chivalry, understood the meaning of romantic love. It is a great temptation to write at length on the books he liked, and how he fought for them, and explained them, and lived with them. Thinking of him, the most constant of book-lovers, I can only say, "Farewell and Hail!"

Thus ends Maurice Egan's *Confessions of a Book-Lover*; but in it there is not a word of the well-authenticated incident, that, in the intimacy begun when this adept in the lore in which Roosevelt revelled was summoned to the White House to interpret and discuss these Irish sagas, the President discovered his future Minister to Denmark. It was, in truth, a discovery, and not a creation by appointment; for real diplomatists, like poets, are born, not made. The unerring tactfulness, the correct judgment, the double capacity for speech and for silence, the clairvoyance to find the true meaning between the lines of written words, patience with impetuosity, the serenity of conscious rectitude,—all these are gifts of nature, phases and projections of that inborn chivalry, that *noblesse* of intelligence, that is not derived from titles and cannot be conferred by kings.

Superficially regarded, it seemed to many incongruous to send a Roman Catholic envoy from the United States to a Court where Protestantism is the established religion. And yet Maurice Francis Egan, transferred directly from a Catholic University to a capital where Lutheranism is the official religion of the State, from 1907 to 1918, nearly half of the time during a war that shook all the foundations of Europe and in which his own country was eventually a participant, while he was the dean of the diplomatic body, not only preserved his own equanimity, but maintained intimate personal intercourse with his colleagues, friendly relations with society, and the status of *persona gratissima* with the Danish King and his Court! This test of his quality was so satisfactory in Washington that he remained as Minister at Copenhagen not only through the administrations of President Roosevelt and President Taft, but continued under that of President Wilson until, after more than ten years of service, he resigned from his post on account of his failing health. As a further mark of the appreciation in which his services to his country were held, he was offered by President Taft, and again by President Wilson, the ambassadorship to Austria-Hungary, which he declined.

Of his diplomatic experience we have an interesting record in his *Ten Years Near the German Frontier*. Its unostentatious chapters, under the guise of a pleasant volume of literature, constitute a revelation of the forces operating to draw Denmark into the maëlstrom of the tragic struggle for Germanic supremacy and are a substantial contribution to the history of the time. But this man of letters was a man of action also. In circumstances of peculiar difficulty from many quarters, it was his tact and his persistence that resulted in the acquisition by purchase of the Virgin Islands by the United States, an achievement that secures to him an honorable place in the history of our territorial expansion.

Already crowned with many academic laurels, after his return from his long mission new honors were accorded him, not only by universities and colleges, but by the King of Denmark and the King of the Belgians. The leading magazines sought and obtained contributions from his pen, and his reviews of books were notable for their learning, their penetration and their comprehensiveness. Among the honors received by him was election, on February 20, 1908, to the National Institute of Arts and Letters, of which he was President during the last year of his life; and, on November 19, 1919, he was chosen in succession to Theodore Roosevelt a Member of the Academy, in which he took an active interest.

Loyal to his friends and colleagues in letters and diplomacy, a man of faith without fanaticism, of convictions without bigotry, of sentiment without sentimentalism, of patriotism without narrow partisanship, Maurice Francis Egan is enshrined in the hearts of those who knew him as a knight "without fear and without reproach,"—gentle, courageous, noble and just,—whose life has shown that all that was admirable in the Age of Chivalry is still possible in the ever-recurrent tournament for the defense of beauty, truth and honor.

WOODROW WILSON

BY BLISS PERRY

WOODROW WILSON was elected a member of the Academy of Arts and Letters in January, 1908. He was then fifty-two, and in the sixth year of his service as President of Princeton University. He had won literary reputation very early. His brilliant treatise on *Congressional Government* dates from 1885. His books on *The State* and on *Division and*

Reunion, his various volumes of literary essays appearing during the eighteen-nineties, and his ambitious *History of the American People,* published in 1902, had brought him deserved praise as a master of English style. He was known to be a gifted teacher, and a speaker, upon academic and literary occasions, of unusual persuasiveness and charm. In any circle of cultivated Americans, at the opening of the twentieth century, the mention of Woodrow Wilson's name excited interest and attention. To the great unliterary and unacademic public he was practically unknown.

But his destiny was to lead him away from the quiet fields of history and literature and political theory into the vexed territory of university administration, and thence into the battlefields of state, national, and international politics. Even at the time of his election to the Academy, it had become impossible to regard Woodrow Wilson as a mere man of letters. He was now an administrator with very definite and radical policies of university reform. They naturally provoked opposition. During his term in the governorship of New Jersey the change of activity from that of the publicist and academic theorist to the practical political leader became more and more pronounced. Wilson's gay and spirited literary essays of fifteen years earlier, and the historical and political studies of the solitary scholar, were more and more effaced from the public mind. It became the fashion to regard him as a wholly new figure in American political life.

The story of his vogue is highly interesting, and it illustrates certain phases of the national character. Critics and historians of our literature have frequently emphasized the curiously composite structure of American literary reputations. They have rarely been won—as Poe's and Hawthorne's, for instance, were very clearly won—by purely literary achievements. Other considerations such as ethics, politics, public service, personal picturesqueness and fascination have played a great part in establishing the fame not merely of Franklin and Jefferson, Webster and Lincoln, but also of

Emerson and Whitman and Mark Twain. Our most characteristic American writing is civic writing, without any stylistic
consciousness, and scarcely regarding itself as literature at all.
The supreme example of it is the "Gettysburg Address."
Neither Lincoln nor Jefferson, neither Roosevelt nor Wilson, after their emergence into public life, can be made the
subject of dispassionate scrutiny as mere writers, any more
than we can think of Anatole France without remembering
the Dreyfus case, or of Burke without remembering his attitude toward the American colonies.

Wilson's fame as a writer has both gained and lost through
this complexity of the standards by which he has been judged.
His distinction as a man of letters was more clearly acknowledged when he was a college professor than when he had become a college administrator, for the obvious reason that his
new and bewildering proposals for university reorganization
provoked sharp dissent from his opponents as well as passionate loyalty from his friends. Colleagues who had once
debated whether Wilson's essay style was too Stevensonian
or whether he quoted Burke and Bagehot too frequently,
now quarreled over the "quadrangle" scheme or the location
of a graduate school. Trenchant phrases sparkling on the
pages of *Harper's* or the *Century* had been one thing, but
here was the phrase-maker suddenly in power, touching
pocket-nerves and vested interests and sanctified traditions.
One had to be for him or against him, style or no style.

His campaign for the governorship of New Jersey and his
achievements while in office served to widen these divergen-
cies of opinion, even among men who had thought they knew
Woodrow Wilson intimately. Was he a dangerous radical,
all the more dangerous because of his admitted skill in controversy, or was he the inspired leader of men into the paths
of what was then called the New Freedom? He became President of the United States, a masterful ruler of his turbulent
party and a spokesman for the nation. Audiences for his eloquent words were amplified. As the underlying issues of the

World War became gradually clearer and clearer, it was this once lonely student of Burke and Wordsworth who was called upon to express them and he was listened to by uncounted millions of men all around the world. Neither Jefferson nor Lincoln ever had such an opportunity to impress mankind by the spoken and written word, and surely it may now be said without any imputation of partisanship that Wilson's greatest messages and speeches challenge in range of thought and beauty of expression the noblest utterances in the political history of our race.

That would be glory enough for any man of letters, but I do not think that Woodrow Wilson, in his later years at least, cared nearly as much about literary reputation as he was supposed to care about it. He always knew, of course, that he could write and speak better than most men, but he had, unlike his famous contemporary Theodore Roosevelt, no instinct for publicity, no dramatic or histrionic sense. He was never the "timid," "vacillating" person of the political caricatures. In action he could be recklessly bold, pitilessly obstinate. But in the hidden recesses of his personality he was shy, sensitive, deeply religious, essentially a solitary. Yet like so many solitaries he had seen a vision. It was a vision, as every one now knows, of a new world order, an era of peace and justice for all men, a veritable, visible Kingdom of God on earth. And Wilson's fate was the familiar fate of the visionary. In the emotional exaltation of the closing months of the World War he really believed that a new mode of thinking had taken possession of the forward-looking minds of Europe and America. He was convinced that no one would dare to place the selfish interests of a single nation or group of nations above the interests of humanity as a whole. He was mistaken. The old order had enough strength left to strike him down. The Europe and America of 1919 were not ready for his gospel, and he sleeps now, the crusader's sword by his side, without having seen the "Holy City" of his dream.

I knew the man long and well. He had his faults of temperament and of method. His physical endowments were unequal to the strain of the enormous burdens which he was forced to carry. His body broke but not his will, nor the flawless clearness of his mind. If his career ended with his burial, as in some stormy Elizabethan play, it would be fitting to call Woodrow Wilson's life a tragedy. Take up the body and let "the soldiers' music and the rites of war speak loudly for him." But in the case of the true visionary, those trumpets of the sad fifth act and the fall of the tragic curtain are impertinences. Upon idealists such as he the curtain does not fall: the play evolves into the eternal drama that makes up the life of humanity. The illogical, impertinent bullet that pierced Lincoln's brain has now become a portion of his glory. "I meet him at every turn," said Thoreau of John Brown after he was hanged; "he is more alive than ever he was." Those who hated Wilson in his lifetime and those who loved him can agree at least in this: that his ultimate fame will depend upon the triumph of the political ideals which he clothed with fitting words. We make our guesses even now, but fifty years hence we shall begin to know something of the verdict of mankind.

HENRY BACON

BY CHARLES ADAMS PLATT

HENRY BACON was born at Watseka, Illinois, in 1866. After completing his general education at the University of Illinois, he went to Boston, beginning his architectural studies first in the office of Chamberlain & Whidden and continuing them afterward in New York in the office of McKim, Mead & White. In 1899 he won the Rotch Traveling Scholarship with which he embarked on a period of two years of thoughtful exploration in France, Italy and Greece. It was by his contacts with Greek architecture that the decisive tendency of his character as an artist was fixed. From thenceforth his style was classic and today he stands in the minds of architects as the embodiment of classic ideals in architecture.

He is best known and will be remembered chiefly for the Lincoln Memorial at Washington, the building to which he dedicated the latter years of his life. The opportunity to design this building is perhaps the finest that has been offered to any architect in our day, the site being at the end of the great Mall which extends from the Capitol to the Washington Monument, thence to the Lincoln Memorial. To acknowledge that Bacon lived up to his opportunity is to give him the very highest praise. The problem was to design a great monument dedicated to a great man, in surroundings appropriate to such a structure. Bacon's accomplishment proved that the work was entrusted to a great architect.

In designing this building, he took as his point of departure the order of the Parthenon, but in fitting the building to its site and uses, he gave the design a form which was his alone. In doing so he showed not only great scholarship but the ability to think along the lines of the highest architectural tradition. His building has grandeur but is not cold. It is his genius which has made the architectural language of the ancients live again.

While this edifice, as I have said, is the one by which Bacon will be chiefly remembered, it stands at the head of a great variety of high accomplishment, consisting of public and private buildings and monuments. He collaborated sympathetically with our most distinguished sculptors. He designed pedestals and statues and provided the necessary surroundings to give effect to this kind of work. It is widely recognized, indeed, that Bacon's invaluable sense of proportion and his instinct of beauty gave nobility to every monument he designed. As a man and an architect Henry Bacon evoked a dual tribute from those who came in contact with him and penetrated the armor of his shy and retiring nature. He won their admiration and their respect. They loved to be in his company. The memory of the man will be long cherished by his friends and his example will be preserved by the architects of this country.

He was elected a member of the Institute November 14, 1913 and passed to the Academy November 18, 1921. His death occurred in 1924.

HENRY CABOT LODGE

BY ROBERT GRANT

HENRY CABOT LODGE, one of the eminent figures of our time, a Senator of the United States from the Commonwealth of Massachusetts for over thirty years and an accomplished man of letters, was born on May 12, 1850 and died on November 9, 1924, in the seventy-fifth year of his age. He was the first occupant of chair No. 39 of this Academy.

Few men in the public life of our nation have been more fortunate in their initial advantages. His parents were wealthy, so that he was free to ignore mere earning power if he chose. In the exclusive circle to which they belonged he learned from childhood to respect intellect and to subordinate the language of mobs to the felicities of pure speech, however caustic. He read with avidity all within his reach and was blessed with a very tenacious memory. His attitude towards life kept him consistently eager-minded all his days, and few obliged to battle for a living have worked harder or with greater zest than he.

The record of his scholarly preparation reads like a catalogue of ships. A year in Europe after graduating from Harvard College. The Law School and admission to the Bar, but with no intention of practising. A Ph.D. degree with Anglo-Saxon Land Law as a thesis. An assistant editorship of the *North American Review* followed by an editorship of the *International Review*. Three years as a lecturer on American history at Harvard. This before he was 30 and in the wake of the avowal: "I had no definite plan, no taste, no aptitude, no mastering passion beckoning me into any particular path. I merely desired to read history and write, if I could."

He was feeling his way. Yet with feet already set in the pathway of two parallel ambitions. Ambitions to which he remained ever constant, and which, though parallel, were advisedly interdependent. He aspired to be a Senator of the United States, and on the way to that goal, whether it proved an *ignis fatuus* or no, to acquire by practice mastery of the English language both spoken and written as essential to the self-respect of one who hoped to be a statesman.

His only defeats for public office occurred on the threshold of his political career. He was 37 before he was elected to Congress, but meanwhile he utilized assiduously the second string to his bow. To this interval belong various studies in history, his short lives of *Alexander Hamilton* and *Daniel Webster* written for the American Statesmen series, the complete works of Hamilton in nine volumes, and *The Life and Letters* of his own great-grandfather, George Cabot, a former Senator of the United States from Massachusetts. In the preface to the last appear the pious words, "A sentiment of respect for the memory of my great-grandfather and a desire to rescue his name, if possible, from complete oblivion, induced me to undertake the work, of which this volume is the result."

During his six years of service in the national House of Representatives Lodge published his *George Washington* in two volumes, a *History of Boston* in the Historic Towns series and his volume *Historical and Political Essays*. In January 1893 he was elected a Senator of the United States. He was but 43 years old. Tenure of this high office, held continuously until his death, with its accompanying responsibilities and power was the crown of his ambition. There is evidence that he never desired any other. It is known that he refused to become Secretary of State. He found from first to last in the legislation incident to the Senatorship a wide and satisfying field for his alert intelligence, positive convictions and vigilant patriotism. He was among the first to warn against the dangers of unrestricted immigration, citing the example of Rome:

> And where the temples of the Caesars stood
> The lean wolf unmolested made her lair.

He fought vigorously for national preparedness, for the fortification of the Panama Canal and the upbuilding of our Army and Navy. Above all, as a member of the Committee on Foreign Affairs he was widely versed in all that concerned our relations abroad, and played an increasingly controlling part for thirty years in the settlement of policy and the drafting of treaties between the United States and foreign countries; notably in the Hay-Pauncefote Treaty and the adjustment of the boundary line between Alaska and Canada.

In those ripe and busy years following his election to the Senate, he found continuously until his death time for the books, and the published addresses and speeches, the first fruits of which were his title-deed to membership in this Academy. Henry Cabot Lodge not only wrote well and graphically and was, especially after middle life, a forceful, finished orator, but was universally recognized as that oft imagined, but in this country hitherto fabulous product, the scholar in politics. In his spontaneous but never failing power of reaching back into memory and so adorning whatever he said or wrote with apt and pregnant illustrations from the concrete wisdom of the past, he had no equal in public life and left no successor. In his posthumous volume *The Senate and the League of Nations* appears his own admission of this gift in the passage, "For a lover of literature and letters instinctively and almost inevitably thinks of the words of the poet or great prose writer which express better than he can in writing or speaking the idea he is trying to enforce."

The audiences whom he constantly addressed were no

greater admirers of this happy faculty than his colleagues at
Washington. The scholarly grace of his forensic speeches
rivals that which he displayed on more purely literary occasions. Together, for he published most of his speeches and
addresses seriatim in book form, they charm by their lucidity
and knowledge of the subject presented and by their delightful diction. He was the orator-elect of many special occasions, both political and academic. Within the confines of
this brief appreciation there is no space to particularize, but
titles so varied as *Abraham Lincoln, The Value of the Classics, A Great Library,* and *The Pilgrims of Plymouth* testify
to his literary versatility. One could cite many passages of
distinction, but none more felicitous than his eloquent apos-
trophe at Symphony Hall, Boston, when his reëlection was at
stake in 1911:

> I received from my predecessors the great traditions of the Senator-
> ship of Massachusetts as a sacred trust, and they shall remain in my
> hands or pass from me to my successor unstained, untainted, unim-
> paired. I would at least have the people of Massachusetts able to say
> of me that
> > "I nothing common did or mean
> > Upon that memorable scene."
>
> I am a Senator of the United States. My first allegiance as an Amer-
> ican is to the great nation founded, built up, preserved by heroic sac-
> rifices and untold treasure. My first loyalty is to that bright flag in
> which the stars glitter and to which we bare our heads in homage as
> it floats above our soldiers and our sailors, and the sight of which
> dims our eyes and chokes our throats when we see it in a foreign land.
>
> But I am also a Senator from Massachusetts and that last word
> touches the chords of memory with tender hand and moves the heart
> of all to whom it speaks of home. I was born and bred in Massachu-
> setts. I love every inch of the old State, from the rocks of Essex and
> the glittering sands of the Cape to the fair valley of the Connecticut
> and the wooded Berkshire hills. Here my people have lived before
> me since the days of the Massachusetts Bay Company. They lie at rest
> in the graveyards of Essex, on Boston Common, beneath the shadow
> of Park St. Church. Here I have lived all my life. Here my dead are
> buried. Here I hope and pray my children and my children's children
> will always live and serve the State in peace and war as best they may.

Henry Cabot Lodge's distinguished and unbroken part in
our national public affairs is the more remarkable when we
recall that he seemed to hold himself aloof from the common
run of men. His intimates were but few. To them he was
firmly bound for life as with hoops of steel, and to any one
whom he cared for or found congenial he was most loyal and
sympathetic. But he would have been the last to term himself
spontaneously democratic. He was popularly deemed cold,
and to many who knew him it seemed that every fibre of his
being recoiled,—as indeed it did recoil,—from the promiscu-
ousness of the "glad hand." In his *Early Memories* (1913)
he records, "The society into which I was born and of which
I became a part was, aside from politics, in its standards and
fashions, essentially English. The Colonial habits of thought,
very natural in their proper time, still held sway." That he
himself was an aristocrat in his social make-up was obvious.
Yet at the same time,—and this was the secret of his success
as a leader who for a generation was able on the stump to
arouse the enthusiasm of the rank and file and whose word
was potent if not law in party conventions,—he was known
to be intensively patriotic, especially in his jealous and vigilant guarding of American interests in our dealings with foreigners. It was not necessary to agree with him on all occasions in order to subscribe to this.

To those who knew Lodge well there was no one exactly
like him. His conversation, sardonic when he chose, but always stimulating in its vigor and freedom from the commonplace, drew listeners in any company, for his reservoir of apt
information never ran dry. He was singularly fortunate in
his home surroundings. During his prime his house was the
most delightful centre in Washington. His opinions were
clear cut and forcible; he never equivocated or shilly-shallied.
There is no denying that he was a good hater, but no more so
than the majority of his critics.

With one side regarding the matter as unsettled and the
other claiming victory, one need not discuss here the merits

of the great controversy which focussed national attention on him during the last six years of his life. Too many clouds hang over the arena to permit one to feel too sure which was politically right, but only to remember that the contest was a conflict between two antipodean temperaments. To carry the intensity of conviction into the shadow of the grave may seem vengeful to some, to others merely the purpose of a determined statesman to lay his case before posterity. At all events, whatever individual judgment or sympathies, even his detractors will admit that Henry Cabot Lodge stands among the positive spirits of our Republic and not with the spineless time-servers.

That he could feel so strongly beneath a calm exterior is evidence of vitality. As to the other side, the depth of his capacity for affection and disinterested admiration, another posthumous volume, partly from his pen, is proof eloquent. Lodge's relations with Theodore Roosevelt were known to be preëminent among the friendships of distinguished public men. But it was not until the two volumes of personal correspondence between them was published that more than a few realized the full quality of their intimacy. This especially with respect to Lodge. Throughout Theodore Roosevelt's career he was not merely his closest friend and more completely in his political confidence than any other adviser, but never hesitated to influence him by plain spoken counsel when he differed from him or thought his proposed course prejudicial to his best interests. That Roosevelt was deeply aware of and grateful for this devotion appears time and again in the correspondence. It is easy, to be sure, for one perusing the letters to apply to them the term mutual admiration, even to the extent of quoting the ironic couplet used by Lodge elsewhere:

> Ladling butter from their mutual tubs,
> Stubbs butters Freeman,
> Freeman butters Stubbs.

It is true that they did praise without stint each book or article that the other printed, and were slow to detect a blemish in one another's speeches. But when it came to vital affairs of statesmanship, the application ceases. It is no less easy to discern in these pages the deep-seated fondness of the older for the younger man reveal itself in constant desire that he should do or say nothing to mar his greatness. To one who reads with care this record of unselfish and ever solicitous attachment is one of the bright chronicles of human friendship.

1925

GEORGE WASHINGTON CABLE
BY ROBERT UNDERWOOD JOHNSON

I AM GOING to violate two accepted rules of composition:
first, that comparisons are odious, and, second, that one
should reserve his climax until the last; and these precepts
shall both be violated by one sentence, to express my conviction that, with the possible exception of Hawthorne and Poe,
Cable is the greatest figure in American fiction. Hawthorne
and Irving had more continuous suavity of literary method;
Poe a more arresting fancy; Mark Twain subtended a larger
arc; Henry James vibrated a more purely intellectual gamut;
Bret Harte was more uniformly, though often artificially, picturesque: but Cable seems to me to share all these qualities
in a combination not found in any one of the others. I base
this judgment only on a recent study of *Old Creole Days* and
The Grandissimes, but, the altitude of mountains being reck-
oned from the top, I have no hesitation in saying that, in my
opinion, in George Washington Cable a great writer has
walked among us whose greatness our generation has not
recognized.

Style, of course, is the essence of the writer, and, in Cable,
this quality is composed of many qualities: grace, force,
range, suggestiveness, imagination, large and unconventional
vocabulary, shimmering humor, easy movement, contrast,
tenderness, surprise and dramatic progression to an adequate
climax. Thus his style has intense personality. I cannot find
for it any provenance: it seems to derive from no master of
literature.

When we turn to the substance of Cable's writing it is not
less notable. Here was a man of Puritan instincts who could

interpret the Cavalier as no other author has ever done. He portrayed women as understandingly and as sympathetically as Tolstoy. He knew the Creoles by heart, and gives us all the sparkling facets of their attractive character. Raoul Innerarity deserves a place beside Tartarin of Tarascon and is of finer fibre. In English fiction, even in Thackeray, there are no more charming women than Aurore and Clotilde Nancanou. Palmyre, the voodoo witch, is a masterly creation. The grimness in *Belles Demoiselles Plantation* and *Jean-ah Poquelin* make *The Fall of the House of Usher* seem fantastic. The historic background of *The Grandissimes* is touched in so lightly that it never seems to rush to the footlights. Processions and crowds and Creole halls are painted with the bold, unfumbling stroke of genius. Nothing human is foreign to Cable, and he dramatises inanimate things, such as the Mississippi River, the jungle of swamps and the old-time mansions, saying of one that it had "an immense veranda about its sides and a flight of steps in front spreading broadly downward as we open arms to a child." He is never commonplace but always keeps the reader on the *qui vive* by the piquancy of his narrative, the natural drift of which carries along his touches of color as lightly as leaves are carried on an autumn brook. Marcel Proust has said that "the writer who does not naturally think in images is far better without them." Here lies part of Cable's strength: instinctively he thinks in images, apposite and precise, and, therefore, is free from artificiality.

When I said that Cable is the greatest writer in American fiction, I forgot part of my climax. I believe the final verdict of criticism will be that *The Grandissimes* is not only the greatest American novel to date but that it stands in the front rank of the fiction of the world. It is amazing in the bigness of its plot, its grasp of human nature, the charm of its execution, the suffusion of atmosphere, its firm dramatic construction and the sculpturesque roundness of its figures. Who in our national literature has equalled the tragedy of the death of the giant slave, the savage prince of his own country, the dreaded Bras-Coupé, who in his last moments, for the reverence he feels for its mother, holds the white babe tenderly in the hollow of his arm, and who when asked if he knows whither he is going gives assent and says with his last breath "To—Africa"!

Cable's gentleness, lovableness and integrity as a man have made us take his talent for granted. His associates of the Academy owe it to his memory to

> Reweigh the jewel and retaste the wine.

We shall then discover that he had not merely talent but genius.

WILLARD LEROY METCALF

BY ROYAL CORTISSOZ

WILLARD METCALF was elected to the Academy on November 20th, 1924. He died in New York City on March 9th, 1925. It was thus for only a short time that he was possessed of a chair in this institution. But he was all his life long governed by the spirit of the Academy, the spirit of fidelity to sound standards. This was a leading source of the success he won as a member of the American school of landscape painting.

He was born at Lowell, Mass., in 1858 and received his earliest training in the school of the Boston Museum of Fine Arts. The master in that city whose name he loved to recall was George L. Brown, whose paintings had once a high repute. Better even than his work was Brown's teaching. I well remember Metcalf's talk about it. He served something like an apprenticeship under Brown. It was his business to keep the studio in order, to tend the fire and so on. It was in a true workshop that he was reared and it was a place in which discipline was constantly operative. It was intensified when master and pupil went out along the countryside in search of subjects. Brown would teach the lad the essential, constructive elements in his profession. Composition was dwelt upon, the real building of a picture. Most of all did he teach Metcalf the importance of the minutiae of form in trees, shrubs and the earth itself, the shapes and densities of clouds, the structure, in short, of the visible world. He insisted upon all these things being clearly seen and truthfully drawn. By the time Brown got through with him Metcalf was nothing if not an accurate observer and a skilled draughtsman. He knew thenceforth how to put a picture together and how to leave upon it the stamp of a peculiarly efficient craftsmanship.

In his boyhood he had developed traits which stood him in good stead at this time. He was a resolute bird's nester, which I know meant in his case a positive passion not only for the eggs he found but for the songs and other characteristics of birds. He cared for nature instinctively and in the years of his prime, when fishing was his favorite sport, half his pleasure in woods and streams was in what he saw, in the feel and fragrance of the natural world. All this was carried into his art. He painted landscape with a deep sympathy. He was not a dreamer. He never poetized or romanticized his subject. But with sensitiveness, with insight, he plucked the heart out of the scene he set himself to depict. The indefinable elements which make our brooks and pastures intensely and unforgettably American are curiously eloquent in his pictures. He would do more than paint the portrait of a place. He would so interpret it that it disclosed the essence of our countryside everywhere. I know of no painter in the American school, save Twachtman, who could so consummately capture the beauty of a snowy day. The things that so many Americans know in their childhood and always remember, the physiognomy of an old barn, the rise and fall of a rail fence, the grace of the birch and the magic of the maple in spring, he would set upon canvas with the raciness that Lowell achieves in his verse, with the raciness if not, as I have said, with the specifically poetic touch.

By some strange play of circumstance, the secret of which I have never been able to discover, Metcalf started life more as a painter of the figure than as a painter of landscape. He proceeded to Paris, where he studied under Boulanger and Lefebvre. They confirmed him in his habit of good draughtsmanship and formed him in the mode of sophisticated picture making which we associate with the Salon. I have a vague recollection of an interior with a sorrowing figure that he painted in this phase of his career. It was a capable but not otherwise a particularly interesting performance. When he was at work in the eighties he did not give any very clear sign that he would detach himself from the general company of clever Americans benefitted by French training. Nor, for that matter, did he give immediate tokens of high accomplishment when he turned to landscape. When the group of artists calling themselves the Ten American Painters was formed he was a creditable rather than a salient member. But gradually he got into his stride, and with a steadiness in progress that was remarkable in itself he presently arrived at positive triumphs.

The old virtues inculcated by Brown made themselves felt with increased force and he profited enormously by the impressionistic hypothesis, never becoming a crass disciple of Monet but giving more and more attention to problems of light and air. In the transitional period leading up to his mastery of those problems he especially impressed his friends by the ardent industry and the inner energy of his labors. He would leave the city as for a campaign and bring back his sheaves with something of the air of a fighter who had conquered another step in his march. Year after year the quality of his art rose higher and higher. If ever a man had the principle of growth in him it was Metcalf. Long before he died he had made himself one of the most authoritative as well as one of the most charming celebrants of the American scene. I return with special appreciation to the Americanism of his art, to the sincerity and force with which he put familiar motives before us. He got into his canvases the simple, lovable truths which, perhaps, only an American can feel to the uttermost in our apple trees and our winding streams. This clairvoyance it was that made him of the line of George Inness, which is to say an inheritor of the very essence of American art.

He did his work—let us remember with a peculiar gratitude—with a magnificent honesty. None of the freakish movements in modern art could ever touch him. In design, in color, in drawing, he was, if I may use the expression, on the side of the angels. He believed in good workmanship and he practised it. There was always something tonic, something even austere, about his endearing personality. It was his artistic integrity showing through. He will be remembered as a painter of great gifts. Also he will be remembered as an artist who had principles and stood up for them.

JOHN SINGER SARGENT
BY EDWIN HOWLAND BLASHFIELD

THE DEATH OF John Sargent was sensational. The Keystone cannot drop out of the great triumphal Arch of the Graphic Arts, but an important member of that segment which comprised the portrait painters had fallen, and we could scarcely realize that no more contributions would come from him to our contemporaneous exhibitions. The thought created a sort of void, a depression in our outlook, for the impress of the man had been emphatic, his influence had been pervasive.

Already some writers are paying the tribute to him which consists in trying to explain that he was not really as great as we thought him, that his qualities were beginning towards the end of his life to pass in favor of new adventure in Art. I am firm in the belief that his niche is permanent and in the topmost row, and that the qualities inherent in him were of the kind that will not pass with any new adventure of the future.

What were those qualities? Perhaps in a very summary way his superiority may be established upon five fundamentals: his capacity, instinct even, for characterization, his sense of values, his dazzling technique, his style, his originality, or if you prefer, his unusualness, his difference from other men.

To me nothing in his performance was more assuring than his almost miraculous sense of values in nature; values—the things that give roundness, depth and existence to objects.

Sargent was sometimes a little indifferent to color,—it was not what compelled him most, temperamentally, though superb color passages are often to be found in his work,—but he never slighted the values. As for his technique, it was based on knowledge first and therefore was sound, quite sound, yet was in manipulation akin to sleight of hand, to wizardry—the kind of handling before which each of us says, "How under the sun did he do it?"

I appeal for confirmation to our fellow-member Professor John C. Van Dyke in memory of the two occasions when as we stood together before the Wertheimer portraits in the National Gallery of London, we felt that there were canvases in the room painted by other artists, but that Sargent's people were alive. As for his originality, one may cite almost any of his works—the difficulty would be to find one of them that lacked it. Notable examples are his furniture tobogganing down from a very high point of sight in his portraits; his amazing rendering of protective coloration in the picture called *The Hermit* in the Metropolitan Museum of Art; his little girls lighting the lanterns; his Ellen Terry holding the diadem of Lady Macbeth above her head; his Prophets; his Confusion of Religions; indeed practically all his canvases in the Boston Public Library.

JOHN SINGER SARGENT

He painted portraits, decorations, genre, landscape, in oil, water color, pastel, black and white and was a leader in all. Probably he will live longest as a portrait painter, but some of his really magical passages occur in small water colors, apparently just records done for fun, while his mural paintings, all unusual, are sometimes unforgettable.

Sargent was born in Florence in 1856. I met him there for the first time one day in 1871 on the Carraja Bridge. He was with his mother, whom I remember better than the boy himself. Of him I have but the faintest memory of a slender American-looking lad—how I should have looked at him if any hint of his future could have been conveyed by his appearance and had opened a vista.

Five years or so later, we men of the Montmartre group of Art students in Paris were stirred by rumors which blew across the Seine from the *Rive Gauche*, tales of a pupil of Carolus, so clever that all his comrades envied him and that the master, very proud of him, was perhaps a bit envious too.

Carolus was given a big oval ceiling to paint in one of the galleries of the Louvre, his pupils worked with him, and portraits of two or three Americans including one of Sargent himself, appear among the figures in the decoration and in passages look more like the latter's work than like that of Duran.

The pupil's portrait of his master next took us all by storm, and then his full length of Madame X, a well-known American-Parisian beauty, set Paris to talking and made the painter and the lady famous in a day. Again, as was the case later with many of his works, it was one of those productions which look as if they had been brushed in in a few moments by a Goya or a Hals, leaping into creation almost as the photograph follows the flashlight—yet which in reality were the fruit of sustained observation and repeated experiment. It was just the painting of a profile, much powdered, outlined rather crisply and of a white evening gown with a train—an *impression* you would say, swiftly seized and recorded—then let alone. But Sargent showed me in a portfolio a number, many indeed, of the profiles done in pencil or color, each differing from the other very slightly but very subtly. Here was no impressionist satisfied with his throw and not risking disturbance by second thought, but a man steadying himself by second reference, correcting his impression and extracting the essence.

And then while society was saying in Paris, "What a future this young portrait painter has here," Sargent crossed the channel. Perhaps the young painter was wiser than the conversational badauds who wondered why he deserted them. Of course his early portraits were reminiscent of his master, but Sargent was to better his instructions, that was patent already to those who saw far, and it is possible that the situation may have bred sensitiveness in Carolus. If it did and if Sargent perceived it, and we may well believe that little escaped his astounding perceptiveness, the pupil was too chivalrous ever to be anything but generous in his appreciation of the man who taught him, or at least laid the foundations of the younger artist's brush-work and draftsmanship. At all events there he was, a foreign-born New Englander with a Philadelphian admixture, with the souvenirs of his first youth spent in the Italian Athens under the influence of the most elegant and subtilized art produced since that of the Greeks, with a French technical training to back and complete his natural advantages, and now arrived in a country where from the walls of public buildings and private houses, Reynolds and Gainsborough, Raeburn and Lawrence, Hoppner and Romney could speak to him of the special branch of Art which was to be the main basis of his career. He so used his gifts and opportunity that in a short time he was a popular, perhaps *the* popular portrait painter with an ever growing clientele recruited from those at once who wished and those who deserved such immortality as the brush can confer. The remark has been made that after all, Sargent was only an impressionist with a natural feeling for characterization and an extraordinary facility in handling his medium. He was all that, but that he was only that is an untenable proposition. The picture bought by the Chantrey Fund for the Nation and representing two little girls in a garden, lighting Japanese lanterns tied to flower stems, is a good example in point.

It was painted in 1887 in Broadway, Worcestershire. I had the good fortune to see the execution of it from start to finish and it showed one interesting and indicative side of its author's methods. Each evening at twenty-five minutes to seven, Sargent dropped his tennis racquet and lugged his big canvas from the studio into the garden. Until just seven, that is to say while the effect of light lasted, he painted away like mad, then carried the thing back, stood it against the studio wall and we spectators admired. Each morning, when after breakfast we went into the studio, we found the canvas scraped down to the quick. This happened for many days, then the picture, daughter of repeated observation and reflection, suddenly came to stay.

Now the comment adduced above might be true, that this was an impression set down in twenty-five minutes in its essentials, but it was the sum of a dozen times twenty-five minutes of impression, with hours for reflection left between each one of those periods and its successor. The picture became thereby the result of a developed thought, emended, pruned, corrected. Sargent undoubtedly did not say with Goethe, "Stand, ye are perfect," for he was not poetizing, but he paused for the same reason, namely that his creation had reached the point which he felt able to attain. His swiftness was a precipitation of thought, not merely a habit or inclination or instinct.

And I am reminded of a story about him, true or untrue. When still quite a young man, in France or England, he was walking in the country by the side of a stream. A fisherman, an 'Arry or a Gugusse, called him opprobrious names, possibly as a relief from boredom or vexation owing to the unsuccessfulness of his catch; he did catch something even-tually. Sargent continued his walk for a time without turning his head—disappeared even, but reappeared, handled the fisherman in such a way that the latter remembered the inci-dent, after which, he—Sargent—resumed his promenade. The reflection, swiftness and thoroughness of the artist's methods and technique may all be seen in the story.

Said my master, Léon Bonnât, to me, one day, *"Pour faire vraiment bien, il faut faire tout du premier coup,"* and added after a few seconds of reflection, *"et encore on ne peut rien faire du premier coup."* Sargent showed by the manner of his attack that he agreed with the first half of Bonnât's dic-tum—and the cracking and color-changing on some of his canvases where overpainting had occurred, proved the truth of the latter half of the French painter's insistence. And yet and yet—some of Sargent's water colors, some surfaces where the painter could not fumble without our detection, seem al-most to demonstrate that he could achieve the impossible—and *finish* "du premier coup."

"Are you a man or a meeracle," said the soldier to Kipling's Mulvaney when the latter rode the mad elephant. "Betwixt and bechune" said Mulvaney, and so Sargent in some of his water colors approaches the miraculous. One has seen notices of more recent water colors by other men, calling them finer than Sargent's because "more direct." That is because their authors had stopped short on the road, which *he* continued upon. Stopping is the beginner's refuge, and is backed by the answer heard in every art school to the question, "Why did you not go further?" "Because I was afraid I should lose what I had already." Now assuredly nobody knew better than Sar-gent that over-elaboration kills the vital look of a work, but Sargent could go further than most people before over-elabo-ration was encountered, and one likes to feel with him and with Robert Browning, "Ah, but a man's reach should exceed his grasp."

Although portrait painting occupied most of Sargent's

time, some of his close friends declare that his love for mural painting was great, early felt and persistent. It has been maintained that he did not feel the fundamental architectural requirements in mural painting. One is inclined to reply that Sargent instinctively rebelled against convention (above almost anything he disliked the banal, I once heard him imply as much), and although architectural requirement is something bigger than conventions it does include some of the latter. The greatest mural painters in the greatest period of mural painting and in the country where it reached its highest point, namely in Italy, and, say, for a period covering much of the 14th and 16th centuries and all of the 15th, grew up in mutual practice with the architect, often indeed were architects themselves, and they understood that desirability of thrust and counterthrust which may be suggested and felt even in painted lines and masses.

Raphael in such works as the Disputa and the Theologia, both in the Vatican *Stanze,* probably carried composition to the ultimate as related to the shapes of the spaces given him to decorate.

In a way he settled and prescribed the general ordering of a decorated lunette or medallion—but even as early as the day of Giotto, there was much understanding of the filling of geometrical spaces by more or less flat painted forms.

Sargent once said in speaking of mural painting, "I understand Giotto and I understand Paolo Veronese better than I do the intermediate work." But by that he undoubtedly meant that the flat unmodeled treatment adhered to by the earlier artist and the frankly pictorial decorations of the Venetian were in either case legitimate and, in a way, settled procedure—while the intermediate work whether reactionary or progressive was hampered by side issues of anatomy, perspective, chiaroscuro and much besides.

Beyond question Sargent was conversant with all this, and if he did not always use the knowledge we may believe that it was because he thought of producing a striking and unusual effect, of being original and himself, before he thought of obeying an architectonic requirement. That in the cycle of Boston decorations there are more or less unrelated parts is undeniable, the horizontality of the frieze of Prophets does not melt into the "Confusion of Religions" above as it might and perhaps architectonically should. But what unusualness, how it all catches your surprised attention; where among the so-called Old Masters do we find finer presentation of the Prophets than in the figures which our artist has marshalled along one end of the hall in the Boston Library? They are not as tremendous as Michael Angelo's seated figures of the Sistine vaulting, not so traditionally "Biblical" looking to us as some of Dürer's Apostles. Sargent's creations seem to derive rather from a mixed souvenir of Syrians or Fellaheen, muffled against the sun of the desert, or of those monastic-looking, heavily-hooded figures that support certain medieval Burgundian Sarcophagi in European museums; but at least this painted threnody of wild, arm-tossing creatures is a new presence in mural art of the last three hundred years, the product of a mind with a quite outstanding visualization. At the other end of the Gallery the artist, years later, filled the lunette with his "Trinity" in solemn, balanced, ordered opposition to the "Confusion." Again it seems a little unrelated to the rest, does not entirely flow into the sequence—although one must admit that in this case the want of relation is not more marked than in hundreds of examples of ancient masters.

And what interest is in the relief work modeled we are told by the artist's own hands! What a puzzling, suggestive mélange of hints that refer one's remembrance to the tangle of beasts and people and ornament, on the lintel of Moissac for instance, or other kindred Romanesque churches of southern France; or again to a Spanish souvenir, as if Our Lady in the Archivolt had journeyed thither from some altar of Santiago da Compostela. And the row of Angels with the instruments of the Passion,—the make of them, their *facture*, is so interesting; they are washed in, one might almost say swashed in, as with a broom; there are two of them almost entirely of a first rubbing of Indian red with a few touches of the blue and liberal touches of gold; again there are nearly blue angels with just a little of red and gold. And their type is beautiful, they are all alike, androgynous looking, as angels should be, one would say, and suggesting in their faces both classical antiquity and good fifteenth century panels.

In the lunettes of the side walls, the compositions are extraordinarily daring and personal, especially in the one where the young Christ triumphantly advancing towards the spectator is apparently mounting an incline in a manner that seems almost a preparation for an Ascension. The color in all of the side lunettes is very simple in scheme, being hardly more than blue and a sort of golden cream color, the design is intricate and full of style, rhythm and decorative quality.

In the cycle of the Museum of Fine Arts at the Fenway, the treatment is quite different. The power and solemnity of the Library figures reinforced by rich dark color, is set aside in favor of a light and almost gay scheme harmonizing with the grey stone and stucco surrounding and recalling Pinturicchio, Primaticcio, Luini, in those cycles of their work in which they told tales currently and cheerfully, rather than set moral lessons framed in deep, rich marbles. The distribution of the ovals, lozenges, and lunettes placed against the light-colored masonry almost imposed the cheerful scheme which Sargent used here, but he certainly seems to have liked it and to have worked in a joyous spirit. It was impossible for him to be vulgar at any time, but here he made refinement doubly sure by renouncing variety of color and keeping away from any cheapening boudoir-suggestion of pink and light blue.

The whole is almost cameo in character. A handsome dark blue abounds as background in the spaces to be filled and gives, as it were, the word of command to steer clear of insipidity. The figures are in one or two tones of cream-color and white, and are often quite delicious in drawing and design. A Greek vase painter coming direct from Attica or Asia Minor and down twenty-four centuries would have approved the Danaides. As for Apollo's chariot—we have said that Sargent rebelled against convention, but he well knew where and how to use a worn example; the group recalls antique gems and coins—the Rospigliosi casino and a sublimated, magnified Wedgwood all at once, and the artist has made it his by the exquisiteness of his drawing. And again, à propos of rebellion against the banal, it is interesting to see how Sargent was forced by the architectonic situation to use the focal figure (usually a lady) who for centuries has owned the central place in the dominating panel of a cycle, most surely of all, in a semi-dome. When a world-master paints a Sistine Virgin or a Madonna del Sacco, or an Assunta for the Frari, she becomes a world-figure to be sure, but to the mural painter compelled to always harbor her, she may become also an irritating figure because of her tyrannous prerogative of being the linchpin, as necessary as hub to wheel. So there she is, in the semi-dome of the Art Museum—the Lady Athene who is sheltering the Arts under her big shield. The low relief figures in stucco which act as supporters to the panels or simply as space-fillers are remarkable as indices of the painter's versatility and thoroughness combined, but they are less effective perhaps and certainly less original than some of the Library relief work. Returning to the color-scheme, it is difficult to know why Sargent put his seated Philosopher (Poet?) and Scientist in colored draperies instead of limiting them to a share with all the others in the cameo tints. They seem to *détonner* a little, and perhaps that is one reason why they are the least interesting things in the series.

The static appears to have appealed less to Sargent than the dynamic, even in his portraits, where there was a chance for the latter, and his best results in the majesty which may come with big repose are perhaps most seen in his prophets in spite of their spiritual struggle and their arm-tossing.

Take them altogether, the Fenway Museum and the Library should be places of pilgrimage, above all the Library. After each visit one goes away realizing more the singular good fortune of Boston and the far-seeing wisdom of McKim which brought Puvis and Abbey and Sargent under one roof.

For all the sensation that greeted the Prophets on their arrival among the Puritans, and for all the fascination of his water colors, it was Sargent, the painter of portraits, who has most preoccupied the public in England and America. From the time when he gave a fillip to the visitors to the Paris salon in his characterization of a white gown, down through the forty-years-long series in which he often delighted, sometimes immortalized and occasionally alarmed his sitters, characterization has been admittedly his most marked quality. Its achievement is a part of the whole Sargent legend, perhaps it culminated in the Wertheimer portraits. Perhaps his sitters were not always and unreservedly grateful to him; perhaps the story that he diagnosed in paint a malady in his subject so insidious that it baffled the physicians, is a true story, and perhaps it is not.

Perhaps acquired momentum of impression counted for much; but that the impression was great and the characterization penetrating and forceful—a cloud of witnesses could rise up to testify. And style informed everything that he touched, one may even say that no matter how plebeian the subject, the treatment of it, the conception and painting of it, are patrician. Lately on the wall of the Grand Central Gallery hung the portrait of a social leader. Her type was aristocratic. He had made her look as distinguished as a race-horse or an empress, an empress as one would like her to look. Near by upon another canvas was a lady prominent in a great educational institution; she was round, rosy, comfortable, with plenty of keenness behind the comfort, not like a race-horse or an empress, but very capable of being a modern Hrotswitha, say, able to write Latin plays, and wearing her mortar board like a crown after all, and in her own fashion, terre à terre if it became necessary, but unmistakably a lady.

Said my companion, again a lady, as we stood before the canvases, "A man who can invest two such types with style and character, making both sympathetic, is a very big interpreter." And he knew how and when to seize the character and make it precipitate suddenly. He could not press this button of precipitation for a time with Wertheimer. "Finally," he said, "I deliberately asked his opinion of a certain investment—then I *got* him."

My comrades of the Academy of Arts and Letters will recall the kindred story which President Butler of Columbia told us at the last annual meeting of the Academy. Sargent and Roosevelt together were seeking a portrait background in the White House upstairs and downstairs and unavailingly. The President, tired of the search, said, "Sargent, the trouble with you is you don't know what you want." "The trouble with you, Mr. President, is that you don't know how to pose," was the reply. "What!" said the combative Roosevelt, "I don't know how to pose?" turning back upon the stair-case as he spoke. "That's right; hold still now; I've got you," said the painter.

Sargent the man conquered nearly all suffrages, certainly of those who knew him well. Though I met him a good many times in New York, the only period during which daily comradeship with him came to me was that of the summer of 1887 when my wife and I passed three months in the little Worcestershire village of Broadway, which Frank Millet, Alfred Parsons and Laurence Hutton discovered for Americans, which Sargent and Abbey helped so importantly to make popular and memorable, and which became the permanent home of Mrs. Mary Anderson de Navarro. I had never seen much of Sargent in Paris, for the Seine was a kind of Rubicon between Montmartre and the Pays Latin, so that he seemed almost new to me when with Mrs. Millet and one or two others he drove over to Evesham to meet us, since in those days the locomotive did not go to Broadway. Almost my first impression was of a certain aristocratic suggestion in his manner and his speech, yet he was wholly simple and kindly and therefore was attractive. Later we learned to know him as essentially modest in spite of his already well-grown popularity as a coming painter of both the "upper and upper middle classes." Years after, having made a two hours' call at his Chelsea studio, my wife remarked as we left Tite Street, "And did you notice that Mr. Sargent is still shy?" And shy he was, though by that time his acquaintance list must have numbered most of the worth-while people in London. In fact he seemed to have had an honest dread of the kind of trivial function which is little more than the result of gregarious instinct and of a craving for such excitement as shall make no draft upon grey matter. He must have known his own value but he had the simplicity which a certain mental stature insures. We are told that Degas once said to another American artist: "So and so, why do you act as you do? *Vous vous comportez comme un monsieur qui n'a pas de talent.*"

Neither Degas nor any other would or could have said that to Sargent. The latter was a contemner of hyperbole. When the lady asked him, "Who *are* those be-you-tiful creatures in your lunette?" he replied, "Just Blokes dancing," and probably concealed a grin. But if any one had countered with, "Well! if *they* are just Blokes, why, so were Titania and Oberon," he might well have grinned openly and admittingly. It was pleasant to see Abbey and Sargent together, working in the studio with Millet, or with all of us in the flower garden or the fourteenth century "Grange" in Worcestershire. One memory remains to me of an afternoon's sitting in the dazzling poppy patch. Sargent's study was better than those of the rest of us, but he finally shut his sketching easel and carried it indoors remarking, "Well, I'm stumped." We all followed suit and very presently a shower approved our self-judgment.

195

Abbey and Sargent seemed not only mutually sympathetic but also good foils,—Abbey with his *intarissable* fun and non-sense,—Sargent so much graver, yet both so entirely and deeply in earnest. Music was a great preoccupation with Sargent. In 1887 Bayreuth was, as to time required in reaching it, further from London than it is now, and pilgrims were not so abundant, but he left his studio more than once to go there. Mr. John Johanssen has said of him that he might have had a career as pianist; he had not quite reached that point in 1887, but he read music fluently. The Millets, who gave a dinner party almost every evening, sometimes had an overflow of guests. On such occasions Mrs. Millet sent Sargent or Abbey to dine with us in our rooms at the old Inn, the Lygon Arms. Sargent came more often than Abbey and after dinner was apt to linger over the piano playing delightfully from the Ring, or the Mastersingers, until we all struck our tents and went up to the Millets at Russell House for the rest of the evening. He certainly was a very perfect Wagnerite, but he was not a bit *précieux,* and played for our dancing, evening after evening. To be sure in those jazzless days, Strauss (the great Johann) reigned and the best of Wagnerites could afford to play Strauss.

He was intensely preoccupied with his work and there were stories of how it enabled him to cast off the petty annoyances of routine—of how for instance, at one time in leaving for the ship to take him to England (or America) he left also a large packet of letters and telegrams with the simple written direction to his Chargé d'Affaires: "Open and answer as you think advisable." But he could play also, and was quick to seize the technique of anything new. We all had our tennis daily, and though he called himself wholly unaccustomed to it, he was good at once, particularly at the net. His sense of humor was quiet but keen. One day he said to us of a sitter, "His portrait is finished and he doesn't know it, tomorrow I shall have to break it to him." Again he had painted a lady who showed in face and bearing the fine dig-

JOHN SINGER SARGENT

nity of the grief of a recent bereavement; he remarked with
a rueful smile: "The family said of my portrait, 'Yes, that is
Mother, but couldn't you make her a little more cheerful
looking?' " In fact the humor of a situation was probably an
occasional solace to him, and he summed all up in saying
that upon every painter's tombstone there should be the inscription: "There was something about the mouth." As late
as 1918 he said to me: "Portraits!— never again! never again!"
and raised both hands in deprecation; he evidently was tired,
but fortunately for his friends he continued to draw now
and then, crayon heads, so quickly and easily done that they
seemed to be a relaxation to him.

In person, he was, in his younger years, tall, slender, and
exceedingly good looking. In later life he became so full-
blooded that he said to me: "When the heat of the American
summer comes, I am frightened, I want to get away to the
top of a mountain where I can breathe." Beautiful studies
made in the neighborhood of Aosta and Carrara are the fruit
of some of his mountain journeys. He was at once so sought
after and so reserved that a whole legend grew up about him.
There were dozens of stories and all to his credit. Some of
them, which I know to be authentic, related to actions of a
very kind and generous character, performed with a really
chivalrous delicacy.

Recently the oldest self-governing body of artists in the
United States celebrated its centennial birthday. That one
of the most grievous losses in the Art World of those last
hundred years should have come through the death of an
American painter is not a little noteworthy in its relation to
our pride and our place in the development of Nations.

At the time of his death, John Singer Sargent was the
senior by election of our American Academy of Arts and
Letters. We may look back with profound self-congratulation
upon having had in our ranks one of the great outstanding
figures not only of contemporaneous art but of Art of all time.

PAUL WAYLAND BARTLETT

BY ROYAL CORTISSOZ

ALL THE CIRCUMSTANCES of Paul Wayland Bartlett's birth and upbringing were favorable to his development as an artist. His father, Truman H. Bartlett, was dedicated both to art and to art criticism, he was both a sculptor and a writer. When Paul was born at New Haven in 1865 he breathed, literally in his cradle, the atmosphere which was to be his all his life. He was taken to Paris as a boy and was only fifteen when he entered the École des Beaux-Arts. From that moment his career was fixed, that of a sculptor whose natural aptitudes were to draw from environment and opportunity exactly the stimulus needed to make them effective.

He studied at various times under Cavelier, Frémiet and Rodin. They taught him much but he was possessed of an individuality which saved him from the imitative drift which any of them, and especially Rodin, might have promoted in a weaker type. The most interesting thing about Bartlett is that from beginning to end he was his own man. He was that by virtue of character and technique. Doubtless his surroundings in Paris fostered his inclinations but the latter had deep roots and would have grown anywhere. I remember talking with him once about the little bronzes of fish, serpents and so on which he had cast himself *à cire perdue*. The impression he left on me was of the very spirit of plastic art. His way of taking up one of the bronzes and fondling it as he turned it about and about for my inspection was indescribably the way of a sculptor. He talked *patinas* as a painter might talk colors. Bronze was to him an ineffably ductile and even sensuous medium. Its genius had entered his soul.

He was a born craftsman, a modeller and chiseller by favor of the gods. I was always delighted, and a little puzzled, by his escape from the influence of Rodin. The latter so often seems to have modelled just for the fun of modelling. The young American had the same gusto, but he would

198

not deviate into mere virtuosity. He had a sense of organic structure saving him from that. One trait he had in common both with Rodin and with that distinguished *animalier* Frémiet, a faculty for the picturesque. A figure by Bartlett is bound to seize the attention, it is vivid, sharply defined, significant not only of form but of movement. He had a seeing eye and his statues are extraordinarily vitalized characterizations.

There are many of them for he was a devoted workman, ceaselessly active down to the time of his death on September 20th, 1925. I do not pretend to survey them all in detail. But one or two of these achievements of his I must signalize, notably the "Michael Angelo" and the "Columbus" in the Congressional Library, and the "Lafayette" in Paris. The "Michael Angelo" is a really brilliant evocation of personality. There is something about the head to suggest, faintly, the seer, but chiefly I think Bartlett summons up the mundane presence of the great master, his originality and his terrific power. The note of power, above all, is struck with splendid precision. I cite the "Lafayette" for its grace, its delicate distinction. The horse and its rider are bodied forth with exactly the elegance that belongs to the eighteenth century tradition.

He had, indeed, the light touch in inspiring measure. He knew how to be monumental, as is shown by numerous heroic figures of his. He did not know how to be heavy-handed or dull. Vivacity rather than depth is the mark of his art. Yet he was penetrating enough to be always sure of the merit I have mentioned, the merit of seeing his subject truthfully and sympathetically. If he was vivacious he was in no wise shallow. It was rather that art meant, for Bartlett, the nervous force, the kindling interest, of life. He simply couldn't lapse into convention. Each work of his was a fresh, ebullient conception. In the best sense of the phrase he energized his sculpture. He was elected to the Academy on May 18th, 1911.

1926

JOSEPH PENNELL
BY JOHN CHARLES VAN DYKE

ALMOST EVERY one who is elected to an Academy such as
this has some friendly casuist to inquire how he of all
men happened to be chosen for academic distinction. Doubtless that inquiry was made about Joseph Pennell when he
became a member of this body in 1921. He was thought to be
a radical, a reformer, a progressive, a flouter of constituted
authority—in short a most unacademic person. But those who
did such thinking imagined vain things. All his life Pennell
was a pronounced conservative. Again and again he and
Whistler wrote and talked of the preëminence of tradition
in art. It was their joint hobby. Neither of them advocated
revolt but rather a bettering of that which had been received
from the past. Pennell had neither love nor respect for ultra-
modern art because it was not founded in craftsmanship—
the tradition of the shop. It had thrown aside training and
skill and had taken up with superficial effect. As for illustration and printing, with which he was directly concerned,
the machine had ruined both of them. The rush and greed of
modern life had spoiled everything. Neither he nor Whistler
at any time criticized academic institutions but rather those
members within the institutions who were nullifying principles and making sport of tradition. Pennell regarded his
election to the American Academy of Arts and Letters as
the highest of many honors he had received, and I have reason to know that Whistler up to the day of his death would
have accepted eagerly an election to the Royal Academy, the
members of which he had scoffed at for the better part of his
life.

JOSEPH PENNELL

Pennell was born a Quaker in Philadelphia, in 1860, and by heritage was a man of peace. The actualities of war when he came to see them on the French front were so revolting that they made him ill. He could do no work there and came away empty-handed. Even in verbal warfare he was ill at ease and rather unhappy. Only those who knew him intimately could quite appreciate his caustic comment and his often bitter criticism of society, government, literature and art. He knew what was the right thing to do and how it should be done and it was the Quaker in him that would tell the truth and shame the devil. He exaggerated, to be sure, but he needed the exaggeration to make the truth apparent. It was no waspish or bearish nature that was making itself manifest. He was the kindliest of souls and the most faithful of friends, as his long years of devotion to Whistler should bear witness. Those who knew him were not disturbed by his candor even when it was directed against themselves. They recognized under it the truth and honesty of the man.

As for his denunciation of modern life in America it was leveled against those who had thrown overboard the decencies of the eighties and nineties for the indecencies of the newer twenties, and not against America itself. Only yesterday, in writing a note for his Memorial Exhibition at Philadelphia, I had the chance to say: "He loved America best of all and scolded about her because he loved her." There is hint of this in the last chapter of his last book, *The Adventures of an Illustrator*. At the head of the chapter he placed a reproduction of his mezzotint of the Statue of Liberty—the great figure looming splendidly against the light of the setting sun. The title he gave it was "Hail Columbia." And in his will he left (with Mrs. Pennell's consent) all his collections, all his prints and plates, and a not inconsiderable fortune in money to the Library of Congress—to America. A superficial view of either Pennell or Whistler will not do because —well, because of its superficiality.

The Adventures of an Illustrator is autobiographical and

in it more than once Pennell insists he was a *born* illustrator. If that be not entirely conceded it must be admitted that he was precocious beyond his years. At sixteen his drawings got him into the School of the Pennsylvania Academy of Fine Arts, though they were at first rejected, together with some marines he had sent to an Academy exhibition. That is not so remarkable perhaps as the fact that at this time, through Stephen Parrish, he saw, admired and tried to follow the etchings and drawings of Fortuny and Rico. They were the very best of pen-and-ink men and Pennell's immediate acceptance of them was almost a stroke of genius. He did not know then that Blum, Brennan and Lungren were following the same trail, and that Alexander Drake, Art Editor of the *Century Magazine,* was lending them practical aid and comfort. But he was shortly to meet that group and to work with Drake whom he never after ceased to praise.

In 1880, armed with a letter of introduction (which he forgot to deliver), he bearded Drake in his den and showed him some sketches he had made for an article, "A Day in the Marsh." Drake approved of them, and took the young illustrator down to the editorial rooms where he met Robert Underwood Johnson, and got an order for the article. Pennell had already chosen a colleague to write the article and the editors even approved of that. It was a great day's work and Pennell, after a luncheon with Drake, went home with his head in the clouds. In recalling that early adventure he writes with jocose humor: "It is extraordinary how much sense I had, but then I was a born illustrator. And I think R. U. Johnson might, in his *Remembered Yesterdays,* have said as much of me." But he had nothing to complain of at that time. He was well started, under the best of influences, with the best of editors, and with the best of methods. Many an artist has spent the first half of his life getting back to the point where Pennell started.

Once launched he made rapid progress. The *Century Magazine* sent him to New Orleans to illustrate Cable's

Creole Days and in 1882, when he was twenty-two, he started on his first European trip to illustrate (for the *Century* again) Howells's *Tuscan Cities*. He was at first somewhat overwhelmed by London and Paris but he kept his eyes open and his fingers busy. He worked—all his life he worked—without ceasing. The immediate goal in Europe was Italy and the work in hand the illustrations for the Howells book, but he did other and independent sketches for *A Canterbury Pilgrimage* and *Our Sentimental Journey,* books done with Mrs. Pennell writing the texts. He saw all kinds of art, and met artists, authors, publishers,—all kinds of people from Böcklin to Vernon Lee. In the summer he went up to Venice, met Duveneck, Bunce and the group of American artists studying there, and in the autumn went on to London to meet Gosse and Lang and more artists. Returned to the United States he was married to Miss Elizabeth Robins (the "E" of the *Adventures*) and together they went back to Europe, he to do the illustrations for *English Cathedrals* for which Mrs. Schuyler Van Rensselaer furnished the text and the *Century Magazine* the press.

His success with the *English Cathedrals* series was immediate. His drawings were not only illustrative but they were picturesque, dramatic, more than half-romantic. Infallibly he picked the right spot, the salient group, the proper light. He was working with pen-and-ink more than with wash and getting effects of brilliant light by forcing the blacks sharply against the whites. It was the Fortuny-Rico method which he had adopted. But before he had finished with this series he saw that the light effects were truer to Spain and Italy than to England and that he was not getting the subdued light, the atmosphere, the envelope of the North. A change began then and there. The next series, *The French Cathedrals* with Mrs. Pennell's text, shows not only a change in the light and air but also the more frequent use of the washed drawing and the etching. He was to go on with changes in method and medium to the end because he was never satisfied with his work and was always reaching out for some newer means of expression. Perhaps Whistler, whom he met in Paris at this time, had some influence in turning his attention to tone—to the envelope. But Pennell was little beholden to any one for his art. He was partly "a born illustrator," as he asserted, but perhaps more largely a self-made one.

His versatility in theme, method and medium, as we look back upon his work, seems extraordinary. During the succeeding years he sketched palaces, temples, sky-scrapers, factories, coal breakers, canal locks; he pictured gardens, streets, waterways, canyons, mountains, and he did them in ink, pencil, charcoal, pastel, wash, etching and lithograph. The illustrations that he made for books by Henry James, Maurice Hewlett, Marion Crawford, Philip Gilbert Hamerton, John Hay, and a dozen others were not mere repetitions of the same manner and medium. Each series was different after its kind, each an attempt to break out a new sail and run a shorter or a better course. And his *Wonder of Work* series, which he had in hand up to the last, was always an outlet for experiment. He made up books of his own with texts and plates of Greek temples, London streets, Panama locks, Pennsylvania coal mines. The wonder was not about his subjects but about his treatment of them—how he could picture familiar themes over and over and yet each time give a new view and lend a new interest.

And quite aside from the quality of his output, the quantity of it seems enormous. It was not merely illustrations for fifty books and two dozen magazines but huge lithographs of current happenings for newspapers, series of etchings for exhibitions, war posters for different governments. His activities reached out into many departments. He wrote six volumes of his own and collaborated with Mrs. Pennell in writing nine more. While in London he was connected with the *Daily Chronicle* and other newspapers, wrote art criticism, succeeding Bernard Shaw as art critic on the *Star*, and fought in his column for Aubrey Beardsley and Whistler. In addition he was for a time Professor in the Slade School of Fine Arts and also lectured elsewhere in London, as later in New York and Chicago. In more recent years he had an etching class in the Art Students' League, talked at the Metropolitan Museum, and wrote letters of protest to the *New York Times* while doing etchings from his Brooklyn window, working in watercolors and oils and writing his *Adventures of an Illustrator*. His energy was unabated to the last.

I suppose it is proper to admire the person of one idea who does one thing and does it supremely well, but what about the person who does a hundred things and does all of them well? A dash at fame with an early masterpiece and a succeeding silence of long years may be counted as at the least worth while, but what about the carry-on for fifty years and a growth in power with each succeeding year? Had Pennell died at thirty we should have had his brilliant clear-cut Cathedral drawings. Those would have placed him close to Rico and Vierge and his etchings would have been ranked with the early Whistlers which he so much admired, but we should have missed the sombre power of his later charcoals, the richness of his mezzotints and the loom and quality of his lithographs, the massive lift of his sky-scraper etchings. The exactness of his early work gave way gradually to a wider vision, a broader handling and an increased mastery. His later work is the better and perhaps the more enduring.

I am disposed to make this statement even regarding his writing, because there has been here and there in the daily press some shallow criticism of the style of his *Adventures of an Illustrator,* and because he was a member of this Academy and something Addisonian in sentence was perhaps expected of him. I should like to say with such positiveness as I can command, that his *Pen Drawing and Pen Draughtsmen,* his *Etchers and Etchings,* and his *Lithographers and Lithography* are the best and most informing books on those subjects in existence. As for their style, if one turns to the earliest volume, on *Pen Drawing*, he will find it written in quite calm and faultless English. In the *Etchers and Etchings* he became somewhat more colloquial, in the Scammon Lectures given at the Art Institute of Chicago he was conversational, and in his last book, *The Adventures*, he was so intent upon color that he practically sacrificed form.

Now this change of style can not be put down to ignorance of the language, for I believe it was a designed change. Pennell was an artist and the primary business of art is expression and effect. He knew very well that the *Discourses* of Sir Joshua Reynolds were not the best models of style wherewith to reach the youth of today. They were written to be read, not talked at an audience. He needed the spoken rather than the written language. This he used in the Scammon Lectures. They were the most informal talks imaginable but I venture to think that the student audience got more information from those talks than from any course of lectures ever delivered from that platform. They reached the student mind and had the desired effect. Just so with *The Adventures*. It was written as Pennell himself talked in conversation and reveals his pronounced personality. And everyone who reads it must concede that it is most readable, interesting, and colorful. Well, what value is there in any book that is not readable, interesting and colorful? And after all does not the end justify the means? Pennell thought so at least and who shall say he was not right?

Joseph Pennell was not only an excellent illustrator, etcher and lithographer but he was a forceful writer. In addition he was an energetic speaker and a famous character in the art and life of his time. He was something of a crusader, if you will, but that was entirely to his credit. He spoke for the truth, and the right, and fought for common decency, common honesty and common sense in American life. That may not be the primary aim of this Academy, but such things are surely not beside its purpose. Not one of us but honored his convictions and admired his bravery in setting them forth.

And so I am returning to my initial contention that he was an Academician at heart and that all the supposed radicalism of his art and life was merely the artist's method of expression—a way of attracting and holding interest in the theme in hand.

STUART PRATT SHERMAN

BY HAMLIN GARLAND

STUART PRATT SHERMAN was elected to chair 49 on the 22nd of February, 1923. He was at this time the head of a department of Literature in the Illinois State University and the youngest member of the Academy. Although a New England man by birth and training, he had been for nearly seventeen years a citizen of the Middle West.

He was known to few of the Academy personally but all knew and valued his work. From his cloistered life in Urbana he had, from time to time, sent to the Eastern press volumes of critical essays whose grace of style and careful scholarship had won for him wide distinction. He was accepted as an admirable link between the Old Criticism and the New, between the East and the West. My acquaintance with him was limited to a few meetings at luncheon or at the Club. For the personal items of this brief memorial I am dependent upon those who were his companions and his students in the West.

That his work as a professor in the University of Illinois was valuable, Dr. Babcock, Dean of the College of Liberal Arts, bears witness: "Sherman was more than a great, gifted, penetrating essayist and critic of literature. He was a forceful, versatile, incisive and understanding critic of life, a nobly stimulating teacher, and a loyal colleague and friend, who shared generously the riches of his spirit and sympathy."

At the time of his death much was said of his popularity as a teacher, and of his presence and his power in the lecture room. Allan Nevins, one of his auditors, writes: "He possessed a quality of personality which caused him to stand out from the general faculty ranks. Stern, reserved, a little sardonic in bearing, he had none of the ordinary professorial arts of popularity. He sought no contacts with students not registered in his courses. Within his classroom, he was impersonal, businesslike and averse to any display of wit, geniality or eloquence.

"His method of conducting the one advanced course which I took under him was to read careful lectures in a monotonous voice without encouraging discussion. He was never electric, and he was certainly not an absorbing teacher, yet, in an austere sense, he was infinitely stimulating. His fine seriousness, his intensity of purpose, the beautiful precision of his mind, his recurrent moments of profundity and his ironic scorn for the shallow or insincere, gradually kindled all of his students who were worth kindling."

Although a man of books, an insatiable reader, a devoted student, Sherman was a lover of woodland life. He puts this in his note book: "Where did it come from, this taste for the wild? I have not been accustomed to think of myself as a nature lover, but when I come to review the times I have spent in camping and tramping in one place or another, I see that the strain of liking for out-of-door life runs pretty much through the years from the first."

It was this liking for the primitive which led him to build a summer home in a secluded colony on the eastern shore of Lake Michigan. This cluster of cottages as simple as pioneer cabins, was known as "The Professors' Colony" and stood in the midst of an unbroken forest of birch, beech and maple, on a grassy bank overlooking a wide, clean sandy beach.

In a quiet, almost lonely spot he built his cabin, "and there, of a summer morning, he could be found at work in his little study clad in khaki trousers and a soft shirt, with a flowing magenta-colored windsor tie, filling unending pages with his minute script."

"It is surprising even to one who was in intimate contact with him through all these summers," writes Franklin Scott, "to find on reflection in how many ways he was active. One summer he covered the walls of his cottage with crayon drawings of the flowers to be discovered in the woodlands and meadows of the region. Another year, he piled up in his study innumerable boxes of insects; a fairly comprehensive collection of the multitude available. He was very fond of a few games. He would pitch horseshoes by the hour. He was a good tennis player, and his desire to add that game to the resources of Dunewood led him to take the initiative in building a concrete court. He worked tremendously at this task, trundling in a wheel-barrow all of the material from the mixer to the workers who were laying the floor.

"No one was more at home in a canoe than he. He made one trip of fifty miles along the winding and dangerous Manistee River. He enjoyed using his strength not only in the ways already mentioned, but in chopping wood and in gathering piles of driftwood on the beach.

"He was a leader on all occasions that brought the community together. In the blueberry picnics, in the community suppers on the beach, and in the Sunday evening 'sings' held in the only cottage that afforded a piano. He had been a member of the glee-club in Williams College and of the Choral Society of the University of Illinois, and he lost no chance to enliven an evening with songs of which he knew an astounding number. One of the regular features of our summer life in Dunewood was the impromptu singing around the great fire of driftwood after the beach supper was over. With a piece of driftwood as a baton he would stand in the circle of his friends and with his deep bass voice lead the singing until all other voices failed.

"He liked to organize and take part in costume parties and dramatic performances. He played with great spirit and effectiveness the part of Jacques in a beautiful production of *As You Like It*. In a more rollicking spirit he took the part of Juliet in a burlesque of *Romeo and Juliet* and on rainy evenings he often read aloud to the assembled neighbors from whatever book he happened to be interested in or working on at the time."

In this pleasant and peaceful round of winter teaching and summer recreation and writing, he spent nearly twenty years, steadily refusing to consider any change, but in 1924 an offer of such magnitude came to him that he was forced to accept it. That he did so with a painful sense of doubt is evidenced by these words which he put into his diary: "When last night there came over me like a strong wave a sense of all I should leave and lose in personal relations to the young men who are coming here, and the good eager students, and some of the devoted townspeople, and one's old friends and colleagues, and the University itself, with its fine promise of natural growth and expansion, and now this morning that the lilacs and spires are beginning to bud and the larches are vivid green in the forestry, and the clean blue of the sky overhead,—it hurt."

In reading these lines, I realize, as I did not at the time, the pain which preceded his removal to New York. I recall writing to him a letter of congratulation and a prediction of a larger usefulness, for I believe that in taking an editorial position of such distinction he was mounting to a larger pulpit than any university could offer. In his answer he raised a note of question which I did not fully understand then but which is clearer to me now. He was suffering the agony of being uprooted at a time when youthful adaptability was beginning to fail.

He was cordially welcomed to the East by his journalistic associates but some of his readers feared a decline from the dignity, restraint and grace which had made his books so notable. I think he had some such fear himself, for he gave to his reviews such labor that they kept the high level of his essays—they were essays—written in the seclusion of his study, unhurried and serene. With the scholar's love for style, and standing for nobility of purpose, he maintained, even in the midst of increasing critical tumult and confusion, the high standards of a lineal descendant of Emerson and Lowell.

He was not profoundly affected by the journalistic trend of his time and his continued defense of the founders of American literature is distinguished by its loyalty as well as by its delightful humor. He was the Puritan man of letters broadened by contact with the West and stimulated by the opposition of his cynical contemporaries.

He was a believer in progress but he demanded an orderly progress. He believed in honoring those who had built acceptably in the past and he, himself, built on his predecessors, secure in the knowledge that permanent forms of national literature are not dependent upon momentary acclaim. That he was influenced by contemporary judgments is true, but no critic of his day kept so high a plane of reasoned praise. He knew other ages, and other literary fashions. He was in possession of comparative estimates which kept a check on his enthusiasms of the moment. He sometimes wrote of these habits of thought but he was too much the student of history to shout with the crowd. He felt deeply the spirit of the time but a humor which sprang from comparative ideas kept him to a course which the future will largely respect.

In almost the latest entry in his note-book, he registered a vow: "I am going to write, so far as possible, for the rest of my life, about happiness and where it is, and how to get there, and any paragraph that I write shall have the word, or the record of happiness in it. This I went out in the wilderness and dwelt forty years to learn." It is our misfortune that his untimely death made these resolutions of such short service.

In all that he said he remained soundly and nobly progressive. A citizen of the New Time rather than a citizen of a new place, he succeeded in winning the respect even of those who are disposed to make light of scholarship. As I read the wit, the grace, the humor of his comment he seems as much alive as when I knew him. It is not safe to predict long life to any man's books in these days of the radio and moving picture, but Sherman's critical estimates have in them something akin to the master spirits of the past. He voiced a certain phase of criticism and can not be overlooked in any estimate of our time.

One of the few meetings I had with him was on the top of a Fifth Avenue bus, and, for some reason which I do not understand even now, he opened his heart to me in such fraternal spirit that I, during that hour, added affection to the admiration in which I already held him. I saw him in something the same guise as that in which his neighbors at Dunewood beheld him, a homely, sincere and unassuming Midlander, homesick and dreaming of his quiet camp above Lake Michigan. A few months later when I read in the morning paper the news of his tragic death by drowning, I was glad of that last confidential talk, for in it I got beneath the critic and found a neighbor and a friend.

1927

JAMES FORD RHODES
BY ROBERT GRANT

LESS THAN a year has gone since the ashes of James Ford
Rhodes were borne from Boston where he had lived
continuously since middle life to Cleveland, the city of his
birth. It was on January 22, 1927, that he died. But already
the facts of his career have been set down by scholars of other
Academies with the fullness of personal devotion, and his
life is being written by the biographer named by him as his
choice twenty years ago in a memorandum left for his son and
confirmed at a later date by word of mouth. A tribute at this
time may therefore more fittingly take the form of an estimate
from affection and understanding rather than a sequence of
detail; and this, especially, because my own intimacy with him
did not begin until he had published the first two volumes
—issued together in 1893—of his great history, and, having
given up his sojourn in Cambridge, was, after an intervening
year in Europe, beginning to be a familiar figure to the resi-
dents of the "inner Boston" that lies between "the Athenaeum
on Beacon Hill and the Historical Society's building on the
Fenway. Not all of Boston" (as Bliss Perry continues), "but
it gives plenty of room for a triumphal procession."

I know only from others of his childhood's dream of writing history, and that this, fostered undoubtedly by living almost within earshot of our Civil War,—for he was born in
1848,—remained in leash for over twenty years from pru-
dence and the exigent realities of iron and coal, his father's
business. Yet it appears that he was sent abroad on the eve
of his apprenticeship to study how these minerals were handled in England, Wales and Germany, attended a course of

lectures in the Collège de France, and was European Correspondent for the Chicago *Times*. He returned with a good reading knowledge of French and German to supplement his earlier studies for a single year, when he was seventeen, in the physical sciences and history as a special student in the University of the City of New York. That "the flighty purpose never is o'ertook unless the deed go with it" should be not less true of the steadfast one, and arguing from this equipment it would not have been strange had the inchoate ambition to be an historian remained latent if not been quenched. More readily so from the practical course of events which establish him again in Cleveland in 1870 as a partner in "the firm of Rhodes and Card, producers and dealers in coal, iron ore and pig iron." Tradition, accredited by Dr. Harvey Cushing, pictures him at this time as "a dapper young man with the fashionable flowing side-whiskers he had cultivated in Piccadilly." Shortly after, too, he married the daughter of his father's partner and "set up housekeeping handsomely and happily in a large house directly opposite that of his parents," who lived in a fashionable neighborhood. If not born with a silver spoon in his mouth, he had golden opportunities for mere accumulation at his fingers' ends from early manhood. His father, Daniel Rhodes, who had "migrated as a lad from Sudbury, Vermont, to the Western Reserve shortly after the completion of the Erie Canal," and was prosperous, changed the name of his firm in 1874 to Rhodes and Company. Among the new partners taken in at approximately that time were his son James and Mark A. Hanna, who married James's sister. For more than twenty years he remained in business, though all the while an inveterate reader who kept "a series of commonplace books with notes and clippings" which he called his "Index rerum." A characteristic form of wisdom led him to subordinate his real tastes to the importance of amassing a comfortable fortune before he gave himself up to them. He withdrew from the firm in 1886, but to begin with went to Eu-

rope for a year, where incidentally he busied himself with
the translation of a French novel by way of practice in the
art of composition. On his return, with his first two volumes
already undertaken, he removed from Cleveland to Cambridge, partly so as to be nearer to his material and partly because "his son at the early age of fifteen had just entered
Harvard." Rhodes himself was at this time thirty-nine.

We, his friends of this Academy, know the rest, for his
election to the Academy in May, 1905, less than six months
after that of William D. Howells, chronologically first in
order, did not occur until six of the seven volumes of the
History of the United States from the Compromise of 1850
were already in print and academic honor after honor had
been conferred on him in eager recognition of a work of
first-class literary importance by a fellow countryman. This
fame, augmented by each addition until the earlier title was
merged in the *History of the United States from the Compromise of 1850 to the Final Restoration of Home Rule at
the South in 1877,* soon became European as well as national
and his graphic, judicial, eminently readable chronicle of
our national development had won him by accord a place
among the great historians of the world. This title equally
secure at his death as at the height of his production was all
the more grateful to his admirers because of the charm of his
genial disposition, the perfect honesty of his opinions and
his outright habit of disclaiming knowledge of that in which
he was unversed,—a trait exceptionally rare among the mentally elect. Indeed, great simplicity and entire freedom from
pretence or affectation were leading traits.

In his inaugural address as President before the American
Historical Association in 1899 he said: "Holding a brief for
history as do I your representative, let me at once concede
that it is not the highest form of intellectual endeavor; let
us at once agree that it were better that all the histories ever
written were burned than for the world to lose Homer and
Shakespeare." How eminently characteristic. He had a

shrewd, just humor, never acid, yet never disproportioned or self-deceiving. He goes on in the next breath to add: "Yet as it is generally true that an advocate rarely admits anything without qualification, I should not be loyal to my client did I not urge that Shakespeare was historian as well as poet. We all prefer his *Antony and Cleopatra* and *Julius Caesar* to the Lives in North's Plutarch which furnished him his materials. . . . It is true, as Macaulay wrote, the historical plays of Shakespeare have superseded history." Yet who was more loyal to his chosen field? More industrious and self exacting? His lauded models were the masters of history who still live, particularly Thucydides and Tacitus, also Herodotus and Gibbon. In his own method of preparation, though not the very first to do so, he utilized largely, and especially for the decade from 1850-1860, newspapers as sources. "While considering my materials," so he publicly wrote in 1908, "I was struck with a statement cited by Herbert Spencer as an illustration in his *Philosophy of Style:* 'A modern newspaper statement, though probably true, if quoted in a book as testimony, would be laughed at; but the letter of a Court gossip, if written some centuries ago, is thought good historical evidence.' At about the same time I noticed that Motley used as one of his main authorities for the battle of St. Quentin the manuscript of an anonymous writer." Moved by observation that all newspapers both north and south for many years had been full of the absorbing slavery and abolition conflict, Rhodes, as Mr. John T. Morse, Jr., has vividly pointed out, "plunged with splendid courage into this extensive sea of information. With astonishing persistence he passed weary days, weeks, months in turning and scanning the dusty, musty leaves of the clumsy folios; more tedious exploration can hardly be imagined, but he found that the harvest amply repaid the labor of the reaping. . . . All this panorama he found thus spread before him at life-size, as it were, in these newspapers; and he could have seen it nowhere else."

JAMES FORD RHODES

Rhodes was devoted to the interests and believed in the purposes of this Academy, enjoyed greatly its exercises and the social opportunities it provided for enduring friendship. He was among the earlier members chosen, and he has often told me of the pleasure he had in the dinners of the Academy at a time when nearly all present were in their prime and death had taken scarcely one. In more recent days—for my membership in this body dates only from 1915—we used to come on together from Boston for a number of years to attend the meetings of the Academy and the National Institute of Arts and Letters. Who could have had a more delightful companion than he was? His entertaining but ever rational conversation, his shrewd humor, the charm of his smile, his genial presence, a veritable breeze from the West, radiating friendliness with a big, far-carrying voice,—how familiar were these characteristics to all who knew him. The charcoal drawing by Sargent, although not done until 1920 when age had begun to silver him, is life-like in its portrayal of his intelligence, sense of humor and kindly graciousness. He entertained this Academy at least once at dinner at his hospitable house, 392 Beacon Street. Among the many honors which he received was the gold medal of the National Institute of Arts and Letters in 1910. Harvard and then Yale conferred on him the degree of Doctor of Laws. Three years after the last of his first seven volumes appeared Oxford gave him the degree of Doctor of Letters. President Lowell has well epitomized his later career as follows:

The ambition of his youth had been fulfilled in 1906, when the seventh volume of the history carried the reader to the year 1877 and the abandonment by President Hayes of the policy of Reconstruction. But until his health began to fail he continued to study and to write. He published his *Historical Essays* in 1909, his Oxford Lectures on the *American Civil War* in 1913, a short history of the war in 1917, and then carried his former history of the country from the administration of Hayes through that of Roosevelt.

We of this Academy think today with reverence and affection of James Ford Rhodes as the great native historian of his time, and a most delightful character.

ALBERT JEREMIAH BEVERIDGE
BY BOOTH TARKINGTON

AT THE BEGINNING of the Twentieth Century two important citizens of Indiana were the most boyish looking men in the state, James Whitcomb Riley and Albert Beveridge; and of the two the Senator looked even younger than the poet. In those days, when it was still a great thing to be a Senator of the United States, people who saw Mr. Beveridge for the first time were startled by what seemed a miracle of precocity; it was incredible that he should have attained to such an office at his age. But what is best in youthfulness marked him all his life; he was ever elastic, buoyant, generous, unfailingly ready with a leaping and ardent enthusiasm.

It was always impossible for him to imagine the failure of anything in which he believed; but he never made a cause his own because he believed in its success. He was simply and profoundly honest in all his faiths; he was, in fact, a man of complete belief in what he conceived to be right, and so, seeing a thing as right, he could never doubt that it would prevail. When he became a Progressive in politics, and thus lost his place in the Republican party, and, in the end, his due reward as a partisan leader, he was convinced that the Progressive movement led straight toward triumph; but that was not why he believed in it. He believed in the triumph after he believed in the cause. That was his way; and he remained with the cause when triumph was no longer possible; he remained with it until the cause no longer existed. For he had a quality not commonly allied with the habit of vehement enthusiasm, and this was steadfastness. He was no more able to be an opportunist than he was to practise in politics the art of trimming sail to the wind.

ALBERT JEREMIAH BEVERIDGE

The strongest partisan mechanism of his state was against him; he could not be part of it, for it accomplished nothing except what was personally selfish; that is to say, it contrived to remain in power for the sake of being in power; but Beveridge, in or out of power, was a man of heart. He cared about children's labor, for instance, and not because what he did for the alleviation of poverty-stricken children would make more votes for him at home. As a matter of fact, his service to humanity gained few votes for him; precinct committeemen are usually somewhat indifferent to that type of service.

He was a man who did difficult things thoroughly. He had a furious energy for work; but the fire never flashed in the pan. For all his hearty, swift impulsiveness, he had the unremitting persistence of the slower, dogged type of worker. He had always been a tireless bookman, a haunter of libraries, and his oratory was backed by an accurate memory of encyclopedic range. It was natural, then, that once out of politics and free, he should have sat down to the work that enriched American biography. He mastered an historical period; and "mastered" is the only word: he worked upon his exhaustive manuscript as few men have had the power and devotion to work upon anything. When his *John Marshall* was finished, there was a man, his life and his times, complete upon paper.

Then, after a little time, Albert Beveridge set the same energy, the same persistence and power and devotion, the same exhaustive thoroughness of research for the truth, to work upon his life of Abraham Lincoln; and while he was still in the midst of that absorbing toil of his, suddenly, one day, he was gone—a thing difficult to believe of him, he was a man always so vividly alive.

He was so alive, as we say, that we can never believe him anything else. I was his neighbor, and sometimes I would meet him, of a winter afternoon, in the hour of the exercise that he took to fit him for work far into the night, and when I saw him tramping through deep snow with the same driving vigor that he did everything, I marveled at his aliveness.

The snow would melt from branches of the trees quickly enough; the trees themselves would some day fall; but it seemed to me that such a man must be imperishable.

He was above personal rancor, not only because intellectually he disdained it, but because his nature was incapable of it. He could neither cherish wrath nor keep any man his enemy. He was kind. He was, indeed, indomitably kind. He had learning; he had scholarship; he had, too, what is called sophistication, yet had faith in the goodness of men and in the goodness of life. His head was as high when he led a forlorn hope as it was in victory; and that was because no good hope ever seemed to him a forlorn one. His statue is to stand in the capital of his State; for the man, like his work, indeed does not perish.

1928

WILLIAM RUTHERFORD MEAD
BY ROYAL CORTISSOZ

WILLIAM RUTHERFORD MEAD, who died on June 20th, 1928, had been a member of the Academy since 1910. When he was elected to this body he brought it into relation with an architectural tradition of singular importance. He had aided in the renovation of an art in the United States.

He was of old New England stock, born in Brattleboro, Vermont, on August 20th, 1846. He received a thoroughgoing education, first attending the Brattleboro High School, then spending two years at Norwich University, and entering Amherst College in 1863. He was graduated in 1867, with the degree of A.B. For this college he had a tenacious, life-long attachment. He was President of the Alumni Association in New York City from 1899 to 1909. In 1902 his Alma Mater gave him an honorary degree of LL.D. In his later years he especially interested himself in plans for the introduction of art study at the college. No memoir of him would be complete without some allusion to his fidelity to the seat of learning which had finally fitted him for life. It sent him forth into the world with fixed habits of straight thinking.

He began the study of architecture under Russell Sturgis in New York in 1868. Three years later he went to Italy, staying chiefly in Florence, and spent some months in diverse European wanderings. On his return to America he was ready to embark as a practising architect and in 1872 formed a partnership with Charles F. McKim. Stanford White joined them in 1878 and under the firm name of McKim, Mead and White the careers of three men were merged in a unity extraordinarily effective, as I have indicated, in the making over of American architecture.

It needed rehabilitation in the late '70's and all through the '80's. Public and private buildings erected just before and directly after the Civil War denoted a sad level in artistic taste and skill. The new firm, starting with an attack upon domestic problems, substituted for the old "Queen Anne" country house, with its fearsome roof and jig-saw decoration, a charming type of dwelling, faintly suggestive of the picturesque French manor farm, and in urban architecture Mead and his colleagues replaced the "brownstone front," of ugly memory, with a kind of house fairly exquisite in its delicate proportions, its restrained ornamentation and its judicious arrangement of well chosen materials. More than one of these beautiful designs has disappeared but many New Yorkers will recall, for example, the Coleman Drayton house on Fifth Avenue above 34th Street, which demonstrated the really artistic potentialities of stone and brick. One monument of peculiar salience in the annals of McKim, Mead and White happily remains to this day, the great cluster of houses on Madison Avenue, back of St. Patrick's Cathedral, which revives the dignity of a Renaissance palazzo.

McKim, Mead and White had immense success—and a commensurate influence upon the architecture of their time. I may cite briefly here a few of their buildings: the Boston Public Library; the Rhode Island Capitol; the Madison Square Garden; Columbia University Library; the Pennsylvania Terminal in New York; the Municipal Building in New York. These do not begin to exhaust the list of their achievements and on many things in that list, like the Tiffany Building or the Gorham Building, the University Club or the Morgan Library, it is tempting to pause for particular analysis. But my purpose is rather to emphasize the effect which the whole great mass of work had upon a period in American architecture.

It counted heavily in the development of the younger generation. The architects who received their training in the office of McKim, Mead and White and have worthily carried on the principles of their masters form a resplendent company. And the firm did more than raise up a school. It refined and steadied public taste. It put ideas of architecture as a fine art into the air. It contributed mightily, in short, to the creation of a new epoch.

Through all these operations Mead carried himself with a notable efficiency and generosity. Like McKim and White, he was helpful, inspiring, to the men in his office. He was that, indeed, to the entire building fraternity. When the Gold Medal of Honor was conferred upon an architect for the first time, in 1913, "for distinguished service in the creation of original work in architecture," it went naturally to Mead. When in 1909 he was made President of the American Academy in Rome there could have been no other choice for the office. Inevitably he received constant testimonies to the regard in which he was held by his fellow architects. They knew his steadfastness, his uprightness, his artistic rectitude. He endeared himself to a host of friends through his qualities as a man, a personality, and through the work he had done in a long life to maintain a noble architectural standard.

WILLIAM CRARY BROWNELL
BY BLISS PERRY

MR. BROWNELL, who died July 22, 1928, in his seventy-seventh year, had been for more than twenty years a member of the Academy. He was elected on January 28, 1908, and was the first occupant of chair thirty-four. In choosing him for membership, the Academy honored for the first time a professional critic, for though Henry James, Lounsbury, Burroughs and Higginson had all written literary criticism, it was incidental to their other work. Mr.

Brownell was known in 1908 as the author of three significant volumes of criticism: *French Traits, French Art* and *Victorian Prose Masters*. Born in New York in 1851, he had had a sound training at Amherst College, had worked for two years under Godkin on the *Nation,* had spent three years abroad, chiefly in Paris, studying foreign art and literature, and after his return had taken his desk with Charles Scribner's Sons, where he remained, as literary adviser, for nearly forty years.

A few members of the Academy can remember him there in the eighteen nineties. A man of fine reserve, and thought by some to be austere, he could nevertheless welcome an unknown author with gay cordiality, and the memory of his beautifully penned and witty comments on the galley-proofs of one's first books is something still to be treasured. One of Mr. Brownell's younger associates in more recent years, Mr. Robert Cortes Holliday, has written this delightful sketch of him:

The first literary adviser to a publishing house I ever beheld was W. C. Brownell. I regarded him as omniscient. The calm, unconscious nobility of his presence, the classic sculpture of his head and greying beard, the philosophic detachment of his bearing, suggested to my mind a somewhat confused blend of Socrates and Marcus Aurelius. His volumes "Victorian Prose Masters" and "American Prose Masters" I read as the stone tablets of the law. And I have not ceased to read them now as the very wise commentary of a full, disciplined, and beautiful mind on human life. Innumerable times a day he would stroll in and out. He would move up and down the sidewalk to smoke—smoking being outlawed in the building; or stand for long periods of time gazing in at the window display. But I do not believe that at the end of the day he could have told you a thing that was in the window.

Is not that a charming portrait of a thinker?

For it was primarily as a thinker that Brownell won and held his place among American men of letters. "Criticism," he said, "is not the product of reading, but of thought. To produce vital and useful criticism it is necessary to think,

think, and then, when tired of thinking, to think more." His first book, *French Traits*, published when he was thirty-eight, was a triumph of straight thinking. In theme it was one of those national character studies which have been familiar since Madame de Staël's *Germany*. He was saturated with his material; but the keenness of observation, the sympathy for the French character and the admirably vivid style are less remarkable, after all, than the clearness and orderliness of Brownell's analytic mind. He had thought his subject through, and though the book appeared nearly forty years ago, it has not been superseded. *French Art*, published three years later, is likewise a beautiful example of expository criticism. The clarity and plastic quality of his theme give order and movement to his thoughts, while the precision and charm of his diction, and a sort of sunlight upon every page, make this volume the most winning of all his books. It does more than convince; it persuades.

Mr. Brownell's friends were aware of those circumstances which compelled him for many years to spend his evenings in solitary reading, in search of some occupation for an anxious mind. He read endlessly, and endlessly did he reflect upon, analyze, compare and weigh the great writers of his own time. *Victorian Prose Masters* (1901) and *American Prose Masters* (1914) were the result. It was perhaps natural that he assessed the English writers first. In 1901 the word "Victorian" had no connotation of obloquy; and Brownell owed so much to Arnold and Carlyle, he admired Thackeray so boundlessly, he was so much interested in George Eliot and Meredith, he was so sure that Ruskin ought not to have written about art at all, that he could not help writing a book about them. If it was not exactly epoch-making criticism, either in its method or in its influence, it was nevertheless dispassionate and penetrating, and it prepared his readers for the richer and more original volume, *American Prose Masters*, upon which Brownell's reputation with the general public may ultimately rest. For this book contributed significantly to that revival of critical interest in our own authors which has characterized the last fifteen years. The chapters are a succession of masterpieces. The one on Lowell reveals the whole of Brownell's own temperament and critical philosophy as he points out what Lowell, in spite of all his gifts, failed to achieve. How fresh and robust is the chapter on Fenimore Cooper; and with what delicacy of appreciation does he analyze Cooper's exact opposite, Henry James! The chapter on Emerson would be memorable if only for Brownell's account of his boyish memory of Emerson as a lecturer. The unimpassioned and somewhat cool examination of the substance and style of Poe and Hawthorne was resented by many admirers of these writers, and no doubt Brownell's predominating intellectualism made him indifferent to the glamor of those romantic qualities by virtue of which Poe and Hawthorne continue to weave their spell. It is true that his personal love for poetry was keen and lifelong. He carried in his pocket a copy of *A Shropshire Lad* until it was quite worn out, and he knew his Keats and Shelley and Swinburne and Wordsworth by heart. The poets were to him a deep source of private happiness, but as a professional critic he had not much to say at any time about poetry and the poetic imagination. The public knew him as a prose-man, a prose-man by nature and by preference; a tough-minded realist; and for all that fascinating but dubious borderland between prose and poetry, he had a refined but clear-cut contempt. One cannot "weigh," he declared, "imponderable iridescence."

Yet this very restriction of his field, though it may have limited the range of his influence, certainly heightened his authority upon those two memorable occasions when he read before the Academy and the Institute his masterly not to say magisterial addresses entitled "Criticism" and "Standards." We listened to those addresses with the keenest intellectual delight. How transparently clear it all seemed as interpreted by the voice of the author! What delicious shadings of irony, what trenchant wit! Nevertheless one captivated listener, at least, confesses his perplexity over the fact that as he reads these discourses,—and he has read them dozens of times,—he finds their style extremely difficult. One must force himself to follow the trail of Brownell's thought, if he is to understand the central issue of modern critical controversy, yet the trail lies well up above the timber-line, and it is undeniably hard going. It may be that Brownell realized for the first time that he was on the defensive,—that he must guard and qualify and distinguish and define warily,—and that his style suffered in consequence. In his *French Traits* he had quoted Joubert's maxim: "Make truth lovely, and do not try to arm her." But now he did arm her for a battle whose outcome seemed doubtful, and the bright face of truth peers somewhat grimly through the slits in the riveted steel.

When published in book form, these addresses were widely read by the judicious; but the injudicious, who are always in the vast majority, have so persistently misunderstood and misstated Brownell's position, that one is forced to the conclusion that few of his opponents have ever taken the pains to master what he actually said. Standards were to him neither dogmatic rules nor inherited conventions. They arise insensibly in the mind of the cultivated public. They are to be tested, however, by principles, and to examine and set forth these principles is the function of criticism. Taste must, in short, be rationalized. "In literature and art there are no longer any statutes, but the common law of principles is as applicable as ever."

If this is a fair summary of Brownell's views, it is evident that he is as far from the dogmatic critics who sit, or once sat, on the extreme right, as he is from the impressionistic critics who lounge upon the extreme left. Yet inasmuch as the very word "standards" has become obnoxious to many of our contemporaries, Brownell knew that he was challenging the present drift of a sensation-loving age. The question in which our whole discussion ends, he wrote, is this: "Are art and letters to be sentimentalized out of their established standards by the comprehensive and militant democratic movement of our time?" I doubt if he really thought that sentimentality and sensationalism would ultimately prevail, but it is certain that he did not intend to let them win without a fight, and it is equally certain that if they cannot win without answering Brownell's arguments, their victory will be long deferred.

Few shadows of this conflict, however, and singularly few of the natural shadows of old age, fall upon the pages of his last books, published when he was more than seventy, namely, *The Genius of Style* and *Democratic Distinction in America*. In his expert analysis of English prose style, Brownell exhibits his ripest qualities. In the last two chapters of his book, discussing the present day uses of style in art and letters, he draws sword once more against what our lamented colleague Stuart Sherman used to call the "Party of Nature," and lays about him with the skill of a veteran and the vigor of a boy. In the book on *Democratic Distinction*, which is dedicated to the memory of Stuart Sherman, Brownell had one immense advantage over most debaters of this question. He was himself a born democrat of the Jefferson and Lincoln school, and this tendency had been fixed by his long residence in democratic France. And he was likewise, and with equal naturalness, a man of distinction who believed in distinction. He had therefore no self-conscious worries about either distinction or democracy. He took them for granted. His task was to discover in our present-day American democracy the forces that are making for distinction, and he found them in abundance. Of course he chaffed the enemies of progress and ridiculed superficiality and egotism and vainglory. But the book is not an old man's Jeremiad; it is a bland, urbane, quizzical survey of the actual and hopeful American scene.

Such, all too briefly summarized, was the achievement of this thinker. He had some public honors, but not many. He was supposed to be a traditionalist; and one must admit that he was born in 1851, that he knew his Arnold and Sainte-Beuve, and that he often quoted the Bible. It is true that he understood the traditions of the elders; that was one part of his professional business. But he was not in the least a traditionalist. His mental life was not lived in the past. He was intensely modern. Like every fertilizing critic, he lived in the present and worked for the future. He spent a life-time of rare intellectual energy in the presence of beautiful objects of art and literature, striving to comprehend them in all their relations and in reference to the principles upon which they are based. He accomplished his task more fully than most men. He had the felicity, not merely of handing on the torch to the younger generation, but of filling the torch anew. The secret of his power,—one may be permitted to suspect,—is betrayed in that sentence written at the end of his life, with an eloquence all the more moving for his habitual reserve, in which he contrasts self-indulgence and self-assertion with the self-reliance "born of faith in the absolute and eternal."

WILLIAM MILLIGAN SLOANE

BY HENRY VAN DYKE

BY THE DEATH of William Milligan Sloane the American Academy of Arts and Letters has been deprived of its second President and one of its most distinguished and delightful members.

He was born, of good Covenanting stock, on November 12, 1850. He received his bachelor's degree at Columbia in 1868, his doctorate of philosophy at Leipzig in 1876, and subsequent honorary degrees from Rutgers and Princeton. From 1873 to 1875 he was personal secretary to the Honorable George Bancroft, the American Minister in Berlin and a celebrated historian of the United States of America. This intimate early association doubtless strengthened Dr. Sloane's natural inclinations to the study and writing of history. It also brought him into contact with many famous scholars and statesmen of Germany,—a contact which was always gratefully remembered, and which was repeated on a larger scale when he was sent to Berlin in later years as American exchange professor from Columbia University.

In 1876 he entered the faculty of Princeton, where he served with great efficiency for twenty years. It was while I was a student in the Seminary there that I had the good fortune to begin a friendship with him that lasted over half a century. In 1896 he was elected to the Seth Low Professorship of History in Columbia University. In this position he did a great work, not only as head of the historical department, but also as a promoter and illustrator of right-minded methods of research and production in the field of history throughout the United States. He was not superficial and sensational in gathering his materials, nor was he dry and tiresome in presenting his results. His aim was to base his work upon a careful study of all the documents, monuments, and records available, and then to draw his own mature conclusions and set them forth in a broad picture which would have the two marks of veracity and vividness.

This was the method which he followed in his *magnum opus, The Life of Napoleon Bonaparte,* published first, in part, by the *Century Magazine,* and then, in four massive and richly illustrated volumes, by the Century Co. in 1896. During the years which he devoted to this congenial task, he went through the enormous mass of Napoleonic literature which had accumulated in several languages; he unearthed and studied original materials which had never before been used; and then he gave his own view of one of the most remarkable persons and the most extraordinary career that can be found in secular history.

Let this American historian of Napoleon speak for himself in regard to his aims and methods:

"Until within a very recent period it seemed that no man could discuss him or his time without manifesting such

strong personal feeling as to vitiate his judgment and conclusions. This was partly due to the lack of perspective, but
in the main to ignorance of the facts essential to a sober treatment of the theme. In this respect the last quarter of a century has seen a gradual but radical change, for a band of
dispassionate scientific scholars have during that time been
occupied in the preparation of material for his life without
reference to the advocacy of one theory or another concerning his character. European archives, long carefully guarded,
have been thrown open; the diplomatic correspondence of
the most important periods has been published; family papers
have been examined, and numbers of valuable memoirs have
been printed. It has therefore been possible to check one account by another, to cancel misrepresentations, to eliminate
passion—in short, to establish something like correct outline
and accurate detail, at least in regard to what the man actually did. Those hidden secrets of any human mind which we
call motives must ever remain to other minds largely a matter
of opinions, but a very fair indication of them can be found
when once the actual conduct of the actor has been determined."

Now, of course, it is inevitable that a work produced in
this way and with this purpose should at times move somewhat slowly, with conscientious caution and reserve. It is not
to be expected that it should have the pervasive pepper, the
oleaginous cocksureness, and the vinegary delight in the mistakes and failings of the great, which serve as French dressing to some recent histories and biographies and give them
an instantaneous vogue as "best sellers." Undoubtedly they
have their place and use. But Sloane's book belongs in a different class and is marked by other qualities. It is first of all
a work of scholarship, patient, unpretending, thorough, non-
explosive. Then it is a work of human letters, broad-minded,
unpartisan, generous in scope and judgment,—a work aware
of the great mystery which underlies all human life and
which took such weird and tragic forms in the era of the

French Revolution and of Napoleon's meteoric rise to a world-wide imperatorship, half beneficent and half malign.

But if one wishes to know how well and with what variety Dr. Sloane could write, one should not stop with the *Life of Napoleon,* but go on to some of his later books which are based upon his travels and his personal experiences: *The Balkans, a Laboratory of History* (1914); *Party Government in the United States* (1914); *The Powers and Aims of Western Democracy* (1919); *Greater France in Morocco* (1924). Here are chapters full of clear observation, wise inference, and vivid comment.

But it was not in his books that the very best of William M. Sloane was revealed to those who knew him. It was in his rich and racy talk, his warm friendship, his active and genial cooperation in the tasks of life and in the pleasures that belong to the avocation of a confirmed angler. Here he shone. He knew so much of books and men; his fund of stories, true or well-imagined, was so inexhaustible; his sympathy with good things was so wide and hearty, his detestation of bad things so frank, fearless and witty, that a talk with him in a camp beside Moosehead Lake, or in his book-room at Princeton, or around his dinner-table in New York (where ladies were always present, and reporters absent), was a joy to the heart and a liberal education.

In 1920 he was elected President of the American Academy in succession to the well-beloved William Dean Howells. The duties of this office he performed with dignified efficiency. In its social accomplishments he was a large and easy master. The Academy has had many loyal and devoted members whose names will be long remembered in its halls. But to no three men does it owe more than to William M. Sloane, its second president, Robert U. Johnson, its first secretary, and Archer M. Huntington, its generous benefactor.

In the autumn of 1925, Dr. Sloane was struck down by a grave illness which left him physically helpless. With a clear mind and an indomitable courage he did his best to regain his health. In this to some extent he succeeded by sheer pluck and the favor of Providence. He was able to enjoy his family, the visits of his friends, and long daily drives in the country. His mind was clear though his nerves were broken. His sickroom was a cheerful place. The award of the National Institute's Gold Medal for History, in November, 1927, gave him a well-earned joy. His days of working were done, but not his days of loving.

For three years he waited thus, in Christian patience and manly fortitude, resigned but never conquered. On a calm September day in 1928 the word of release came to him, and he went into the world of light. America has lost a fine scholar, an upstanding man; and we have been parted, for a little time, from a loyal friend, a dear comrade.

1929

BRANDER MATTHEWS
BY NICHOLAS MURRAY BUTLER

T HERE ARE MEN who do important and interesting work in the world, whose personalities loom larger through the years than do any of their performances. Brander Matthews was one of these. No matter what he wrote or how excellent it may have been, no matter what he taught or how abundant an inspiration it was, the personality of the man puts it all into the shade. His manner, his merriment, and his charm were all his own, and were never failing. By good fortune he wrote for us an autobiographical sketch which he called *These Many Years*. He gave to it, as subtitle, the words "Recollections of a New Yorker." And a New Yorker he certainly was, in some respects the last of his kind.

Those mingled Scottish and English strains which gave to America its possibilities as well as its ideals and so much of its competence, united to produce this charming man and to guide his feet toward the metropolitan city which he truly loved and mightily adorned. One does not easily think of Brander Matthews as finding the home of his father's origin on Cape Cod, but there it was. From a parentage in which New England and Virginia were mingled, our dear friend and associate of so many years was born in New Orleans when the Nineteenth Century had just passed its middle point. But neither Cape Cod nor Virginia nor New Orleans was the suitable setting for this amazing personality. He was a cosmopolitan by his very nature and through his every taste, and it was only one of the world's capitals which could lure and hold him.

He probably was the first youth, and doubtless one of the

234

very few youths, to be consciously educated and trained for the highly exclusive profession of millionaire. His father, who was a man of immense wealth as fortunes were counted in those days, and who would be deemed a very rich man even now, told his son repeatedly that he need never work for a living, but must fit himself to care for the great properties which his father possessed. All through his undergraduate days in Columbia College, and during his subsequent study of the law, Brander Matthews was fitting himself to pass through life as an educated gentleman possessed of a vast fortune which he should be competent to manage. Hardly had he entered upon this attractive task, however, when the fates decided that his life was to be something wholly different. They swept away his father's fortune, reduced the family possessions to practically nothing, and invited the young man to turn his attention to making a living by his own efforts. Most men confronted by such a situation would almost certainly lapse into a state of despair and helplessness, or become bitter cynics with no interested concern for life or for their fellow men. Not so Brander Matthews. He paid little more attention to this astonishing happening than if he had merely stumbled and fallen while walking through his father's garden. He picked himself up, metaphorically tightened his belt, took pen in hand, and started to make a living by the practice of the art of letters. His early travels in England and in France, the delightful acquaintance with men of letters and of the arts which he had been enabled to make, all now stood him in good stead. His dominant interest was the literature of the drama, whether creative or critical. With the French drama, both classical and contemporary, he became quickly familiar. With the playwrights of the day, whether to be found in Paris, in London, or in New York, he was speedily intimate companion and friend. His name as author became known, his reputation grew, and the livelihood of which he had gone in search came into his happy possession.

No one ever heard Brander Matthews refer to the dashing of the cup of gold from his lips, save with philosophical detachment or in amused contemplation. Even had the Golden Calf been in his possession, he was not the sort of man ever to fall down and worship it.

Forty years ago, when Columbia University was in the building, it was my fortune to propose to the governing authorities that provision should be made to have English literature taught and interpreted not simply by academically trained scholars, but also by men who were themselves of established and growing reputation in the world of letters, whether critical or creative. Once this proposal was accepted, it was yet my official duty to seek for the individuals who might best satisfy the requirement which had been set. The two who were selected, George Edward Woodberry and Brander Matthews, both became members of the Academy, both became distinguished in high degree, and both wrote their names high on the roll of honor of the University which was so fortunate as to secure their glad and notable service.

Brander Matthews hugely enjoyed his academic life and associations. He formed every sort and kind of intellectual contact. He attracted to his lectures and intimate discussions the most ambitious and eager students from all parts of this country and from many other countries as well. He never permitted himself to be cast in the traditional academic mold. He did not know how to be solemn or aloof or distant or coldly disinterested. That rich and delightful personality of his poured itself over everything which he said and did. At one moment those who were following his words were convulsed with laughter; at another their eyes were fixed upon him with rapt attention.

Brander Matthews knew and had known every man of letters of importance in this country, in Great Britain, and in France, for full forty years. He could relate personal anecdotes concerning them, each and all. He described incidents of their lives and work which made them live again, really live, in the hearts and minds of the younger generation which crowded about him. His friends were legion, and on their roll are many names celebrated in more lands than one. This delightful man moved through the years on intimate terms with Mark Twain and Howells, with Lowell and Henry Cabot Lodge, with George William Curtis and John Hay, with Richard Watson Gilder and Thomas Bailey Aldrich, with Edward L. Godkin and Edmund Clarence Stedman, with Edwin Booth, Coquelin and Henry Irving, with Henry James and Austin Dobson, with Andrew Lang, Thomas Hardy and Laurence Hutton, with Sir Martin Conway and Edmund Gosse, with H. C. Bunner and George Du Maurier, with Florence and Sothern and Crane and Gilbert, with Theodore Roosevelt and Rudyard Kipling. What other life than his was set in such a firmament of brightly shining stars? He instructed, inspired and stimulated, not tens or hundreds, but actually thousands, of the ambitious youth of this land who had a wish to gain some true insight into the significance of letters, and to be led up to the high places from which they could look out upon the undying achievements of the spoken and the written word.

Brander Matthews took the keenest interest in his fellow workers in letters. He was an unfailing ornament of the old and famous Saturday night gatherings at the Century, and never missed a stated dinner of the Round Table. He was a familiar figure at the Saville Club in London and later at the Athenaeum. Literally he rocked the cradle of the Authors' Club, of the Players, and of this Academy. His place was never vacant when the members of the Academy assembled, and no mind among all its membership was more alert than his, to seek out ways and means of new and broader and higher usefulness.

Brander Matthews was truly a New Yorker. He loved the metropolitan city, its good cheer, its joyousness, its liberality, its openmindedness, its varied companionships, and its enjoyments. Isolation had no charms for him. The country was merely a delightful place from which to come back to town. He wished to be where men were, where power was generated, and where great deeds were planned and done.

There are men of letters, fortunately, of every sort and of every kind. It would not be easy to trace relationship between an Emerson and a Whitman, or between a Browning and a Kipling. Yet they are each and all men of letters of the highest order of excellence, and each and all have carved their names on the undying roll of literature's immortals. Brander Matthews eludes classification or comparison. He was unique—unique in the circumstances of his education and early training, unique in what the world thought was the calamity which overtook him, unique in the fashion in which he turned himself with persistent cheerfulness to his new and unexpected task, unique in the quality and character of his academic service, unique in his odd and inviting intermingling of creative and critical writing with many-sided and keenest human interest, unique in his good humored faith in mankind, unique in the strong affections which his friends had for him and he for them, unique in the place which he holds in the hearts of all of us and on the rolls of this Academy.

FRANK V. VAN DER STUCKEN
BY HENRY HADLEY

IT IS OUR privilege today to pay tribute, sincere and deserved, to a man of great achievement, great influence, talent and personality—Mr. Frank van der Stucken, who became a member of the Academy of Arts and Letters two years ago.

All Americans hold a justifiable pride in the works of this man and his ideals, so pure, so noble and so unselfish. Not because he displayed any eccentricities peculiarly American, but rather because he was entirely cosmopolitan, and in every phase of his work maintained a standard which compared favorably with the best abroad, do we feel this pride.

Although the impression exists in the minds of many that music is a young, undeveloped art in America, it must be remembered that in this, as in all arts, we inherit the traditions and achievements of our forbears.

The musical heritage of America is therefore just as rich as that of Europe—being identical.

However, comparatively few Americans have had the privilege of such close personal contact with so many of the great masters as van der Stucken, and from these masters, the privilege of absorbing their ideas at first hand and also the enjoyment of the unconscious influence of the truly great.

Mr. van der Stucken was the happy possessor of the friendship of such men as Liszt, Grieg, von Bülow and others.

"Not all of me shall die," cried the poet Horace. "Not all of me shall die" is echoed by the valiant spirit of Frank van der Stucken.

When a man passes on something to the succeeding generations which helps and inspires them, that giving is itself a symbol of immortality, for whatever contributes to generous, pure, high-minded human living is of God.

Once, when approached by one of a group of those who had gathered about him absorbing that about the art of music which is never learned in the classroom or out of books, he was tactfully asked what recompense could be made for all the time and effort which he bestowed gratuitously upon them. He replied: "What I have, I give you unreservedly, with the hope that when the opportunity presents itself, you will give it to others, and in the same spirit as I now give it to you, for this is my idea of immortality." Nothing could more clearly reveal the character of the man than this sincere, spontaneous response.

Frank van der Stucken was born in Fredericksburg, Texas, on October 15th, 1858, into a family of affluent circumstances, gentle and cultured.

He showed a great predilection for music at an early age, and when only eight years old, was taken to Antwerp, where he might acquire free use of the French and German languages and study music at the Conservatory. He was a diligent student, and in 1881 went to Leipsic where he met and studied with Grieg.

Shortly after he met the great Franz Liszt who became so interested in him that he arranged a concert in the Ducal Theatre at Weimar for van der Stucken.

Only those engaging qualities which were peculiarly his own, the rich sense of humor, and above all, his innate refinement and fastidious intellect which rendered him irresistible to the lowly as well as all others, could have made such distinguished friends for him.

Among this group he considered von Bülow the father of modern orchestral conducting.

After a prolonged stay in Europe, with thorough schooling and much experience as a conductor, van der Stucken was invited to come to New York City as conductor of the "Arion," a well-known men's chorus of that time. He was recommended for this post by Max Bruch and once related how it came about. Quite out of a clear sky he received an invitation to visit Max Bruch one afternoon. With mingled anxiety and curiosity as to the object of the visit, he presented himself to this old, distinguished master. He was invited to walk in the garden where they talked of books, philosophy and everything except music. After a charming hour's chat he felt that his visit was over and took his leave. It was only from its members in New York much later that he learned how the music committee of the Arion Society had written Bruch enlisting his aid in securing a conductor. Needless to say Bruch was favorably impressed and wrote accordingly.

So he began his career in America, with which country he was ever afterwards identified.

While conducting the Arion he gave orchestral concerts to introduce novelties, and at these concerts never forgot to include the American composers of that time, who were struggling for recognition.

After having aroused his chorus from its state of complacency with vigorous, exacting rehearsals and ambitious programs he performed a miracle which up to that time was undreamed of. He took his chorus on a triumphant tour throughout Europe, a fact scarcely less to be marveled at to-day than it was at that time.

In 1889 he did what in those days was positively heroic, giving an orchestral concert in Paris composed entirely of American compositions, including MacDowell's D Minor Concerto, which the composer himself played. Not only then, but throughout his whole career he was the champion of the American Composer.

In 1885 the Cincinnati Orchestra was formed, giving only three concerts the first season with Anton Seidl, the celebrated Wagnerian, and van der Stucken as conductors. Van der Stucken shortly after became the permanent leader of the Symphony Orchestra and remained in that post until 1907. In 1905, after the forming of the great festival chorus, he became its leader, thereby forming the basis of that signal influence which the chorus has exerted upon that community for years.

He raised the festivals to a place of artistic beauty and magnitude which is unchallenged to-day, and his memorable performances up to the last were a brilliant climax to his career.

His flaming enthusiasm, glowing personality, perseverance, kindliness and his high musical standards swept his singers on irresistibly and neither distinguished soloist nor the most inconspicuous member of his chorus would ever dream of giving less than his utmost—more than he had to give—when Mr. van der Stucken conducted.

It was by presenting such monumental works as Bach's "St. Matthew's Passion," the majestic "Missa Solemnis" of Beethoven that he served the community for thirty years by forming its musical taste.

With his usual daring and courage he gave the first performance anywhere of Pierné's "Children's Crusades"—thus paving the way for the many performances of this beautiful work which followed.

One of his devoted admirers—one who sat at his feet for years—paid a tribute to Mr. van der Stucken, which I can do no better than repeat to you:

"We are most concerned with the *spiritual* values which were the outcome of all these efforts and doings. Thousands of lives have been enriched and touched by direct contact with his genius—many children who have sung with him and felt —although they did not realize it—the measure of his musical enthusiasm—and only think of the thousands of students who were taught the inexorable law that only *sincerity* and *honesty* in art can prevail, and that the one open sesame to the realm of genuine achievement is in the one magic word —*Work!*"

It was when he began rehearsals for the festival of 1929 that his strength failed, and after much persuasion on the part of his devoted family and friends, he very reluctantly gave up his work. Shortly afterward he was stricken, but his indomitable will and strength rallied to such an extent that he determined to set out for Europe with the "idée fixe" that he could be cured by one of the famous baths. But he only reached Hamburg, where he entered a hospital not long after landing, and in a few days died. He is buried outside that city in a quiet resting place which is *home* to him, for he was so much a citizen of the world that he belonged to all countries.

Just after the large celebration in New York of his seventieth birthday, an event which gave him great satisfaction, he wrote an intimate and devoted friend, "I've still many things to do—but in any case I feel that I can march down the valley of the Shadow *sans peur et sans reproche.*"

His compositions, consisting mostly of songs, symphonic poems, choral works, etc., belong to his early career for the latter part was devoted principally to *choral* conducting in which he became preëminent. The letter from a Cincinnati friend continues, "It has been the privilege of this entire community to have learned its artistic credo from this man's teachings and his example.

"We know our ideals and what we owe them. We know that—high as they are today—they must be higher tomorrow; and that, come what may, our artistic conscience must remain inviolate and the integrity of our convictions must be unimpaired.

"There will ever remain with us the all-pervading idealism of those fundamentals upon which we have been taught to build, and what greater gift—what finer heritage can any man bestow? It has added and will continue to add richness and beauty to our lives."

THOMAS HASTINGS
BY ROBERT UNDERWOOD JOHNSON

THOMAS HASTINGS, architect, was the seventh of that name in direct line, all of whom were of the Presbyterian faith, his father being a distinguished preacher and president of the Union Theological Seminary in New York City where "Tom," as he was usually called, was born. From his grandfather, Thomas Hastings, who was a well known composer of sacred music, we have the beautiful "Rock of Ages" and to this background, in a measure, may be due the grandson's scholarly approach to his architectural work.

Hastings's greeting to his friends was a virtual benediction, so full was it of geniality and good will. At his office he would come bustling out to greet a visitor, grasping both hands in his and establishing at once an understanding of friendliness. He was thus a man of temperament and enthusiasm. His sense of honor and his integrity were not confined to the affairs of his profession, but were the controlling influence of his life. He was one of the most attractive figures of his time in New York City in artistic circles. He was much beloved by those who worked with him, and his generosity to his associates and employees is attested in these not altogether trifling lines:

There was a hard master named Hastings,
Who gave his staff regular bastings.
If one had a cough,
He would give a year off,
And charge it to savings and wastings.

It was while a student at Columbia that he received his first impulse toward education in architecture. This was after meeting a gentleman named Maybeck, at the office of Herter Brothers, who suggested to him that he should go abroad to study. This he did in 1880, when he entered the École des Beaux-Arts, studying in the atelier of Jules André. While in Paris, he made the acquaintance of John M. Carrère. Upon his graduation and receipt of the French government diplôme, in 1884, he returned to New York and entered the office of McKim, Mead and White, then the leading architects, where he found Carrère already at work. In 1886 the two formed a partnership, and in 1887 they were approached by a friend of Dr. Hastings, Henry M. Flagler, who had a project for developing Florida. From this contact came their first important commission for the design of the Ponce de Leon Hotel, and later the Alcazar in 1888.

These hotels were recognized by the profession generally as a novel success in American construction. They were, indeed, a sensation, and turned the attention of other architects to the resources of the Spanish style as adapted to the Southern climes of the country. The firm immediately took its place among the leading architects of America, and its success grew rapidly, as did the range and variety of its work.

It is always difficult to distinguish the individual activities of the members of an architectural firm. But, in the case of two men so sympathetic as were John M. Carrère and

Thomas Hastings, one will not go far afield in assuming an intimate collaboration in their work. Mr. Carrère's death in 1911 left Mr. Hastings in supreme control of the work of the firm. In general, changing fashions and economic conditions produced a growing departure from the strict French inspiration of the earlier work of the firm, and the Tower of Jewels at the Panama Pacific Exposition at San Francisco, 1914, was characteristic of this trend in its use of the classic orders to give the note of gaiety for an exposition building. The Memorial Amphitheatre in the national cemetery at Arlington, Virginia, is in a style almost Palladian Classic, with its sweeping, elliptical colonnade. It is one of the many monuments designed by Hastings. Among other buildings with which he is particularly identified, besides many churches and private dwellings, are the House and Senate office buildings in Washington, the New York Public Library, and the Frick residence. In the last few months of his life he completed the work on Devonshire House, London, a palatial apartment house.

On June 26, 1922, Hastings was awarded the Royal Gold Medal of the Royal Institute of British Architects, an honor only twice before conferred upon an American.

In one of his published essays, Hastings made the following statement with which I may appropriately conclude this all too cursory tribute:

There is beauty in nature, because all nature is a practical problem well solved. The truly educated architect will never sacrifice the practical side of his problem. Emerson realized the truth when he said, "It is a rule of the largest application, true in plant, true in a loaf of bread, that in the construction of any fabric or organism any real increase of fitness to its end is an increase of beauty."

Hastings further said, "The practising architect, if he continues, as he should, to be a draftsman all his life, must realize that beauty of design and line builds well in construction, and with greater economy and endurance than construction, which is mere engineering. . . . Following the natural laws of the survival of the fittest, if undertaken in art, beauty will predominate in the end, and so deliver us from the defacement of nature."

Such were the ideas and ideals of Thomas Hastings who was deeply interested in our Academy, and was for several years a devoted member of its Board of Directors.

1930

GEORGE EDWARD WOODBERRY
BY ROBERT UNDERWOOD JOHNSON

IN PAYING this tribute to our colleague, one of America's foremost men of letters, I feel derelict, almost disloyal in its inadequacy. Woodberry's literary activity subtended so large an arc that I have only been able to encompass a small part of its flowing beauty. I am the more chagrined by knowing that, were the situation reversed, he would be more just and comprehensive in his judgment of me. I purpose however to do his memory at least one service: to quote a little of his engaging rhyme and a little of his mellifluous prose, so that, absent though he be, he may speak for himself.

I doubt if there ever was a poet, however distinguished by his prose—Shelley, Arnold, Emerson, Lowell, Stedman—who would not prefer to be judged by his verse. A wider appeal and a surer permanence are given to imagination and emotion by that form of music we call poetry. Knowledge and the power of presenting it in its relations to life carry immensely farther in meter than in criticism.

Woodberry had above everything else the conscientiousness and candor of the true critic, and this is felt in every line he wrote. He saw steadily and whole the authors of whom he wrote. He lived a life of frugality, knowing how

To scorn delight and live laborious days,

but with abundant joy, in Nature, in his art and in the passion of the spirit. Thus he touched and inspired all whom he taught.

His poetry is rich in the fortunate traits of imagination and emotion. Rereading it in part, I am struck particularly by the

Elegy on the death of Edwin Booth, which I heard pronounced in the presence of the great Salvini. I recall that one of our colleagues,—not a poet,—spoke slightingly of it, and that, at that time, I thought it ineffective, this, as I now think, being chargeable to the author's weak delivery, which I am told was not characteristic of his lectures. I wish now to recant that impression of a dirge of rare nobility and feeling. Speaking of Booth's *Othello* he says:

> Alas, our eyes have seen,
> As if no other woe than this had been,
> The heartbreak of the Moor, and, dark behind,
> Traced frank Iago's intellectual stealth
> And panther footfall in the generous mind.

How fine that is! Again after a masterly passage on *Hamlet*, and on the startling likeness between the tragedian and the character, he closes this strophe thus:

> He held the mirror up within the soul,
> And from his bosom read the part alone,
> The infinite of man within him sealed,
> And played himself—Oh, with what truth exprest!
> He plucked the mystery from the master's breast,
> But ah, what mortal plucks it from his own?

Once more he says with a burst of emotion that is more than glowing rhetoric:

> Cease, flood of song, thy stream! now cease, and know
> Thy silver fountains from all hearts do flow!
> Cease now, my song, and learn to say goodnight
> To him whose glory lends thy stream its light!
> The last great heir of the majestic stage
> Has passed, and with him passes a great age;
> Low with his elders lies his honored head,
> And in one voice are many voices dead.

Woodberry's sonnets are technically all that the sonnet should be—clear, firm, unified, moving easily to a climax of gentle surprise. Of the two entitled *At Gibraltar*, both already distinguished, the first shows the author at his best:

> England, I stand on thy imperial ground,

GEORGE EDWARD WOODBERRY

Not all a stranger; as thy bugles blow,
I feel within my blood old battles flow—
The blood whose ancient founts in thee are found.
Still surging dark against the Christian bound
Wide Islam presses; well its peoples know
Thy heights that watch them wandering below;
I think how Lucknow heard their gathering sound.
I turn, and meet the cruel, turbaned face.
England, 'tis sweet to be so much thy son!
I feel the conqueror in my blood and race;
Last night Trafalgar awed me, and today
Gibraltar wakened; hark, thy evening gun
Startles the desert over Africa!

But he also knew how to adapt the sonnet to measures that
rival his facile lyrics of love and regret. One of these songs
may stand for many in its poignancy:

Why wilt thou make, O Wave,
    Forever in from the bay?
Dost thou seek on the beaches' grave
    To cast thy life away?

Why wilt thou blow, O Wind,
    Forever out to sea?
Is it death thou, too, wouldst find,
    O winged eternity?

I told my love unsped
    To both in the eventide;
The wild Wind moaned, and fled,
    The wild Wave sobbed, and died.

Sonnet, lyric, dirge, ode, or epigram, whatever form Woodberry's poetic nature takes, one is impressed by its sincerity
and its natural utterance. He never yields his conviction of
the supremacy and permanence of the ideal. Let me quote
one stanza—a poem in itself—from his beautiful dirge for a
friend, *The North Shore Watch*. It is quite in the grand
manner of Wordsworth or Shelley.

Beauty abides, nor suffers mortal change,
    Eternal refuge of the orphaned mind;

Where'er a lonely wanderer, I range,
  The tender flowers shall my woes unbind,
    The grass to me be kind;
And lovely shapes innumerable shall throng
  On sea and prairie, soft as children's eyes;
Morn shall awake me with her glad surprise;
  The stars shall hear my song;
And heaven shall I see, whate'er my road,
  Steadfast, eternal, light's impregnable abode.

That would not be out of place in the *Adonais*. Again and again I find myself thrilled with the felicity of such lines as this:

The Colors make the Country whatever be the sky;

or these

And sowing Persia through the world the rose
Reddens our Western vales.

Let us turn now to his prose,—an immense body of penetrating and inspiring writing. His amazing range of scholarship had the two indispensable qualities of profundity and precision. He is not merely an expositor of what lies before him, a commentator of intelligence whom one comes to trust implicitly, but a formulator of principles. Leaving aside his editing of Shelley and Poe, I take his essay on Virgil as an example of what literary criticism should be. It is so comprehensive in its view of the antique world and of humanity in many epochs that one may construct from it a sheer philosophy of life. Woodberry is not content with giving you an analysis of Virgil's poetry, the alliances of his mind and the sweep of his emotions; he makes you feel the background of character, mind and emotion in the old world and the new. One is reminded of what Froude said of history, that its chief value consists in "sounding across the centuries the eternal note of Right and Wrong." Woodberry shows us not merely Virgil but all that he stood for.

This power of generalization I take to be the test of a

critic. Woodberry gives us not only the facts concerning the Roman poet, but also the atmosphere and background of Poetry itself, of subtle and perennial interest. He says of Virgil's universality:

"Of no other poet can it be said that his lines are a part of the biography of the great: of emperors like Augustus and Hadrian, of fathers like Jerome and Augustine, of preachers like Savonarola, churchmen like Fénelon, statesmen like Pitt and Burke; and among the host of humble scholars, of schoolmasters, the power he has held in their bosoms is as remarkable for its personal intimacy as for its universal embrace. No fame so majestic has been cherished with a love so tender. Virgil thus blends in a marvelous manner the authority of a classic with the direct appeal to life."

He goes on to say of Virgil's method what might almost be said of his own:

"He used for his artistic method a selective, partial description, subordinating individuality and detail to social and general presentation, and he employed episode, suggestion and the emphasis that lies in enthusiasm to enlarge the theme and qualify it with greatness; in particular, he intended no exhaustion of the subject, but only of the feeling of the subject, which is the method of great poetry, and hence come the rapidity, the variety, the completeness of impression which are the most obvious traits of the changeful lines."

This essay alone might well be recommended for college and university education, whether in the study of Latin verse or of English prose composition.

In conclusion I wish to say what I believe Woodberry would wish to have said. In common with many other American poets, he was so sincere in his art that he threw his leaves upon the stream of Time without any care whether they were found by the public or not. He was not a self-advertiser, but left to the future the appreciation of his verse. This very modesty of the poets of the Academy who have passed away puts upon it, in my conviction, an obligation to do what it can to see that they are not forgotten. We carry as our insignia the figure of Pegasus: what are we doing to fortify in the minds of an eager but bewildered public the fine traditions of Poetry which that figure implies? These colleagues of ours have poured out their heart's blood in patriotism and emotion. Even though

> Things are in the saddle
> And ride mankind

I believe a better day is coming. We can do much to hasten it by laying public emphasis upon their best achievement, and in thus honoring them we shall honor the Academy, and promote the purposes, intellectual and spiritual, for which it was founded.

These lines are not a farewell but a greeting to a knightly gentleman, a tender lover of children, a devoted friend, a conscientious artist, a captain of the soul. Let us thank Heaven that he has lived and that he has contributed so much of beauty and inspiration to the world.

ARTHUR TWINING HADLEY
BY JOHN HUSTON FINLEY

THE LEGEND that Arthur Twining Hadley came into the world speaking Greek suggests the origin of some ancient myths. His brilliancy of mind was such that stories were invented to account for his genius. But as some ancient said of Plato's *Phaedo*, "If Plato did not write me there were two Platos;" so if Hadley did not say these things there were two Hadleys, which is not to be imagined, much less admitted. God made no replica of his quick and quickening wit.

He must have been born full-panoplied. The son of the famous Greek scholar "remarkable for the extent of his acquisitions," he seemed to support the theory of the transmission of acquired character, so extraordinary an acquaintance did he show with a variety of subjects even in his earliest years. He led in everything to which he gave himself and had an intellectual range astounding to the ordinary man. He could use many languages effectively, improvising even on occasion, and he possessed a basic knowledge of every liberal discipline. The old Greek poet Alcman had a word for him, phrasidorkon (φρασίδορκον) one "that looks with the mind," not only in memory backward but forward in prevision. And it also suggests one who looks "quick-sightedly" and "accurately," as a gazelle,—one who speaks and acts from quick, clear sight. "No prophet," said Professor Seymour in his admirable memorial address, "ever translated his principles into actual life more completely than he. . . . He constantly preached the necessity of intelligence; he invariably utilized it and flexibly." He carried in his writings and conversations "the flower of Socratic talk."

When elected President of Yale University he was regarded as a very young man for the position, but such was his reputation for scholarship, his acquaintance with practical affairs (being considered even then as a foremost authority on transportation) and his popularity with students and alumni, that he overcame the handicaps of slight experience in academic administration. He was even assisted and endeared by the very eccentricities of mind and body which would seem to a stranger to disqualify him.

My first memory of him recalls him at the last baccalaureate service of President Dwight, just after his own election, when the voice of Old Yale called down the blessing of Heaven upon this nervous young scholar. And I can't forbear to speak of the next, in which President Hadley appeared again, this time as leader, and men protected by oilcloth capes (Otto Bannard, his classmate, 1876, foremost among them) carried the old-fashioned smoking torches in procession in a cheering lampadedromy.

He justified his selection. The shining of his intellect,

which was as a star of the first magnitude, drew men of scholarly tastes to Yale, and the soundness of his judgment in economic matters kept the academic house in order. It was a period of laying foundations for an expanded and enriched institution. But with it all he was not so overwhelmed by the myriad details as to lose sight of the ideals. They were fixed in his own fortunate heritage and his own university disciplines, and he was true to them to the end. In the memorable closing words of his last baccalaureate address he set forth the crowning values of life as he, a foremost economist, a very practical man of affairs, estimated them:

> So to live and so to think that those about us will have more courage and self-sacrifice and larger and truer vision of what is required of man—these things are more important than all the scientific principles we can discover or all the material results we can achieve.

It is not strange that he should have dwelt so much of late upon the freedom of the individual; for his philosophy always emphasized the mind of man and its release for its own highest functioning. He was an expert of high authority in certain economic fields, but his lasting fame will be associated with his distinguished, humanistic direction of Yale University, and his speaking from that platform to an audience that reached around the world.

His effectiveness in speech was not in grace of utterance with coordinate gesture, but in the perfection of phrase and the appeal of his clear thinking. He seemed at times as primitive man, but of powerful mind, fighting for the future of mortal breeds. His bodily exuberance of expression was compelling because it had back of it the conviction of his whole mind and soul. There could not be the slightest shadow of dissimulation in anything that he said or did, and there never was "a whisper of envy."

Simonides, in a fragment that has survived the centuries, laments the passing of one whom the lot of death overtook wandering in a distant sea because he failed "of sweet and dear home coming." But President Hadley was not a stranger in any part of the earth, and by his very death in a far land he brought it nearer to us and ours to it.

Μέγα γείτονι γείτων

(Neighbor is great thing unto neighbor),

So long as Yale herself is known
Will be remembered his high labor.

1931

EDWARD CHANNING
BY A. LAWRENCE LOWELL

Handicapped in childhood and youth by ill health and lack of a parental home, Edward Channing by force of character made himself a great historical scholar and substantially completed the work he had projected in early manhood. In Harvard College, where he graduated in 1878, and in the following years he came under the influence of Justin Winsor and Henry Adams from whom he derived methods that were of much use to him in his research and teaching. Before the end of his junior year he had decided to make the study of history his career, and by the time of graduation his interest had become centered in the history of this country. He therefore spent two years in working on the subject for the doctorate of philosophy, which had been established not long before. A year of travel in Europe was followed by the usual miscellaneous efforts, disappointments and success, in securing a foothold in the teaching staff of the University. A *succès d'estime* he made early by a prize essay on Town and County Government in the North American Colonies, which brought his election to the Massachusetts Historical Society; and by 1887 he had worked his way up to an Assistant Professorship, leading ten years later to a permanent chair. Meanwhile he was gradually concentrating his teaching on his favorite field of American history.

As a teacher he was not less remarkable than as a writer, although in a somewhat different way. From Henry Adams, his earliest master in the field, he had acquired three methods of dealing with his students, waking them up by shocking their prejudices, giving them subjects to study and report upon, and looking up their ancestry to find topics in which they would be likely to take an hereditary interest.

The shocking was deliberate. In fact, Adams is reported to have said of one of his classes that he had ridden roughshod over all their prejudices but could not stir them up. Channing did the same,—in the case, for example, of Plymouth Rock and the Washington Elm—until he was regarded as an iconoclast who reveled in discrediting the revered traditions of our people. Although he did not object to that reputation, it was by no means justified, and much of his criticism of popular legends may be resolved into the meaning of words. The landing of the Pilgrims, or Washington's taking command of the army, implies in the common conception a ceremony such as would never take place save for publicity or posterity, which neither Bradford nor Washington had in mind.

The practice of assigning to both graduates and undergraduates topics to be worked up in the library and made the subject of a report began, so far as I am aware, with Henry Adams and was brought to a high state of perfection by Channing. In his undergraduate course there were two of these a year, carefully selected with regard to the probable interests of each student, with whom the assistant in the course had three conferences, before, during and at the completion of his study on the topic. This at least was the procedure at the turn of the century; and the result was more work by undergraduates in this course than in any other of its kind in the department.

The topic, as already noticed, was selected with special reference to the probable interest of each student. This was a matter to which Channing gave peculiar attention. All the men were required to fill out statements in regard to the antecedents of their families and these Channing and his assistant examined, spending several evenings assigning subjects that would be likely to have some hereditary or geographical attraction for the students to whom they were allotted. The plan was excellent and in many cases had a highly stimulating effect.

All this shows how keen an interest Channing took in his students, how much labor he expended upon them, and in fact the writer was always impressed with how well he knew so large a body and remembered them years afterwards.

As a lecturer he was highly successful, and at times very impressive. One of the persons present remembers in particular his lecture on Anne Hutchinson, to which the students listened with rapt attention and sat silent for an appreciable time after it was over. Yet these lectures were delivered in a quiet, discursive tone, without the slightest attempt at oratory; and indeed, Channing would not tolerate and sternly repressed on the part of his students any demonstrations such as were then too common in college courses. So much for Channing as a teacher. It was a kind of work that may leave a permanent impression and may develop—as in Channing's case—scholars who become eminent in the next generation, but which is often forgotten. Its effects are written in the minds of men, not on pages that are carefully preserved.

As a scholar he will be chiefly remembered by his History of the United States which as he tells us in the preface to the first volume, he designed should begin at the earliest discoveries and continue to the end of the nineteenth century. The labor of writing such a book from the sources was of course colossal, and it would have been still more difficult had he not made his researches and his teachings cover the same period. After he was fully established at Harvard, his two great courses for undergraduates and graduates covered the Colonial times until he had worked up all the material thereon for his book, and then he progressively took up one period after another, giving out to his students the result of his labor. Indeed, when the writing on his book had covered any period, he took little further interest in it, and did not care to discuss it.

Channing had a thoroughly independent mind. He be-

longed to no school or type of thought, and would have resented being classed as a conservative or a radical. He was
himself first, last, and all the time, and it is hard to discover
in his talk or his books a prevailing slant of thought in the
direction of any philosophic current at the moment popular
or otherwise. For that reason he made scholars but not a
school. His own philosophy of history on this continent was
that it was a progressive evolution, each condition giving rise
to the next by a natural succession; civilization being a
growth, not a series of shocks or fresh starts.

He was continually searching for facts, working up any
trails that he came across, and he always had a new one in his
mind which he brought out in conversation even more sharply than in his History, for he was quick to see the bearing of
a significant fact on an obscure situation. An example of this
was his search, in connection with the Trent affair, for the
meaning of the request of the British Consul at Portland for
leave to transmit officers' baggage to Canada, and Seward's ·
answer thereto. To determine what had been actually sent to
Portland he examined the manifest of the ship and discovered, to his surprise, that she brought a large amount of cotton. This led him to examine the cargoes of other ships about
that date, and he found that, far from being short of cotton,
the British were sending it over in large quantities for sale in
New England at a time when the Confederate States were
relying on the lack of cotton in Europe as a motive for inter-
ference in the war.

An evening with Channing was a delight, for he always
had something new that he had unearthed, about which he
liked to tell and we liked to hear, and he told it in a more
pungent way than he wrote it afterwards. Great as the volumes of his History are, from a scholarly point of view, they
are not as interesting as his conversation was. That is partly,
I think, because he felt that committing a thing to print was
a serious matter, and that history should be written in a judicial attitude; with the result that his writing was more re-

strained, more carefully considered, than his talk, and thus lost some of the sparkle. Moreover, he entirely disapproved of the treatment of history as a form of literature. It was to him more nearly a science than an art, and he would have repudiated with scorn Macaulay's ambition to drive with his history the last novel from the lady's dressing table. Perhaps this was carried too far, for while its scholarly value would not have changed, his History might have had a wider and a longer popularity. For students it will always be essential, but the public likes bright colors.

Personally, Channing had a shell about him, and many people saw little else. They thought it hard and prickly, and so it was superficially; but some of those who came nearest to him thought it largely a protective envelope to shield a shy and sensitive nature, due, perhaps, to the lack of an early home. His mother had died when he was three months old and his father was a wanderer whom he scarcely saw. Evidently a lonely child, unwell, and near-sighted, he seemed to shrink from contact with the outer world and with other people; so he appeared to be encased in reticence and even gruffness. Yet he was very affectionate and indeed devoted to his friends. He thought about them when he was away. To one I know he never forgot to come on the morning of his birthday, and also brought him from abroad gifts that he knew would be appreciated. To the casual observer he appeared to be one who could live satisfied in his own household, without need for other people. He attended meetings of learned societies very little, and only when he had to speak. He tended to shun general society; but this was not true of the companionship of his intimate friends, whether they were working in the same lines as himself or not.

Apart from travel, his only recreation appeared to be in boats, and he was an excellent sailor, threading the mazes of the shoals of Cape Cod without touching keel or centerboard. He had a real love of the sea, and understood both it and the craft of seamen, a knowledge that helped him greatly in the maritime part of his History, especially in its early period. With rare fortune he lived to complete a great and very laborious work, that may be said to have occupied his whole life, for he carried his plan from the first discoveries through the Civil War. All that was unfinished of the original design were the last few years of the nineteenth century; and this would have left no natural place to stop. His History is a rounded whole, an achievement that in its scope and detailed study of the sources will never be repeated.

GEORGE WHITEFIELD CHADWICK

BY HENRY HADLEY

WITH THE passing of George W. Chadwick on April 4th, 1931, a definite period in our national musical history was closed—a period rich in achievement and adorned with a goodly number of illustrious names.

Of the New England School of Composers it may be said that it was to music what that of Hawthorne, Emerson, Lowell and all the other writers of their periods were to our national literature. And of this particular epoch, it is Mr. Chadwick who made an indelible impression. There is scarcely any phase of musical experience which was not his —composer in all forms from songs to symphonies, teacher, organist, lecturer, conductor of choral societies and orchestras. And to this full and well-rounded experience, we must attribute the characteristic sureness and conviction which marked everything he said and did.

His integrity as a man and musician, his gift of humor, his wit—sometimes caustic, but underneath always intensely human—are well known, while the depth of his emotions, the spontaneity of their expression, are abundantly reflected in his works.

My experience and friendship with him began when, as a lad of fifteen years, my father took me to Mr. Chadwick's home in Boston and arranged for me to have lessons in counterpoint with him. These hours which I spent every week at the South Congregational Church, where Mr. Chadwick played the organ and where he had a little studio, were and still are lovely memories, very precious to me. George Chadwick did much to instill in my young mind the love of all things beautiful in Art.

As a teacher he was painstaking and thorough, and never failed to interpolate his instruction with witty remarks and anecdotes drawn from his inexhaustible knowledge of the masters. He could always illustrate his points most aptly with examples from the great writers, and in many subtle ways he enlarged the vision and stimulated the imagination of his students.

He had fine taste and sure judgment and always chose the richest, the most expressive colors from his musical palette. I well remember the beauty of a certain passage in his "Lovely Rosabelle," a ballad for solo, chorus and orchestra which he had just then published. He had adroitly combined the low quality of the altos of the chorus with the high register of the tenors, and by thus blending them to the text in unison, he produced a passage with a peculiarly ghost-like, unearthly effect—a very impressive and indescribably beautiful one. And so in all his works, he constantly achieves startling effects through peculiarly skillful instrumentation, and his profound knowledge of the possibilities of the orchestra and voice.

Naturally I eagerly anticipated all of my lessons and never failed to take away something very substantial.

It was my privilege later in life to claim him as colleague and friend. His summer home on Martha's Vineyard Island was close to my own, and there we have spent many happy hours together. As the years passed, a broad humanitarian spirit possessed him and all his views in regard to musical conditions in this country mellowed. His advice was always valuable, and to him I often repaired for sage counsel and sympathetic understanding, in which he never failed me.

His interests were not limited to music. He was a voracious reader—especially of history. He loved painting and sculpture, and numbered among his friends highly distinguished artists and poets. His companionship with the American painters who, at that time, were studying with Duveneck in Munich, led him to a realization of the proximity of the art of color-tone.

George Whitefield Chadwick was born in Lowell, Massachusetts, on November 13th, 1854, and comes in straight line from the old New England stock of 1630. His mother died when he was born, but his father cared tenderly for his little boy. Although Alonzo Chadwick was a farmer he taught a class of singing for many years, marrying the second time a member of one of these classes.

George's elder brother, Fitz-Henry, who was fourteen years older, gave him piano lessons. A family orchestra was later formed with the help of the neighbors and from Fitz-Henry, George learned to play the organ.

Graduating from the high school, he was allowed to study with Carlyle Petersilea who had the advantage of study with European masters. Later he attended the New England Conservatory of which he was destined to become the Director later in life.

At a very early age he was selected as head of the music department of Olivet College, where he taught piano, organ and harmony. With his manifold duties as teacher and leader of the Glee Club, he gave weekly recitals and lectured on music and aesthetics, in all of which, in spite of his youth, he acquitted himself with much distinction.

He had an ardent desire to study in Europe and, overcoming the objections of his family, he went abroad in 1877. He went to Leipzig where he studied with Reiencke and Jadassohn, the latter declaring that Chadwick was the brightest student of his class. It is said that of Jadassohn he learned to write what has been styled "significant counterpoint" and there is no doubt that through Jadassohn's encouragement to write a capella and in four parts he acquired the technic of his flawless choral style.

He was also encouraged to write chamber music, but the orchestra held greater charm for him. He profited greatly by his study in Leipzig and here produced his String Quartet in C Major and his overture to Rip Van Winkle, both of which were highly praised.

He especially loved the form of the overture and has designated some eight of his compositions by that name, "Melpomene" being best known because oftenest heard.

Upon leaving Leipzig he went to Munich (after a very short stay in Dresden) to study with Joseph Rheinberger. Who can say what the joyous, carefree life in Munich contributed to his inner life and imagination? Here he found free musical utterance. He left Munich about the end of March, 1889, and returned to America to compose, teach and play the organ.

In 1885 he married Ida May Brooks of Boston and two sons were born to them, Theodore and Noël.

He wrote his first symphony in 1882, and became conductor of the festival choral societies in Springfield and Worcester, Mass.

Among the outstanding works by Chadwick are *Angel of Death,* Symphonic Poem; *Aphrodite,* Symphonic Poem; *Symphonic Sketches;* the Three Symphonies; *Tam O'Shanter Symphonic Ballads;* Overture, *Melpomene; Piano Quintet in E^b; Phoenix Expirans.*

His compositions number well over four hundred.

His death at his home in Boston marks the span of fifty years with an indelible stamp and this contribution we acknowledge with pride and affection.

The recognition of thirty-five years of work at the New England Conservatory is adequately given in the resolutions of the Board of Trustees of the Conservatory which expresses its sincere appreciation of his long and faithful service, his wise, just and fearless counsel, his friendly help and sympathy for students and faculty alike, his great musical accomplishment and his stimulating force of character and gift of leadership in building the artistic standards of the Conservatory to their present high plane.

EDWIN ANDERSON ALDERMAN

BY JOHN HUSTON FINLEY

THE LAST TIME President Alderman sat in this room, he came from the train a little late (in the tweeds of travel) and (as he had not remembered his assigned seat) he took the one at my side to which I beckoned him. This is for me an especially proud memory. That the seat was also next to that occupied at one time by that Jovian member, Dr. Basil Gildersleeve, makes the incident the more memorable for me. They two now lie in the same yard in Charlottesville, Virginia,—an academy in which the mortal puts on immortality, whose motto is furnished by the epitaph on the great Greek scholar's tomb: "The Bivouac is over."

I speak first of Edwin Anderson Alderman in that association in which he will always be most intimately remembered, as first President of the University of Virginia, though he had a valiant and brilliant record before he entered upon that office. He used to tell the story of a Virginia lady who hesitated to ask a stranger where he was from for fear that he would have to confess that he was not from Virginia—which he said would make an awkward pause in the conversation. But though Dr. Alderman was not born in Virginia, he was as to the manner born. Even Virginia was proud to claim him and did so without an awkward pause.

President Wilson, under whose father's sturdy Presbyterian ministry Dr. Alderman was spiritually nourished as a boy, said when search was being made for a President of the University of Virginia that he must incarnate the spirit of the South and that the ideal man was Alderman. Dr. Curry's statement of Dr. Alderman's aim became a prophecy: "To democratize the point of view of an aristocratic society."

Thomas Jefferson was the first "Rector" of the University of Virginia, but not until 1904 did it have a President. It was long administered by the faculty and its chairman, under the direction of "The Board of Visitors" and its Rector. Jefferson designed a collection of schools, each gathered about a professor—a plan of organization to which, in modified form, the great universities are looking today. But the administrative affairs of the collective institution grew in scope and complexity till the need of an executive office became imperative, and the choice fell upon one already known throughout the South as the "evangel of public education," Dr. Edwin A. Alderman—a modern Abelard heralding a full renaissance that should illumine the South.

When still a young man, he and Charles Duncan McIver and Charles Brantley Aycock, afterward Governor, went up and down the State of North Carolina proclaiming the need and duty of the Commonwealth to give an education to every child within its borders, "whatever its class or color." They were as young troubadours in education in those early days, as the mediaeval troubadours were in song, "who tuned their pipes for no fee," but for love of their ideal. He said of himself many years later that the first vote he ever cast was for the public school and that no joy had come into his life comparable with that of associating himself with this sort of service to the public. He held that the universities must also interest themselves in the things which concern the people, no matter how homely or prosaic—"the Negro's cabin, the factory child, the village library, the prices current, the home, the field, the shop." The old idea that it was the duty of the State to care for the university was in his administration turned about, making it the primary duty of the university to care for the State. The University of Virginia under his inspiring leadership during more than a quarter of a century has come to be more than a "secluded nursery for the production of scholars and gentlemen." It still performs that function, but it has come to be an institution to which all the people of the State may look for practical instruction and guidance.

But he has done more than enlarge and improve Jefferson's institution and lead it into a new era. He has been democracy's most eloquent voice. He has often spoken for America in shining and stately sentences that will be permanently preserved in American literature. And notably in his memorial oration before Congress on Woodrow Wilson. I have reread beside it the oration of Pericles and there it deserves to be kept. I am sure that Pericles could not have spoken with a more melodious voice. It was as that of a well-loved viol, fashioned "in mellow shapeliness" through which the lofty thought spoke, as the late Poet Laureate would have said, with "incantation of strange magic to charm the dreams that undreamt lurk in the unfathomed deep of new unfeatured hopes" of youth and "uttermost forms of all things that shall be." One remembers that it was broken for years but by our Northern airs it was repaired so that it was even mellower. The living voice that moved multitudes also "bears the colorless photography of print." Such sentences as this will illustrate this added tribute:

To live in liberal and lofty fashion with hearts unspoiled of hate, eyes clear to see the needs of a new and mighty day, in a new and mighty land.

When a character in Michael Ireland's story of *The Return of the Hero* was dwelling upon the virtues of this great hero (the son of Cumhal, the son of Tremor, the son of Subhalt, the son of Baoiscne, of the offspring of Nuada Necht) he said with pure Celtic imagination that if he were to stretch himself out in a lengthy tongue from where he stood to distant Iorrus and if his audience were one ear from that self-same place to Loch Lein of beautiful shores, it would fail him to tell a small part of the wisdom that his hero spoke, and he added:

For him to speak was a matter of right place and fortunate inclination not to be won by sweating. Wisdom is a beautiful shaping of life. It lives in the spoken word.

Dr. Alderman had that wisdom, won without sweating as it seemed. There was with all his temporal responsibilities a beautiful shaping of life in him, and it showed itself most entrancingly and powerfully in the spoken word, by which he moulded his world to the dream of his heart.

Oliver Wendell Holmes in his story of his hunt after "The Captain"—the captain being the son who became Justice of the U. S. Supreme Court—describes a young wounded Southern officer from North Carolina upon whom he came in his search "as of slight, scholastic habit"—who spoke as one accustomed "to tread carefully among the parts of speech." But while this son of North Carolina was of scholastic habit, he trod with swift step among the parts of speech. They marched with instant, accurate and loyal response to his aid in every battle into which he flung himself with spirit and with what would seem to an ordinary speaker abandon. And they never failed him.

The art of speech, which is having illustration here today, suggests that the type of oratory which had its flowering in him may not blossom again. While the magic of the microphone—what Milton would have called the sounding alchemy—gives millions to a speaker (instead of hundreds or thousands) for an audience, the manner of speech can not be quite the same, lacking two elements in Cicero's definition of delivery, countenance and gesture. Dr. Alderman's last great speech was delivered with its aid. I hope that the words have been preserved in his voice. It will tell future generations what manner of speech crowned our language in our day. It will say to them: *"Qualis vir, talis oratio."* For us, all that he was escapes our telling to those who have not seen or heard him.

So completely did the man become words which in turn compelled deeds, that we in thinking of his life praise the word of spirit rather than the material result. And Mr.

Archer Huntington has in one of his poems given us lines that might well be inscribed upon the cenotaph of Dr. Alderman:

> Not human deeds in cenotaphs we sing,
> Nay, to the fleeting word that is man's ghost
> We build our honours to enshrine the dust.
> Man fades and all his shrunken time is lost,
> Yet ever on its argent pinions floats
> The grandeur of the word that was his soul.
> Not to the deeds of men are cenotaphs.

TIMOTHY COLE

BY ROBERT UNDERWOOD JOHNSON

EMERSON SAYS that nothing great is ever accomplished save when many work together as one. Something akin to this condition appears in the revival of wood-engraving in the United States in the twenty-five years before 1900, when, as a movement, it may be said to have reached its climax of beauty. Led by the *Century Magazine* (then known as *Scribner's Monthly*) and inspired and directed by Alexander W. Drake, art-editor of that periodical, rightly called the father of American wood-engraving, more than two score American craftsmen, artists of the burin, were engaged in friendly emulation. It was a veritable epoch of delight. As one of the editors of the magazine it was my fortune to be a witness of the spirit of generous rivalry and comradeship with which this work went on, every engraver hailing with joy each new accomplishment. It was like a Florentine guild of the Renaissance. To the present generation, the value and importance of this movement are a closed book, only to be opened by those who care for beauty as a principle.

The artistic value of the results is not obscured or impaired by the fact that, due to commercial considerations, wood-engraving in America is now virtually a lost art. Years ago the

wood block was superseded by the cheaper half-tone processes of reproduction. The skilled engravers held out bravely
against the decline of popular interest in the art; a few craftsmen are still at work, but the men of distinction are gone.
The last and the greatest of these was Timothy Cole.

While the American public of those days was not lacking
in appreciation of these engravings, the most cordial recep-
tion came from critics and connoisseurs of France and England. *L'Art*, then the leading authority in esthetics, reprinted
cuts from a portfolio issued by the magazine, adding highly
laudatory comment. The distinguished critic of England,
Philip Gilbert Hamerton, wrote in his volume *Graphic Arts*:
"The development of delicate and versatile wood-engraving
in America is due to the managers of *Scribner's Monthly*,
who worked resolutely with this definite end in view . . .
There can be no question that the Americans have far surpassed all other nations in delicacy of execution. The manual
skill displayed in their wood-cuts is a continual marvel . . .
The two superiorities in American wood-engraving are in
tone and texture." After speaking of the "almost unlimited
ingenuity" with which our engravers vary the tone, he adds,
"As for texture they seem able to imitate anything that is set
before them."

Against such a background of general achievement the
work of Cole stood out in uniform excellence. I remember
the sensation that each succeeding block of his created in the
offices of the magazine. The editors and publishers were con-
voked to see the newly arrived proof, which was greeted with
enthusiastic expressions of "Well, he has done it again!"
Others may have failed now and then; Cole never did: he
was a Homer that never nodded. For each commission he
seemed to have invented a new method. At one time it would
be a long graceful line sweeping across the block, now a black
line, now a white, with as much charm of detail as of the
resultant mass; again, beautiful effects of shadow would be
attained by stippling that fairly danced with motion, or by

masterly, well-modulated cross-hatching. But all his methods had for their object the production of tone. This was his distinction—the distinction of all great art—that he had style, but no mannerism. He never fumbled and this resourcefulness never deserted him. To the last, his blocks are marvels of technic directed by fidelity.

Putting aside his method, let us consider the range and content of his work. He was famous long before his *magnum opus,* the five famous series of the Old Masters. There was no si bject which he touched that he did not adorn,—portraitι :e, landscape, painting, sculpture, everything found its equat on of beauty in the divination of his mind and the skill of his hand. And then one day there came one of those rare occasions which are turning-points of fate. Mr. Lewis Fraser, associate of Mr. Drake in the Art Department of the *Century,* displaying to me one morning a new proof of Cole's, said, "Johnson, it is a crying shame that such ability should be wasted on a subject so unimportant; that man should be sent abroad to engrave the Old Masters." This remark struck my imagination and, pondering it, I said, "Fraser, I want fifteen minutes of your time. Your idea about Cole is a fine one. Come with me and propose it to the publishers and I will second you." We went at once, and when Mr. Drake, who that day had happened to be absent, returned to the office, the suggestion struck fire with him and he threw his whole force behind the project, which, warmly supported by the editor-in-chief, Richard Watson Gilder, was promptly adopted by the publishers, with the result that Cole was sent to Italy in 1884 for a year or two, as we thought, to reproduce examples of the great painters. Who could have fancied that this enterprise would extend to a period of twenty-six years, comprising five series of Old Masters, those of Italy, France, the Low Countries, England and Spain! The project was a success from the beginning and was accentuated by each succeeding block, printed with admirable subtlety by the De-Vinne Press. Cole suffused himself with the personality of each painter and with the individuality of each canvas, sitting before it, first in study and then in execution, verifying everything as he virtually repainted it in black-and-white upon the block on which it had been photographed, and thus corrected the mistakes in "values" which were made by the photographic processes of that day. He caught with equal facility the austere naïveté of the pre-Raphaelites and the mellow suavity of the Venetians. He held the mirror up to Beauty and has left us a supreme and glorious record of those treasures of art. When the work in foreign galleries was finished,—having succeeded Mr. Gilder as editor-in-chief,—I enlisted Cole in a supplementary series of "Old Masters in American Galleries." When I left the *Century* in 1913 I made a last request that Cole should be retained upon its staff, but commercial considerations prevailed. However, he soon found appreciative hospitality in the *Art World* ably edited by the sculptor Frederick Ruckstull, to which he contributed larger blocks; after that vigorous and admirable periodical was discontinued, his activity was confined to private commissions. His last block, a portrait of a young woman by Gainsborough in Mr. Widener's gallery, marked the brilliant culmination of an epoch and of a unique personal career.

George Eliot held that the receptive faculty is greater than the creative: Cole possessed both to the degree of genius. Love makes us wise, and if ever a man loved his work it was Timothy Cole. His outstanding personal qualities were sensibility, gentleness and spirituality. He lived a life apart, in the seclusion not of a monastic but of a devotee, and was not affected by the misleading and so often empty activities of urban life. The sweetness of his character played a large part in his achievement. He was not only the simplest but the kindest of men, inexhaustible in his generosity, and without taint of jealousy or envy. He gave to his work, and in turn his work gave to him, the happiness that comes from a deep devotion to any art. I believe—why should I hesitate to say it?—that in the history of Art he deserves to be considered among the great.

DANIEL CHESTER FRENCH

BY ROYAL CORTISSOZ

T HE American Academy of Arts and Letters was founded
in 1904. Daniel Chester French was elected a member
in the following year. He was thus early received into this
body in the very nature of things. He was thoroughly in
harmony with its spirit, moved in all that he did by a high
feeling for tradition but convinced in his soul that "the letter
killeth," that tradition is only fruitful when it fertilizes and
enriches the personal, creative energy with which the true
artist is endowed. He was born, at Exeter, New Hampshire,
in 1850. He died on October 7th, 1931. It was a long life
and it was a happy one, happy for him, and inspiring for his
fellow countrymen, because it was dedicated from beginning
to end to the production of noble work.

A rich source of the distinction which French achieved
as a sculptor resided in the resolution with which, in his
youthful, formative period, he "hitched his wagon to a star."
It was the star of high thinking, of an idealism which looked
through and above the phenomena of the visible world, and,
without ignoring the claims of realism, gave to what he saw
a certain elevated significance. The vitalized bust of Emerson
which he modelled at the outset of his career has a dual
status. It is, in the first place, an authentic portrait of the
man. "Yes, that is the face I shave," said the sage. But it is
also a souvenir of French's insight into the imponderables of
the philosopher's character, of his alliance with what was
finest in the old cultural habit of New England. He was himself a born Emersonian, which is to say that he was a thoughtful, sensitive individual, delicately tinctured in the fibre of
his being. He had imagination and a flair for spiritual values.
A beautiful seriousness of purpose animated him.

Along with the subtler elements in his cosmos there went
a lively, racy faculty for the interpretation of character. He
was in his early twenties when he produced "The Minute

Man," which launched him, but even then he knew as though by clairvoyance the traits of the essential American and in statue after statue he confirmed the promise given by his initial work of an art rooted in our soil. The stately, symbolical figure in his *Death and the Young Sculptor* is not more eloquent in its solemnity than is the figure of the artist in its manly vigor. By the time French came to model his *Lincoln*, in the great Memorial at Washington, his mind, and, indeed, his whole nature, had become saturated in human character as it functions in American life. He was a singularly penetrating interpreter of the types it fell to him to commemorate.

As a sculptor pure and simple, as a stylist, he practised an art flowing from the older and more or less classical phase of the American school. He was all for simplicity and a grave, measured handling of a problem, he drove absolutely at poise and dignity. To the newer generation, for which sculpture started with Rodin and was continued by Bourdelle and Maillol, he made no appeal. He was, in its prejudiced eyes, flatly "academic," and that summarily settled the matter. As a matter of fact he had abilities far transcending any merely "academic" formula. I once asked him why there was so much bad sculpture scattered about. Humorously he replied —and I may say in passing that French's sense of fun was one of his most attractive traits—"Why, don't you know? It is because sculpture is the easiest of all the arts." He went on to speak of the facility with which the veriest dabster could worry a lump of clay into resemblance to this or that object— and then he went on to talk of the difficulty with which the qualities that make good sculpture are brought under control. French mastered these latter qualities, qualities of imaginative evocation, of design, of style and so on, through innate power, but also through devotional hard work. He had his reward in the emergence of some memorable images from under his hands.

One of the noblest of them is the *Memory* at the Metropolitan Museum, a seated nude reminiscent of antique ideas. The first impression one receives from it is that of a figure of great dignity and loveliness. On closer scrutiny one sees also how much the statue owes to learned research into form, to art in composition, to authority in the development of line and in the nuances of modelling. First and last, in looking at this serene marble and at numerous other productions of French's, one is conscious of his idealism, of his reverence for beauty and the loftier issues of his craft. Sculpture was not "easy" for him, for he made it an affair of depth and emotion. At every stage of his long, successful life, he was faithful to his star.

1932

DAVID JAYNE HILL
BY NICHOLAS MURRAY BUTLER

A N INDUSTRIOUS and many-sided career of public service, marked always by conscientious devotion and useful- ness and often by distinction, was that of David Jayne Hill, who died at Washington on March 2, 1932, in the 82nd year of his age. Dr. Hill came of the solid, straight-thinking and high-minded stock which has fortunately been so well repre- sented in the history of American life and letters. A native of New Jersey, he obtained his formal education at Bucknell University in Pennsylvania, at the University of Pennsyl- vania, and later at the Universities of Berlin and Paris. When but twenty-nine years of age he undertook the work of educational administration as president of Bucknell Uni- versity, and after nine years spent in that post passed to the University of Rochester, which important institution he served as president for eight years. Following his resignation from the work of educational administration, Dr. Hill spent several years in studying the public law of Europe, and made himself a master of it. In 1898 President McKinley called him to official public service as Assistant Secretary of State, and in the Department of State he served side by side with John Hay for five years. Then in succession he became Min- ister of the United States to Switzerland, to the Netherlands, and Ambassador to Germany, which distinguished post he held from 1908 to 1911. Dr. Hill was a member of the Amer- ican Delegation to the Second Peace Conference at the Hague in 1907, and labored effectively to carry out the in- structions of Secretary of State Root that a genuine Court of International Justice be brought into being to promote the peace of the world. Upon retiring from official service Dr. Hill made his home at the national capital, where his studies and literary work were carried forward eagerly and assiduously until his final illness overtook him.

Dr. Hill's sound scholarship, his knowledge of men, and his long experience in official life made him a valuable and valued adviser, both official and unofficial, in all that relates to international intercourse and international coöperation. His stout volumes on the History of Diplomacy, unfortunately never completed, are a fine monument of scholarly endeavor and ambition.

Dr. Hill's life represents that type of American career in public service, both official and unofficial, which is the pride of our people and one of its chief glories. It is fortunate indeed that there is so often to be found an open path between public service in the sphere of liberty and public service in the sphere of government, and that scholars and wise men are found ready to tread it.

Dr. Hill was elected to the Academy on November 17, 1920, as the fourth in succession to occupy chair No. 31. He greatly valued the associations and the opportunities which the Academy offered, and when his health permitted was always an eager and interested attendant upon its meetings and public exercises.

GAMALIEL BRADFORD

BY ROBERT GRANT

GAMALIEL BRADFORD was chosen a member of this Academy at its annual meeting on November 12, 1931, but, because of illness which prevented his traveling, he never occupied the seat to which he was elected. He died on April 11, 1932, at Wellesley Hills, Massachusetts, in the house where he had lived almost continuously since 1866 and under the shelter of which his literary laurels were won.

He stood by direct descent in the eighth generation from Governor William Bradford of the Plymouth Colony, whose grandson Honorable Gamaliel Bradford (1704-1778) bore the Christian name which was to be held seven times in succession. From his father, a banker, and also a protagonist of political reform, he inherited ardor and considerable keen facial resemblance. From his mother, Clara Crowninshield Kinsman of Newburyport, besides her sentitiveness to beauty, the physical frailty which suffered him to attain just short of three score years and ten only by the most steadfast of regimes and rigorous eliminations. His mother died of consumption at the age of 29 and his own delicacy was so obvious that, to give him every chance against the New England climate, some of his winters were spent in Washington, and, when he was fifteen, one whole year in Europe. From the latter dates the beginning of his thorough knowledge of French, German and Italian which broadened the horizon of his intensive studies of human character, and incidentally provided the cue to his own method. For in his essay *Psychography*, which opens his volume *A Naturalist of Souls*, he quotes from Sainte-Beuve, with whom he was more deeply imbued than by any analyst, the formula *"J'analyse, j'herborise, je suis un naturaliste des esprits."*

It was of his own soul that Gamaliel Bradford was first of all a searcher from youth upwards. When possessed by illusion, he was honest to the core in owning it to be delusion if on further scrutiny he was so convinced. He was continually asking questions of himself while considering his problems. He had a constitutional tolerance which enabled him, as his sonnet to Sainte-Beuve brings out, to "pray with saints yet press the sinner's hand." Though blessed with sanity and a financial competence inherited from his mother, he could turn the shield and murmur "I sometimes wish I had the courage and the character to be a rebel myself." The wistfulness in this instance was à propos of Thomas Paine, the rebel; but on the threshold of his career the same capacity to sympathize with both sides is illustrated by his confession in *Saints and Sinners*, the book published on the eve of his death. He was writing of St. Francis d'Assisi, and the context runs:

"When I was twenty and was engaged to be married, my love and I came to see the world for the time something as Saint Francis saw it. We, too, felt that we should give up luxury and wanting, should discard the comforting equipment of material life, to which we were accustomed, but of which so many millions were destitute, and adopt voluntary poverty for the good of the world and our own souls. As a letter of that time expresses it: 'We should give up everything, live not only simply, but in poverty, with the poorest of clothes and the simplest of food, giving up everything material, everything tending to outward things, not because we want to be ascetic, but because we will have nothing to draw us from the life within and because we want to set an example of forgetting all the luxuries and comforts of the body. We want to build a little house somewhere, perfectly plain and poor, and live there in every way just as peasants would live.'

"We were twenty, and simple, and foolish. Our parents and relatives and friends ridiculed us and scolded us and reasoned with us, and in the end forced us to let our ideals go —for better, for worse?—I wonder." . . .

It has been well written since Bradford's death that his "whole life was the triumph of a brilliant intellect over a frail body." He himself has set down that he "was educated by ill health, by a vagrant imagination and by vast, vague and utterly erratic reading." It is true that he was forced by lack of vitality to withdraw from Harvard at the end of the third week of his Freshman year, and that though his soul was in study and creative writing, he tried for a while to interest himself in his father's business. But his natural bent overcame all obstacles, and after a marriage to the girl of his heart, whom he had known from childhood, he settled down within the limits of tastes which they had in common to a life of letters. Although this decision continued forever to isolate him from the world of surface affairs, the quality of his tastes bore witness to the truth of Shakespeare's warning: "Keep up your bright swords, or the dew will rust them." He was devoted to music and no mean performer; he followed with zest in the company of his neighbors the beauties of nature and the literature of all ages; it was out of his weekly habit of reading with a group of friends the plays of the great dramatists and discussing them that the power of disintegrating character which made him famous was conceived.

Spirits are not finely touched but to fine issues. His was a "fight for glory," as he has himself recorded with peculiar frankness. Recognition was slow in coming. He wrote many poems, eight novels, of which three were published and five rejected. Turning to play writing, he completed some fifteen plays. Of these one was printed, but not a single one produced. "My creative work," he wrote, "has failed from my utter lack of contact with the surface of life." Yet he could sing valiantly:

> My prose is for others,
> My songs for myself.
> The slow dust that smothers
> My Poems on the shelf
> Inflicts on my haughty
> And insolent nerves
> The treatment such naughty
> Exposure deserves.
>
> My prose is decorous,
> Or strips other men,
> Discreetly sonorous
> On things that have been.
> My verse tears the curtain
> From shuddering me,
> Pale, haggard, uncertain,
> As souls should not be.
>
> My prose is large, sunny,

And pleasant to touch;
It brings me some money,
Though, damn it, not much.
My verse bares my pocket
As well as my heart;
Yet, love it, or mock it,
To sing is my art.

When success arrived with the appearance in 1912 of *Lee, the American,* he was fifty years old. This biography not only brought him fame, but determined the course of his subsequent output. With but three exceptions, Mr. Bradford for the remaining twenty years of his life kept ardently, if a little unwillingly, to the field of what he chose to call psychography. He had found an eager and loyal public, and its applause was a stimulus to the production of that gallery of portraits—more than a hundred in all—which followed. There was no affectation in what he wrote to a friend as late as 1928: "I do envy you, though, your work of direct creation. I like to tell myself at more enthusiastic moments, that there is a certain element of creation in what I do. But there is a lot of pure drudgery that has to go with it that I do not much care for. What I revel in is the pure joy of making characters out of my brain; but, alas, I never have been able to make one that others reveled in at all. I wish I knew how you do it. If I did, I would never do anything else."

With more conviction another passage written to the same friend less than a year before his death sets in relief both his enthusiasm and his own conception of his aim. "This fascinating problem and puzzle of human nature! I am plunging into it more deeply than ever with the book upon which I am perhaps most rashly embarking, *Saints and Sinners,* a collection of extreme types of vice and virtue, from which I am trying to distil the essential humanness common to all of us. I have already done Caesar Borgia and Saint Francis and am just now entirely absorbed with Talleyrand, meaning to follow him with à Kempis, Fénelon, Casanova, and Byron.

You see what a precious, delicious medley, and I am so wickedly, or curiously, organized that I find one lot about as fascinating as the other. I only wish I had more life and strength for tackling them."

Bradford was able to compress into a single paragraph the tolerant, dispassionate yet ever exacting attitude of mind which brought him an increasing host of grateful readers: "The art of the psychographer," so he writes, "is to disentangle the habits which combine to make character from the immaterial, unessential matter of biography, to illustrate by touches of speech and action that are significant, and by those alone, and thus to burn them into the attention of the reader, not by any means as a final or unchangeable verdict, but as something that cannot be changed without vigorous thinking on the part of the reader himself." He had won the affection of the South by his understanding portrayal of the personages of the Civil War. By the gallery of world figures contributed subsequently he secured international attention which was at its height when he died. His own blithe response to success must not overshadow, however, the wide erudition, thoroughness and exacting judgment which controlled every word he published. Nor can one exaggerate the patient disability under which he worked or the self-imposed power of concentration which kept him master of his forces. For periods all of his work was done in bed. His actual writing day under favorable conditions was never more than two hours, and during spells of fatigue and sleeplessness would be ten or fifteen minutes. Yet so ably did he husband his strength that he studied his subjects in the intervals, so could write rapidly at the typewriter,—for he rarely used a pen,— with the result that he never revised and seldom cancelled a word.

That Bradford had kinship with Sainte-Beuve and Lytton Strachey both in his purpose and method is hardly to be gainsaid. Though this has been too much dwelt on, it is to be remembered that he acknowledged his debt to the former by copious references in his notes to the authority of the great French critic, and that he dedicated his *Daughters of Eve* to his brilliant English contemporary. But though the vein was similar, his individuality is readily distinguished. Bradford was neither a cynic and bitter, nor was he a devastating satirist. Ironic he could be, if either his sense of justice or standard of values were offended, but it was the irony of one seeking to qualify, not to overwhelm, and his pen though diamond-pointed had no barb.

This almost Janus-like quality of open-mindedness, often conveyed at the end of his psychographs by a wistful epigram of extenuation of the lost or defeated soul, was just as noticeable when one talked with him. He was a most delightful companion, fluent of speech and never without an opinion, but always tolerant of what others thought, as if he were eager to own that when the best was said for what passed for truth life still remained a puzzle. This temper of mind radiated too a gaiety which lying always just below the surface welcomed the opportunity to become sparkling merriment in congenial company.

It was significant too that one whose body was so frail should have such zest in life. He was intensely engrossed by the why and wherefore of the creature man and by his own ego which aspired to know. Orthodox explanations of the future were never for him infallible. As late as 1924 he wrote:

"Meantime, the world, as I see it, seems to me to need desperately some form of religion; but I am in no position to suggest one, having none of my own. I have groped and wandered through years of vague speculation and have finally abandoned the abstract for the passionate study of concrete individualities, which are inexhaustible in interest and charm. The only inconvenience is that one has, after all, an individuality of one's own, which will not be wholly nor always appeased by the objective, but cries out most inconveniently for some solution of the eternal problems. And no solution comes." It was characteristic, however, of the intensity which kept him so young in heart that he should express the wish for parts of *Adonais* to be read at his funeral. Who among the mourners filling the little chapel but felt these immortal stanzas to be singularly appropriate to the inquiring spirit that had passed:

> Peace, peace! He is not dead, he doth not sleep!
> He hath awakened from the dream of life.
>
> *
>
> He has outsoared the shadow of our night.
> Envy and calumny and hate and pain,
> And that unrest which men miscall delight,
> Can touch him not and torture not again.
> From the contagion of the world's slow stain.
> He is secure:
>
> *
>
> He lives, he wakes—'tis Death is dead, not he;
> Mourn not for Adonais—thou young Dawn,
> Turn all thy dew to splendour, for from thee
> The spirit thou lamentest is not gone!
>
> *
>
> He is made one with Nature. There is heard
> His voice in all her music, from the moan
> Of thunder to the song of night's sweet bird.

GARI MELCHERS
BY CHILDE HASSAM

Some members of this Academy have spent so many years in Europe, going there early for the supposed advantages of the schools, that they are almost accounted Europeans.

It was indeed thought, fifty years ago, that one had to go to Europe to get an education in the Fine Arts. So it is not strange that Sargent, Whistler, Pennell and Henry James spent the greater part of their lives in Europe.

These men were all intensely American. We know that Whistler, Sargent and Pennell were, and I have no doubt that Henry James was. A good many Americans sympathized with his magnificent gesture towards the mother country England during the war. It is perhaps just the thing an artist would do!

There is a deeply rooted belief in the minds of many that, we being a "new country," the arts of painting and music are undeveloped here. But we are not a "new country," in the sense of civilization, for ours is as old as Europe's to the last tick of the clock. We inherit the traditions of our forbears; their achievements belong to us as much as they belong to Europe, for we are Europeans; our languages in the Americas are European languages; our art is European, wholly European, and can nowise be anything else.

A very able librarian organized and built up a splendid library in Newark. He was engaged in other cultural activities and gave exhibitions of paintings—native art. He came to the conclusion, actually knowing nothing about painting, that the most important contribution to American Art was made by the obscure and untrained painters and print makers, mostly lithographers, though there were some wood blocks— often printed in color. In this way he made his contribution to modernistic obscurantism, and whether he knew it or not he helped to foster the cult of the incompetent, now known as the Ellis Island School. Cortissoz had years ago called these European absurdities Ellis Island Art. It is now a school and it tears down, or rather tries to tear down, all of the older established art, quite like the Italian futurist who decided that the only way to progress was to burn down all of the European Art Museums. They point to a French caricaturist and distortionist who painted very few canvases, but who made literally thousands of caricatures and drawings, as the greatest artist of the nineteenth century. It is so easy to make the caricatures and distortions that they are still doing it, but not one of them can do a competent technical performance in painting, let us say in bad smooth painting, like a Bouguereau, for Bouguereau, however bad as an artist, was a competent and sound technician in bad smooth painting; not that I think for one minute that bad smooth painting is any worse than bad rough painting; the so-called strong painting with the coarsest texture is just as bad if not worse, as it is more confusing to the eye at the first glance. However this may strike you, I think that this man and his like—he has left some understudies—having carefully confused the issue at the start, are responsible for the mural decorations that have just been put up in a public building in Detroit, the native city of Gari Melchers, to whom I am to pay this short tribute here today.

This distinguished member of the American Academy of Arts and Letters might almost be accounted a member of that group of famous men of whom I spoke at the beginning, but he like Pennell came back to America in 1914 and spent the last twenty years of his life here. For he was an American; his father Joseph Melchers came from the stock that has given us some of the very best Americans, one of the German revolutionists of 1848. A sculptor and decorator, he made his way to Detroit, married an American, settled in the small town and taught in the early Art Schools.

Gari Melchers was born in Detroit August 11th, 1860. His unusually wise father sent him to Europe at the age of seventeen, so that he might have all the advantages he himself had enjoyed. Wise—he had been in the Paris schools—he sent his boy to Düsseldorf.

It was thought absolutely essential to begin early in life to study the Fine Arts. As we glance backward, there was the boy Van Dyck, the most striking instance of beginning early, and one of the finest examples of fruition. He was apprenticed to a painter in an Antwerp studio at the age of ten, which means, though not actually, that he was a pupil of Rubens at that early age and as he became later in fact.

No other American painter except John Sargent, who was born in Florence, had earlier privileges of study in what was then considered, if not now, the best of the European schools

and in the art centers of Rome, Paris, Munich and Düsseldorf—to name them in their rank of that period. The schools
of London were just as good, no doubt better than any, but
London was not the fashion in art schools for some obscure
reason. There was that persistent patter about the Latin race
though there never was any such race in the world. The
whole modern movement of that time in painting was due to
English artists, Constable, Girtin, Turner, Bonington and
all the English water color painters who were the first to work
out of doors with a clear palette; the very medium called for
clarity with its white paper, and no oil and varnish to turn
dark brown. It was not French, it was English, but the
French profited and learned from it. The so-called Barbizon
or French school of 1830 was due entirely to John Constable.
Equivalent and contemporary to what Wordsworth and the
English poets did with words and a clear and simple vision in
looking at nature, it was another new note of clarity and truth.

You cannot account for fashion, or any of the present vagaries in the arts. If we could we should all of us be able to tell
you why a Mexican is permitted to put up in a public building in Detroit the most astonishingly distortionate mural
decorations—to use a polite euphemism to so describe them.

If I again use this dark shadow in this paper it is to contrast
with the bright geniality and unusual humanity, amounting
to popularity among his fellows, of this good painter and
essentially kindly man. To come to his career, and the wisdom on the father's part that sent his son of seventeen to the
fine old town of Düsseldorf where the boy was as well
grounded in the rudiments of his art as he could have been
anywhere. If it were all to do right over again, could it be done
better? It was better than Paris! Now you would hold him
here!

Today, coming back to mere fashion and caprice in the
arts, there is nothing so dead as the Düsseldorf school, unless
it may well be Munich. Rome is dead enough and Paris is
going on the way.

Paris, fifty years ago, where the young man next took up his always serious study, was a very different place from the Paris of today. You could not then take your visiting card and affix it to a plain panel in the Autumn Salon, make a few free brush marks around it with the primary colors, and be acclaimed a genius who invents his own forms and has no need to look at poor old Nature. As always, you were surrounded with poor painting—the Paris Salon always was and continues to be the largest and worst exhibition in the world; the Autumn Salon is more shocking but actually no worse. But there was good painting being done, the French themselves little suspecting it, any more than they suspected or supported their two great men of 1830—Corot and Millet. The one sold his first picture at the age of fifty-five, his old father's surprise in an extant letter is on record; and had it not been for the Boston painter, William M. Hunt, the other would have starved to death.

Good painting was being done by a Dutchman, Jongkind; the American, Whistler; a South American, Pissarro; an Englishman, Sisley; and notably by several Frenchmen. French painting was at its best but it took the French over forty years to find it out, just as it took them fifty years to find out that Corot was a figure painter, and one of their best figure painters. You may not have noticed, but it is none the less a fact, that Whistler and Sargent are now claimed by the British school, as Sisley and Pissarro are claimed and listed as French.

The father's sound sense and good judgment bore fruit in the fact that this young man just of age had his first success, and was noticed and rewarded in Paris. This almost immediate recognition marked him as a painter of large achievement. It was official to be sure, but possibly nowhere else could he have had just that stamp put upon his work.

It should not be forgotten that a young man growing up and making his first successes in a city that was a world center had the advantage of making pleasant contacts with other artists, absorbing their enthusiasms and ideals. Out of something of this kind came the admirable art motto "Waar en Klaar" (true and clear), that he put over his studio door in Holland.

Truth and clarity ever bear away the victory. It makes one think at once of the many fine portraits by Frans Hals made at Haarlem, not far away. In fact nothing in the way of fine private and public collections was far away from this little town on the North Sea where Melchers was to paint many of his best canvases in the old small simple churches, and where he was to spend his last pleasant summer—at work.

There can never have been many young men who had such free contact with the masterpieces. In looking at those of Hals, he must have thought that their very name was lucidity; and so true are they that no one ever thought of a mere question of their truth.

He was in the birthplace of painting in oil, the principal medium of expression for the painter ever since the days of van Eyck. He could read his Fromentin, *Maîtres d'Autrefois,* and about that other great Dutchman who had done his life's work in Amsterdam not far away. Whatever other qualities you may write or read into Rembrandt, and with which we would no doubt all of us agree, in "Waar en Klaar" Hals has never been surpassed. As Fromentin very truly says, "Nobody ever painted more easily or better, and nobody ever will."

This was in effect the art creed of Melchers, and that he followed it throughout a long life was apparent in the splendid exhibition of his work held here in the Academy of Arts and Letters. He has pictures that hang permanently in most of the Museums of the world. No one has perhaps received more medals and honors than he. He lived in Holland, Germany, Italy, France and America over extended periods. He made various visits to America to do portraits, and to make mural paintings in the Library of Congress and at the World Fair in Chicago before coming here to live permanently in 1914.

GARI MELCHERS

He was tolerant of men and manners, most tolerant of his fellow artists and only intolerant of sham, mildly impatient of the insincerity of many if not most of the modernistic canvases, which he knew would not last out another decade. He was very appreciative of other living painters' work. He greatly admired John Twachtman, J. Alden Weir and Eakins, to mention his American contemporaries only. He had many friends in France and Germany amongst the painters and greatly admired the work of the good painters of the period.

Being an honest and masculine man himself, his humanity was only impatient with the incompetent. Even at that he was more patient than most good men are. He felt keenly the misfortunes of his fellows and willed that his estate finally be dedicated to the Artists' Fellowship fund.

As surely as there are various kinds of bad painting there are various kinds of good painting. As I see it I am to speak in appreciation of the kind of good painting that Melchers did. No involutions, no circumlocutions, no abstractions, far, very far from any distortions. Frank, masculine and direct, well composed and constructed, a natural and very true clear color scheme, often in a cool suite of greys, and a fine grey picture is as much of an achevement as a most gorgeously colored one,—true, clear and cool like a Vermeer.

Every true aesthetic is an implication of nature. Something of nature is inevitable in any painting that is not a geometrical abstraction. If music is sublimated mathematics, should one begin by the study of cacophony though it be a recognized part of a musical composition? And in the most important language in the modern world, with the most splendid literature in any one language known to man, should one begin by studying the obscure dialect of the North American Indians? The absurdity of the cult of the incompetent is brought out into the full light of day when we contrast the results of that cult with the achievement of Melchers.

To sum up, his work was so sound and sane and clear that if we could come back and look at these pictures three hundred years from now (we are that distance away in time from the great Dutch masterpieces) we should see them as they are today; and I will end by saying that his very last picture was one of the very best canvases that he ever did, and a fine performance for any painter anywhere.

He must have firmly believed in Menzel's dictum on the encouragement of Art—for it is the classic answer to those who think that mere money and museums can help Art, "You may help artists in many ways but only artists can help Art."

JOHN CHARLES VAN DYKE

BY HAMLIN GARLAND

Although I had been meeting John Van Dyke for many years in New York at the Authors' Club and at the dinners of the National Institute of Arts and Letters, I had only a vague notion of his origin and his career. I thought of him as a native of New York, an art critic and historian with no especial interest in the West. He first claimed keener interest by the publication of a small volume called *The Desert*. In this fine book he entered my field. I at once recognized the truth of his observations and the beauty of his interpretations.

When next I met him I asked him how he got his material for this book. "You must have lived on the sand and camped besides the cactus clumps among horned toads and rattlesnakes." He replied, "I did. I went out into that country for the benefit of my health, and to amuse myself, or rather to occupy my time I studied the climate and the fauna and flora of my surroundings."

This led to the discovery that he had lived as a youth in Minnesota at Wabasha on the upper Mississippi River and that he had made studies of the Sioux and other tribes whom

I had visited and of whom I had written. In short, so far from being merely the art critic and the librarian of Rutgers College, he was a traveler who had roamed widely in Western America and knew the life and the landscape of many states. No one had written a better book on the desert than his and when he announced a companion monograph called *The Sea,* I hastened to obtain it. I found in it the same power of description and similar directness of vision.

These two essays, for they are hardly more than essays, won my outspoken admiration and led to a better understanding and a more intimate friendship. Of his controversy concerning the spurious Rembrandts I knew little, although in the Louvre he pointed out to me certain true and false canvases. I knew enough of the sea and its moods to find in his descriptions of wave and sky something of the same vivid pictorial power and much of the essential poetry which had so delighted me in his desert essay.

In his later life he bought a house in Onteora and became my next-door neighbor during the summer and many were the discussions we had on art, war, politics, literature, red men and pioneers. We dwelt oftenest I think on the beauty of the old-time prairie and gave much time to analyzing the qualities which the wilderness had developed in our fathers. He looked the part of a Western pioneer, for he was of heroic figure, six feet in height and nobly proportioned, graceful and powerful, much the fashion of man I conceive Hawthorne must have been.

Each winter of his later years he left New York and wandered far among "faery islands forlorn" and each spring he brought to us the manuscript records of his travels. The West Indies, the East Indies, Egypt, Java, Sumatra, each of these regions yielded a series of delightful sea-scapes and many colorful sketches of life and character. In truth, he was always the painter in his descriptions. He never blundered with his color and his sense of values was as subtle as it was accurate.

His interest in the Academy was keen and we often conferred on matters concerning its works and membership. His advice was sound and constructive and as an officer in the National Institute of Arts and Letters he was always for action.

I once visited him in his office in Sage Library and at his home which overlooked his boyhood valley, the valley of the Raritan in New Jersey, just to the east of New Brunswick, where he labored for many years. He told me that this valley and the marshes opposite his door had furnished the material for a third monograph called *The Meadows*. In this old-fashioned dwelling he lived for many years alone with an elderly housekeeper to maintain a certain degree of order in his life but in Onteora he had the companionship of a beloved niece and her understanding husband, Walter Parr of Columbia University.

The painter and the poet were strongly evident in all that he spoke or wrote and the walls of his library could not confine his body, much less his thought. His hunger to know the world increased with years. He loved the good old Earth and he especially loved his home up there on the heights (more than two thousand feet above the Raritan) and often as I passed his gate, I could see him sitting on his porch looking out toward the hills darkening against the sunset. At such times he resembled a gray old eagle who, having flown far over the sea, had come back to rest upon his native crag. His eyes at such times had the look of one who remembers with regret the far away islands of the West. I am sorry that I did not oftener join him on that pleasant porch.

1933

HENRY VAN DYKE
BY JOHN HUSTON FINLEY

Henry van Dyke was first of all and foremost the preacher, though a man of "many tasks of different kinds," done all with high distinction and supreme grace—a preacher and a teacher, poet, diplomat, fisherman, yet ever a preacher whose voice (in Tennysonian phrase) the "rolling air" still keeps in the memory of the living. And he was a doughty fighter in these several fields: in the pulpit, in the press, in the stream, in the lecture room, in public affairs.

In his later years when occupying the chair of English Literature in Princeton University he was wont to speak of himself as a "teacher of reading." He who is truly able to teach reading and incite a love of it, as he did, "should have rank," as some one has said, "at the head of the entire teaching faculty." Virginia Woolf says in her *Second Common Reader,*

> I have sometimes dreamt that when the day of Judgment dawns and the great conquerors and lawyers and statesmen come to receive their rewards—their crowns, their laurels, their names carried indelibly upon imperishable marble—the Almighty will turn to Peter not without a certain envy when He sees us coming with our books under our arms: "Look, these need no reward. We have nothing to give them here. They have loved reading."

I have here the "dummy" of a little book which I myself printed, entitled *Books, Literature and the People,* a discourse which he made at the first meeting of the National Institute of Arts and Letters. There is time for only two short paragraphs in definition of literature:

> Every one knows what books are. But what is literature? It is the

ark on the flood. It is the light on the candlestick. It is the flower among the leaves: the consummation of the plant's vitality, the crown of its beauty, and the treasure-house of its seeds.

Literature is made up of those human writings which translate the inner meanings of nature and life, in language of distinction and charm, touched with the personality of the author, into artistic forms of permanent interest. The best literature, then, is that which has the deepest significance, the most perfect style, the most vivid individuality, and the most enduring appeal to the human mind and heart.

Henry van Dyke was most widely known as a lover of nature—of forest and stream, mountain and sea. But with all his love of the out-of-doors, he was a man of the city. Even in his *Out-of-Doors in the Holy Land* he sings his Psalm of Great Terrestrial Cities, as John sang of the Celestial City in the solitude of Patmos. "How wonderful are the cities that man has builded," he exclaims—

Their names are like mighty enchantments. . . . They shine from far, sitting beside the great waters. . . . They spread out their splendor along the rivers. . . . Yet every one of them is full of trouble and toil. . . . And their makers run to and fro within them. . . . Abundance of riches is laid up in their store houses. . . . Yet they are tormented with fear of want. The cry of the poor in their streets is exceeding bitter.

And then he exclaims: "O God of wisdom, Thou hast made the country. Why hast Thou suffered man to make the town?" God's answer as he heard it, was: "Surely I am the maker of men. And in the heart of man I have set the city."

He did not, when first called to the City of New York, decline, as did the prophet Jonah when commanded to go to Nineveh, "that ancient great city." Nor did he sit in an academic booth, as did Jonah, to see what would become of the city, when it had not done all that the preacher had demanded of it. This city was indeed set in his heart and though he spent his later years outside of it, he was ever turning his face toward it and considering its salvation. He was man of the multitudes as well as of the solitudes. He sought the latter not to escape from responsibility but to prepare himself to serve the former with greater joy and power. Voices may cry in the wilderness but they must reach the cities before their gospel can become a great moving spiritual force in the world. Euripides said that it was requisite to one's happiness to be born in a famous city. That is no longer true, if ever it was. Yet it is significant that the place of ultimate happiness is pictured as a city.

But he was, too, a world-citizen, known and beloved of many peoples. The Netherlands received him proudly as minister from the New Netherlands. France remembers him as a lecturer in her universities. Britain gave him her highest academic degrees. But above all he was a pilgrim-citizen of the world. In one of his poems he wrote:

> Thou hast taken me into the tent of the world, O God,
> Beneath thy pavilion I have found shelter.
> Therefore thou wilt not deny me the right of a guest.

And the Lord of the Tent made answer:

> In this tent of the world I will be brother to thy bread
> And when thou farest forth I will be thy companion forever.

In the season when the tulips used to bloom in Union Square we remember how weary seemed to him the parade, how weary books and weary trade and how he wished for fishing, for which the month of May was made. But, after all, that was but his brief avocation, his "off days." He was first and last a "fisher of men," and, as was happily said by the New York *Sun*, St. Peter must have given him special and a double welcome.

A "minister" he was in the noblest import of the word, a "minister of God," a minister of his country, to which he gave distinguished service in the administration of his some-time neighbor, Woodrow Wilson, a minister of humanity in his eloquent spoken and written word.

He sent me his last poem (and when he wrote it he said to his son that it would doubtless be his last, as it proved to be) addressed to the President of the United States, "To Our

New Pilot," and published only three weeks before Dr. van Dyke's death. As a Lieutenant-Commander in the Navy during the War, and as the teller of the tale of *Gran' Boule*, he knew the language of the sea and ships. It is his last word to his country and his captain, beginning

> O Pilot, in this dim, distressful day
> Called to the helm, let nothing you dismay!

Nearing port at eighty, last November at the Academy meeting, as you may recall, he said of life that it was "well worth the cruise." And no doubt what he said of the Other Wise Man he would have said of himself: that if he could live his earthly life again he would not have it otherwise than it had been. At any rate, that is what we, in gratitude and praise, would say today.

Of all that he wrote I should wish to have written the poem "The White Bees" which he read to me before its publication and in it (as I re-read it after his death) I found lines that sing what I should wish to have written as his epitaph:

> Friendliness and blessing followed in his footsteps;
> Happier were the dwellings wheresoe'er he came;
> Little children loved him and he left behind him in the hour
>   of parting
> Memories of kindness and a godlike name.

IRVING BABBITT

BY HENRY DWIGHT SEDGWICK

FROM TIME TO TIME men rise up full of purpose to make the good life more accessible to all men; some of them act from ambition, conscious or unconscious, some from coiled energy within, some from the stimulus of serving a large cause, and most plunge headlong into action; only a few set themselves apart to study, to think, to reason, only a very few consecrate themselves by a long vigil, as it were, beside their arms. Without the incentive of religious belief such self-discipline is rare. Of this scanty band Irving Babbitt was one. He believed that there were deteriorating forces in the world —in the United States, in democracy, in Harvard University—and that it was his business to combat them; and, as we all know, his formula of battle was the great tradition of Humanism.

During the long flow of European history many high causes have come and gone, leaving behind them as their most abiding monument the memory of the zeal and generous purpose by which they were upheld and defended, and I think that we may be sure that, whatever fate befall this doctrine of Humanism, the name of Irving Babbitt will be remembered as that of a man who bore himself like a crusader. "One should not be moderate," he says, "in dealing with error." His books are so many combats, all full of honorable contention, *Literature and The American College* (1908), *The New Laocoon* (1910), *The Masters of Modern French Criticism* (1912), *Rousseau and Romanticism* (1919), *Democracy and Leadership* (1924); and in his chair at Harvard College for nearly forty years he manifested the same zeal, the same generous purpose.

These books, I am ashamed to say, I had never read till lately, and I was hardly well in them when, following that tendency that a truant mind too readily follows, my thoughts became more absorbed in the spirit behind the ideas than in the ideas themselves, and there flashed into my mind the memory of the charming verses in the *Hartsreise* in which Heinrich Heine describes his visit to a charcoal burner's hut. The old people have withdrawn themselves, and the poet sits talking in front of the fire with their little daughter. His emotions have been touched by the quiet of the mountain top, by the solemn forest, by the pious simplicity of these mountain folk, and he is troubled because the little girl suspects his Christian piety. So he explains to her that even as a little boy he believed in God the Father, and later on in God the Son, and at last also in God the Holy Ghost. You remember the scene. The girl gazes at him with wondering eyes, while he tells her how the Holy Ghost is engaged in the hard task of purifying the world and how thousands of knights ride forth to fight under His command. And as the poet's emotions rise at the thought of the Holy Ghost he bids the girl look at him, and not be afraid, for he himself is one of the knights of the Holy Ghost.

> Nun, so schau mich an, mein Kindchen,
> Küsse mich und schaue dreist!
> Denn ich selber bin ein solcher
> Ritter von dem heil'gen Geist!

From what I hear of Irving Babbitt, he always acted as if he, too, were a knight in the service of a great power for good, which he would not have called the Holy Ghost, but "Our Higher Intuitions," "The Higher Will," or to quote his own words, "Positively one may define it as the higher immediacy that is known in its relation to the lower immediacy—the merely temperamental man with his impressions, and emotions and expansive desires—as a power of vital control (*frein vital*)." This definition is admirably expressive of his own self-controlled, puritanical character.

I use the word puritanical, and yet I do not wish to be misunderstood. A Puritan Irving Babbitt appears in his books, very serious, a little stern, but those that knew him personally did not find him so. In conversation he allowed himself a freedom which he denied himself when writing; then, he let himself run into picturesque exaggerations, he was witty, humorous, brilliant, full of ideas, stimulating. Young men delighted to go for a walk with him and hear him talk. But to that side of him I cannot do justice, as I did not have the honor to know him, and so I return to his achievement.

As I have said, Irving Babbitt was troubled at heart by the deficiencies and failures and misbehaviour of poor, wayward humanity, and he went to work to put right the matters that seemed to him the most out of joint. Some of us, I speak it to our shame, are content to stand aside and watch these human waywardnesses, as we do the course of tortuous rivers, with a sort of amused indifference. Not so he. He was a scholar, a profound scholar, one of the most erudite that America has produced, he stalked familiarly through ancient, mediaeval and modern literatures, seeking, selecting, analyzing, defining, and compacting the ideas that he wove into his doctrine of Humanism, in order to provide all those that would accept it a high and healing philosophy of life.

The doctrine of Humanism varies to a certain degree, I suppose, according to the predilections of those that entertain it. It hails from the scholars of the Renaissance who interested themselves in the classical civilization, with its comparative indifference to the supernatural and its emphasis upon the dignity of man. Aristotle had laid stress upon the line of separation between the rational man, who recognizes the authority of reason, and the instinctive man who obeys his impulses, and he had asserted that man's chief good does not lie in mere animal existence, but in the recognition of the lordship of reason, in the supremacy of intellect and will. After long ages, this rational man of Aristotle's reviving during the Renaissance, and continuing on, gradually evolved into the Humanist with his Aristotelian qualities, enlarged and elaborated. As I understand it, this doctrine lays down three categories. The category to the right includes those who believe in a supernatural order, who tend to subordinate reason to faith, and diminish man's human importance by regarding his life on earth as a mere fragment of a larger existence. The category to the left contains a more varied company. It includes those who disregard the cleavage which Aristotle marked between man the human being and man the animal, those who disregard Emerson's pronouncement that there is a law for man and a law for thing, those who, absorbed in scientific specialties, look upon humanity as of the same stuff as the substances they study in their laboratories, and all those who treat man as part and parcel of the natural order; it includes humanitarians, who pay tithe of mint and anise and cummin to men's physical needs and neglect the weightier matters of the will and intellect; it includes romanticists, who give loose rein to sensation, sentiment, sympathy, instinct, temperament, and in general all one-sided people who float along on the flux of phenomena.

In the path between these two categories walk the Humanists, head erect, creatures of will and intellect; they believe in a well-rounded life, in discipline and self-restraint, in the golden mean; they avoid the excess of supernaturalism to the right and of naturalism to the left, they value form, measure, proportion, discrimination, selection; they seek the permanent in the whirl of change, reality in the mists of illusion, unity in multiplicity; and, more than all else, as the foundation stone of their philosophy, they believe that there is in man "a restraining, informing and centralizing power that is anterior to both intellect and emotion," and that this power, this Higher Will, should hold a tight rein over man's loose, wandering, uncharted desires, should be a law-enforcing policeman to all such physical rowdies. And they claim that the best traditions of the world are with them, that Confucius was one of them, that Sophocles, Aristotle, Cicero, Horace, Erasmus, were of them. In short the humanist stands on the dignity of human nature, on the creed that intuition reveals to him a Higher Will, and that he is capable of self-dedication to that Higher Will. But in order to do this men need standards that are set above individual caprice and the flux of phenomena. "We must (to quote his words) strive to get at standards positively and critically, and such striving might best be defined as Socratic, Aristotelian and Christian, and should put prime emphasis on definition, for the sake of clear thinking, on habit, for the sake of character, on humility, which is measuring oneself by high standards." And so, in this manner, he looks out beyond the little horizon that bounds the sight of ordinary men, up at high encircling mountains that he could see beyond.

I am sorry, I am no philosopher, I flounder in the flux of multitudinous impressions, and perceive no patterns but those of human experience, and, as you see, I cannot do this high ethical theory justice. Yet, as I look beneath the rich brocaded drapery of erudition with which Irving Babbitt presents his theory, what I do understand is this, that the humanist is very similar to what the Greeks called καλὸς κ' ἀγαθὸς and the English call an honorable gentleman. Babbitt himself says, "After all to be a good humanist is merely to be moderate and sensible and decent."

I repeat that through ignorance, or mental or moral indolence, or lack of intelligence, I do not go along with all that Babbitt says, but his teaching reminds me of the words spoken by Socrates to Charmides, and I seem to hear Irving Babbitt saying in his kind, dogmatic way, these same words to me: "Wisdom or temperance I believe to be really a great good . . . and I would advise you . . . to rest assured that the more wise and temperate you are, the happier you will be."

Humanism may, or may not, lead us into a promised land but the austere, firm, upright, puritanical personality of Irving Babbitt will always be a burning and a shining light.

CHARLES ADAMS PLATT
BY HERBERT ADAMS

IT WAS THE happy destiny of Charles Adams Platt to achieve eminence in three fields of art. This by itself was much, but this was not all. An etcher in his youth, a landscape painter in his early manhood, and an architect in his consummate final period, he had the added felicity of becoming a pioneer in two movements of high importance in the development of our national art. Both movements were democratic. One concerned itself with our dwelling-places and gardens; the other, with our museums.

His early work in architecture gave a vital and timely

impetus to the harmonious designing of a structure and its immediate surroundings to fit its allotted landscape, if any. The structure might be a little two-story home, or a lordly villa; a summer-house or an art library. He maintained that no matter how modest, no matter how monumental the design, a three-fold wholeness of beauty, order, and fitness should always be sought, and could almost always be found. We had indeed been fortunate in our landscape architects for many of our great public parks; but until Charles Platt created a few summer homes and gardens of thrilling beauty in Cornish, New Hampshire, under the benevolent eye of Mount Ascutney, in Vermont, we had hardly realized that the basic principles of landscape architecture could be happily domesticated at our own dooryards.

Perhaps we had foolishly imagined that such principles were the exclusive right of civic grandeur, or else of great riches. All very well, we said, for Versailles, or the Villa Lante, but not for us! Charles Platt, more abundantly than any other man of his day, showed us our error. And having produced half a dozen shining examples of house-and-garden beauty, in more or less simple guise, he thereupon created designs on a grander scale; designs now of private, now of public importance.

Enthusiastic appreciation of his work spread from New England and New York to the South, the Middle West, the Far West. His style was his own. It held within itself the best of that which is traditional, always provided that the tradition harmonized with his profoundly imaginative conception of the beautiful possibilities that might magically flower from a bare problem.

Certainly the movement for ordered beauty about our private dwelling places was democratic. No less so was the trend toward a higher fitness to purpose in planning our public museums of art. Thus an aristocrat (for in the noble root meaning of the word Charles Platt *was* an aristocrat) served the ends of democracy. The Freer Gallery in Washington was our first really notable example of an art museum designed from within rather than from without. We had many fine museum buildings antedating the Freer. Too often, however, our architects had stressed a grand exterior rather than a practical interior. A change of ideals was needed. Then came a fortunate circumstance. In designing the Freer Museum, so monumental without, so friendly within, Charles Platt the painter and Charles Platt the lover of fine craftsmanship stood at the elbow of Charles Platt the architect, never for a moment allowing him to forget that things of beauty must be thoughtfully placed and fitly lighted in order to be seen aright.

That "form should follow function" was to many a discovery; with him it was an instinct,—a feeling neither to be overlooked nor yet to be overworked. His plans for the new wing of the Corcoran Gallery are thoroughly practical. He was commissioned to make preliminary designs for our National Gallery, an enterprise still in abeyance. To this he gave much research and study.

After my forty years of cherished friendship with this great artist, I look back with unceasing wonder at his full half-century of achievement. The mere volume of work accomplished would have been remarkable in a man of robust physique, but our dear colleague's physique was never that. When people spoke to him of his success, he would often say, with his whimsical twist of eyebrow, "I was lucky." Doubtless his greatest piece of luck was that first, last, and always, he was an artist in every fibre of his being.

He was born in New York, in 1861, son of a distinguished lawyer. His mother belonged to the Cheney family, noted for the artistic manufacture of silks. When a young boy, he eagerly chose his career. There was never any doubt or hesitation. As a natural activity, he drew, he painted, he made cardboard models of houses and things. Excited by a visit to the studio of John Rogers, of Rogers group fame, he even went so far as to make plaster casts from life, from

hands and faces of obliging friends. However, later, a somewhat unsuccessful experiment on the countenance of Laurence Hutton, collector of life masks, completely dashed his
ardor for such adventures: Hutton had a mustache. But
"sculpture per se," as Charles himself would say, always held
his keen interest. In the various groups and statues in which
I had the joy and honor of his collaborations as to pedestal,
placing, and planting, he gave to each problem, however
modest, his best and richest thought.

His formal education in art began in the schools of the
National Academy of Design, and in the Art Students
League. He studied etching under Stephen Parrish, and at
twenty, produced a delightful plate, Gloucester Harbor. His
subsequent fame as an etcher is well known. In 1882 he
went to Paris, where he drew and painted under Boulanger
and Lefebvre. He took what he needed from these masters,
his own nature being in profound sympathy with the seriousness in study inculcated by both. At that time the Impres-
sionists were making many a dent in the academic armor.
He noted their thrusts, and balanced the good and ill of their
efforts. He profited by intercourse with the young students
in architecture. He painted in Holland, he traveled, he exhibited in the Paris Salons.

Returning home in 1887, he was at once welcomed into
the reasonably insurgent Society of American Artists and
other groups. He formed close friendships with the leading
artists of the day: Saint-Gaudens, Dewing, Brush, Thayer,
Walker, Cox, Alexander, Metcalf, Twachtman, Hassam; a
host! His fame as etcher and as painter increased; honors and
prizes were his. His next sojourn abroad was in Italy, where
with his brother William he made exhaustive studies in the
magic of Italian gardens, the majesty of Italian buildings.
The Renaissance rather than the Baroque charmed him.
Much of his scholarly research is embodied in his book on
Italian Gardens, published by Harpers in 1924.

From this period onward, all his previous studies became

his great gain in his architectural work. His mastery of light-and-dark in his etchings, his assured line-and-color composition in his landscapes were his willing servants. It is a mistake to say that he "took up" architecture. "Versatile" is far too flimsy a word to describe his endowment. And it was precisely because of his unusual endowment, joined to his unusual variety of artistic experience, that he was a power and a glory in our architecture. He loved beauty too deeply to overadorn a design. Yet with all his passion for beauty, he never forgot fitness to purpose. Hence the fine integrity, within and without, of his city structures, such as the Hanna buildings in Cleveland, and his New York houses,—designs of necessity developed without benefit of landscape background, yet with their own characteristic comeliness, as well as practical arrangement.

Some of his most impressive work is found today on campus grounds, as at the University of Illinois, at Deerfield, and at Phillips Academy, Andover, Massachusetts. At Andover he constructed anew, rearranged the old; and always in the spirit of the place. His chapel and art gallery are gems of loveliness. Fortunate indeed are the Andover students, to dwell in such an environment.

He was consulting architect for the new architectural development at Dartmouth College, and had much to do with the new Baker Library, and with making its beautiful setting at the head of the campus. For the sake of those who knew Mr. Platt's position at Dartmouth, and valued his opinion, I may state that he was *not* consulted as to the fitness of the much discussed Mexican murals, now covering some thousands of square feet of wall space in that library.

His integrity as man and artist knew no compromise, but controversy as such was distasteful to him. We think rather of the harmony of his life. We recall his unfailing generosity, his singularly lovable personality, his many-sided genius, his enduring contribution to our culture. On a door into a room of our New York Public Library is an inscription, "Art and

Architecture." As if the two were quite separate chapters in the story of art! In Charles Platt's work the two were one. He could never have been the architect he was, if he had not been the artist he was: dedicated to beauty, fitness, and order; and believing in the discipline which helps us to create these things.

1934

PAUL SHOREY
BY JOHN HUSTON FINLEY

THE NAME with which one most often associates that of
Paul Shorey is Plato's. The first product of Shorey's enthusiasm and study, which won for him his doctorate in the
University of Munich and carried him to a "position of
world authority" was a thesis under the title *De Platonis Ide-
arum Doctrina*. His last great contribution to the world's scholarship was his book entitled *What Plato Said*. In an airplane
journey to California nearly two years ago I carried with me
this volume and despite the cotton in my ears I could hear
Shorey repeating passages of Plato across the continent or making incisive comment upon them. And who would not be a
Platonist in heights where earthly things become, as Plato
contended, "shadows of ideas laid up in the House of God"?

I assume that Shorey must have been first of all a mathe-
matician or a geometrician, for it is remembered that Plato
had this inscription placed upon his door: Ἀγεωμέτρητος
μηδεὶς εἰσίτω ("Let no one who is not a geometrician enter.")
But if Shorey was not, I am sure that could Plato but have
heard his fine voice, speaking his own tongue with marvelous sense of rhythm, reading aloud the hexameters of
Homer, the lyrics of the dramatists or the lyric poets, he
would not have required of him even the demonstration of
the Pythagorean proposition. Dr. Shorey was like Chaucer's
Clerk of Oxenford in that he loved above all to teach, but
the books that Shorey had at his beddes' head were the books
not of Aristotle but of Plato. He was himself a Platonist in
the definition of Platonism that I recently came upon in a
book by an English scholar:

Platonism is a mood of one who has a curious eye for the endless variety of the visible and temporal world and a fine sense of its beauties, yet is haunted by the presence of an invisible and eternal world behind (or, when the mood is most pressing, within) the visible and temporal world, sustaining both it and himself, but inwardly lived by him as that with which in moments of ecstasy, or even habitually, he is become one.

Shorey was born in the Middle West town of Davenport, Iowa, was graduated from Harvard and was admitted to the bar in Chicago. But the practice of law made little appeal to him and he went to Germany to study. He himself said of Gildersleeve (in his address before the Academy eight years ago) what another might say of him: that he "was not dominated by the erudition of Germany."

He was, when he pleased, a scholar of the German type, but he never succumbed to the weakness of its more recent developments, the pyramiding of hypotheses and the suppositing of conjectures by misconstruing Greek. He knew Greek too well for that.

Shorey was one of that group of brilliant scholars whom Harper gathered about him in refounding the University of Chicago. He had spent several years in teaching philosophy and Latin at Bryn Mawr (and he later dedicated an edition of Horace to its alumnae), but to the Greek he gave himself to the end of his days, ranging "sympathetically and exactly," as one of his peers in learning has said, however, over the entire field of humanistic culture (both ancient and modern) which had its first home in Greece, where, as Dean Woodbridge has said, that "peculiar kind of curiosity" which we call "philosophy" began.

President Norlin, himself one of the foremost of Greek scholars and at the same time president of a great State University, the translator of the writings of Isocrates (who was called the "Old Man Eloquent" and the first great publicist of his day), speaking at the university service in tribute to Shorey, said that while he had himself sat under many distinguished scholars and lecturers both in this country and abroad, Shorey was the greatest teacher he had ever known. He had a catholicity of mind, a wealth of incidental allusions of the best thought in the world (he had a prodigious selective memory and a genius in mastery of languages: French, Greek, Latin, Swedish, Dutch, Italian, Spanish) and a "sparkling wit." We remember especially his charming words at the Virgilian celebration, when he began his address by saying: "We are met to celebrate the abiding power of poetry." He gave ever a sense of the "great fellowship of the human spirit through the ages." Here is his last will and testament concerning humanism:

The study of the human spirit that creates and dissolves all systems abides. And the study of the human spirit is not planetary or biological evolution or the anthropology of the pre-human man. It is neither the psychology of the laboratory nor the metaphysics of the school; it is neither science nor pseudo-science—it is humanism.

The prayer of Socrates must have daily been his:

Help that I may prosper in the inner man
And grant that what I have or yet may win
Of those the outer things may be akin
And constantly at peace with those within.
May I regard the wise, the rich, and care
Myself for no more gold, as my earth-share,
Than he who's of an honest heart can bear.

Like the scholar in Browning's *The Grammarian's Funeral*, he was "working against time." Like him who settled *Hoti's* business, properly based *Oun* and gave us the doctrine of the enclitic *De*, when death was creeping toward his heart ("Dead from the waist down"), so Shorey worked on even after the warning stroke came. There is a memory of the death of Socrates, as related by Plato, in Norlin's tribute to him:

O heart of gold, grown suddenly cold,
It was not time to go.

His last public address was a lay sermon spoken in the

chapel of the University of Chicago, afterward published in the *Atlantic*. Here is his last look back across the ages and then into the age about him:

There were eloquent immoralists at Athens. There were festivals in which instincts were unleashed and human nature sought relief from the restraint of conventional moralizing. There were comedies which travestied and made a mock of the gods. But literature as a whole was sane, and the greater classical writers were, as a whole, on the side of the angels. But I think any sober observer would be justified in saying that never in any literature has there been such a carnival of unreason and immoralism as that which disports itself in the print that most of us have been reading in the past twenty or thirty years and in the films that children have been looking at.

I can go no farther in this fragment of a tribute to his memory. So we leave him as he did those who bore Browning's grammarian to his high sepulture:

Leave him—still loftier than the world suspects.

CASS GILBERT

BY ROYAL CORTISSOZ

CASS GILBERT was born in Zanesville, Ohio, on November 24th, 1859. He died at Brockenhurst, Hampshire, in England, on May 17th, 1934. His long and distinguished career as an architect was begun back in the eighties, when practitioners of the art were confronted by more than one type of leadership. Richard Morris Hunt stood for both academic and romantic ideas of French origin. H. H. Richardson was committed to the Romanesque. McKim, Mead and White adopted classical motives as they had been filtered down through the Italian Renaissance. It was the last mentioned firm in association with which Gilbert launched himself, young, tall, handsome, and in his whole ebullient personality giving evidence of the character which was to win him authority and repute. He was to affirm himself through the realization of large, monumental conceptions.

These were destined to justify themselves through illustration of classical elements, handled broadly and boldly, but Cass Gilbert had more than one string to his bow and proved it, on occasion, with brilliance. In the Gothic Woolworth Building he gave free rein to his more exuberant impulses and exploited them so ably that this remains one of the vitalized architectural landmarks in New York, a singularly picturesque and impressive skyscraper in a city of skyscrapers. He could design also, in the vast structure for the U. S. Army Base, in Brooklyn, a building whose bare mass, austere lines and obvious practicality must commend it to the most exacting modern taste. Outstanding things like the building of the New York Life Insurance Company, on the site of the old Madison Square Garden, and the approaches of the Washington Bridge, are likewise of his versatile designing, yet his instinct for the column and the arch would not down. Antique precedent determined the nature of the buildings which counted so heavily in the development of his fame, such as the Minnesota State Capitol, the New York Custom House, the building of the United States Supreme Court at Washington. These achievements, especially that at Washington, possess the Roman amplitude and dignity which were the principal ingredients of Gilbert's art.

In 1931 the Society of Arts and Sciences gave him its gold medal for reasons which drew from him a reiteration of his faith in the skyscraper as a form of architecture. But the salient note which he struck on the occasion of this award was one which went deeper. He put in a plea for beauty and sincerity as the indispensable factors in the evolution of architecture. He held fast to an elevated ideal of art and labored not only as an architect but as an executive to maintain it. Never was any one more active in the promotion of organized artistic effort. In 1881 he and a handful of others founded the Architectural League. In 1908 he was chosen to head the American Institute of Architects. In 1926 he was made president of the National Academy of Design, the first architect in the history of the institution to fill that office —and most devotedly he filled it. Some years before, in 1914, he had been elected to the American Academy of Arts and Letters and at the time of his death was a member of its Board of Directors. To all these bodies, and to others, he brought enthusiastic and wise service.

I knew him over a long period of years and can well remember his stalwart presence and the energy that went with it. He was clever in little things, in the making of travel notes in water color, for example, but he was much more than clever in the fundamentals of his busy and constructive life. There he was a follower of the grand style, rising to the great opportunities offered to him to design buildings on an heroic scale, and the last impression he leaves is one of force, tempered by scholarship. He aided the cause of American Art generously and effectively. The recognition that came to him here and abroad was for work well done. He will be honorably remembered.

BRAND WHITLOCK

BY ROBERT UNDERWOOD JOHNSON

WHEN ON THE 11th of January, 1918, Brand Whitlock was elected a member of the American Academy of Arts and Letters, he was the youngest member of that body, being 49 years old. It may be interesting to recall here that eight members of the Academy (including myself) were particularly interested in his candidacy at the time, namely: W. D. Howells, John Burroughs, H. M. Alden, Augustus Thomas, A. Lawrence Lowell, Theodore Roosevelt, and Owen Wister.

His chief literary work had not been produced, but the quality of his writing was well known through his numerous novels written before that time, and he was recognized as a distinguished addition to its list. In turn, he was very proud of the honor and often spoke in appreciation of it, as the following incident shows:

While abroad, the sculptor De Vreese asked Whitlock to sit for him for a medal. De Vreese also extended a similar invitation to the Marquis de Villalobar, Ministre d'Espagne. The Marquis, as usual, posed with all of his decorations. Whitlock, modest American citizen, had not at that time been decorated, and confessed this to the sculptor. But he turned the lapel of his coat, indicated a small insignia—that of the American Academy of Arts and Letters—and said with pride, "That's enough."

Whitlock was born on the 4th of March, 1869, at Urbana, Ohio. His political inclinations however took him to Toledo where he became affiliated with Tom Johnson, a liberal public figure, and later he was elected Mayor of the City for four consecutive terms. In his first campaign, he was chosen without the support of a single local newspaper. A fifth election was declined by him, and soon after President Wilson nominated him for the post of Minister to Belgium.

While he was Mayor of Toledo, he took a trip abroad to familiarize himself with municipal institutions and criminal procedure in foreign countries. Not long after this tour, his well known volume *The Turn of the Balance* appeared.

One of the greatest of his many services to the City of Toledo was the purification of the water supply. During the contest in Congress for the water of the Hetch-Hetchy Valley which San Francisco ultimately obtained, Whitlock said to me, as recorded in my memoirs:

Why don't they employ the filtration system? When I was Mayor of Toledo we had our water from the dirty, yellow Maumee—as forbidding a source as could be found. We installed a filtration plant and obtained as good a quality of water as that of any other city in the world—so pure that the trained nurses in the hospital complained that they had no more typhoid cases to take care of!

314

His administration in Toledo was of a non-partisan type
and brought great attention to his public work which was
in the interest primarily of the people to whom he was devoted, and by whom he was greatly beloved. His character
in this work is indicated by a text which he underlined in
his Bible at the age of nine:

We then that are strong ought to bear the infirmities of the weak,
and not to please ourselves.

In saying goodbye to him, when he left for his post in
Brussels, Mr. Bryan, then Secretary of State, said:

You'll have nothing to do but rest and show Americans the battle-
field of Waterloo.

Who could have foreseen that Whitlock would for the
greater part of the War be in a storm center, unique in the
history of that conflict? He aided the Belgians in saving the
integrity of the City of Brussels and his firm stand for justice
and humanity has made him one of the foremost diplomatic representatives of his time. He had to make the most
important and urgent decisions on his own responsibility,
and he acted with promptness, tact, and firmness.

In the case of Edith Cavell, shamefully hurried to her
death for an offense that any other commander would have
treated with leniency in one who had been an angel of kindness to her nominal foes, Whitlock, ill in bed, did all he could
to avert the calamity.

Whitlock was a diplomat by chance, as it were, because
his friend, President Wilson, at the time himself very weary,
appointed him to the post in Belgium knowing that he would
have repose concerning that country with Whitlock representing America. He was not, however, unprepared for such
a post, for, as I have indicated, a number of years before the
World War he had made a trip abroad for the specific purpose of becoming acquainted with municipal institutions, so
that when President Wilson offered him the assignment at
Brussels, he accepted at once. Later, when the legation was

raised to the rank of an embassy, Whitlock was appointed our first Ambassador to Belgium. His entire diplomatic career was marked by phenomenal success because he was first and foremost an artist obeying his finer sensibilities, rather than the rigorous traditions of international law. He knew the Belgians, their history and their traditions, and he loved them.

After the conclusion of the World War, it remained for him to produce his magnum opus in literature—his life of LaFayette. A biographer must love his own subject, and Whitlock shows throughout this glowing work his admiration for the young Frenchman. Someone recently said that LaFayette was no hero because he took no risks. This absurd statement is refuted by the whole of the two volumes of the adventurous life of the Marquis, who, from the moment of his clandestine departure for America on his chivalric mission, to the very last of his imprisonment in Germany, showed his indifference to danger in his devotion to the country whose cause he had espoused and served devotedly as a youth. Whitlock's style is at its best in this work which, had we an Academy that crowned works of literature, should place above it the seal of its approval. It is, indeed, America's best tribute to LaFayette's glorious career and it does honor not only to the author, but to the American Academy of Arts and Letters.

Four volumes—*The Thirteenth District* (our greatest political novel at the time of its publication); *Forty Years of It; The Turn of the Balance;* and *Lincoln* were written in America. His other volumes were written either at Brussels, Le Havre or Cannes.

Whitlock's personal qualities were of such an engaging nature, that to rehearse them here would be to anticipate history. I have endeavored to do this suggestively in the following sonnet, which I modestly submit as part of this all too incomplete tribute.

> Why should tears fall if mine fall not for thee—
> Thou gentlest of the brave I ever knew,

Thou bravest of the gentle and the true,
Knight-errant of our modern chivalry;
Champion of her whom pitying dawn could see
At her last prayer; foe to the pitiless crew
That warred upon the weak, thou with the few
Fronting the swarming hosts of cruelty!
Noble thyself, what record thou hast made
Of nobleness, that keeps the world in heart
And shames us out of silence into speech—
Standing henceforth with LaFayette apart
Thou summonest the heavens to our aid
Bringing the star of glory within reach!

AUGUSTUS THOMAS

BY HAMLIN GARLAND

AUGUSTUS THOMAS was born in 1857 of a fine St. Louis family of moderate means, and early became a bread-winner for the family. As a page in the state legislature of Missouri and later in the House of Representatives at Washington he earned ninety dollars per month, all of which went to help out the folks back home. Passing from this to newspaper work, he had small opportunity for an academic education. He got his learning as he went along the road.

In the newspaper office he began to write plays, and from writing plays he naturally passed to the acting of them. The earlier years of his career were alternately spent in acting in other men's pieces and in struggles to produce his own. His first success came with *Alabama,* in 1891, a success which he confirmed by another local color piece called *In Mizzoura.*

Nothing like these plays had been done of the South West, although New England had produced *Way Down East* and *Shore Acres.* He continued in this vein by writing *Arizona* and *Colorado.* His distinction lies in work of this character although later in his career he won almost equal praise for two plays with psychical content, *The Witching Hour* and *As a Man Thinks.*

In his autobiography he tells us definitely that these two plays were based upon his experiences as a young advance man for Bishop, the mind-reader. He once said to me, "Bishop started me thinking of the hidden world." He also points out in *The Print of My Remembrance,* that his experiences as an actor on the road and as railroad clerk and newspaper reporter furnished him with a fund of dramatic material upon which he drew throughout his long life as a dramatist.

He wrote and saw the production of more than sixty plays, and these productions put him at the top of the American playwrights of his day. Whatever else critics may say of them, they were built of native material. They were of the new world, his world. Nearly all of them were wholly his own creation, but he dramatized several books—as in *Colonel Carter.* Five or six of them are of enduring quality, landmarks in the history of the American drama. *New Blood* and *The Copperhead* are serious studies of sociological material. Humorous character comedy, however, was his strong point.

Although following his career with keen interest I did not come to know him till in 1898 when Charles Dudley Warner, president of the newly formed National Institute of Arts and Letters appointed him with me on a committee, with instructions to draft a Constitution and by-laws for the organization. Our work on the committee led to a warm friendship which lasted throughout his life and led to many meetings of delight and profit to me.

He was at this time the conquering prince of the theater, handsome, witty, polished and dangerously suave. He was in high demand as an after-dinner orator, and his skill as a presiding officer was unexcelled. He knew everybody and met everybody with smiling, imperturbable humor. He carried himself with grace and natural dignity and his richly modulated voice was a delight to the ear. His spoken English was singularly free from any provincial stridency and his use of words was seldom wrong. His knowledge of French and German, his residence in France and England, and especially his association with the great actors of his day, had made him a shining exemplar of what American speech should be.

All this is the more praiseworthy when it is held in mind that he had at most no schooling of the customary sort, and that his education in writing and speech had been acquired along his busy and variant way. It was because of this noble blend of English and American "accent" that I asked him to serve with me on the committee which the American Academy had authorized and empowered to award a medal for good diction on the radio.

His mind was catholic in its interests and generous in its outgiving. I never knew a more alert intelligence. He had seen so much, read so much and done so much of vital interest that conversation with him was a delight. He was witty but never at the expense of pain in others. His humor was kindly. In our later years we spent many hours discussing literary problems and feeling our way along psychical paths —always to my advantage. I never talked with one more sympathetic in understanding or swifter in seizing upon my half uttered thought.

He spoke better than he wrote—or so it seemed to me. He would have made an admirable diplomat. He should have been sent to France or England where his polished oratory, his wide experience and his handsome face and figure would have presented to the old world the most admirable type of self-made man, original dramatist and tactful orator. He was representative of the best self-cultured new world intellectual aristocrats.

1935

GEORGE PIERCE BAKER
BY WILLIAM LYON PHELPS

GEORGE PIERCE BAKER was born on the fourth of April, 1866, at Providence; he was graduated at Harvard in 1887, the next year was appointed Instructor in English, was subsequently promoted to the Professorship, and taught at Harvard from 1888 to 1924, when he accepted a call to Yale as Professor of the History and Technique of the Drama, and Head of the new University Theatre. He retired owing to ill-health in 1933.

In 1907-1908 he was James Hazen Hyde lecturer in Paris at the Sorbonne.

He was elected a member of the Academy in 1925.

In addition to his academic work at Harvard and at Yale, Professor Baker himself wrote and directed historical pageants in various towns in America, which are a contribution to our social history.

His most important books are *The Development of Shakespeare as a Dramatist,* and *The Technique of the Drama.*

From early childhood to the day of his death Professor Baker's chief interest was the art of the drama, and its relations with the theatre. When he began teaching in 1888, there were no opportunities offered at any university for the study of modern drama; and for many years Mr. Baker spent the major part of his time and energy in teaching English Composition, especially in the field of forensics. He performed this difficult task not only conscientiously, but with such energy that he elevated it almost to the position of a creative art. There are hundreds and hundreds of Harvard graduates who remember with gratitude and affection this prolonged grind in argumentative composition; for they came in later years to realize its value.

Fortunately for all concerned and certainly for his own spiritual welfare, he was from the start given a course in Elizabethan Drama, which field he had mastered as a scholar and taught as an apostle.

When I entered the Harvard Graduate School in 1890, I took this course, so that I have the honor of being enrolled among his pupils.

When he began to teach the art of play-construction, he made an academic number famous all over America—the number 47. The 47 Workshop was the title of the course directed and taught by Professor Baker; it was an absolutely practical course in the writing and stage production of plays. Students travelled from every part of the United States to become his pupils; many called but few were chosen. The number was ruthlessly kept down and only the elect were admitted.

Among these were Eugene O'Neill, Sidney Howard, Philip Barry, S. N. Behrman, playwrights; Winthrop Ames, Maurice Wertheim, Theresa Helburn, George Haight, Henry Potter, Kenneth MacGowan, producers; many stage designers and dramatic critics, among whom is Walter Prichard Eaton. It should also be remembered that among those whom he advised *not* to write plays are Heywood Broun and Thomas Wolfe.

From this 47 Workshop flowed a spirit of passionate enthusiasm for the theatre, incarnate in many young students, who devoted their lives to it.

> Bliss was it in that dawn to be alive,
> But to be young was very heaven!

It is interesting to remember that the years of Professor Baker's career included the greatest period of British drama since the death of Shakespeare and the only period of importance in American drama.

The thirty years from 1895 to 1925 saw a creative outburst of genius in the British theatre unprecedented since the spacious times of Queen Elizabeth. When this mighty tide began to recede, the American theatre, which had never enjoyed a period of distinction, rose to its present flood. It is probable that more good plays have been written in the United States since 1925 than in any other country in the world. The theatre, in all its manifestations, has shown more progress in America since the World War than any other form of intellectual or artistic endeavour. There is simply no comparison between the present condition of the American theatre and that of any period in our past.

I love to remember the prophecy of our beloved American dramatist Bronson Howard. The ancients believed that often in the last hours of life men were given the power of prophecy, like Hector at the gates of Troy. Bronson Howard died in 1908. Shortly before his death he spoke these eloquent words:

> The brilliant indications shown by our younger writers for the stage who are now crowding to the front, eager, earnest, and persistent, with their eyes on the future and not the past, coming from every walk of life, from universities and all other sources of active thought, are the basis of my prophecy. It is this: In all human probability the next great revival of literature in the language will be in the theatre. The English-speaking world has been gasping for literary breath, and now we begin to feel a coming breeze. I may not live to fully enjoy it, but every man of my own age breathes the air more freely already. Let us hope that the drama of this century will yet redeem our desert of general literature. The waters of our Nile are rising.

The part played in this tremendous movement by Professor Baker was significant. When he began his course of instruction in play-writing, there were very few American original plays of serious value; when he retired, the American theatre had reached fruition. There can be no doubt that his life devotion to the cause, with the large number of his successful pupils, counted for a great deal. And if there were any doubt, the individual testimonies of leading American dramatists would dispel it.

During the last eight years of his career, from 1925 to 1933, Professor Baker was the Head of the Yale University Theatre, which is a branch of the Department of the Yale School of Art. Here, thanks to the generosity and foresight and wisdom of Edward S. Harkness, Professor Baker had a modern theatre, fully equipped in every respect; his school of drama had found a home worthy of the art and of the man who taught it. The devotion of his pupils and of the staff of teachers became even stronger, if such a thing were possible, in these last years; and his death brought expressions of grief and loyal affection from every state in the Union.

It is impossible to speak of the work and influence of Professor Baker without a tribute to his wife. He was married in 1893 to Christina Hopkinson of Cambridge. She was his daily inspiration.

EDWIN ARLINGTON ROBINSON

BY WILLIAM LYON PHELPS

ONE DECEMBER DAY in the year 1896 I received through the post a thin paper-covered booklet called *The Torrent and the Night Before* by Edwin Arlington Robinson. (Gardiner, Maine, 1889-1896.)

On the title-page was printed a disarming ironical quotation from François Coppée—

> *Qui pourrais-je imiter pour être original?*

and at the foot of the title-page, instead of a publisher's name was the statement

PRINTED FOR THE AUTHOR · MDCCCXCVI

and across the title-page was written in ink

W. L. Phelps,
with compliments of E. A. Robinson
9 December, 1896

323

The printed dedication of the tiny volume was humorously modest:

This book is dedicated to any man, woman, or critic who will cut the edges of it.—I have done the top.

I have no recollection of reading this book, and none of acknowledging it; but I must have done both, for the next year (1897) I received a bound volume of 123 pages, called *The Children of the Night,* A Book of Poems by Edwin Arlington Robinson. (Boston, Richard G. Badger & Company, MDCCCXCVII.)

A publisher's note preceding the title-page said

This first edition of The Children of the Night consists of Five Hundred Copies on Batchworth Laid Paper, and Fifty Copies on Imperial Japanese Vellum

and on the fly-leaf was written in ink

> W. L. Phelps
> from E. A. Robinson
> 4 December, 1897

I read every word of this volume, as is proved by a note I made at the end of it, only a few days after I received it.

For more than twenty years these two precious volumes disappeared from my sight; during that interval we moved twice. One day, somewhere in the nineteen-twenties, I found the two resting quietly among a lot of old papers, wholly uninjured by their prolonged slumber.

I mention these facts, because the first of these books is now one of the most valuable to collectors in American Literature, and the second fetches an exalted price; both being autograph copies adds to their value.

I never saw Robinson until Yale gave him the honorary degree of Doctor of Letters in 1922. I had a good talk with him then. He was quiet, reticent, modest, and produced an impression of absolute sincerity.

Edwin Arlington Robinson was born at Head Tide,

EDWIN ARLINGTON ROBINSON

Maine, 22 December 1869 and died in New York, 6 April 1935. He was never married. He was three times awarded the Pulitzer Prize in Poetry. He was elected a member of the Academy on 10 November 1927.

His fiftieth birthday, 22 December 1919, was celebrated all over the United States; one of the very few occasions in the history of our country, when the birthday of a poet had a nation-wide commemoration during his lifetime. It is unnecessary to say that he took no part in it, nor made any public appearance.

The year after his death, 18 October 1936, a tablet to Robinson was unveiled at Gardiner, Maine, in the presence of a large assembly. The exercises were as simple as they were dignified. Hermann Hagedorn called him a beloved figure in the American Pantheon, "the anchorite, outside space and time, conscious of an eternal eye upon him and upon the work of his hands."

This tablet was presented to the city by Henry Richards, husband of Laura E. Richards, author of the little book giving all the information we have of Robinson's childhood and boyhood in Maine.

It is interesting, in view of the facilities for publicity in the twentieth century, that during his entire career Robinson did everything possible to avoid attracting attention. No one could secure a photograph of him or any biographical data from himself; he refused to appear in public, he did not read or discuss his poems before audiences, he remained solitary and inaccessible. Yet he was generally acknowledged as the foremost living American poet; raised to that eminence by the sheer merit of his verse.

When in the year 1928, he was awarded by the National Institute of Arts and Letters the Gold Medal for poetry, he wrote me this characteristic letter:

Dear Phelps,

I am writing to you as President of the Institute of Arts and Letters to express my sincere thanks to all concerned in my receipt of

325

the Gold Medal for Poetry this year. It is certainly a source of great pleasure and satisfaction to me. At the risk of appearing a little ungracious, may I ask if anything in the nature of a formal presentation may be omitted? As I grow older I find myself less inclined, if possible, to indulge in the luxuries of publicity. I am still human, however, and am glad to know that there are several people somewhere who like what I have done, or some of it.

Yours sincerely,
E. A. Robinson.

His statement, "As I grow older I find myself less inclined, if possible, to indulge in the luxuries of publicity," has a humor all its own.

In this same year the *Letters* of Thomas Sergeant Perry, a truly great scholar, and an intimate friend of both Mr. Robinson and me, were published, with an Introduction by Robinson. I wrote him again about the Medal and about these letters, but I lamented the absence of an index. He replied as follows.

Dear Phelps,

Thank you for your letter of the nineteenth regarding the award of the medal. Your consideration is much appreciated, and you have my gratitude.

Your approval of the Letters and the Introduction gives me great pleasure, as you know. The lack of an index has called down curses on my head, and with reason, as I have to admit.

Yours very sincerely,
E. A. Robinson.

When Robinson began to publish his poetry in the late nineties, the times were not favorable; but the true poet should have genius for the inopportune. These two early volumes attracted very little attention; and apparently they were doomed to speedy and complete oblivion, the inescapable fate of ninety-nine books out of every hundred.

But about fifteen years later, in the revival of poetry in America, Robinson came into his own; and he deserved his fame, both for the excellence of his work and because he was one of the leaders in this renaissance. The dates are significant. *The Torrent*, 1896; *Children of the Night*, 1897; *Captain Craig*, 1902; *The Town Down the River*, 1910; *The Man Against the Sky*, 1916; and *Merlin*, 1917.

His original play, *Van Zorn*, is not only very fine as drama and as literature but it exhibits a side of his talents usually unknown; it had the bad luck to appear in 1914.

I confess that I made two errors in estimating his work. I thought that when *Merlin* appeared, he was on the wrong track, that he had better let those legends alone. It seemed to me as if he were trying to dilute Tennyson; and to dilute Tennyson won't do at all. My second error was my belief that the value of Robinson's work was analytical and intellectual rather than emotional. In 1918, I wrote,

It is of course possible that Mr. Robinson wished to try something in a romantic vein; but it is not his vein. He excels in the clear presentment of character; in pith; in sharp outline; in solid, masculine effort. . . . He is an excellent draughtsman; everything that he has done has beauty of line; anything pretentious is to him abhorrent. He is more map-maker than painter.

Then, to my amazement and delight, he proved me wrong by producing in 1927 his masterpiece, *Tristram*. It not only is his best poem, it is the best poetic version of that immortal story that has ever appeared in English. It glows with passion and is radiant with beauty. And indeed, perhaps its closing lines about the other Isolde, Isolt of the White Hands, leave on our minds the deepest impression. For here he rises from the particular to the universal.

> Isolt of the white hands,
> Isolt with her gray eyes and her white face,
> Still gazed across the water to the north
> But not now for a ship. Were ships to come,
> No fleet of them could hold a golden cargo
> That would be worth one agate that was hers—
> One toy that he had given her long ago,
> And long ago forgotten. Yet there she gazed
> Across the water, over the white waves,
> Upon a castle that she had never seen,

And would not see, save as a phantom shape
Against a phantom sky. He had been there,
She thought, but not with her. He had died there,
But not for her. He had not thought of her,
Perhaps, and that was strange. He had been all,
And would be always all there was for her,
And he had not come back to her alive,
Not even to go again. It was like that
For women, sometimes, and might be so too often
For women like her. She hoped there were not many
Of them, or many of them to be, not knowing
More about that than about waves and foam,
And white birds everywhere, flying, and flying;
Alone, with her white face and her gray eyes,
She watched them there till even her thoughts were white,
And there was nothing alive but white birds flying,
Flying, and always flying, and still flying,
And the white sunlight flashing on the sea.

CHARLES MARTIN LOEFFLER
BY WALTER DAMROSCH

IT IS DIFFICULT, if not impossible for me to give anything like a worthy and impartial analysis of Charles Martin Loeffler—this aristocratic composer and man. His death has been too recent and I was too closely bound to him by years of friendship and admiration. Besides all this, I lack the literary skill to enable me properly and adequately to express my estimates and analysis of him as a musician and composer. Permit me therefore to give you just a few random reminiscences and appreciations of him.

Loeffler came to America in 1881, and presented to my father a letter of introduction from the great German violinist, Joachim, who had been Loeffler's master. My father was immediately strongly attracted by his high musical ability and an indescribable personal charm. He immediately took him into his orchestra and every Sunday afternoon during the winter he came to our house for afternoons of chamber music, playing the viola in a string quartet of which the other members were my father as first violin, Sam Franko as second and Karl Bergner as violoncello.

A great friendship soon sprang up between Loeffler and myself, which lasted through the years. He was only a year older than I, but our birthdays were on the same day, January 30th. Two years later Major Higginson of Boston founded the now famous Boston Symphony Orchestra, the first orchestra to be maintained by a yearly subvention from the generous purse of Higginson, which enabled the members of the orchestra to devote themselves to daily rehearsals and weekly symphonic concerts. This noble venture preceded other similar organizations by several years, and we honor Higginson's memory as the great and bold pioneer in this important field of music. This Boston orchestra immediately attracted the best players of Europe as well as America because its members not only could devote all their time to the cultivation of symphonic music, but their yearly salaries gave them a certain assurance of existence. Loeffler was among the first to be chosen and made Boston the centre of his musical activities until the end.

It is interesting to delve into his student years. He was fourteen when he decided to become a professional violinist. Joseph Joachim was his first great teacher and inspiration. But after achieving remarkable proficiency under this master, he decided to go to Paris in order to acquaint himself more thoroughly with the French school of violin playing of which Massart, a pupil of Wieniawski, was the great exponent at the Conservatoire of Paris. At the end of his studies, Massart recommended him to one of those fantastic and rich Russian noblemen of the pre-Soviet period—Baron Paul de Derviss, who not only possessed two magnificent country places in Switzerland and Italy, but traveled from one to the other with a complete symphony orchestra of seventy musicians, which he maintained for his personal pleasure. This orchestra rehearsed and played daily for their rich employer, often with the Baron as the only listener. At these concerts Loeffler not only played at the first violin desk of the orchestra together with Caesar Thompson who later on shared violinistic honors with Ysaye in Brussels, but also as soloist.

Needless to say Loeffler's nationality and all these varied early surroundings and impressions had a strong influence on his creative mind as a composer. He was an Alsatian, born at Mulhouse, at that time under French government. When the Franco-Prussian War began in 1870, the family fled to Russia in the province of Kiev, and it was there on his eighth birthday that Loeffler received a little violin as a birthday present. Then came his studies with Joachim in Berlin and with Massart in Paris. Then the two years with the erratic but musically generous Russian nobleman—Switzerland and Italy, and then in 1881 Loeffler's migration to America. Musical historians of the future can easily demonstrate these influences in Loeffler's creative works. Carl Engel, the noted musicologist, has already done so in a very interesting biographical sketch published by him in the *Musical Quarterly* of July, 1925.

Musical Boston received Loeffler with open arms. Major Higginson, the founder of the orchestra, Mrs. Jack Gardner, Mr. and Mrs. Montgomery Sears, John Sargent, the conductors of the orchestra—George Henschel, Wilhelm Gericke, Arthur Nikisch, Carl Muck, all became devoted friends and admirers. His personality was quite unique, for the most contrasting characteristics seemed to melt in him into complete harmony with each other. An aristocrat to his finger tips, he was democratic in his intercourse with others. His musical beliefs were very decided but he was always ready to acknowledge merit in his colleagues and to listen to their arguments. He loved to stress their good qualities and to ignore their failings. He always had a gentle and affectionate smile even when he maintained his views on a beloved or hated composer in some heated discussion with me or some other friends. He hated mediocrity and insincerity in Art and was quick to detect them, but he was always eager to discover and to proclaim real talent.

He was deeply sensitive to outside impressions and surroundings. His early associations with France resulted in an intimate acquaintance with her literature and music, and for a time the genius of Debussy attracted him strongly. I remember in 1907 I went to Paris to engage six woodwind players, as New York was strangely deficient in them, and it irked me to think that the Boston Orchestra was in that respect superior to mine. To my surprise and delight I found Loeffler there living in absolute seclusion in a little hotel on the *rive gauche*. Some mysterious soul trouble had sent him abroad into voluntary exile for the time being. We were together daily and he told me with great excitement of the new opera at the Opéra Comique, *Pelléas and Mélisande* by Debussy. He had already heard it three times, but insisted on accompanying me so that he could enjoy my pleasure in hearing it for the first time.

As his nature was never static but always developing, his enthusiasms for various composers changed from one to another. Brahms who was his early God was discarded for the more delicate evanescent nature poems of Debussy and so on.

His childhood in Russia became an inspiration for an orchestral work, *Life in a Russian Village*, published in 1925, which is like an exquisite dream memory of the long ago, in which childhood and Russian musical idioms are very artistically developed.

I do not think that the ultramodernists attracted him very much although he was always interested in their efforts and keen in detecting the fakers from the genuine devotees among them. He was interested in George Gershwin and I remember his coming to New York especially to hear my first performance of Gershwin's *An American in Paris*. Even the singing and playing of negroes in the night clubs of New York was not beneath his interest. I can never forget his

331

suddenly appearing at the first performance of my Opera *Cyrano* at the Metropolitan Opera House in 1913, returning that night to Boston to carry on his musical duties there the next morning. A few days later I received a long letter from him, so affectionate and so laudatory of my work, that it was but another proof how strongly his convictions were emphasized and influenced by his personal feelings. But he did put his gentle finger very firmly and properly on certain faults in my music even though he couched them in words ever so gentle.

In 1903 Loeffler retired from orchestral playing in order to devote himself more exclusively to creative work. He retired to his New England farm at Medfield, Massachusetts, and generally came to Boston but once a week to teach a few favored pupils. Several very talented and very pretty girl pupils simply adored him as some of them confessed to me in later years. Occasionally he would prepare some interesting program of chamber music with them and would have it performed in his very lovely music room in Medfield, to which a few of his Boston friends received highly prized invitations. It was in this period that the mystic Gregorian chants of the Roman Catholic Church attracted him so strongly that he formed a little choir and every Sunday conducted them in the Catholic service of the little country church in Medfield.

Loeffler's occupation with this mediaeval music left a strong influence in some of his writings, especially in his string quartet and in the symphony *Hora Mystica*.

As a composer he was exceptionally critical of himself, and many of his works were revised again and again. An interesting example of this is his *Pagan Poem* which is a musical peroration on the eighth Eclogue of Virgil. This work began as a piece of chamber music for pianoforte, woodwinds, horns, trumpet and a few strings. Afterwards he rearranged it for only two pianos and three trumpets, and finally it developed into an orchestral symphony. Many of

us consider this his finest work. But I always loved to conduct his *La Villanelle du Diable* and *La Mort de Tintagiles*,
a symphonic poem on Maeterlinck's drama.

As his soul shrank from violent contacts, his music, though
it depicts the deepest emotions of life with sensitive understanding, is always refined, and perhaps for that reason does
not always make an immediate vivid impression. But repeated hearings disclose a wonderfully poetic and sensitive
artist whose contributions to our art must be considered as
very important.

The last letter I ever received from him was in 1930. Loeffler was evidently engaged on some orchestral composition
for which his beloved classic Greece formed the background,
for he wrote "Have you any idea where I can find a Pan-
pipe? Or have one made for a short orchestra piece? I am
utterly at loss. If you know all about it, please let me know.
The example here enclosed is what I should like in tone
and compass. Ever yours, Martin."

The musical scale which he sent with it was so strange
that it sounded as if in some occult fashion he had trans-
ported himself back 2400 years and had heard God Pan
himself play it upon his pipe.

In answer I wrote: "Dear Martin: Please do not think me
a pig for not answering your wonderful letter more promptly,
but I have been so terribly rushed owing to our sailing tomorrow, that I have not had either the time or the peace of mind
to tell you how deeply I appreciate your letter and above all,
your long and loyal friendship. I have always felt that it was
good to know that there were at least a few like you in the
world—real artists and finely sensitive human beings.

"I have, however, inquired high and low, especially
among my woodwinders as to a Pan-pipe, but I am afraid that
with that famous birthday on December 25th, nineteen hundred and thirty years ago, the last tune of Classic Greece had
been piped and Pan vanished to make room for the Christ,
and taking his pipes with him. You, if any one, may be able

to reconstruct one, and above all, with your magic art of music, bring back to us 'the glory that was Greece.' The scale which you sent me is so intriguing, that I am naturally keen to know the rest of it."

Loeffler's life at Medfield gradually closed in upon him more and more. He became more of a recluse. The creative artist must commune with himself, and Boston society, concerts and friends saw him less and less. This loneliness or aloofness was accentuated during the last years by his illness. I confess that I missed our very friendly contact, his charming wit, his exquisite understanding and sympathy. He was altogether a unique spirit in the musical life of America.

CHILDE HASSAM

BY ROYAL CORTISSOZ

CHILDE HASSAM, a salient figure in American painting, was in nothing more significant than in his individualism. He had the American way of profiting by European example without falling a victim to European convention. This statement is borne out by the facts of his career. Born in Boston, in 1859, he grew up at a time when the young artist inevitably went abroad to complete his training. When, after some study at the Boston Art School, he proceeded to Paris in 1883, it was the most natural thing in the world for him to fall under the influence of Boulanger and Lefebvre. All young Americans launching themselves in that period, turned as a matter of course to such academic teachers. It did them, and it did Hassam, unmeasured good. The discipline they received directed their talents into habits of sound drawing and composition. There is an early figure piece of Hassam's, called "Autumn," a full length of a shambling old harpist, which shows with what thoroughness he had mastered the rules of technique then governing the Salon—in which, by the way, his work was exhibited in 1888. But even thus early it was apparent that he was feeling his way toward a path of his own and when at a later date he awoke to the evangel of Claude Monet and the principles of modern impressionism he gave to a foreign tradition a new and peculiarly personal accent.

He was able to do this in part because he had been drilled in the ways of good craftsmanship but even more because there surged within him a passion for the beauty existent in his native land. "New York," he once said, "is the most wonderful and most beautiful city in the world. All life is in it." All life was, for him, in the whole American scene when he returned from Paris, all life to be expressed in terms of light and air and color. "Gusto" is the word for Hassam, a kind of joyous energy which vitalizes everything he did, the pictures of the New England coast, studies of flower-lit spaces or of grassy rock-strewn shores, war time paintings of flag-bedecked New York, interiors done in the studio or elsewhere, or, in his later years, pictures of figures and the sea developed at Easthampton, where he died in 1935. He let his fancy range when he came to these last designs and gave them romantic titles—"Sunset from the Grove of Nemesis," "The Wild Swans Sacred to Apollo," "Diana the Huntress Finding Graffiti of Poseidon," and such like. But it was not really the enchantment of pagan myth that lured him. It was, rather, the enchantment of sheer nature, of a nude figure gleaming through a thicket or seen against sea and sky, of trees and clouds, of life as it ministers to the pleasure of the eye. He was prodigiously industrious, forever exulting at work, and he poured forth an endless quantity of paintings, water colors and etchings, as was made apparent when an exhibition of his work was held at the Academy in 1927. But in this great mass there is never perceptible a slackening of his ardor, there is never a sign of any cooling of his warm, emotional response to truth and beauty.

If one quality more than any other promises to keep his art alive it is that springing from his force as a colorist, working always with taste, with restraint, with a finely tempered brilliance. His is color heightened by light, strained through atmosphere. It is, finally, the color of a painter who had originality and style.

Childe Hassam was elected to the Academy in 1920 and was a faithful participant in its deliberations down to the time of his death. His interest in the organization did not cease then. By the terms of his will all the oils, water colors and pastels remaining in his studio were bequeathed to the Academy, the proceeds of the sale of them to be held in perpetuity as the Hassam Fund. The income from this fund is by his instructions to be devoted to the encouragement and promotion of painting and etching in the United States and Canada, through the purchase of American and Canadian works of art. These works, he also stated, might be presented to any museum in either country. The gift was characteristic of his large and generous nature. His fellow-Academicians mourn in Childe Hassam not only a distinguished colleague but a singularly loyal friend and lovable man.

1936

EDWIN HOWLAND BLASHFIELD
BY ROYAL CORTISSOZ

WHEN EDWIN HOWLAND BLASHFIELD was elected to the Academy, in 1908, the organization received into its fellowship an artist peculiarly dedicated to its spirit. He was an embodiment of tradition. What is tradition? Nothing is more foolish than to think of it as a dogma, a formula. It is simply the tribute which the genuine artist pays to the wisdom of the finer souls in the art of all ages. "Painting," John La Farge once said, "is, far more than most people think, a matter of brains." Blashfield was true to the pith of that axiom. He mixed brains with his colors, enriched his art by all the elements which flow from culture, from really enlightened travel, from the adventures of the imagination as well as from the trained exercise of the hand. "The old masters grow bigger and bigger to me," he wrote to a friend not long before the end. He was born in New York in 1848. Thus when he died at his summer home on Cape Cod, on October 12th, 1936, he had lived a long life. From the beginning it had been formed by high thinking, by devotion to an elevated ideal.

He took such an ideal with him when he went to Paris in 1867, intent upon studying under Gérôme but presently enlisting, instead, under the banner of Bonnat. He could not have encountered a more sympathetic master. Bonnat was a rigid disciplinarian and strengthened the young American in the draughtsmanship which was thenceforth, through all his days, to be characteristic of him. Moreover, while Bonnat held his disciple to a severe standard of the painter's craft, he gave him the stimulus emanating from a rare intelligence. The Frenchman was a connoisseur and collector, a

337

lover of tradition. His influence made not only for the betterment of Blashfield's drawing and design but for an enlarge-
ment of his horizon. All the conditions of his time abroad
were conducive to the broadening of his outlook. The sway
of the romantics and of the Barbizon school still endured and
men like Manet, Monet and Degas were coming into view.
Blashfield was caught up into a stream of artistic energy and
ideas. He steeped himself in it for considerably more than a
decade, painting historical subjects, exhibiting at the Salon
and at the Royal Academy, and seeing much of Italy as well
as of France and England. When he came back to the United
States it was as a mature painter of carefully thought out
easel pictures. His traits in that character will be remembered
from the exhibition of his works which was held at the Academy in 1928. But it was not as a painter of easel pictures that
he was to win his fame.

That was to come to him in the field of mural decoration.
The subject was already active here at the time of his return
from Europe. La Farge had decorated Trinity Church, in
Boston, in 1870, and his superb altar-piece in the Church
of the Ascension in New York dates from the '80's. Long
after that La Farge was still dominant, the unique leader.
But Blashfield in his turn became a leader, a pioneer, when
mural painting in America received a special impetus at the
Chicago Fair in 1893 and in the Congressional Library at
Washington. From the rather tentative work that he did at
Chicago, when a new movement, essentially experimental,
was launched, Blashfield rapidly emerged as an expert in the
solution of the problem of filling a given space upon a wall so
that it became part and parcel of an architectural fabric. A
long chapter would be needed to describe the art, the dignity
and the beauty with which he adorned public buildings all
over the country. It is sufficient to say here that Blashfield
made a memorable contribution to the art of his time, a contribution teeming with historical and allegorical ideas,
marked by great distinction in the painter's conception of

form and color, noble in composition and altogether expressive of that regard for tradition which was mentioned only a moment ago.

It is important to recognize the play of ideas in Blashfield's work, the flowering of his life-long experience in the world of great achievement. Whatever his theme, whether an episode from the career of Washington or the symbolization of the state of Minnesota, he rose to it with equal imaginative and technical power. Allusion is not inappropriate at this point to the fact that Blashfield was elected to the Academy on literary as well as artistic grounds. One of his most notable achievements—in which he had the collaboration of his first wife, the late Evangeline Wilbour Blashfield, and A. A. Hopkins—was the editing and publication in four volumes of seventy of Vasari's *Lives*. One more evidence, this, of his alliance with tradition. And with that alliance there persisted one of the warmest, most engagingly human influences known in the art of our day. In sympathetic encouragement, in helpful criticism, he was the comrade of every young artist with whom he came into contact. With his personality and his wisdom he was a force to be remembered, a tower of strength to mural decoration and to all the arts in America.

One word more must be added, in appreciation of his long service to the Academy. In 1916 Evangeline Wilbour Blashfield established a fund at the Academy "to assist in an effort to determine its duty regarding both the preservation of the English language in its beauty and integrity, and its cautious enrichment by such terms as grow out of modern conditions." In 1918 Blashfield substantially increased the fund. Annually the addresses delivered under it recall both her name and his, a name synonymous with good will for the things of the mind.

LORADO TAFT

BY HERBERT ADAMS

LORADO TAFT held a unique position among American sculptors. Important as his own creative work was, his influence through the spoken and written word was no less so. That influence was wide-spread. From coast to coast, he aroused public interest in the art of sculpture, and in its proper use in civic development.

He was born in Elmwood, Illinois, April the 29th, 1860. His father, Don Carlos Taft, was professor of Natural Sciences and Geology at the University of Illinois. As a boy, Lorado showed a decided aptitude for modelling; but it was not until after his graduation with honor from the University that he devoted himself whole-heartedly to the study of sculpture. In 1880 he went to Paris, where he studied and worked for five years. On his return to his native land in 1885, he settled in Chicago. At that period, he found the Middle West a barren field for sculpture, and there were long, lean years for the young artist.

Nevertheless, progress was being made in aesthetic matters. The Art Institute of Chicago was developing an important art school, in which Mr. Taft received a position as instructor. He evidently found it easy to express himself in words (a rare gift among sculptors). Within a few years, he was made a lecturer in the Extension Department of the University of Chicago.

From then on to the very end, he was in demand as a lecturer in the field of art. The subject called forth his enthusiastic devotion. He did pioneer work in the Middle West, but as his reputation increased, his addresses on sculpture and civic art were eagerly sought in all parts of the country. From this it must not be inferred that he gave the major portion of his time and talent to the lecture platform. Quite the contrary. He was a distinguished practitioner, and produced many important works.

It was the Centennial of 1893 that gave him his first real opportunity as a sculptor, through a commission to make sculptural decorations for the Horticultural Building. A little later came the Black Hawk monument, a colossal figure forty-two feet in height, representing an Indian chief who gazes out over the beautiful valley of the Rock River at Oregon, Illinois. Following this, he created the group called "The Blind," a work which added materially to his fame, and led to the commission for the heroic bronze group for "The Fountain of the Great Lakes." Then came a succession of memorials, fountains, and statues, placed in widely separated locations.

Lorado Taft was by nature a religious man, with a heart full of compassion for human suffering, and in sympathy with human joys. His faith took the practical turn of good will toward his neighbor. His particular creative interest was in symbolic themes, expressive of human experience. What he earned by his lectures and commissions went back into these ideal creations. His great "Fountain of Time" on the Midway of the University of Chicago is the most ambitious of his many subjects developed in sculpture. The group was inspired by Austin Dobson's couplet,

> Time goes, you say? Ah, no!
> Alas, Time stays. We go.

His hope for the future of art in our country lay in the aesthetic education of the young. It was a subject he often dwelt upon. For years he struggled (let us hope not in vain) to bring about the founding of a great historic museum of architecture and sculpture. He used to speak of it as the dream of his life.

His idea was to have in such a museum a reproduction of every fine piece of sculpture and of some fragment from every noble work in architecture known to the world. Whatever was shown should be properly arranged as to period, and furthermore, should be suitably lighted. He often discussed the vexed question of lighting sculpture, and maintained with perfect truth that a sculptor's work is seldom lighted so as to reveal its full beauty.

A visit to his studios made one think of the workshops of the Renaissance artists. There one found Lorado Taft surrounded by his pupils, some of them working on projects of their own, with an occasional suggestion or criticism from the master, and others acting as his assistants in the time-honored way. One saw a happy family of artists cooperating with enthusiasm toward a common end. It was unique. I know of no other workshop like it.

His lectures never seemed to distract his mind from creative effort in his studio. You would see him absorbed in his modelling. Some one would say, "It's train time!" "All right, I'm off!" And away he goes.

On the platform, or before the microphone, he had a friendly, natural manner,—a way of capturing the interest of his audience. He never indulged in artistic jargon or in modernistic phrase-making. He used words that meant something to his hearers. His attitude toward his contemporaries in art was unfailingly generous. He looked for the good in everyone's work and in every school of sculpture; at the same time criticizing with frankness that which he felt was false or unworthy. His writings on sculpture have definite importance. His monumental *History of American Sculpture,* first published in 1903, is still, in its revised edition, the standard work of reference on the subject.

Most modest as to his own attainments, magnanimous in his whole outlook, he remained young in spirit to the last. When his end was approaching, he meditated on one of his great conceptions, a work which for a long time had been in process of development. He called it "Creation," and intended it as a companion to his "Fountain of Time." On October the 30th, 1936, Lorado Taft asked to be taken to his studio once more. With this farewell to earthly achievement, a noble spirit left the world but a few hours later.

1937

ELIHU ROOT

BY NICHOLAS MURRAY BUTLER

IF PERICLES delivered the truly great speeches which
Thucydides ascribes to him, he was the first in the Western World to achieve greatest eminence both as statesman
and as man of letters. This has not often happened in the
history of statesmanship and of literature. Caesar was a
nation-builder and a man of letters, while Cicero was a man
of letters and a publicist of highest authority. When our own
nation was in the making, there was an extraordinary revelation of the possibility of combining political insight and public service with literary skill and fine literary form. The writings of George Washington, of the two Adamses, of Jefferson
and of Hamilton demonstrate this beyond peradventure.
Burke had already made his mark in both fields of endeavor,
and Thiers, Disraeli and Gladstone were shortly to do the
same. Bismarck, although the fact is little recognized, would
have been a distinguished contributor to the literature of his
people had his literary skill and productivity not been over-
shadowed by his stupendous achievement in the field of
practical statesmanship.

Elihu Root was another statesman of similar type. The
farsighted vision, the human understanding and the power
of interpretation which marked his state papers and his public acts, were all revealed in a literary form which has made
these a permanent contribution to the literature of our language and which brought him the distinction of membership
in the American Academy of Arts and Letters. Literature
and literary power are not and need not be something apart
from other personal characteristics and attributes, but un-

happily they are too often looked upon as such to the disadvantage both of literature itself and to that of achievement in other fields of endeavor.

Elihu Root was one of those fine and rich personalities who would not and could not detach his private pursuits from the public welfare. Before he was a teacher or a lawyer or a statesman, he was a good citizen. He measured his public and professional activities in terms of the highest standard of American citizenship. His attachment to the college which bore the name of his hero, Hamilton, on the campus of which he was born and near the campus of which he lies buried, grew with the years and nothing affected him more directly or more deeply than its welfare and its repute. His reading was of the now unhappily old-fashioned type which included the best that had been written in any language. The ancient classics were familiar to him, as were the outstanding contributions to English, to French and to Italian literature. He reflected this knowledge not only in his frequent quotations, but in his own direct and persuasive literary style. There were few topics upon which he did not touch in the course of his long and active life. Some of these called for charming and tender sentiment, and he furnished it. Some of them called for learning and precise knowledge, and he furnished it. Some of them called for courage and vision and outstanding leadership, and he furnished it.

History will confirm the judgment of Lord Bryce that Root was the greatest Secretary of State in the history of the American nation, among all the long list of names which begins with that of Thomas Jefferson. Of our Secretaries of War, he was easily the most distinguished and his five Reports, made while incumbent of that post, are, as Lord Haldane described them, the last word on the organization and administration of an army in a democracy. That he had no peer as a diplomat was the judgment of Sir Cecil Spring-Rice, which judgment is fully confirmed by his long record of outstanding achievement. In his adjustment of the diffi-

344

culties between the United States and Japan, in his work for
the pacification of Cuba and the Philippines and their good
government, in his emphatic insistence upon upholding our
treaty obligations against discrimination in the Panama
Canal tolls, in his work at the Washington Conference for
the Limitation of Armaments, and in his plan for the Permanent Court of International Justice at The Hague that
brought into existence the tribunal which, one of these days,
will be looked upon as a ruling influence in the peaceful
guidance and development of the world's organization, he
made permanent contribution to the history of modern civilization. His letter of instructions to the representatives of
the United States at the Second Peace Conference at The
Hague in 1907 is a classic document and marks an epoch
in the building of the institutional life of an organized family
of peaceful and cooperating nations. When the history of the
world's difficult and painful struggle to put international war
behind it and to establish a peaceful and wisely organized
world comes to be written, the name of Elihu Root will lead
all the rest.

One must go back across well nigh a century and a half to
find in Alexander Hamilton that American to whom Elihu
Root's mind and life and type of public service are most analo-
gous. The truly great oration in which the Reverend Dr.
John Mitchell Mason, Pastor of the First Associate Reformed
Church in the City of New York and later Provost of Columbia College, paid tribute to the memory of Alexander
Hamilton when speaking before the Society of the Cincinnati at Federal Hall in New York City on July 31, 1804, may
be in large part repeated at this hour in memory of Elihu
Root:

One of his (Hamilton's) primary objects, (said Dr. Mason) was
to consolidate the efforts of good men in retarding a calamity which,
after all, they may be unable to avert; but which no partial nor temporary policy should induce them to accelerate. To these sentiments
must be traced his hatred of continental factions; his anxiety for the
federal constitution, although, in his judgment, too slight for the

pressure which it has to sustain; his horror of every attempt to sap its foundation or loosen its fabric; his zeal to consecrate it in the affections of his fellow citizens, that if it fall at last, they may be pure from the guilt of its overthrow—an overthrow which may be accomplished in an hour, but of which the woes may be entailed upon ages to come.

With such dignified policy he joined the most intense application to his professional duties. . . . How he resolved the most intricate cases; how he pursued general principles through their various modifications; how he opened the fountains of justice; how he revered the rights of property; how he signalized himself in protecting the defenceless; how judges, and jurors, and counsel, and audience, hung on his accents; let them declare who have entrusted their fortunes to his hand.

With these words of historic judgment called to echo over the greater part of a century and a half, we may leave Elihu Root's well-earned fame to be confided to a grateful people's care.

PAUL ELMER MORE

BY WILLIAM LYON PHELPS

Paul Elmer More was born at St. Louis on December 12, 1864, and died at Princeton, New Jersey, March 9, 1937.

He took the degree of B. A. at Washington University in 1887, and received honorary degrees from Glasgow, Columbia, Dartmouth, and Princeton. Although his entire life was devoted to scholarly research, his official connections with academic life were brief. For one year he was Assistant in Sanskrit at Harvard and for two years Associate in Sanskrit at Bryn Mawr.

For five years before the war he was Literary Editor of the *Nation* in New York, when that periodical was conservative.

Doctor More belonged to the most select class of the intellectual *élite*, to a class smaller relatively in the United States than in any European country. I hasten to explain that I mean by this that for most of his life he had no professional occupation; he was not a university professor, he was connected with journals in an advisory editorial capacity only for a comparatively brief period; and he never earned his living by belonging to any kind of organization. He was an independent scholar, completely untrammelled, free from committees and all the complicated machinery of education. He loved learning for its own sake and might never have produced so many books if it had not been that he also loved humanity with equal passion; so that he felt it necessary to give to others the results of his learning and meditations.

Doctor More was one of the most learned men in the world; at a time when there are so many short cuts to information, and when many are content to know only enough of a subject to conceal their ignorance from others even less fortunate, Doctor More always wrote from profound and thorough knowledge. He was a scholar in Sanskrit and in some other Oriental languages; he was a first-class scholar in Greek and Latin, and of course at home in the principal modern European tongues; he was familiar with the history of human thought from the dawn of philosophy to the latest contemporary conjecture; he was prodigiously well read in English literature and was not, like some great scholars, illiterate in everything after 1850, but was well acquainted with the novels, poems, plays, and essays of living writers.

His long series of volumes called the *Shelburne Essays* were penetrating and brilliant illustrations of literary criticism at its best; founded on thorough knowledge, displaying qualities of sympathetic insight and gentle irony, and sparkling with wit and humor.

The range of his mental interests is shown by the fact, that although his heart lay in the study of philosophy, metaphysics and theology, he wrote a biography of Benjamin Franklin, who, disgusted with the uncertainties of those studies, said that he quitted them for others more satisfactory.

347

PAUL ELMER MORE

Doctor More was one of the greatest living authorities on the history of the early Christian Church; and during the last twenty years of his life, Christian faith held complete possession of his heart; for where your treasure is, there will your heart be also. And there is not the slightest doubt that the most precious treasure in his mature and in his closing years was his belief in the Incarnation, which he had come to believe after a long early period of agnosticism.

The series of books he wrote beginning with the year 1917 and continuing to the last moments of earthly consciousness, for he corrected the proofs of his latest publication on his deathbed, were concerned with the highest and the deepest thoughts that can enter the human mind. These books were *Platonism, The Religion of Plato, The Christ of the New Testament, Christ the Word, The Demon of the Absolute,* and *The Catholic Faith.*

Although these works were original and profound, they were written in a language so clear that they could be understood by any men or women of fair intelligence, even if they were themselves without formal education.

For I happened to be intimately acquainted with an old man in Michigan who had spent most of his life since boyhood on the Great Lakes as a sailor, rising from the humblest position to that of Captain; for many years he had been a sea-captain and now in a comfortable old age, he had retired. He had had only a very little schooling; and was as near to the position of a self-educated man as one could very well be. In the middle watches of the night on many a voyage he had reflected on many things; and in his last years he read many books. One day I came upon him as he was absorbed in reading; and to my surprise, I found that the book that held his attention so closely was *Christ the Word,* by Paul Elmer More. I expressed to him my own delight in that book, and Captain Ludington replied, "On the subject of religion, More is my favorite writer."

The two little books—little in size—that he produced in his

last years, *The Sceptical Approach to Religion* (1934) and *Pages from an Oxford Diary,* which appeared immediately after his death, are masterpieces—masterpieces in thought, in learning, and in expression. The former is an attempt to see how far the human intellect can rise to a belief in God and in the divine order of the world, without any special revelation or mystical intuition; it is the finest work of the kind I have ever read.

The latter consists of meditations that filled his mind in many hours of happy solitude during a winter in Oxford; these pages are confessional in their religious belief, with a frank consideration of obstacles; but they are fortunately also a confession of the tremendous passion and of the emotional excitement that filled his whole being.

For just as I believe that there are in the world no commonplace persons, but that those who seem to us commonplace seem so because we are ignorant; so I believe that there are no great research scholars who are really coldhearted, no matter how lacking in demonstrativeness their manner may be. Doctor More was often called cold; and he considers this curious misapprehension in that last little book—and almost laughs aloud at its ineptitude; for his heart was a furnace of emotion.

He was not a good lecturer, not a good public speaker; this may have been because he was not a professional teacher, was not accustomed to facing college classes, was not used to oral expression; and I can see how those who heard him speak in public may have believed he was both arid and glacial.

But even as those who explore hitherto unexplored regions in the remotest places of the earth, do so because they prefer excitement to security, so there are solitary thinkers whose minds, advancing far out on the distant frontiers of human thought, find such enterprises filled with wild emotions; for, as Henry James said, "there are no adventures like intellectual ones."

The mind of our great philosopher was true to the central

fact of religion. The greatest contribution of Christianity to the world, he said, was Hope. With an absolutely sure instinct for the significance of religion, he felt the fatal error made by many clergymen and theological schools today was the substitution of social propaganda for spiritual regeneration. Even as science is powerless to save the world and has fallen into a bankruptcy more desolating than any financial depression, so no new system of economics or change in political government can either redeem mankind or renew the individual.

His books are among the most important of modern times, for they show how a fervent religious belief can not only be accompanied with intellectual self-respect, but can have its foundations in thought. Doctor More was a living example of the statement of Thomas Aquinas, that the faith of a man is better than the faith of a child.

FREDERICK MacMONNIES

BY JAMES EARLE FRASER

FREDERICK MacMONNIES will live through his art as long as people cherish beautiful form in sculpture, and guard it in sacred places,—although his death means the loss to the world of a great and colorful artist.

He was a man of rare charm and wit, shy, perhaps, at times, but to his friends a delightful companion.

His early life was filled with acclaim, much affluence, and finally, too little recognition. It is sad to realize that such high appreciation showered upon him here and abroad should be even slightly dimmed.

Much of the reason for this is the result of varying fashions in art, and a great deal to a change in his own style of work.

This leaves him none the less the great artist—and I am honored to pay tribute to his genius and personality.

FREDERICK MacMONNIES

The youth of MacMonnies became a tradition to me when I assisted Saint-Gaudens in his Windsor studio, and listened to his account of the young man's aptitude for modelling, and his ability to make beautiful and completely comprehended sketches at the age of seventeen.

From that period on, he developed with an amazing rapidity, enhanced in large measure by his early training in a great sculptor's studio, such a training as was given to the young artists of the Renaissance, with the opportunity to see and aid in the making of real works of art.

His promise was carried to an early realization,—he was considered a prodigy,—an unusual occurrence in the complicated art of sculpture.

He had the gift of the musician or poet, to produce extraordinary work at an early age.

By the time MacMonnies had reached the age of thirty, he had completed many remarkable sculptures.

Among them was the colossal Columbian Fountain, at the World's Fair in Chicago, in 1893, a symbolic ship of state, guided by Father Time, with the amazing total of twenty-seven heroic figures.

The modelling of the nudes, and general grouping of the composition immediately stamped young MacMonnies as one of the strongest sculptors of the period.

Even before this colossal work, he had completed a figure of Diana, a Faun with a Heron, and three very unusual portrait statues, namely: the Nathan Hale, Stranahan, and Sir Henry Vane.

There are extremely few portrait statues which can be classed as works of art, and the ability to create them is rare, but the successful portraits go down the ages as surely as the Elgin marbles. The Sophocles, Demosthenes, Gattemalatta, the superb Colleoni, are examples worthy of such comparison.

MacMonnies showed his particular genius in this exacting and difficult phase of sculpture in four statues which are deservedly well known.

The statue of Nathan Hale in City Hall Park, which I have mentioned, modelled superbly with masterly ease, is one of the finest statues in America.

Sir Henry Vane, in the Boston Public Library, a beautifully modelled swashbuckling dandy of the Colonial period, excellent in character, and admirably designed, is in direct contrast to the Stranahan portrait,—conceived and executed with severity and power.

The Shakespeare is the fourth portrait statue in this group. It was executed for the Congressional Library, along with the bronze doors of the same building.

With the exception of the Congressional sculpture, this very remarkable output was accomplished, I must repeat, before he had reached the age of thirty. To the layman, this may not seem extraordinary, but I know of no other sculptor who has had such a record.

From his thirtieth year his activity continued unabated, with the Bacchante and Infant; three figures for St. Paul's Church; a Victory figure for West Point; the Shakespeare; and the sculpture for the Brooklyn Memorial Arch, crowned by a Quadriga, one of his best architectural pieces of sculpture. In this work he attained flowing design, with a fine restraint.

His versatility is further shown in the Baby with the Duck, humorous, impish and playful. Saint-Gaudens said that it was comparable to the best Pompeian sculptures, with an entirely modern approach.

In the same year came the huge groups of horses in Prospect Park, richly modelled, immensely animated, but retaining fine and powerful contours.

All of this remarkable sculpture was accomplished in ten short years, and before he was thirty-seven years old. It was inevitable that such a pace could not be sustained, and a breakdown in health forced him to give up work.

When he was allowed to resume, he began by painting. It came easily, his handling was fluid, his color good, and his drawing superb. The French painter, Gérôme, spoke of his drawings as worthy of Holbein. In 1903 the Paris Salon conferred upon him a medal for painting.

After 1905 he created numerous major works, with a noticeable difference in style; a monument for Denver; the Washington at Princeton; Civic Virtue; two equestrian statues; and finally his last work of importance, the huge monument for the battlefield of the Marne, in France, a group of fiercely protesting figures, carved in stone, towering over sixty feet in height.

During this splendid but fatiguing rush of work, he found time to talk with and aid the struggling students who sought his criticism, and there are many artists who remember his valuable advice, and who will always be his strong admirers.

Many of you are familiar with his great charm, his wit, and handsome, engaging personality. He had a talent for friendship, and was much sought after, but with all these enviable distractions and artistic qualities, he never gave up the habit of constant work, a frenzy of enthusiasm for actual work,—so that he regularly spent his days, from early morning until there was no more light, in his studio.

He lived in Paris for over twenty years, and was highly considered by the French artists, who took him into their hearts as one of themselves. He fully merited his popularity here and abroad, and accepted his renown with infinite good taste.

He received many high honors, among them an honorable mention, at twenty-six, and in 1891 a silver medal, conferred for the first time on an American, at the Paris Salon. A gold medal at Antwerp; the decoration of Chevalier of the Legion of Honor by the French Government, when he was thirty-three; the Chevalier of St. Michael of Bavaria at Munich; election to the American Academy of Arts and Letters in 1915; and the grand prize of honor at the Paris Exposition.

Contemplating thus, with appreciation, the results of MacMonnies's life work, it is evident that his fame can confidently be left in the critical and just hand of time!

WILLIAM GILLETTE

BY WILLIAM LYON PHELPS

WILLIAM GILLETTE was born at Hartford, Connecticut, July 24, 1855, and died there April 29, 1937.
His father was Francis Gillette, United States Senator from Connecticut; his mother Elizabeth Daggett Hooker. He studied at Trinity College, Hartford, and took his B.A. at the Massachusetts Institute of Fine Arts.

He grew up in Hartford at the Farmington Avenue corner where dwelt Mark Twain, Harriet Beecher Stowe, Charles Dudley Warner; and he was filled with literary ambition, especially in the field of drama. During his boyhood he produced plays in the attic of his father's house; and his father, somewhat alarmed, tried to discourage him from a stage career. But while still hardly more than a boy he went to St. Louis and got a place in a stock company. For this work he received no pay but gained a knowledge of the theatre that came to fruition in later years in his triple success as playwright, actor, and producer.

He went with the stock company to New Orleans and when twenty years old returned to Hartford. His neighbor, Mark Twain, was deeply impressed by young Gillette's talents and encouraged his desire to become an actor. It was Mark Twain who secured a position for him at the Globe Theatre in Boston. Here Mr. Gillette made his first appearance September 5, 1875, in a play called *Faint Heart Ne'er Won Fair Lady*. One of his earliest great successes was his acting in *The Private Secretary*. Beginning with 1881 he was playing in his own compositions, among the most famous of which were *Secret Service, Held by the Enemy,* first produced in Brooklyn in 1886 and which made a tremendous success; *Too Much Johnson,* and his dramatization of *Sherlock Holmes*. In 1897 he appeared at the Adelphi Theatre in London in his own play, *Secret Service,* and repeated the success he had enjoyed in the United States. Very seldom has anyone connected with the theatre been so successful in the combination of writing plays, acting them and producing them. He will always be remembered as the lean detective in *Sherlock Holmes,* a part for which he was adapted physically and mentally.

After he retired from the stage, he built a great castle at Hadlyme on the banks of the Connecticut River, which he called "The Seventh Sister." A good part of this castle he built with his own hands, showing great ingenuity in the construction of doors and locks and other pieces of furniture. He also built a railroad and drove the engine himself. In this castle he lived peacefully, with six pet cats.

Although his original plays do not belong to literature, they showed extraordinary knowledge of the art of the playwright. I remember at a dinner given to Henry Arthur Jones in 1907 where nearly all the guests were dramatists or actors, Paul Armstrong rose and said that William Gillette was the greatest living American playwright.

In addition to the composition of many plays, after he retired to his castle he wrote an excellent detective novel called *The Astounding Crime on Torrington Road.* This book showed such talent in detective fiction that it is a pity he did not follow up its success.

William Gillette had an absolutely unique personality. His conversation and his letters were filled with wit and humor. Everyone who knew him loved him, but I think he found in his own mind the best company of all; for in the English edition of *Who's Who* where every person is requested to give his favorite recreation, Mr. Gillette wrote, "doesn't like any recreation whatever." Those who knew him best will understand that remark which was absolutely sincere. I think he was continually amused and entertained by his own mind.

WILLIAM J. HENDERSON

BY WALTER DAMROSCH

IN WILLIAM J. HENDERSON, America lost one of its foremost writers on music, and I lost in him a dear friend, who, however, never allowed friendship to interfere with his criticism of my public work.

To give proper expression and estimate of the life work of such a man would need a skilled literary pen, and with the exception of my appreciation of him from the standpoint of a musician and friend, I feel that I cannot adequately do justice to him.

He entered the world in 1855 and left it at the age of eighty-two and therefore was able to give us a long life of noble endeavors in his profession. The gods were kind to him at his birth and endowed him with many and diversified talents, all of which he developed so assiduously that he became expert in all of them. But early in his career music occupied most of his interest and activities.

His father was a theatrical manager in New Jersey and that gave him easily and naturally a practical knowledge of the stage and of the art of acting. It was the first representation here of some of the Gilbert and Sullivan operas that awakened in him an interest in the right combination of words and music—a combination so perfect that even today these masterpieces can be studied profitably by librettists and composers.

Journalism must have attracted him very early as a field in which he could develop his talents, for as soon as he was graduated from Princeton at the age of twenty-one, he worked as a typical cub reporter, first for the *Tribune* and then for the *Times,* writing up general news in excellent fashion. As yachting and the study of seamanship had been among his recreations during his student years, he was assigned to all manner of naval happenings besides the usual murders, burglaries and general catastrophes of the night life of New York. Also such incidental musical events as could not be covered by the one musical critic whom the papers of that day employed but grudgingly on a subject which they did not then deem of great interest to their readers.

It was not until 1883 when the Metropolitan Opera House began its first season under Abby, Schauffel and Grau, while at the same time its older rival, the Academy of Music, was still giving music under Colonel Mapleson, that two musical critics were appointed by the *Times*. One of these was Henderson, and it was this opportunity which gave him the chance to develop what proved, after all, to be the greatest of his talents and predilections.

Two years later, when he was covering the cruise of the New York Yacht Club at Marblehead, the *Times* appointed him principal musical editor, and from then on began his career in that field, which in importance and high quality, musicianship, literary skill and fairness, is perhaps unequalled in the annals of our city.

He joined the *Sun* in 1902 and from then until the day of his death June 5, 1937, he worked daily, unceasingly, and with an incredible freshness and impartiality at this task.

You, my colleagues of the Academy, can hardly realize what that meant. Whether it was an opera performance at the Metropolitan, a symphony concert at Carnegie Hall, the first appearance of a young aspiring instrumentalist or vocalist—in all this flood of music, which begins in October and ends only in April, Henderson was always at his post. And whether his comment consisted of a short paragraph or of a lengthy dissertation, it always expressed the gist of the musical events with the clarity of a Dr. Johnson and with the background of an extraordinary knowledge of musical history and musical forms.

It is natural that I as a musician should be most interested in the great work which he accomplished as a writer on music, both as musicologist and as chronicler and critic of the daily musical events of a crowded New York season.

357

I am totally incompetent to weigh his accomplishments as a writer on naval matters. I cannot sail a boat and cannot even differentiate between the larboard and starboard of a ship. But those who know tell me that he was an expert on yachting and navigation and that one of his books on this subject was extensively used in the naval training classes as a text-book during the Great War.

His many works on music are important. His book *The Art of the Singer* proves him to have delved deeply into the history of this important part of music and its great exponents of the past. It is of inestimable value to the vocal student and artist of today. I believe that not only every singer, but every serious musician can learn much from a careful study of Henderson's research and knowledge of this branch of music.

That he was constantly expanding his horizon is proven by many other of his own publications on The Story of the Orchestra, Richard Wagner, and so forth and so on.

His fine literary training combined with complete understanding of the combination of words with music, made him for me an invaluable collaborator in my composition of an opera on Rostand's *Cyrano de Bergerac*. He knew how to retain all the wit, the pathos, the local atmosphere of this great French dramatic poem that were suitable for a musical version, and I count my association with him during the long period which it takes to write an opera, as among the happiest of my life.

But notwithstanding his many and diverse talents, his many books and lectures, his greatest influence on the musical public of New York was undoubtedly his daily chronicling and criticisms of musical performances on the concert and opera stage. In these the idealist as well as the practical realist, the critic as well as the teacher, the great lover of music as well as the cynic in regard to some of the abortions or imperfections of its exponents, expressed themselves in impeccable English, in absolute clarity and without any personal bias whatsoever. A perusal of these articles from the daily files of the *Times* and the *Sun* will give the reader a perfect picture of the musical life of New York, from almost its first beginnings, its gradual development up to its stupendous activity of today.

We who knew him well will always miss the personal contact with him, his wit, his devotion, and the clarity of his mind, but his noble efforts in connection with the art of music in our country will make themselves felt for many years to come.

WALTER GAY

BY ROYAL CORTISSOZ

WALTER GAY was elected a member of the Academy on November 8th, 1934. He died at his home in Paris on July 13th, 1937. As he spent most of his long life in France his personality was comparatively little known here, but he is affectionately remembered by his friends on both sides of the Atlantic, a man full of an endearing charm. His work was made familiar to New York by repeated exhibitions. One, well representative, was organized in his memory at the Metropolitan Museum in the spring of 1938. It was composed of pictures of interiors, a few painted in New York, but most of them done in his own homes, illustrating the dix-huitième which he loved. They, like Gay himself, had great charm.

In 1930 he wrote his *Memoirs* and had them privately printed in a slender volume. He gave me a copy and from it I can recover a little of the story of his artistic career. "About 1895," he says, "I began to give up painting large figure pieces. Medals and honors were all very well, but to obtain them I was obliged to make too many concessions to the public in the way of subject and of treatment. Besides, I felt that I could be more personal in small ones. Added to this I had a sentiment for the past: it meant much to me. So I painted many studies at the Château de Fortoiseau, without exhibiting them, showing them only to sympathetic people who could understand what I was trying to do. I was searching for the spirit of empty rooms—interiors."

What he sought he found and placed upon canvas with a singularly sensitive touch. I have a vivid recollection of his "interior" in the Rue de l'Université and of that which made his château of Le Breau, down near Melun, enchanting, and I can testify to the perfection of his transcripts. Both places were vibrant with the beguilement of eighteenth century France, not only through the architectural and decorative motives present but through the drawings and bibelots which Gay had collected with unerring taste. And the envelope that he had fashioned for himself meant more than tangible things, it meant the sentiment of which he speaks. It is this impalpable element that comes back to me as I look at his pictures. He caught veritably "the spirit of empty rooms," because they were not really empty, a spirit inhabited them. An especially felicitous word on his evocations has been spoken by his friend Louis Gillet, of the Académie Française, and I must quote it from the essay published shortly after Gay's death:

He found his style; he organized little fêtes, a sort of ballet or quiet fairy tale where objects took the place of vanished figures; he composed little sonatas, a delicate kind of chamber music where the table, the curtains, and the old armchair balance each other and play the part of violin, flute and double bass and sing their song without the help of features or words, while light streams in or the moonbeams circulate with noiseless steps between the old pieces of furniture. He expressed the atmosphere and filtered light from shade and caught the little secrets which inanimate things record when they are alone, and translated delicate shades by the illusion of the unsaid, and marked the pulse of time, the regret and sadness by an absence of living figures.

There is, as the foregoing fragment subtly suggests, a certain romanticism implicit in these interiors. Yet for all his emotional response to his subject Walter Gay kept his eye on the measurable fact. It was not for nothing that he had been trained under that strict disciplinarian, Léon Bonnat. He developed the soundest of techniques. He was always an able craftsman. And from the very beginning he pitched his standard high. On going abroad long ago he went first to London, and there, he says, "I spent three happy weeks studying the pictures in the National Gallery." Arrived in Paris, he continues, "I went every day across the footbridge over the Seine to the Louvre." He had, also, stimulating comrades. In the night school at Bonnat's he came to know Sargent. At Auvers-sur-Oise he painted with Daubigny. Inspiring figures moved across his horizon, Manet, Boldini, Puvis de Chavannes. He knew Whistler, Miss Cassatt and Degas, who received him in his studio and came to Gay's. Then Bonnat sent him to Spain to study Velasquez. Out of it all came the pictures of what seemed at the time only a typical Salonnier. But in due course Gay was to gather up all his inner resources and find himself, to paint "the spirit of empty rooms."

The pictures of those rooms and the pictures of his earlier career do not offer the only contrast in his biography. On the first page of the *Memoirs* he makes this statement: "There have been three great events in my life: going West in 1872 at the age of sixteen, going to Paris in 1876, and my marriage to Matilda Travers in 1889. I have never regretted any of them." The first pages of his book deal with the roughest kind of Western life, with Indians and buffaloes. He looked back with a wistful memory upon that youthful experience. Yet after its adventure he was to be made over by France, where he was to spend happy and fruitful years. The sportsman in him survived and he was a good shot at the pheasants, down practically to the end of his days. But the fastidious artist prevailed, the artist who was a connoisseur, saturated in knowledge and in taste. It was a great privilege to sit with him and Mrs. Gay in the garden at Le Breau and later to explore the château, with its *boiseries*, its furniture, its graphic souvenirs of the eighteenth century masters. Walter Gay had a most engaging way with him, gentle, exquisitely courteous, as though there lived again in him the tradition of that period of culture to which he was devoted. Traversing his pictures I have been moved by the beauty with which they reproduce interiors I have known and others strange to me. At the same time I have been conscious of the beautiful nature out of which they proceeded, the man who was as lovable as the artist.

EDITH WHARTON
BY ROBERT GRANT

THERE WAS an interval of twenty years between the death of Julia Ward Howe, the only woman until then a member of the American Academy of Arts and Letters, and the election of Edith Wharton on November 13, 1930. *The House of Mirth, Ethan Frome, The Age of Innocence* and her finest short stories had already been published. Much of the best American fiction of the last fifty years has been contributed by women. Yet despite honied words, this world is still managed by men, and the policy of the Academy, like that of many other learned bodies, has been to throw the burden on the other sex where membership is concerned. The choice of Mrs. Wharton sprang from enthusiastic recognition of her genius as a novelist and as a consummate artist in the use of pure English. Long before her death our world of letters was aware, subconsciously at all events, of the truth of the estimate which Professor Arthur Hobson Quinn put into words in his *American Fiction,* published in 1936: "With Edith Wharton the supreme artist in modern American fiction emerges, belonging to no movement or group, following her own standards and, while assimilating more richly than any other American novelist except Crawford the culture of France and Italy, remaining essentially American in her choice of material and in her artistic point of view." This eulogy in my opinion should not make an exception of Crawford; indeed if any exception is to be considered should it not rather be Howells or James?

I have heard from a reliable source that Mrs. Wharton's literary executor is not likely to sanction any formal biography for the reason that she has herself set down in *A Backward Glance* with delightful precision yet delicate restraint all that she wished posterity to know of her life and literary processes. Extraordinarily sensitive to the atmosphere of Europe, especially of Italy, from the early age of four, and ever an ardent traveler, she lived during her youth and the first ten years of her marriage mainly in her native land. It was from her select family and their circle, to which she accredited an aimless life, except for elegance and a deep-rooted devotion to absolute correctness in every-day speech, that she acquired her familiarity with the New York society of the seventies which she satirized so artistically and keenly. Her winters were passed in New York City, her summers at Newport, which bored her.

Italian wanderings in the spring and a visit to London were a foil to this conventional mode of life. But shortly prior to the publication of *The Valley of Decision* in 1902 the Newport house was sold and one built near Lenox. This was named in memory of her great-grandfather Stevens's place The Mount. Here she lived and gardened and wrote contentedly during summer and autumn for ten years, and here it was, as she has gayly recorded, that she received the terse and vigorous letter of an amateur critic: "Dear Madam, have you ever known a respectable woman? If you have, in the name of decency write about her."

It was from the proximity of The Mount to the remoter parts of Massachusetts and New Hampshire that her famous *Ethan Frome* and the later novel *Summer,* to which Mrs. Wharton was ever partial, were written. Her residence in that neighborhood refutes the early frequent query "What

does she know of her subject?" "For years," so she declares,
"I had wanted to draw life as it really was in the derelict
mountain villages of New England, a life even in my own
time, and a thousand-fold more a generation earlier, utterly
unlike that seen through the rose-colored spectacles of my
predecessors, Mary Wilkins and Sarah Orne Jewett. In those
days the snow-bound villages of western Massachusetts were
still grim places, morally and physically: insanity, incest and
slow mental and moral starvation were hidden away behind
the paintless wooden house-fronts of the long village street
or in the isolated farm houses on the neighboring hills; and
Emily Brontë would have found as savage tragedies in our
remoter villages as on her Yorkshire moors."

My long friendship with Edith Wharton dates from very
shortly after her marriage in 1885. We had previously exchanged a letter or two, but the first time I met her was at
Groton where she was visiting with her husband, Edward
R. Wharton of Boston, at the house of a mutual friend.
Teddy Wharton was thirteen years her senior, a friend of
my boyhood and a college classmate. I was struck by his
bride's refinement, but was kept a little aloof at first by her
reserve,—for even as late as this she suffered in the presence
of strangers from what she has termed "the long cold agony
of shyness." Because Charles Scribner was my own publisher, I had the opportunity to observe her modest, yet wonderfully swift development under the discernment of Edward
L. Burlingame, editor of the magazine, and his colleague,
William C. Brownell, adviser of the publishing house. They
accepted her first short stories, recognizing in them the touch
of a new artist in letters. There was an interval of only two
years between her venture *The Decoration of Houses* written
with Ogden Codman and the appearance of *The Greater
Inclination* (1899), the book of short stories which caused
the London bookseller to say to Mrs. Wharton incognito as
he handed it to her, "This is what everyone in London is
talking about now." Three years later appeared her first

novel *The Valley of Decision* of which she has written so revealingly. "I have often been asked whether the writing of *The Valley of Decision* was not preceded by months of hard work. I had never studied hard in my life and it was far too late to learn how when I began to write *The Valley of Decision;* but whenever I make this reply it is received with polite incredulity. The truth is that I have always found it hard to explain that gradual absorption into my pores of a myriad details—details of landscape, architecture, old furniture and eighteenth century portraits, the gossip of contemporary diarists and travellers, all vivified by repeated spring wanderings guided by Goethe and the Chevalier de Brosses, by Goldoni and Gozzi, Arthur Young, Dr. Burney and Ippolito Nievo, out of which the tale grew. . . . My years of intimacy with the Italian eighteenth century gradually and imperceptibly fashioned the tale and compelled me to write it; and whatever its faults—and they are many—it is saturated with the atmosphere I had so long lived in."

Three years later (1905) appeared *The House of Mirth,* that compelling yet touching satire on New York society within the memory of many who read it, and Mrs. Wharton's reputation as a fearless and veracious artist was made. To my mind *The Age of Innocence, The House of Mirth* and *Ethan Frome* are her best books and in the order named. It is the fashion to speak glibly of *Ethan Frome* as her masterpiece and the book stands high on the list of books to be read by college students. But compact and thrilling as it is, I was told by the author and we have her words in print that far from thinking *Ethan Frome* her best novel, she was bored and exasperated when told that it was.

Because of our kindred tastes I was one of the group who from time to time visited at The Mount, delighting in its abundant hospitality and the sparkling talk we heard there. The group was small and of different ages. It was a trait of the hostess to like devotedly the people she fancied and disregard the outer world. In the best sense of the word she was fonder of the society of men than of women. Even then and oftener in the years to come I heard Mrs. Wharton spoken of as cold and unpatriotic. But invariably it was by women who did not approve of her analytic mind. In *A Backward Glance* she has alluded to her especial friends, but any memorial which did not refer to the debt which she felt she owed to Walter Berry would be inadequate. With a fervor from which there is not time to quote she tells how he taught her to write and safeguarded her literary style from her first volume of short stories to *Twilight Sleep*, the novel published in 1927 just before his death.

My last visit to The Mount seemed the happiest at the moment, for each of my hosts gave the impression of being in love with what they had builded, and Edith Wharton spoke gleefully of hoping to pay for a new terrace with the profits of her next book. Within three weeks I heard they had decided to uproot themselves and live abroad. The decision seemed a mystery at the time. Teddy Wharton was an attractive man, debonair, spruce, and amiable. They had many fastidious tastes in common, but he was not intellectual, and his wife had in this sense outgrown him. We have Edith Wharton's printed word for it that his growing ill health was the underlying cause of their emigration. On the other hand the lure of Europe and wider literary associations were fully understandable as one of her motives, and at the moment it seemed as if Teddy would find the boulevards of Paris thoroughly congenial. But he never fitted in and they bored him. On the other hand her eager intelligence derived fresh vigor and atmosphere from the old world and from the contacts her growing reputation brought her. After some wanderings they settled in Paris on the rue de Varenne, and here they remained, except for travels and a few summers spent at The Mount until after the great war. It was in Paris that Edith Wharton sought to assimilate all that was beautiful in the realms of artistic or literary knowledge and simultaneously to produce unfalteringly the brilliant series of novels and stories that have won her lasting fame. During the years of the war she initiated and conducted the bountiful splendid charities in aid of the wounded and tuberculous into which she threw herself with completely unselfish ardor. War weary and eager to escape from Paris, she fell in love in 1918 with a house in its ruined suburbs already named the Pavillon Colombe. "At last," as she says in her autobiography, "I was to have a garden again—and a big old kitchen garden as well, planted with ancient pear and apple trees, espaliered and in cordon, and a pool full of fat gold fish and silence and rest under the big trees. It was Saint Martin's summer after the long storm."

Here, and shortly after in her winter villa Ste. Claire Le Château at Hyères in the south of France, Edith Wharton settled down to the rounding out of her literary career. *A Son at the Front* was conceived in 1917 but not completed for four years. Meanwhile she wrote *The Age of Innocence*, of which Walter Berry, to whom she showed it chapter by chapter, said "Yes; it's good. But of course you and I are the only people who will ever read it. We are the last people who can remember New York and Newport as they were then, and nobody else will be interested." But she writes "It had its fate and that was to be one of my rare best-sellers." Often as she travelled, and paid visits, her literary industry was remarkable. Even so far as in the day at The Mount she wrote in bed with a pencil every morning until luncheon time. With this nothing was allowed to interfere. The rest of the day was free for what she would, motoring, gardening and the joys of conversation or reading.

One may not follow her work further in detail. What is most significant in it from the beginning to the end was the exacting seriousness with which she visualized her art and the transcendent skill with which every situation and sentence was illuminated. My own friendship with her, which might have languished because of her residence abroad, was strengthened by our correspondence. In looking over my sheaf of letters I am impressed again by the warmth, frankness and delightful gaiety which permeated whatever she wrote to those of whose sympathy she was sure. Once when two of her manuscripts had appeared in the same year, I referred to them as "your twin books" and drew from her a plausible explanation followed by the airy not unfamiliar couplet

> The rabbit has a pleasant face,
> Its private life is its disgrace.

I do not pretend to have been within the fortunate circle of Mrs. Wharton's greatest friends, who beginning with Henry James formed a special group, and with whom she was so closely and avowedly allied, especially in her later years. For all of this group she had an intense affection. As far back as 1909 she wrote me: "It is curious that when I was younger and busy with my own slow development, I could subsist on *myself* indefinitely, with only a vague unformulated need of companionship *de l'esprit;* whereas now I find myself greatly stimulated by it, and consequently more and more dependent on having it for at least a few months of each year. Hence my great enjoyment of London and Paris."

It is to be said of this truly remarkable woman that she had two aims from the first, but especially after she transplanted herself. These aims were parallel and independent, but in the last analysis one was subsidiary to the other. Most of her compatriots knew next to nothing of Edith Wharton except for her literary creations. They saw her through the haze of distance writing in an ivory tower at the Pavillon Colombe or Ste. Claire Le Château. They did not realize that in the interval since they had first heard her name she had become one of the most cultivated women of her time. Ever athirst for the beauty in knowledge she had steeped herself in architectural and scenic lore, in familiarity with the masterpieces of foreign art and literature. She had delved with the aid of travel into all that was inspiring or recondite in the thought and scenery of a scholarly past.

All this for its own sake, and yet as a stimulus and aid to the literary portrayal on which her talent was bent. Although her surroundings were foreign and she had facility in the use of French,—as witness her *Madame de Treymes* (1907) and *Voyages au Front* (1916)—her countrymen and country-women and usually the American scene itself were her dearest concern. Her situations kept pace with the customs and idiosyncracies of Americans of her own class which lent themselves to satire or to pathos when weighed in the balance of the eternal fitness of things. Edith Wharton stood in the van of her generation in its readiness to make fun of the smugness and conventions of a not remote past and to idealize the freedom and naturalness of a rapidly changing world. Yet no one had a keener pen for the foibles of the over-rich or self-indulgent intoxicated by freedom, or for the vulgarities of those who gloried in being self-made. Her women were apt to be more sharply drawn than her men, for the reason perhaps, as has been said, that her quasi heroes were generally men of comparative leisure with a small fixed income, or else artists. Except for the sketch of Abner E. Spragg in *The Custom of the Country* she never sought to draw the successful American business man of large affairs.

There was, too, a deeper vein,—one may fitly style it a reservoir,—in Edith Wharton's work, which calls for mention to do her full justice. To say that she belonged to no group or movement is true in a narrow sense, but faulty from the point of view of her own attitude. Groups or eccentric expression counted for nothing in her own conception of literature. For her, there was only one great current of the art of fiction which had its own universal laws from which there could be no deviation. There were the immortal story tellers, —among whom Tolstoi was perhaps her dearest idol,—and it was to be worthy of their company, if only to touch the hem of their method, that her genius directed her.

I have spoken of her learning. Here again one must recognize that she accumulated it not solely from her love of knowledge, but for the purposes of her art. Even if one were to assume that this was unconscious, there would be no denying the atmosphere of culture which enriched all her scene and supplied the *mot juste* to her characterization. Where was there anyone in the field of serious fiction of whom this was so significantly true?

A modern of the moderns in her sympathies, Edith Wharton is sure to rank very high not only for the perfection of her style, but for her fastidious reticence. Looking across the Atlantic from her ivory tower and fully cognizant of disintegrating standards, she veiled her situations so artistically that one could read between the lines what life really is without the aid of aggravating details. This is another way of saying that, though fearless to the core, she told her readers all that it was necessary to know without violating the canons of artistic truth, obedience to which she felt to be a requisite of great literature, the hue and cry of democracy to the contrary, notwithstanding.

JOHN RUSSELL POPE
BY ADOLPH A. WEINMAN

IN THE PASSING of John Russell Pope the American Academy of Arts and Letters has suffered the loss of a member preëminent in American Architecture and of an artist of international reputation. It has been said that death loves a shining mark and he has found it in the taking of this distinguished architect at a time of his life when he was reaching for ever higher achievements in his art, as witnessed by his final work, the designing of the new National Gallery of Art in Washington, though an adverse fate barred his carrying this work to its final completion.

John Russell Pope was born in New York City, April 24th, 1874, the son of John and Mary Avery (Loomis) Pope and a descendant of John Pope who settled in Dorchester, Massachusetts, in 1630. It was early in life that he showed a definite interest in the art of design, a tendency directly traceable to paternal influence, his father having been an artist. The boy received his education in the College of the City of New York and later spent three years in the study of architecture in Columbia University under the able guidance of Professor Ware.

Here he distinguished himself by winning two of the outstanding honors in architecture, the McKim Scholarship and the Schermerhorn Traveling Scholarship, the former giving him the opportunity to study two years as a fellow of the American Academy in Rome. He subsequently studied at the École des Beaux Arts and graduated in two years, thereby establishing a record for a foreigner. This extensive training in draftsmanship and thorough discipline in the art of architecture generally, gained during these formative years, have left their indelible mark upon all his work. This and his wealth of imagination enabled him to express himself freely and forcefully, once he got down to paper and pencil.

His was an orderly mind, capable of perceiving fully in the whole, and his work is its reflection. He was not given to smart effects in his architecture, whether of monumental, utilitarian or intimate design. There was about him that imperturbable calm which reflects itself so well in his most important structures, such as the Scottish Rite Temple and the National Archives Building, Constitution Hall, National Christian Church and American Pharmaceutical Building, all in Washington, the American Battle Monument at Montfaucon, France, the Addition to the British Museum to house the Parthenon Marbles and the new Sculpture Halls for the Tate Gallery in London.

One could continue with a long list of other important monumental buildings and memorials he designed and could add thereto many outstanding utilitarian buildings such as hospitals, gymnasia and railroad stations and the more intimate structures, such as town houses and country homes and one would find upon examination that, despite the wide range, each bears the mark of a designer of distinction. Pope was no specialist in architecture, he played the whole gamut and played it extremely well. Opportunities came to him early in life, not by sheer good fortune, but chiefly through recognition of his outstanding ability. Many of his commissions were won in competition.

It having been my good fortune to have collaborated with him as a sculptor in not only some of his large public work, but also in the work of a more intimate character, this collaborative relation having lasted over a period of nearly thirty years, and until the time of his death, I am enabled to speak with understanding of his profound knowledge not alone of architecture, but of the sister arts, of sculpture and painting, interior decoration and landscape planning, as related to architecture.

It was ever a real treat to discuss with him some problem in which we were both interested and the pros and cons came thick and fast in the sifting process of ideas. He had a way of presenting a problem for discussion, a motif in sculpture, for instance, that soon convinced that it had had his very thorough consideration before he had decided upon its incorporation in the design of a building or memorial, but at all times keeping an open and receptive mind for any suggestions a fellow artist might present.

He loved to visit collaborating artists' studios, sit around and say not a word about the particular work in which he was interested, but talk about extraneous matters until he had fully made up his mind what to say about the work under consideration, and that he said with such perfect tact as to make one feel he was expressing one's own ideas. He was an ideal collaborator, sympathetic to his fellow workers and most helpful through his profound insight and analysis and his keen sense of scale and fitness.

While contributing in full measure to the development of the art of architecture in America on an ever higher plane, he also gave generously of his time and effort to public service, as a member of the National Commission of Fine Arts under President Wilson and President Harding and as a member of the Federal Board of Consulting Architects during President Hoover's administration. From 1933 until the time of his death in 1937 he was President of the American Academy in Rome.

Though conservative by nature and training, his work, through beauty and freshness of design and bigness of conception, or intimate charm, never failed in its appeal to the discerning. He remained steadfast to his high ideals in a period in art where so-called self-expression goes to amazing extremes and where novelty, however crude and shoddy, rather than character and soundness of design, seem to be the order of the day.

In John Russell Pope one can justly say that America has brought forth a talent of a most exceptional order and a personality that has left a high and lasting mark upon the architecture of his time. He was a man without pretence, a great artist and a loyal friend.

HENRY HADLEY
BY FREDERICK S. CONVERSE

THE STORY OF the evolution of serious music in America is an interesting one, and Hadley's influence in its development has been very important and far-reaching.

From the early and successful efforts of John K. Paine as a composer of symphonic works and as the founder of an important department of theoretical music at Harvard College in 1870, down to the present time, there has been a steady growth of ability and accomplishment among our native composers of serious purpose.

In the generation which succeeded Paine, the names of Chadwick, Foote, MacDowell, Mrs. Beach, Whiting, Dam-

rosch, Herbert, Parker, Kelley and Loeffler stand out conspicuously. Their influence as teachers and in some cases as
performers was not less important than their productiveness
as composers.

In the next, or third, generation, speaking musically, one
finds the familiar names of Hadley, Hill, Mason, Gilbert,
David Stanley Smith, Taylor, Griffes, Powell, Shepherd,
Schelling, Hanson, Miss Mable Daniels and many others—
so quickly has the procession grown to large proportions. In
a recently compiled list of New England composers alone,
there were some three hundred names, and who shall say
whether they all deserve the distinction. The sorting of such
a list is a job for Father Time alone to undertake. He is
probably at it already.

Hadley, then, belonged to the third generation of composers, which began to function actively about 1900.

Composers of music are much influenced by the artistic
and aesthetic influences which surround them in their youth.
Beethoven reflected Mozart and Haydn in his early works,
while Wagner showed strongly the influence of Beethoven
and Von Weber, as well as that of Meyerbeer.

Young composers of Hadley's generation were subjected
to the stimulating and overwhelming influence of Richard
Wagner and his cult. The echoes of his revolt against the
pedantic and firmly entrenched Classicism of Germany at
that time were still resounding in this part of the world. One
was almost forced to take sides.

Soon the rich and powerful current of Wagner's emotional
and romantic style carried all things musical before it in an
irresistible flood of gorgeous sound. Young and impressionable natures were gladly enthralled by the strong enchantment. Almost all music in Europe and in America was
tinged with its glowing sunset colors. Was it really sunset,
or was it perhaps a new dawning? No one can yet say.

Then came Wagner's great successor and disciple, Richard
Strauss, to complete the conquest and to show the possibili-

ties of descriptive realism through the medium of orchestral sound. This was a fascinating plaything, which often diverted the attention of composers as well as listeners from the essential value of the musical thought.

At this period hardly anyone escaped these influences, except Brahms, with his sturdy neo-classic style, and after a few years Debussy with his gentler impressionism.

Hadley, like others, was deeply moved by it all. In his early compositions one finds a glowing richness of orchestral tone expressing his own melodic fervor, energy and enthusiasm. The buoyant spirits and frequently exalted sentiments that pervade all his works were already in evidence.

The prodigious extravagances of later days which began to appear in the work of Schoenberg, Stravinsky and their followers had no noticeable influence on Hadley's style. I do not think he liked them, though he seldom criticised other composers harshly, and I am not sure. At all events, he continued to say what he wished to say in a natural, coherent and forcible way, always retaining a broad melodic style.

The late distinguished critic, Henry T. Finck, said of his work:

Few contemporary composers know how to handle the orchestral forces with such supreme command of their possibilities as Henry Hadley. His tone poem "Ocean" being orchestrated with a cleverness that Strauss himself could scarcely surpass.

Says another writer, Mr. H. R. Boardman:

A spirit of lofty idealism pervaded the art of Henry Kimball Hadley. His message is one of joy and optimism, characteristically American, inherently uplifting. The music of this master rings true; sincerity is stamped on every page.

Hadley had the great advantage of musical surroundings from his earliest youth. Both his father and his brother were professional musicians of high standing, and besides these, the sympathetic understanding of his mother, as well as the great musical abilities of his devoted wife, were no doubt of enormous help to him throughout his whole career.

Born in Somerville, Massachusetts, in 1871, he was steeped in an atmosphere of music in his earliest years. He learned very early to play the piano and the violin, and also studied theoretical subjects with George W. Chadwick, the noted composer of Boston, so that by the time young men are usually just beginning to think about a professional career in music as a possibility, Hadley was well advanced on the difficult road to technical mastery of his art. His subsequent studies in Europe broadened his outlook and improved his skill. There he had practical experience in training opera choruses and in conducting an occasional opera,—just the sort of valuable experience that was so difficult, if not impossible to acquire in America at that time. When he returned to this country after several years passed in Germany, France, Italy and England, he was eminently fitted to conduct, to compose, or to teach. All these things he did for several years. He led orchestras in Seattle and in San Francisco, and taught music for a while in St. Paul's Episcopal School for Boys in Garden City, New York. Working constantly at composition all the while, he soon began to receive great encouragement in this field by many performances accorded to his works both at home and abroad. He often spoke warmly of the help and encouragement he received from Victor Herbert in his early years as a composer.

Throughout the succeeding years, his works found their place on symphonic programs everywhere, and are now well established and frequently heard. They have a universal appeal because of their sincerity and frankness, their fervent and beautiful melodic content as well as their skillful orchestral treatment,—qualities which will undoubtedly assure them a long life.

There is another side of Hadley's career which deserves special commendation. It would hardly be possible to say enough in praise of his generous, unselfish encouragement to other composers, both young and old. He seems to have been utterly free from any taint of envy, and was just as

ready to help his contemporaries by bringing out performances of their works as he was ready and anxious to help real
talent, wherever he found it among his younger colleagues.
For the struggles of others he always showed the most sympathetic interest, and provided he sensed a real talent, was anxious to secure recognition for it. His achievements in this
direction, especially as assistant conductor of the New York
Philharmonic Orchestra and later with the Manhattan Orchestra, which was organized, maintained for several years
solely by his efforts for the avowed purpose of encouraging
American composers, were notable.

I have recently learned from one of his Boston friends, a
well-known publisher of music who also has done much for
the cause by publishing many American works, that the now
famous Berkshire Festival was originally Hadley's idea and
that he outlined it to him many years ago; that he also enlisted sufficient interest among his acquaintances in the
Berkshire region to enable him to finance and give two series
of summer concerts there.

Not only in America did he work for the cause of American music, but presented American works in many foreign
countries where he acted as guest conductor, notably England, Germany, South America, and Japan.

Taken all in all, the cause of American music has had no
more able, unselfish or helpful champion in all its history
than Henry Hadley. His name will long continue to be respected and revered as one of its foremost promoters.

He was the recipient of many honors during his long
career, among them a Degree of Doctor of Music from Yale
University and a decoration from the French Government,
but above them all he valued his membership in the American Academy of Arts and Letters. He was indefatigable in
his labors for the musical interests of the latter institution.
Since his death his good work for American music is being
carried on by the National Association of American Composers and Conductors, of which he was the founder and

first President, and his memory has been fitly honored in the establishment of the Henry Hadley Foundation, of which the acting President is Mrs. William Vanamee and the Honorary President, Dr. Jean Julius Christian Sibelius, the great Finnish composer.

ROBERT UNDERWOOD JOHNSON
BY ARCHER M. HUNTINGTON

ROBERT UNDERWOOD JOHNSON was perhaps the most enthusiastic among those who first raised and maintained the idea of the American Academy of Arts and Letters. That group, now disappearing (of which the writer is not one), we must believe will always be honorably associated with the creation of this splendid undertaking which has enlisted the interest and service of so many of the best minds of this nation and which will continue to claim the devotion of many others to come.

In this short statement it seems best to mark chiefly his relation to the Academy which he so deeply loved and leave the scrutiny of some phases of his full and rich life-work to others. All who write of him must credit to him the lifelong endeavor to express and enhance beauty and to bring its influence to bear upon the lives of his fellows, an endeavor which has lifted some men to supreme creation and others to unbounded usefulness. His efforts so often directed to cultural matters of intangible value had none the less a true and practical effect as most material grandeur has its origin in the unrealized and unrequited endeavors of the idealist.

While it is true that men, with a boundless impudence and unfathomable vanity, rediscover as their own the simple truths of living, it may be said of Johnson that he came into life fully armed with a Miltonian concept of the truth and wore away barriers by faithfulness to that concept that others storm and lose. There can be no finer thing said of a man when the great bookkeeper has struck his balance than that his life work has brought a light to flood the shadowed by-ways of living. Hope never left his heart. Steadily, patiently, uncomplainingly he worked and wrote and spoke for those things which to his mind were freighted with import for those about him. Such hope is surely the cloud from which the lightnings of achievement blaze. It is out of the hoping hearts of the world that the healing waters of Horeb softly well.

Johnson paid long and reasoned tribute to the arts and out of that unbroken constancy has risen some added respect, even at a time when respect has grown sick and old and drawn a cloak about her shivering form. So, aside from all his other work as editor, poet, ambassador, we must pay high tribute to his great labors on behalf of the Academy. To him the Academy is indeed greatly in debt.

At a time when we are being told that the arts of the ages are shams it is well to consider that if this be true we who inherit their traditions have a very poor family history. We might just as well say that the average human muscles are failures because of their antiquity and that we must create others at once. Johnson did not believe in all these new voices. He used the old yardstick in judgment, the standard of the endless years, and we may perhaps make as faithful calculations with one measure as with another.

There are those who do not, or say they do not, approve of Academies. The great human movement toward association gives the lie to such beliefs or assertions. Men and women of creative minds do and always will associate for the interplay of the creative spirit; for that sympathy and under-standing which can be had only from brothers in the field, and for that recognition which the general public may fail to render. Prophets who speak only from the isolation of deserts are soon surrounded by a curious hierarchy of un-realities—their own privately created academies of the soul. Exclusive academies indeed are these, for what can be more exclusive than that which does not exist! Nor do the great heroes of the word arise as pallid desert flowers. Shakespeare, Goethe, Molière, Cervantes, and Dante worked with men. Isolation spews forth its devotees in a fierce awakened desire for association, for the great deeds of a Mahomet or a Saint Ignatius.

For many there is need of Tradition, of memories, of tribute and reward; of the gathering about an ideal; of the lighting of ever-burning fires; of raising imperishable monuments and tablets to Art, and those who express it. To Johnson this was the predisposition of a lifetime. We recall his work for the Keats and Shelley Memorial, his defense of the Yosemite, and other examples. He was a great amateur of respect, a singer of tributes, an apostle of friendships. And so when the Academy came into being it was largely this man's influence which fanned the first feeble spark, and kept alive a waning interest and which at last brought renewed enthusiasm to bear upon the plan and gained for an institution the dignity of a temple.

To those who find their hearts leaning to the cold-eyed goddess of criticism, the life of Johnson offers many opportunities to indulge the fancies of that highbrowed sister of Hate. He was simple, "impractical," as many who feel that if a thing should be done it can be done, and filled with the endless enthusiasms which small minds condemn—and fear.

It is the fashion these days to credit no man with an unalloyed seeking after truth. So unbelief in goodness or the qualities of the heart and spirit create in many the urge to meet bad opinion half way—to live up to anticipated condemnation. Johnson was not one of these. So as I speak of him I do so with raised voice regardless of those who pick at the threads of a fabric and criticize their hue without comprehension of the beauty of the textile—or its warmth.

Johnson had little of wealth but a wealth of kindness, little power but the power of generosity, and a love for art as he understood art—which is all that any of us have. At a time when some of us feel that much of the fineness of life is being touched by coarseness, when many of the jewels we thought bright seem to lack lustre, he never doubted that allegiance to his ideal was more essential than the analyzing scepticism which picks all ideals to pieces and leaves no spiritual clothing for the coldness of the heart.

In the days when the Academy was a feeble flame in a great darkness he saw it as a blazing light, so that when it came into its own he was not overtaken by surprise or rendered vain by the blinding glare of achievement unforeseen.

The artist truly flies between heaven and earth. Homage rises to him from below—and if he strive to fly too high he may move in the sunlight of derision—a flame to melt his wings away—and give a new name to one more Icarian sea.

Johnson was not one of those who make poetry the Jazz of a pilfered philosophy. His god was sincerity and sincerity, even half sincerity, casts certain informing high lights. But he was above that falseness which descends to the ringing of little gilded leaden bells for morons.

When we consider the things to which he contributed so earnestly and what they now stand for, we may well be thrilled by the thought that through a long life he did things which bear the stamp of nobility! Let us be thankful for this worker. Men die variously; in a chorus of contempt; in the music of battle, in a vanishing regret. They are buried in their achievement be it good or bad. More than all the others Johnson's spirit lingers in the Academy. Like all of us he will die doubly in the deaths of those who knew him and loved him, and perhaps his name may be for long put aside in a time of fever and semi-insanity—but not be lost, for he gave his life for things which alone will uplift his memory. In a few years all those who knew him will have passed away; there will be no one to say "He bored me with his never-ending enthusiasm for the Academy." But younger men will say "This Academy—how was it brought about? Whose was the devotion which nursed it through long years of discredit?" And then from the dusty pages of old minute books, from files and letters, from memoirs and clippings, from newspapers and magazines there will arise proofs of a devoted life and the name of Robert Underwood Johnson.

1938

GEORGE GREY BARNARD
BY HERMON A. MacNEIL

IN GEORGE GREY BARNARD we are confronted with the life of a very exceptional sculptor, quite as far removed from the commonplace as the mystic William Blake with whom he had certain characteristics in common. An individualist in the highest and best sense. Following as he did "The Triumvirate" in American sculpture, as we were wont to call St. Gaudens, Ward and French, both he and Frederick Mac-Monnies, his contemporary, were brilliant stars in our art life and the more interesting to contemplate together because MacMonnies translated his emotions into form with the eye of an eagle while Barnard, seeing with the inner eye, gave us a new note of deep meaning to conjure with in the realm of form expression. I say *conjure* because when he first exhibited in America his work was so "out of the ordinary" that only the few elect recognized the poetry and power in his work. His work did not quite fit with our practical American natures.

I am reminded of an incident that occurred to another American sculptor who had lived abroad and sensed the admiration of Latin peoples for beauty. On his return to America he was making a memorial. Working on a ground floor in summer time, the door being open, workmen during rest periods would peer in and mutely watch the process of modelling in clay. Finally one of them expressed himself with the remark: "Say, Mister! Is it on wires that's did?" Fresh from the Latin country where the remark of the onlooker would most likely have been "Quanto bello," was it any wonder the contrast of our practical natures struck home?

However, Barnard shortly convinced America. He was given the sculptural decorations of the Harrisburg Capitol to do and although it was not in his nature to be bound by architectural limitations, he achieved through great political and financial stress remarkable groups flanking the entrance. Mass and carrying strength at a distance as well as subtle evanescent modelling when viewed closely is rarely so effectively accomplished.

His birth occurred in Bellefonte, Pennsylvania, in '63. But he was brought up in the West during the period of our great national strife—one section warring against another. In his early years the air must have echoed with the strife that was going on and that must have made a lasting impression on this youth, seared it into his soul, as it were. Through his own early struggles working at jewelry, at which he excelled, to get his daily bread, he craved a larger outlet. Was anything more natural than that he should continue with forms of a greater size and of infinite possibilities? It took courage for one who knew privation intimately to leave his livelihood and try to make good in an unknown field where there was no demand. But, as Elihu Vedder once said: "A man will do what he will do," and Barnard did just that. He left his jewelry work and went into the Art Institute of Chicago to study sculpture. Again he went through years of struggle of a most austere kind to achieve what was in him, to express life as it came to him. Born of a preacher, youth during the Civil War and its aftermath, hard physical struggle for a livelihood, these were the youthful beginnings. Is it any wonder these three conditions gave a lasting bent to his whole being?

From then on through his long life of magnificent productions, his work (always of a high artistic import) was chiefly the outpourings of this vigorous manly soul. Michael Angelo was his one great precursor and Rodin, his contemporary, whom some thought at times he imitated. But Barnard had greater poetic power.

GEORGE GREY BARNARD

Barnard's first great work, "The Two Natures," now in the Metropolitan Museum, was the keynote for his life's work. Like love, beauty or art, it is untranslatable into words, incapable of being expressed by them. Yet, because of its power, Artist, Preacher, Philosopher as well as layman *have* to talk because the contemplation of it touches their very souls. An original conception thoroughly adapted to its medium of marble, Mr. Barnard worked on this group, clay, plaster and marble, from 1888 to 1894. We do not quite agree with Lorado Taft's finding lack of grace or charm of expression in this group, yet gladly quote his otherwise admirable description when he says:

In the conventional sense it is not even a good composition for it looks more like an accidental grouping than like a carefully adjusted harmony of lines. Perhaps it is this very lack of convention which fascinates one against his will, which draws and holds, though it may not persuade. Mr. Barnard's thought is too powerful, his expression too original, to strike responsive chords at once. How could it? What is there within us to respond to such notes as these?—what in our daily humdrum lives to bring us into tune with such Titanic dreams of struggle? And yet there is something of the force—shall we say the uncouthness?—of nature about this work which is irresistible. It is unique and reminds one of no other; nor can one in its presence look at aught else until he has made the circuit of all its extraordinary views. It is the manly and not less artistic expression of conflict, in form so new and yet so intelligible that its primary significance cannot be mistaken nor its intensity ignored. It is the work of a man who is first of all a sculptor.

With all its rugged unrest of line, the group offers absolute repose, though indeed it is the feverish repose of breathless men who must stop for an instant or suffocate. The shadow of the struggle is over them still; the fearful embrace again so near at hand that we do not at once recognize the absolute immobility of the moment. In its every member the composition shows the fervid fancy of a strong man who has *felt* the whole scene. It is almost superfluous to point out the poetical advantage of this quiescent moment over any incident of the actual struggle. To have recreated "The Wrestlers" of antiquity, the usual "Jacob and the Angel," or those bloodthirsty men of Copenhagen, would have been to remove the whole thing from the realm of spiritual interest and to have made of it a prize fight. It would have

385

been an error almost as fatal as to transform this impressive group into a conventionally unified and balanced composition with its comfortable *dénouement* assured by every well-established line.

In its very incompleteness, in the lack of finality of composition, the artist has made appeal to our emotions. He leaves us in suspense. The uncertainty of the outcome is written in the fundamental lines of the group. The issue, as with each of us, is unknown to the end. Herein lies much of the universality of its significance and the potency of its appeal.

His "Brotherly Love," made about this time, ordered by a Norwegian, very definitely shows again this searching of his soul into the unknown. W. A. Coffin says of it: "The 'Brotherly Love' violates some of our traditions, but it is beautiful and possesses a weird, indescribable charm. It is a group intended for a tomb, and shows the figures of two nude young men whose heads are partly buried in the roughly hewn marble which forms the bulk of the monument, and whose hands seem to have forced their way through it and to be searching each other's grasp. I suppose that the marble mass may typify rock or darkness, or eternity, or something else tangible or intangible, and that the brothers are groping through it to join each other after death."

And Mr. Taft truly adds: "It has been said that a poet is entitled to credit for anything that his poems suggest. If the same applies to sculpture, Mr. Barnard may claim on this work a bountiful royalty, for it has been interpreted in many ways: 'Life drawn unto Death,' 'Life reclaimed by Relentless Matter—Earth,' 'For now we see through a glass, darkly; but then face to face,' 'Sympathy' and the like. The original idea of the artist was, however, 'The Unseen Giver,' one who extends a helping hand without hope of recognition or reward."

In this work particularly, some critics in France were stirred to criticize Barnard because he made use of undeveloped or unformed rough marble, as Rodin and Michael Angelo sometimes did. The best answer to that is that the import of these figures would have been expressionless without the unfinished block to grope in, the nebulous effect of a rough block being quite similar to the "atmosphere" in a painting. However, in the Champ de Mars in 1894 Barnard at thirty-one placed before the critic and public the results of his efforts to date in the yearly Salon-Champ de Mars. He was immediately elected an Associate of the Société Nationale des Beaux Arts. Artists and critics united in proclaiming his work the sensation of the year and the sculptor now "made" and famous was fêted and entertained by the great art patrons of Paris.

From now on he made New York his home. Work after work emerged from his hands—impelled by and expressing the deep-toned soul that could not rest. His great humanitarian nature led him to center his interest more and more in a profound study of our President Abraham Lincoln whose nature he thoroughly searched and sensed, and he has left us numerous records of his physiognomy that will probably never be excelled. Of his heroic, much-discussed statue of Lincoln, it is doubtless true that he sought too strenuously to show the elemental, even uncouth rather than the nobler aspect of the man, but nobody can say it was done without profound thought and consummate skill. His last herculean endeavor, unfortunately left unfinished at the time of his death, "The Rainbow Arch," was again the outpouring of his soul toward humanity. Rarely does the record of a life leave us with impressions of such consistency, originality and power as that of George Grey Barnard.

OWEN WISTER

BY HENRY DWIGHT SEDGWICK

OWEN WISTER was born on July 14, 1860; he died on July 21, 1938. His father, Dr. Owen Jones Wister, was a country practitioner living at Butler Place just outside of Philadelphia and a delightful man, with a sweet personality;

his mother was the daughter of Fanny Kemble, one of that notable family of actors, the most gifted that ever was in England and perhaps in Europe. I remember well my first visit to Butler Place, at the end of our freshman year, how, during my first meal, Dr. Wister referred to Admiral X. I said, "I am sorry I have never heard of Admiral X." Dr. Wister replied with a loud guffaw, "He was cashiered from the Navy." "What for, sir?" I asked. More guffawing. "Because he called the Queen of Spain the son of a b-h." (It is evident that the Admiral did not say it with a smile.) I was terribly embarrassed by the expression, and did not know which way to look.

And of Mrs. Kemble, Mrs. Wister's mother, endless stories were told sixty years ago. For instance, she was staying at the village hotel in Lenox, kept by a Yankee, Mr. Curtis. She asked him to take her for a drive. He did so, and began to talk, Yankee fashion, as equal to equal. "Silence, my good man!" she said, in her Lady Macbeth manner, and he shut up. On her bill at the close of the week, after the figures for food and lodging, appeared the item: "Sass,—five dollars. When I takes it, I gets paid for it." Mrs. Kemble was delighted, and the two became fast friends. You see Wister was brought up in a family of marked personality. He was also brought up upon Shakespeare's plays and Walter Scott's novels, perhaps the best of educations to make a civilized gentleman; and Wister did become a highly civilized gentleman of the Eighteenth Century English type. I am aware that this is a contentious term, but Wister was of that type, and they that like it, like it very much.

The tide of Democracy, the legacy of a lawless frontier, the influence of an enfranchised proletariat, the compulsions of universal conformity, with their several enmities to privacy, to reticence, to the old notions of personal rights, cause the mass of our fellow countrymen to decry and deride the type, and, what is worse, render them almost ignorant of it. Owen Wister, in spirit, as I say, belonged to the Eighteenth

Century, and sometimes the consequent maladjustments touched his spleen; but, then, in that century, people sometimes were splenetic. Let me go into some particulars.

Wister set great store on the value of tradition, of manners; he liked form, finish, a touch of ceremony. He believed that human intercourse is a matter of art, that, for instance, little delicacies in the mode of coming forward to greet a guest, whether a new acquaintance, or formal company for dinner, or an old friend—the inclination of the head, the outstretching of the arm, the carriage of the body—are matters of importance, never to be slurred over or neglected, unless on purpose; for Wister could be curt, where he deemed curtness appropriate. And when I speak of good manners I do not mean foppery (as you can see by his admiration for the behaviour of his hero, The Virginian), but the sum of little acts and words that show human kindliness, and a wish to make human intercourse a pleasure. I have often thought that among the most charming acts of courtesy I have ever seen was the way in which Wister listened in conversation. You may hear a hundred distinguished men in America talk, and talk interestingly and agreeably, but you will have to go to the hundred and oneth before you will find a courteous listener, one who foregoes his lion's share of the talk. There was something almost histrionic in Wister's carefulness about these matters, and I fancy that he got this from his Kemble ancestors. He always brought to my mind, by some wayward association of ideas, a multifarious Eighteenth Century background, a hall paneled by the Adams, a ceiling painted by Tiepolo, *fauteuils* by Boulle, a spinet played on by Cimarosa, an armchair with Burke sitting up into the small hours to finish reading *Evelina*, yes, and a touch of Washington at Valley Forge,—for few know with what dogged courage Wister bore a great private sorrow for many years.

He possessed, too, another Eighteenth Century quality, rationality. He was in religious matters an agnostic; had he actually lived in the Eighteenth Century, he would have been a deist. He liked the reasonable, the understandable, the measured, the orderly. I cannot remember definitely, but I feel sure that he preferred Pope to Shelley; and held a vague notion that romantic people overstepped the limits of propriety in the expression of their sentiments. He had,—he could not escape it, born in a Shakespearian family and bred upon Walter Scott,—a romantic strain, as is so obvious in *The Virginian*, but he fancied that that was adventitious, and he did not like to have it thought to be a part of his nature. So, too, beneath his agnostic rationalism, lay a strong Christian sentiment. He was ill for near a year before he died, and on his bed in that great New York hospital, that lifts its glassy magnificence to heaven, like choirs of Beauvais Cathedral piled one above another, he talked to a friend about Jesus of Nazareth, and what Jesus meant in this troubled world, and what would happen to everybody, if science with its insistence upon chemical and physical energies should strip away all reverence for Jesus's supernatural conception of the universe. This unexpected lapse from rationalism—I use the old-fashioned terminology; by rationalism I mean the belief that the mind should dominate the emotions—was due largely to St. Paul's school, where he was educated, and to the influence of Dr. Coit.

Wister had, too, what he used to call the healthy Eighteenth Century attitude toward the unseemly facts of life: he enjoyed the "manliness" in *Tom Jones,* and once, when somebody was deploring the mediaeval humor in Chaucer (which affects the normal civilized being like crossing the Channel in a squall after too many *lemon squashes*) he said, "Well, you know that of course I revel in it." He had adopted what he considered a rational point of view; man stands on his hind legs, but he is an animal and has animal traits, let us be honest and acknowledge it. He believed that the animal side of man should have its place in literature, but he himself never used words that violated the most strict sense of propriety, and I remember hearing him censure the license

in that respect of a distinguished American novelist with
some asperity. Certainly, he was far from being a Puritan, he
thought the Puritanical attitude towards life wrong. He was
a professed Epicurean, in the good, and in what some call the
bad, sense of the word. He delighted in beauty, in what,
following what I suppose is common usage, I call the nobler
pleasures of life, though he would never admit that one pleasure was nobler than another. One pleasure, he maintained,
may be more pleasurable than another, more heavily charged
with enjoyment, but not more noble. He loved to sit in the
Cathedral of Chartres (he always made a pilgrimage there,
on every visit to France), and muse before the storied windows, and under the holy arches of the crossing. I remember
how he stood silent in the cathedral at Burgos, in the Alham-
bra, in the Capella Palatina at Palermo, and at Olympia,
within the sacred enclosure by the river Alpheus, where
under pine trees, mystically musical in the gentle wind, ane-
mones, poppies, and various shy little white flowers adorn
the graveyard of the ancient gods—*i dei falsi e bugiardi*—
and shake his head as if to say how sad that men no longer
create such things, and turn to his companions, as men do in
church, expressing sympathy by communion without speech,
"Yes, this is a holy place." In that temenos thoughts lay too
deep for words.

Wister was true to his century, too, in that he did not like
the proletariat; he had a vague notion that they should, as
the English gentry had thought for hundreds of years, remain in that position of life to which it had pleased God to
call them, where they would not interfere with a gentleman's
fastidious enjoyment of the good things of life, things, under
God's inscrutable Providence, quite beyond proletarian
reach. He thought well of persons who shared his theories
of values—he preferred men educated at a university, who
possessed a smattering of the classics, who knew something
about French literature and Italian music, who acknowledged the greatness of Wagner and delighted in Offenbach,

who recognized quotations from Shakespeare and were familiar with Prosper Mérimée and Henri Meilhac, whose clothes had an English cut, and were horrified when any children dwelling in the same street chewed gum. But he liked and enjoyed his cowboy friends quite as much as he did those who had been university bred, and he was an admirable "mixer."

As I have said, he was educated, as the phrase is, at St. Paul's School, Concord, New Hampshire, and at Harvard College. He graduated with a degree *summa cum laude* in music, and expected to devote himself to music; he then studied in Paris, had an opportunity to play his own compositions to Franz Liszt, and was encouraged by the master to follow a musical career, but for family reasons he was put to business in Boston. His health suffered, and he went to Wyoming for recuperation; and then entered the Harvard Law School, from which he graduated in 1888. He practised law in Philadelphia for a couple of years, but his real bent was for letters, and through his sojourn in Wyoming (very different in those days from what it is now), the West had touched his imagination and his heart. He filled many little note books with careful records of what he saw and heard, and then set to work upon his tales of cowboys. *The Virginian* was published in 1902, *Lady Baltimore* in 1906, *The Pentecost of Calamity* came out during the Great War, and *An Ancient Grudge* not long after. He was a lifelong friend of Theodore Roosevelt, and after the latter's death, wrote *The Story of a Friendship*. His tales of Western life are said to depict, better than any history, various aspects of cowboy life that are now gone forever; and *The Virginian*, I presume, occupies a secure place on a front shelf in American literature. *Philosophy IV* and many other tales are delightful. *The Pentecost of Calamity* was one of the best war books, and *An Ancient Grudge* useful and timely. His style was clear, fresh, and downright. But Wister did not confine his interests to music, literature and the West, he was a public-spirited citizen of Philadelphia, and did what he could to improve political conditions in what he considered an imperfect city. The last public episode in his life was to preside over a meeting, called to protest against President Roosevelt's proposal to make changes in the Supreme Court. In order to interfere with this meeting some supporters of the President's proposal obtained a warrant to arrest him on the charge of violating some local statute, but before the warrant was served, he appeared voluntarily before the magistrate, and the charge was set aside, or withdrawn. I forget which.

So he went through life, learning many hard lessons, bearing a great sorrow with calm, reticent manliness, becoming every year more considerate, more genial, urbane and mellow, diffusing more and more an atmosphere of what the Greeks meant by the qualities of καλὸς κ' ἀγαθὸς, until he became a very accomplished gentleman and a delightful friend.

1939

SIDNEY HOWARD

BY WILLIAM LYON PHELPS

SIDNEY COE HOWARD was born June 26, 1891, and died August 23, 1939.
In the theatre Americans have made more progress in the twentieth century than in any other art. From 1492 till 1919 no play was written in America that combined distinction in literature with theatrical effectiveness. Clyde Fitch wrote many good acting plays, which also have value for the student of society; but they do not quite belong among permanent contributions to literature.

American drama began in 1919 with *Beyond the Horizon,* by Eugene O'Neill. During the twenty years after that date, in addition to a succession of plays by O'Neill, the American stage was illuminated by the work of Sidney Howard, Robert E. Sherwood, Elmer Rice, Philip Barry, Maxwell Anderson, Thornton Wilder, Sidney Kingsley, Marc Connelly, and Rachel Crothers.

Sidney Howard was born in Oakland, California, and received his B.A. degree at the University of California in 1915. The following year he was at Harvard, studying under Professor George P. Baker. The next year he went to France and drove an ambulance on the Western Front and in the Balkans. After the United States declared war, he became a Captain in Aviation.

While on the editorial staff of *Life,* he began to write plays. He was married to Clare Eames, a distinguished American actress. After her death he was married to Leopoldine Blaine Damrosch, daughter of our beloved Walter Damrosch. This was an ideally happy marriage. After three or four dramas that showed potential powers, the Theatre Guild produced in November, 1924, his drama, *They Knew What They Wanted;* this ran for a year, and was awarded the Pulitzer Prize. In 1925 *Lucky Sam McCarver* attracted favorable attention, though it was not so good a play as its predecessor; but in 1926-1927 the Theatre Guild produced two of Howard's plays, *Ned McCobb's Daughter* and *The Silver Cord,* both adding greatly to his reputation, and the latter being one of the finest American plays of our times.

In the twelve years of activity that followed, Sidney Howard showed a steady advance, both in his art and in its intellectual content. *Yellow Jack* was a remarkable and wholly original drama, dealing with the heroic conquest of yellow fever; the scenes and their setting were unlike conventional stage effects and were very impressive. One of the most successful adaptations of a modern novel was Mr. Howard's *Dodsworth,* taken not from Sinclair Lewis's more satirical works, but from what is perhaps his most judicial appraisal and representation of American life. Mr. Lewis collaborated on this play.

Mr. Howard was a cosmopolitan in outlook and in knowledge. He translated and adapted for the stage Edmond Rostand's posthumous play, *The Last Night of Don Juan; S. S. Tenacity,* from the French of Charles Vildrac; *Morals,* from the German of Ludwig Thoma; *Olympia,* from the Hungarian of Molnar; *Marius,* from the French of Pagnol.

Among other important plays were his *Alien Corn* and *The Late Christopher Bean.*

Apart from his work as a man of letters, Mr. Howard took an active part in public affairs. He was President of the American Dramatists Guild, member of the Society of American Dramatists and Composers, and on the Board of Directors of the American Civil Liberties Union. He held strong convictions as a Liberal; but he was first, last, and all the time a creative writer, devoted to the theatre. He was engaged in the composition of a play at the time of his death.

This tragic accident cut short a career that not only had given him a permanent place in the history of American drama, but was full of promise for the future.

Seldom have we seen a man so positive and so sincere in conviction, with so lovable a disposition. Everyone who knew him felt his irresistible charm.

1940

JONAS LIE
BY ROYAL CORTISSOZ

IT IS THREE YEARS, almost to a day, since Jonas Lie was elected to the American Academy of Arts and Letters. That is not a very long period and it was curtailed by his death on January 10th of the present year. But it was long enough to secure for him a firm place in the warm regard of the Academy. All his traits as a man and an artist peculiarly fitted him for membership in a forward-looking organization like this, which is faithful to tradition but accepts it as an inspiration rather than as a formula and would take from the past only those basic principles which promise progress in the present and in the future. When Lie was elected president of the National Academy of Design in 1934 he said to an inquirer: "The Academy must necessarily be conservative. It must stick to the tried and proven. Nevertheless there are certain changes which I think would be for the advancement of the organization." He made them, living up to the liberalism which he thus proclaimed.

Jonas Lie was born at Moss, in Norway, in 1880, the son of a civil engineer. He was named after his uncle, a poet and novelist, with whom he lived and studied in Paris until he was twelve years old. At thirteen, his father having died, he came to the United States and aided in the support of his mother and sisters by working as a designer in a cotton factory for nine years. In the evenings he frequented the classes of the Art Students' League and the National Academy of Design. His first picture, "The Grey Day," was hung in an Academy exhibition when he was only nineteen. Thenceforth his success was rapid. It was in 1913 that he painted a memorable series of pictures showing the Panama Canal in the course of its construction. Twelve of these canvases were presented by an anonymous donor in 1929 to the Military Academy at West Point, in honor of Gen. Goethals, the builder of the canal. There are many public places in which his pictures hang. One of his works is in the White House, a picture of the Amberjack which as a close friend of Mr. Roosevelt he gave to the President in 1933. The list of his paintings in public museums and of the various artistic and other bodies to which he belonged is too long to be recited upon this occasion.

He was an American through and through but it must have been partly an inheritance from his native Norway that enabled him to fill his pictures with lucent air. He painted them in various parts of the world, in Brittany but far more in New England and in the Adirondacks. Wherever he painted them, he gave them the tang of nature studied at close quarters, the atmospheric quality which is half the battle. He had color, too, good color, and American art was made the richer by his luminous, vivid impressions. A favorite motive of his was a stretch of water dotted by the white sails of boats and seen through a frame supplied by gleaming birch trees. He made it beautiful and did so, moreover, not only through the charm inherent in his vision but through a fine technical authority.

He was an able executive as well as an able artist and the National Academy owed him much through his tenure of the presidential office. His administration offered conclusive evidence that conservatism, which he practised in his art, in no wise connotes a narrow point of view. On the contrary, he was a singularly openminded leader, hospitable to the younger generation, the friend of genuine art, no matter where it originated. Also he was a tireless worker, positively heroic in his labors, for example, over the special exhibition that the Academy presented à propos of the World's Fair, in 1939. He made substantial sacrifices of energy in the preparation of that admirable project. And his sympathies extended beyond the interests of the institution which had placed him at its head. He was, in his time, an efficient member of the Municipal Art Commission and he gave his services to many another instrument for our artistic betterment.

Endowed with an engaging personality, Jonas Lie was an always welcome and helpful spokesman for good taste and progress. He had humor, candor and an ingratiating mode of approach to a subject. His life as an artist was full of triumphs, but they never softened him. When illness came he faced its difficulties with courage. He was cut off untimely, in his fifty-ninth year. A wide circle of his fellow artists who rejoiced in his talent, and a large public long finding enjoyment in his work, must join with the Academy in regrets over his passing.

HAMLIN GARLAND
BY BOOTH TARKINGTON

A BIT OF AUTOBIOGRAPHY, offered with apologies, may serve as a slight indication of the size and scope of Hamlin Garland's kindness of heart. After college I'd been writing industriously for years but to no effect whatever except to produce an interminable drizzle of printed rejection slips; and then, one day, suddenly out of the seeming nowhere, came a letter from a stranger, though I'd heard much of him. A magazine editor had handed him a long manuscript of mine, and the letter began with four dumbfounding words that changed everything for me: "You are a novelist." I couldn't imagine anybody's saying such a thing, and last of all could I have believed that an accredited novelist would ever say it; but after I came to know Hamlin Garland I found that nothing was more typical of him than his stopping work to write such a letter to a groping, unknown youth dismally mystified about himself and the art of writing. Hamlin Garland was as indefatigable for people unknown to him as he was for his acquaintances, and he was as warmly in the service of an acquaintance as most of us are in the cause of a close friend.

It is impossible to think of Garland without thinking of his kindness, the greatness of heart that was in all of his work and in all of his life; and I believe that next one thinks of his integrity, his almost incorrigible intellectual probity. Moreover, his eye was ever as clear as his heart was kind and as his mind was honest, and this clarity is in all that he wrote; it is in his selection of words, the words that he used as author and the words that he heard from the mouths of his fictitious people. It's a truism to say that he was a realist. It would have been impossible for him to be anything else. To him realism didn't mean either the "candid camera" or a detective's dictaphone; he practised it as an art, and could write of the soil without using fertilizer for ink.

Hamlin Garland was a middle-westerner who was at home in Boston, New York, Chicago, Louisiana, the Dakotas and anywhere in California. Born in Wisconsin, he lived all over the United States and was every good kind of American. He was an outdoor man and an indoor man; he was a hand on a Wisconsin farm and he was a member of the American Academy of Arts and Letters. He was a novelist, a biographer, a historian, a playwright and a serious investigator in psychic research. As a novelist he now may be known most generally, I suppose, because of *A Son of the Middle Border*, *Rose of Dutchers Coolly* and *The Captain of the Gray Horse Troop*, and I hope that as a biographer he will be remembered as the author of the life he wrote of General Grant, that touchingly true portrait of a great soldier. Yet it could not be more truly and sympathetically the picture of a human being than are the portraits of people in his novels and stories; all his days he was a friendly searcher for the truth about people, about life and about death. I think it's possible that as a realistic novelist, as well

as an inquiring human being, he sought the truth about
death because he knew that without at least some inkling of
it the truth about life could never be comprehended.

The title of one of his books is significant of the time during which this quest was a preoccupation of his—*Forty Years
of Psychic Research.* He was not a credulous man, not a
wishful thinker; he was always a realist. After all those
years his conclusion was that the "case for survival" had to
be marked "not proven." Then when he was well into his
seventies, he came almost accidentally upon new evidence,
and it was of the kind he'd long sought.

The "case for survival" depends of course upon the ex-
clusion from observed psychic phenomena of the possibility
that these are produced by manifestation of clairvoyance projected by a living mind. That is, the dead person must prove
himself to be dead by communicating to the living investigator a fact known to the dead only. I think it was in 1937
that Garland wrote to me of his new discoveries; he rather
more than suspected that he was turning up the requisite
type of evidence, not in a single instance but in quantity.
Later I learned what great physical activity his new research
required of him and how thoroughly and indomitably he
pursued the priceless bit of knowledge that was his objective.
I think that for himself at least he at last obtained it, although
in his published account he carefully avoided the air of triumphant statement.

This account is called *The Mystery of the Buried Crosses,*
and at the end of the book he wrote that he merely presented
"the problems involved in the discovery of these barbaric
buried amulets." Then he added, "Unlike the true frontiersman, few of us who seek the borderlands of human life are
able to overtake the forms which flee, or touch the hands
which beckon."

The Mystery of the Buried Crosses is possibly one of the
most important books ever written. A year ago, in 'Thirty-
nine, he wrote of it to me, "I fear Duttons have given it up

as a failure. I played fair with my readers. I quoted arguments from opposing experts and I left the verdict to my readers. This, probably, counts against its acceptance. . . . As Howells once said to me, 'What have we old fellows to do *but* work?' I keep well and (as my book witnesses) able to climb hills and wallow through cactus—but I am getting old—almost seventy-nine."

I doubt that until then he had often felt his age. He always seemed to be among the most living and imperishable of men. His body, happily, had always been as lively as his mind. True himself, he sought the truth in everything, sought it with unmitigated zeal, dug for it ardently, reached for it earnestly and yet never over-reached for it. When he found it he did not mourn over it, didn't exult over it—he presented it. His interest in death was his interest in life.

JOHN HUSTON FINLEY
BY NICHOLAS MURRAY BUTLER

ONE DAY toward the close of the year 1902, Edward M. Shepard of Brooklyn, then a Trustee of the College of the City of New York, told me that General Alexander S. Webb, who had been president of that college since 1869, was about to retire. Mr. Shepard asked me whether I could suggest some young man who might be considered for this important post. It was on the point of becoming much more important than it had been, because of plans which were making for the development of the college, as well as for providing it with a new group of stately and well equipped buildings. I told Mr. Shepard that I knew a young man of unusual personal charm who was a scholar, an admirable speaker and a good administrator, who was then a professor at Princeton University. I said that it would probably be impossible to detach him from his academic relationship at Princeton, but that he was just the sort of man that I was sure the Trustees of the College of the City of New York were seeking. He whom I had in mind was John H. Finley, then about forty years of age, and already making quite evident the possession of those qualities and characteristics which gave his life its charm, its usefulness and its distinction. After a series of conferences with Mr. Shepard and his fellow trustees, Dr. Finley was offered the presidency of the College of the City of New York, and was installed in that post on September 29, 1903.

It was ten years later, on a hot Sunday morning in August, when I met Dr. Finley walking up Fifth Avenue near 42nd Street. He hailed me and said: "You are just the man I have been trying to see, but I heard that you were on holiday and away from New York. Look at this! I had to answer before I had a chance to consult you." He drew from his pocket a letter advising him that he was to be elected Commissioner of Education for the State of New York, and showed me his letter of acceptance. He said: "What do you think of that?" "Well, Finley," I replied, "it is no doubt a most unusual honor, but I cannot help looking at it as proposing to use a razor to cut down a tree." A quarter-century later Dr. Finley reminded me of that sentence, and said that the years had taught him what it was that I meant.

Dr. Finley's career was certainly exceptional. Not only did he hold the distinguished positions which I have named, but when in 1921 he left Albany to join the editorial staff of the *New York Times* he greatly increased the scope of his influence and multiplied his opportunities for reaching the public mind. He made it plain to his fellow countrymen that he was distinguished not only as educator and as orator but as editor as well. It would not be easy to find in the history of his day and generation a career of greater usefulness or zeal in public service.

Dr. Finley was born in a small town in the state of Illinois on October 19, 1863. He was graduated from the neighboring Knox College in 1887, and then went on to Johns Hopkins University for graduate study in his chosen fields of literature and politics. After several years of service with the State Charities Aid Association in New York, he was for seven years, from 1892 to 1899, President of Knox College, his Alma Mater. Then, in 1900, he became professor of politics at Princeton University. This was the definite beginning of his years of leadership in the instruction and guidance of public opinion. The *New York Times* has testified with strongest emphasis to its appreciation of his service to that great newspaper and through it to the service of the public.

This is not the place to dwell in detail upon all the happenings in Dr. Finley's life. It cannot be long before a suitable biography will be written to record in our literature the story of this most admirable career. After all has been said and done, it will be recognized that it is Dr. Finley's charm of personality and the many-sidedness of his nature and of his intellectual interests upon which those who knew him intimately most like to dwell. The story of some of his remarkable walking expeditions in Palestine and Greece and Scotland as well as in different parts of the United States reveals a human being of many-sided contacts with his fellow-men and their history. The causes to which he gave such generous and helpful service in our modern life were those which have greatest meaning for the happiness and the well-being of mankind.

John Finley's knowledge of the English Bible and of the Greek and Roman classics was certainly remarkable. It was this knowledge which guided his thinking and enriched his literary style. He led an intellectual life which was spiritual and a spiritual life which was intellectual. His strong religious feeling and faith really dominated his life and gave him those satisfactions which religious faith alone can bring. His painless death on March 7 of the present year, without a struggle, brought this life to an end with almost dramatic appropriateness. It would have been sorrowful indeed, had

404

such a nature as his been sentenced to long and difficult illness in preparation for death.

John Finley was chosen to membership in the American Academy of Arts and Letters in 1927, in well earned recognition of his writing and his eloquent spoken words. He greatly valued the associations which membership in the Academy brought to him, and he was loyal and devoted in his membership.

John Finley was one of the few outstanding personalities of our time. His faith was such that he might have been expected to repeat the extraordinary last words of the late Earl Balfour, who, as his eyes closed, whispered:

"This is going to be a great experience."

EDWIN MARKHAM

BY WILLIAM LYON PHELPS

EDWIN MARKHAM was born on April 23, Shakespeare's Birthday, 1852; he died on March 7, 1940, having very nearly attained the age of 88. He was born at Oregon City, Oregon, near the shore of the Pacific Ocean, and died on the shore of the Atlantic, thus illustrating Wordsworth's famous conception of human life—that our life on earth is between two mighty oceans of eternity.

Great poets are more important than great statesmen, great scientists, great military men; for while man cannot live without bread, man cannot live by bread alone. The highest values are spiritual. It is better to have the assurance of immortality, of a great destiny, of the significance of the individual personality, than it is to have any knowledge or any gain outside of these. After the depression of 1929, Christopher Morley called on President Hoover in the White House, and asked him what he thought was America's greatest need. The President replied, "America's greatest need is a great poet." Carlyle said that no nation was great until it had a voice; and we know that Italy is not great today because every little boy is sleeping on his knapsack, but because Italy has Dante and the great painters. Germany is not great because she has conquered some other nations, but because she has Goethe and the great musical composers. Russia is not great because she is theoretically communistic, but because she has Turgenev, Tolstoy, Chekhov, and Dostoevski. England is not great primarily because she has the most powerful navy in the world (though I thank God she has) but because she has Shakespeare and a larger number of great poets than any other nation, past or present.

Edwin Markham in his childhood unconsciously gave a good imitation of David. After the death of his father, his mother took the younger children from Oregon to California, and settled on a cattle range near the Coast Mountains. Here Edwin became a shepherd, and spent long happy days following the flocks and herds in the sunlight, and often slept under the stars.

The public school was open only three months in the year, but there happened to be a teacher who loved poetry, and it was this man who awakened in Edwin a passion for poetry which dominated his life. Later the young man became a school teacher himself, then Superintendent of schools in a little town in the Sierras. Here he happened to open a magazine that contained among the illustrations Millet's famous picture of the Man with the Hoe, the second inspiration of his life.

Edwin Markham was not a man of one poem; but it is certain, no matter what he himself thought of the whole range of his work, that this poem, "The Man with the Hoe," must always remain his masterpiece, because it had more influence than all the rest of his productions put together. As Browning said, we judge of the power of men by the length of the shadow they cast; and this poem threw a shadow across the whole world. It was not written impromptu, nor indeed even in a short time. He began it, worked on it at various places and at various times, and finished it near San Francisco in the Christmas vacation of 1899.

Had he spoken it over the radio, it could not have received more instant acclaim. The response of the world was immediate and tremendous. As a result he spent the rest of his happy life not only in writing, but in visiting every State in the Union, speaking to huge audiences and reading his works. On the occasion of the poet's eightieth birthday, widely celebrated, William Rose Benét made an accurate estimate of Edwin Markham's position in literature:

"Markham has retained unusual vigor, both in his personality and his writing. He has always been a dogmatic poet, but with a great liberality of spirit and an accomplished knowledge of versification. He has never surpassed his 'Hoe' and his 'Lincoln' poems. They were the work he was primarily born to do."

His funeral, in Brooklyn, on Sunday, March 10th, was a national event; and he was buried in Los Angeles, beside the grave of his wife.

ROBERT GRANT
BY M. A. DeWOLFE HOWE

ROBERT GRANT was a man of many books. Thirty-one titles are listed under his name in the 1940-41 volume of *Who's Who*, and there are always fugitive writings which escape tabulation. It was, of course, in his capacity as a writer that he became in 1915 a member of this Academy, to which he proved his devotion through the later years of his life as a most active and energetic member of its Board of Directors. It is not enough, however, to recall his books and his effective interest in the affairs of the Academy. His identification with the life of his time is no less to be remembered.

His books and his life, be it noted, stood in a close relation to each other. This is not merely another way of saying the style was the man, for in Robert Grant's case the substance of his writings, no less than their style, marked them distinctively as his own. It is a truism that every writer is conditioned in greater or less degree by his personal background of experience. With Grant the degree was more than commonly great. Born and bred in the tradition of that Boston which extended itself in his time from Beacon Hill to the Back Bay, and knew not other regions, he was, through his own associations and tastes, a true representative of it, and, in *The Chippendales*, he pictured it to the life.

This book may be regarded as a milestone on the road at one end of which stood *The Bostonians* and *The Rise of Silas Lapham*, and at the other *The Late George Apley*. James and Howells in the 1880's and Mr. Marquand in the 1930's conducted their social studies of Boston, each on terms of his own, and with perceptions and methods quite other than those of Robert Grant. No one of them, however, was so indigenous to Boston as he, and none of them sought more honestly and sympathetically to depict the typical Bostonian of his period—in *The Chippendales* the final decade of the nineteenth century. In his *Fourscore: an Autobiography* (1934) he could write of his young hero, Henry Chippendale Sumner: "I recognized enough of myself in him to be able to depict him exactly as he was, even when prevented by unworthiness from following him." Thus he may be said to have been both the writer and in some measure the hero of one of his most widely read books.

Born January 24, 1852, he first saw the light of day on Beacon Hill. The Boston Latin School, coasting and fighting on the Common, summers at Nahant—through life as in boyhood—Harvard College, with four undergraduate years, three more for a Ph.D. in Philology and three beyond these for the degree of LL.B.—ten years in all—these experiences, as if not enough, were followed in later decades by twenty-four years on the Harvard Board of Overseers. In spite of all this exposure to learning, he was more a thoughtful, and most agreeable, man of the world than a profound scholar. He took much pleasure in his clubs, his cards, his salmon-fishing and golf, his close contacts, through kinship and friendship, with large segments of the circle to which he belonged. As he took pleasure, so he gave it—through the charm of personality that makes for ease in the relations between human beings in every generation.

Like the typical Bostonian of his own fiction he was not merely a private citizen, practising his profession of the law. As a young man he served for a time as Secretary to a Mayor of Boston, the learned Dr. Samuel A. Green, best known for his long, scholarly service to the Massachusetts Historical Society. After five years as Water Commissioner of Boston, Grant was appointed, in 1893, Judge of the Probate Court and Court of Insolvency for Suffolk County, and here he served for thirty years. Each of these posts had for him the advantage that its duties did not prevent a man of native energy and self-imposed industry from following his bent as a writer.

With Grant this was truly a life-long bent. He began to pursue it in college, became an early editor of the *Harvard Lampoon* while in the Law School, and found himself launched as a popular writer when three of his ventures in satiric verse, first printed in the *Lampoon,* were published in a pamphlet, *The Little Tin-Gods-on-Wheels, or Society in our Modern Athens,* illustrated by Francis G. Attwood, famous thereafter for his drawings in *Life.* A year later, in 1880, came *The Confessions of a Frivolous Girl,* the first of many prose studies of the social scene—light as air, now definitely "dated," but notable in retrospect as a starting-point for a long and steady development. Various aspects of the society he knew served as themes for a number of later books, of fiction and of genial observation, as in the Reflections, Opinions, and Convictions, respectively, of a Married Man, a Philosopher, and a Grandfather.

Within the narrow limits of this sketch it would be impossible even to name all these books. One of the best of them, *The Chippendales* (1909), an authentic treatment of that irresistible theme of novelists, Boston and its inhabitants, has already been mentioned. Its validity as a picture of life in Robert Grant's Boston is only confirmed by the last of all his books, *Fourscore: an Autobiography*, a narrative of fact which provides many bits of documentation both for *The Chippendales* and for other pieces of the author's fiction. It should be said, however, that the relation between personal experience and imaginative writing is least discernible of all in the novel generally, and rightly, regarded as Grant's best, and most widely read.

This was his *Unleavened Bread,* published in 1900. Here the scene is laid in a "western city with an eastern exposure," in New York, and in Washington. Boston is not remotely included in its map. Its central figure, Selma White—of a period in which "the war" was still our Civil War—represented a type still new when the nineteenth century was ending, the American clubwoman, humorless and ruthless in the pursuit of her own ambitions, and, thanks to the author's rejection of all sentimentality in dealing with her, triumphantly winning everything she set out to attain. "The novel was written," Grant declared in *Fourscore*, "with more intensity of conviction than any other book of mine. I detested my heroine, but was fascinated by her, for I knew her to be a true creation not hitherto portrayed in fiction." So indeed she was, a detestable figure, relentlessly presented, and standing as a permanent contribution to the gallery of American womanhood in one of its least attractive forms. The satirist whose prentice hand was tried on Frivolous Girls created in Selma White a character who cannot be overlooked by any realistic social historian of the United States at the time when Robert Grant was at the height of his powers.

It was a far cry for him, at seventy-five years of age, retired from the Probate Court, and nearly at the end of his creative writing, to turn to a brief employment which fixed the eyes of the world upon him in an entirely unaccustomed light. This was his service on the Commission appointed in 1927 by Governor Fuller of Massachusetts to report to him upon the fairness of the murder trial of Sacco and Vanzetti. It was an assignment which Grant had neither sought nor desired, and it took him into a field of law in which he and his two colleagues were without direct experience. This is no place to discuss the case or the report of the Commission. Controversy was bound to follow any settlement of the matter. Grant himself discussed it at length in his *Fourscore*. His nature would not permit him to dismiss it as a *fait accompli* calling for no afterthoughts. His frank recital of the facts as they remained in his mind after the passage of seven years stands in clear witness of his personal integrity through an affair of portentous moment.

In the spring of 1938 it was my good fortune to sail from Southampton to New York on the same ship with him. His wife, whom, as Amy Galt of Montreal, he had married in 1883, had recently died, after a singularly happy union of more than fifty years. Accompanied by his secretary, he had been spending a winter on the Riviera. His eyesight and hearing were failing, but an unbreakable spirit of youth and friendliness made him the most congenial of shipmates, and won the hearts of many who had never seen him before. So it was to the end of his days—with old friends encountered in the usual meeting-places, and with new, for even after visiting the Mediterranean at eighty-six he journeyed to Hawaii, with all the zest of a young traveller. He died in Boston May 19, 1940, in his eighty-ninth year, survived by three of his four sons.

FREDERICK J. E. WOODBRIDGE

BY THORNTON WILDER

To some philosophy means a long discipline in abstract speculation; to the man in the street it means little more than resignation; to Professor Woodbridge it was neither abtruse nor passive. As writer, teacher, editor and administrator he felt philosophy to be in constant relation to every man's daily life. Professor Woodbridge was not only a lover of wisdom himself, but he called forth the operation of the philosophic faculty in all who came in contact with him. He lived through the years when the United States was producing a school of philosophy which arrested the attention of the whole thinking world and he played a vital part in that movement, but he freely acknowledged that he was more occupied with its extension than with the formulation of its doctrines. He said of himself: "The principle of realism seems so important to me for metaphysics and philosophy that I have been more busy with championing it than with developing it." This championship was as remarkable for its diversity as for its vigor.

Frederick James Eugene Woodbridge was born in Windsor, Ontario, in 1867. His father was actively engaged at the time in certain movements of political reform in the community, but impatient with the conservatism of his fellow-citizens he presently crossed the border into this country and became the head of an institution of public health in Kalamazoo, Michigan. Frederick Woodbridge went from the schools of Kalamazoo to Amherst College where he graduated in 1889, returning for the degree of Master of Arts in 1898. The thirty-four years of distinguished scholastic and administrative service which he gave to Columbia University did not prevent his serving his own alma mater with signal devotion: he was trustee of Amherst College for nineteen years; and twice he refused the presidency believing, as he said, that "the final executive decision was not his forte" and that he could be more useful to both institutions as teacher and adviser.

For a time Frederick Woodbridge felt himself to be destined for the ministry and he accepted a scholarship at the Union Theological Seminary in this city, then a Presbyterian institution. Though philosophy was to regain its place as his primary interest, a religious emphasis reappears at intervals in his work and in the last book, *An Essay on Nature,* his discussion of the teleological direction in nature derives from a religious viewpoint. In 1898 he made the first of many trips to Europe. He studied at the University of Berlin where he was to return later as the Theodore Roosevelt Professor of Philosophy. After teaching two years at the University of Minnesota he was called in 1902 to be Professor of Philosophy at Columbia University. In 1895 he had married Miss Helena Belle Adams of Chicago, whose wide interests and sympathies found expression in an influential participation in various movements of social and civic betterment until her death in 1935. Professor and Mrs. Woodbridge are survived by four children.

When Professor Woodbridge first entered teaching the temper of philosophical studies in this country may be described as reflecting a liberal idealism. What Santayana calls "the trade-winds of doctrine" were blowing from Kant, Hegel, and the English rationalists. But the tide was gathering for the movement which, stemming from Charles Pierce's influence on William James and reinforced by a world-wide activity in experimental psychology, was to assume and outgrow the name of Pragmatism. William James published his *Principles of Psychology* in 1880, his *Will to Believe* in 1897; and in 1898 he delivered in Berkeley, California, his epoch-making lecture on "Philosophical Conceptions and Practical Results." Josiah Royce followed with his *Religious Aspects of Philosophy* and John Dewey with his *Studies in Logical Theory* in 1903. This tide was to make the tour of the world and to return to us from the University of Vienna

413

as the logical positivism which is the prevailing "trade-wind of doctrine" that young philosophers are facing today.

It was this movement—"the shifting of emphasis in philosophy from pure intellect to perception," as it has been called—which Professor Woodbridge championed, and his gifts and energy opened up ever wider fields of activity. As an author he is best represented by his volumes *The Purpose of History, The Realm of the Mind* and *An Essay on Nature,* the proofs of which he read during his last illness. On his seventieth birthday, in 1937, the philosophical faculties of Columbia, Minnesota and Amherst combined in publishing and presenting to him a volume of his essays collected from periodicals and from his books. Professor Woodbridge's contribution to the movement as an editor was no less influential: in 1904 he founded *The Journal of Philosophy* and soon after *The Archives of Philosophy.* These journals served as vehicles for the increasingly adventurous declarations of the movement, and rereading them today one can recapture something of what Professor Woodbridge remembered as the "excitement" that surrounded their publication. A still more practical outlet was found, however, for his ideas; in 1912 he was appointed Dean of the Faculties of Political Science, Philosophy, Pure Science and Fine Arts at Columbia University, an office he held until 1929. His annual reports to the President were widely read throughout the country; year after year they aroused fruitful controversy and have taken their place among the classical documents in the theory of higher education.

Professor Woodbridge felt, however, that the formation of those students who are now teaching philosophy in all parts of the world was his principal work, and neither editorial nor administrative duties caused any intermission in this task nor diminished the generous vitality he expended on it. His clarity and force as a writer were equally present in his conversation; he possessed to an unusual degree that art of discussion that is called the Socratic method, whereby ideas seem rather to be elicited than imposed and which combines informality with precision.

Professor Woodbridge became a member of the Academy in 1935. In his death we have lost not only the admired thinker and writer, but a wise associate and a valued friend.

FREDERICK SHEPHERD CONVERSE

BY WILLIAM LYON PHELPS

HE WAS BORN at Newton, Massachusetts, January 5, 1871, the son of Edmund and Charlotte Converse. He was a lineal descendant of Deacon Edward Converse, who came to America from England in 1630. He attended the Newton High School, Cutler's Preparatory School in the same town, and in 1893 was graduated from Harvard with highest honors in Music. I myself had the honor of teaching, in a course known as "daily themes" at Harvard, many men from the undergraduate classes of 1892 and 1893, and I have a pleasant recollection of him and of his work. He was married in 1894 to Emma C. Tudor, and after a business career that lasted fortunately only six months, he decided to make music his chosen life-profession. For about a year and a half he studied in Boston under Carl Baermann and George W. Chadwick; and then for two years at Munich at the Royal Academy of Music under Josef Rheinberger.

After his return to America, he taught Harmony at the New England Conservatory of Music, later was Instructor in the Music Department at Harvard, and was promoted in 1905 to an Assistant Professorship. In 1907 he resigned his post at Harvard to devote himself to original composition; but in 1921 he returned to teaching as Professor at the New England Conservatory, was Head of the Theory Department, and from 1930 to 1938, was Dean of the Faculty, retiring only on account of ill-health.

He was awarded the David Bispham Medal for *The Pipe*

of Desire; he was one of the founders of the Boston Opera Company, of which he was the first Vice-President; he was a member of the Phi Beta Kappa and was elected to the National Institute of Arts and Letters in 1908 and to the American Academy in 1937.

He died at his home in Westwood, Massachusetts, on June 8th, 1940.

In the recently published *Memories of the Opera* by the famous Director of the Metropolitan Opera Company, Giulio Gatti-Casazza, whose death in 1940 removed one of the ablest Directors of Music the world has ever known, and one of the most upright and noble characters, I find that he paid tribute to Mr. Converse for having composed the first American Grand Opera ever produced at the Metropolitan Opera House in New York. This was *The Pipe of Desire.* The production took place March 18, 1910, and the six members of the cast were all Americans except one. Gatti wrote, "Learning of the existence of Frederick Converse's opera, which had been given a quasi-professional production in Boston, I myself made the contract for its presentation at the Metropolitan."

Mr. Converse composed more than one hundred pieces, with a large variety of forms: five symphonies, three suites, eight symphonic poems for orchestra, four operas, an oratorio, several cantatas, a fantasy and concerto for pianoforte and orchestra, string quartets, and many other pieces. Among his most distinguished works are *The Mystic Trumpeter, American Sketches,* and *Flivver Ten Million,* which was called *A Joyous Epic for Orchestra.*

Wallace Goodrich, the distinguished Director of the New England Conservatory of Music, who had already furnished me with many facts in the career of Mr. Converse, was kind enough also to send me some personal reminiscences which are of the highest importance in revealing his personality and character and are written with charming intimacy:

416

FREDERICK SHEPHERD CONVERSE

"My own acquaintance with Mr. Converse goes back t the time when we were about three years old and played together on the floor. From that time on, he was one of my closest friends, and during the last twenty years we were associated here at the Conservatory. It would be difficult to express a full estimate of Mr. Converse in a brief space. He was one of the finest characters I have ever known, and from the very first took a most sympathetic interest in the welfare of those about him. In his later years, he became devoted to the Church, and at the time of his death was Warden of St. Paul's Church in Dedham. He was an indefatigable worker, as the number of his compositions will show. He had great success with the latter, but was able to devote a great deal of time to reading and to matters of general educational importance, particularly as related to musical instruction for students; but I know that you knew him well in the Academy, in which he prized his membership highly. I suppose his most prominent characteristics were his uprightness and conscientiousness, his devotion to his family, and his generous thought for all his fellow men."

And, as Mr. Goodrich remarked, "It was fitting that Mr. Converse's last composition should have been a setting of the great hymn of praise—*Te Deum Laudamus*—the tribute of a noble Christian character to the Divine Lord in whom his faith and trust had never wavered."

It is not always that talent and character are so harmoniously united; and it is a pleasure to add that the members of the Institute and of the Academy who came into close contact with Frederick Converse felt the irresistible charm of his unselfishness and good will.

417

1941

HENRY OSBORN TAYLOR
BY FRANK JEWETT MATHER, JR.

Henry Osborn Taylor belongs to the scant but distinguished line of American private scholars in the succession of Prescott and Parkman—investigators, who being able to pay their own way, never offered their necks to the academic yoke.

He was born on December 5, 1856, in New York, on 10th Street when that was still well uptown. His people were in easy circumstances and of the best social position. A boyhood in city preparatory schools offers few features, but the summer exodus to the family farm at Cobalt, Connecticut, meant the adventure of the little steamer that plied from Peck Slip to Hartford, and put a small boy ashore at a deliciously small hour of the morning. From the fine stone farm house, which later became the modest mansion, Knowles House, the fields sloped down gently between groves to reach the Connecticut, where its tides sweep through a forest gorge. The farm itself provided the joys of haymaking, berry picking, comradeship with simple men and patient animals, primal experiences which were later to serve well the future historian of civilization.

The normal progress of a New York boy of Yankee breed towards Harvard was broken by a curious restlessness. At fifteen he persuaded his parents to let him enter a ship-broker's office. There he read furtively Bain's *Intellect and Senses,* Hallam's *History of Mediaeval Literature,* and Gray's *Botany.* To escape ship-brokerage he joined his brother in the Nevada mining town of Austin, serving as a bookkeeper. While finding out that the move was a mistake, he read such books as *John Halifax, Gentleman,* and Flint's *Physiology;* the sixteen-year-old lad reveals the insatiable intellectual curiosity that ever marked the mature man. On August 2, 1873, one reads in his diary that he has decided to "leave this rough life and become a gentleman." Badly interrupted studies involved a somewhat heroic compensatory course of tutoring.

Entering the class of 1878 at Harvard, he passed, according to his own account, a somewhat solitary four years, yet winning the friendship of Barrett Wendell and the future poet-critic George E. Woodberry. In Henry Adams' course on American History, young Taylor gained lasting notions of methods of research; in Charles Eliot Norton's famous course on the Fine Arts he learned ideals of culture. On graduation in 1878 he proudly wore a Phi Beta Kappa key. His senior essay, under Henry Adams, "Constitutional Development in the Colonies," was accepted by the *Magazine of American History.*

Early in his college years he had chosen the law for his profession, with visions of public usefulness and political prominence. A year at the Columbia Law School produced ambitions for broader studies in Europe. Europe to a studious young American in the late 70's meant just Germany, and the young man added to wide and liberating travel two semesters of assiduous study of Roman Law at Leipzig. In far different activities, Taylor never failed to acknowledge the value of these studies—the discipline of following out clear principles to their practical application, as compared with the clever and empirical allegation of judicial precedents. In 1881, at twenty-five, he took, as first honor man in his class, the LL.B. at the Columbia Law School, and set up his office.

Mr. Taylor was never the sort of person who left things as he found them, and it was wholly characteristic that within two years of entering practice he published *The Law of Corporations,* in which he carried through our tangle of

419

ad hoc legislation the clear analyses of the Roman Law. It passed through five editions and I believe is still a standard in its field. The study and practice of the law, while enlisting his interest and promising prosperity, failed to satisfy his ambitions. In January 1885, his twenty-ninth year just passed, he jotted down in his diary what was to be the program for all his subsequent activity:

"The conception of what must be either a great book or a total failure [it was neither, he wrote over forty years later]. In my mind I call it *The Ideals of Mankind*. Its purpose will be to show what men throughout the past have desired as best; not desired trivially or sensually, but what they have thought to be best and highest, of most absolute worth, and therefore aimed at. The thought of the book glows within me. I have begun reading and thinking for it, starting with old Sanscrit Indian thought." After ten years of joyous study, the two thick volumes of *Ancient Ideals, a Study of Intellectual and Spiritual Growth from Early Times to the Establishment of Christianity,* made their quiet but effective appearance. Early in their preparation an opportune legacy had enabled the author to close his law office. There had been a humanitarian adventure of several years' duration, in the leadership of a boys' club on Tompkins Square.

Ancient Ideals, as its author objectively admitted, while not a masterpiece, was emphatically far from a failure. There was the obvious disadvantage that the Oriental chapters had to be written at second hand, from translations. As the survey moves into the Greek and Roman field, where the author commanded the languages, the work gains authority and charm. Even now after forty-six years I doubt if there exists in English a better brief survey of the relation between the Hellenistic philosophies and the formulation of the Christian faith. More important, the author here worked out the method later to be more effectively used—that of letting the ancient sages speak for themselves in abundant and skilfully chosen quotations. In reading this book one should not fail to note that it was finished in years when the writer had temporarily returned to something like orthodox Christianity. But through varying phases of doubt and disbelief in creeds, it would be impossible to find a moment when Henry Osborn Taylor's feelings were other than Christian. His ultimate position might be briefly described as one of devout and prayerful Theism colored by strong Christian sympathies.

After *Ancient Ideals* the small but meaty book *The Classical Heritage of the Middle Ages*, 1901, was an affair of only four years of assiduous labor. The scholarship devoted to the task is thorough and profound, and while, especially in the field of the arts, later research has largely superseded certain chapters, this book remains the best survey in English of what we may call Dark Age culture, and it amply earned the author the accolade of "Master" which it drew from his former teacher, Henry Adams. It passed through four editions, a remarkable record of usefulness and longevity for a book of this sort.

Ten more years of work resulted in the two thick volumes of *The Mediaeval Mind: a History of the Development of Thought and Expression in the Middle Ages*—the author's most widely-read book. Here the boy who in his 'teens was reading Hallam's *History of Mediaeval Literature* came fully to his own. There was and is nothing in English that makes the noble quest of the Middle Ages for a perhaps impossible intellectual and religious certitude, so clearly and persuasively reveal itself. In that moment when the established "philological syndicate" in our universities was romantically exaggerating the generally rather slight value of mediaeval literature in the vernacular, Mr. Taylor went unswervingly to the real point, that the best thinking and choicest feeling of the Middle Ages was with singularly few exceptions expressed in its Latin literature. Thirty years ago it required a kind of genius to form a judgment that now seems obvious, if only because meanwhile there have been thousands of good readers of *The Mediaeval Mind*. For ten years with unfailing gusto Mr. Taylor read up and down the *Patrologia Latina* and kindred massive tomes, giving the gist of chapters where the gist was enough, now and then pouncing on a passage eloquent enough to call for translation—a descriptive and objective method on the whole, but description resting on fine literary discrimination, objectively always conscious of implicit human values and ever fraught with personal sympathy and admiration.

Midway in the preparation of his *magnum opus*, at forty-nine, Henry Osborn Taylor exchanged an apparently confirmed old bachelorhood for the hand and heart of Julia Isham. There had been earlier devotions, candidly and charmingly avowed in his autobiography, *Values and Verities*. Indeed, as he has somewhere written, an ideal devotion to a good and lovely woman was from his youth a primal need of his being. This capacity for devotion was finally focussed in an ideal marriage. Lovely in person and in intelligence, admirably generous and sympathetic in public and private relations, Julia Isham's wealth raised her husband's modest prosperity to something like affluence. The spacious apartment appropriately overlooking the mediaeval mass of Bertram Goodhue's St. Bartholomew's, Knowles House, at Cobalt (enlarged into an unpretentious mansion, with delectable dependencies in the way of guest houses amid gardens) offered a constant and thoughtful hospitality to guests who were personages in science and letters, to guests who were merely aspiring, to guests who needed only quiet with untaxing cordiality. Julia Isham knew the value of her husband's historical works, shared his predilections with the most intelligent sympathy—and left him as free to pursue his scholarly task as he had been in old bachelorhood.

Well before the ink on the proof sheets of *The Mediaeval Mind* had dried, Mr. Taylor had started another comprehensive work which appeared nine years later, in 1920, under the title *Thought and Expression in the Sixteenth Century*. The scope of the book was broader than the title, for the

whole period ordinarily called the Renaissance—a term Mr.
Taylor disliked, as denying historic continuity—was treated.
In comparison with *The Mediaeval Mind* the theme was
unfavorable, in a measure uncongenial. There was lacking
that coherence which religious endeavor had brought to the
Middle Ages; there were already a number of excellent books
on the subject. Mr. Taylor could bring to this well-worked
theme only his rare gift of selective documentation and a
fuller attention to scientific matters than his predecessors
had devoted. So *Thought and Expression* perhaps has made
less general impression than *Ancient Ideals* and *The Mediaeval Mind*. Yet as a specialist in the Renaissance I know of
no book in the field that provides better stealing, while, more
broadly, Mr. Taylor brought out with peculiar emphasis the
prophetic, one may say the incipiently modern quality of
much Renaissance thinking and feeling.

He was now sixty-four, with a life-work, the quantity and
quality of which only a few professional scholars have surpassed, behind him. He had earned release from the long
days at the New York Public Library, and a reasonable
enjoyment of his slowly and solidly won prestige. While I
sometimes regret that he did not round out his survey of
civilization with two more thick volumes on modern ideals,
I believe he was wise in regarding the purely historical part
of his work as finished. Then I recall that in the handful of
small books which were the recreation rather than the task
of his later years, Mr. Taylor after all discussed discerningly
many of the leading ideas and discoveries of modern times.
These little books also represented the need of synthesis, of
pulling together as functioning forces the ideals which he
had earlier treated descriptively. In particular these little
books, which perhaps represent his highest literary accomplishment, gave him the opportunity to express his final religious convictions, and this he did rather by charming and
very personal adumbrations, than by the customary formula-
tions. I feel some treason to my friend in now attempting

even a loose formulation of deep experiences which he chose to leave undefined. Yet the matter is interesting as locating the last ditch of a naturally devout soul in a time of much doubt and negation. Perhaps Mr. Taylor's last ditch was that of such great Victorians as Tennyson. He believed in a God who, while not omnipotent, was good, powerful, and purposeful. He believed in prayer as worship of this God, even if one asked for nothing and was not sure that such prayer was heard. He believed that Christ was our fullest revelation of God as Ruler and Father. He held hope that by some providential economy personal influence may be immortal, but in his latest thinking he felt that the human individual was not fitted for immortality. I fancy his final religious position was not far from that of the God-intoxicated Jew, Spinoza, of whom he wrote with admirable insight and sympathy in *Human Values and Verities*.

As a philosopher he held that the proper human aim was a stable and noble happiness, that such happiness could only be attained by the satisfaction of all our faculties—mental, volitional, emotional. I cannot recall that he ever quoted Pascal, yet I know that he would have agreed with the sage of Port Royal that "The heart has its reasons, which reason does not know." All the same, there was much of the rationalist in him. While unwilling to deny the affirmations of hope and aspiration, he felt they must ultimately be referred to reason as a sort of Supreme Court, but a court that should act not too legalistically, but with tenderness and respect for all human needs.

This is not the time to enumerate these little and charming books. Especially noteworthy among them perhaps is that tiny classic of an autobiography, *Values and Verities*, with its accompanying volume of general commentary under the same title, and his last book, *A Historian's Creed*. The latter contains what seems to me his finest and most personal achievement simply as a man of letters, the essay "The Soul of Archilochus." In it is imagined the soul of the Greek poet surviving through the centuries, ever responding to new and finer ideals. It is a precise and eloquent allegory of the author's own pilgrim's progress through the aspiring ages. It was a fitting valedictory, and the dedication always moves me as do certain ineffable brief lyrics—

TO THE MEMORY
OF MY WIFE
JULIA ISHAM
A LITTLE BOOK
TO
SO GREAT A MEMORY

Mr. Taylor was a tiny, agile, at times peppery man. When I first met him he was in the early fifties, and he seemed to me then to be in hale and frosty old age. Twenty-five years later, and until the illness of his penultimate year, he seemed to me to grow no older in body or mind. He was kindly, but on occasion could be waspish and a little formidable. "My mind is tolerant, but my temper is not," he has written several times and most self-understandingly in his autobiographical pages. He never learned to bear fools gladly. As his contemporaries passed on, he easily made friendly relations with young persons, but he insisted that only such of the young as had read *The Mediaeval Mind* should be asked to tea. In his last two years, after the death of his wife and an almost miraculous rally from a prostrating pneumonia he was ready and even glad to go to an unknown, perhaps to no destination. It was enough that he had lived so richly and abundantly.

He never sought honors, but they came to him manifold, and he frankly enjoyed them—honorary doctorates from Wesleyan, Columbia, and Harvard, membership and often office in esteemed scholarly societies here and abroad. When less than a year before his death I had the high privilege of proposing him for our membership, I found that several of my colleagues to whom I wrote in his behalf supposed he had been long a member, but, like too many of us, had the bad habit of not attending meetings. At our last meeting he made a brief and amiable appearance, but he never physically occupied his chair, No. 47. But for the tablet on chair 47 bearing his name, and that name on our rolls, our annals would be much the poorer.

GEORGE DE FOREST BRUSH

BY ROYAL CORTISSOZ

GEORGE DE FOREST BRUSH was fortunate in his epoch. Born in 1855, he came to maturity in the seventies and shared in the spirit then promoted by the rise of leaders who were destined to give a new lease of life to American art. He was a contemporary of John La Farge, Winslow Homer, George Inness and Abbott Thayer, to whom something like a golden age in our school of painting is due, an age remarkable for its pursuit of beauty and good craftsmanship. He followed that pursuit with intense devotion and it was inevitable that he should have been elected a member of the Academy of Arts and Letters in 1910, entering as by a high prerogative an organization which fosters alike respect for tradition and the play of individuality. In the series of exhibitions which the Academy has held there is none to be recalled as more in harmony with its aims, or more distinguished, than the one of works by Brush which was arranged here in 1933. It illustrated the art of a man whose innate conservatism never quenched his creative fire.

Little biographical information concerning him is available. We know that Shelbyville, Tenn., was his birthplace and that he died at Hanover, N. H., in April, 1941. We know that like so many American artists he was trained in Paris, under Gérôme, and that early in his career he saw much of Indian life in the West, and painted it. We know that he travelled abroad, especially in Italy. We know finally that he lived a long life at his home in Dublin, N. H., and that he was evenly successful, the recipient of many honors. But on the whole personal details are scant. This may be regrettable but his true history is widespread, for all men to see. It is written in his works.

These had their origin in a decisively spiritual nature. Some words of his own, written on Thayer, give a clue to the point of view which he held in his time of pupilage and to which he was ever faithful. "Coming into that strange life of the Paris Latin Quarter," he says, "I know many of the young Americans, along with myself, were stunned by it. It seemed at first a great shock . . . Abbott was the influence that I know must have held many a young man up to an ideal of conduct. It was his stand as against the drift of the Quarter that endeared him to many of us. It is what attracted me to him." He was the more easily attracted to the white-souled painter implied in this passage, the painter who became his lifelong comrade, because his own wagon was spontaneously hitched to a star. Yet this involved him in no hazy dreaming. On the contrary he gave himself up whole-heartedly to the disciplinary admonitions of Gérôme. No remarks of his were ever more characteristic than those which he once made in a lecture: "A student learns nothing until he comes under a master. . . . We must not run after new things. We must find out what the masters knew."

Gérôme was a master of form, draughtsmanship and composition and Brush was so responsive that his early drawing is a little hard, a little inelastic, like that of his teacher, and there is obvious emulation of the latter in one of the first of the American's works, "The Sculptor and the King." It is markedly in the manner of Gérôme. But Brush soon got into his stride, exercising an individualized and very beautiful kind of drawing and in certain of his Indian subjects, painted long ago, like "The Indian and the Lily" or "The Silence Broken," it was clear that he was already his own man. He was as clearly himself in portraiture, in his designs from pagan mythology and in the "Mother and Child" pictures

427

which have done perhaps most to establish his fame. In these he was touched to some extent by the old Florentine and Venetian schools, but it is significant that he was never moved to adopt the Madonna motive from them but left his compositions essentially American, essentially the expression of his own genius. They are lovely studies of their theme and, besides having tenderness, they reach an impressive plane in the matter of technique.

I have alluded to his draughtsmanship but must return to it for a moment. It tells exquisitely in his pencil studies of form and drapery. It might seem exaggeration to bring in at this point the illustrious names of Leonardo and Dürer. In the definition of form he is neither as sensitive as the one nor as powerful as the other. But I cannot help thinking of them as I remember his mastery over the figure or over the fold of a robe, the fineness and precision of his touch, and especially the beauty with which he invested his work, whether in black and white or in oils. It is as a great craftsman and a noble idealist, and, I may add, as a lovable man, that we must bid him farewell.

WILLIAM MITCHELL KENDALL
BY ROYAL CORTISSOZ

I WISH THAT as a prelude to comment on the career of the distinguished Academician who left us on August 8th, 1941, William Mitchell Kendall, I could bring to you some sense of the charm of his personality. We were friends for years, beginning in the office of McKim, Mead and White, where he was a leading draughtsman, and our alliance was broken only by his death. In all that long period, starting in the early '80's, there was never a diminution of the sweetness of his companionship. He had a warm, generous nature and it was enriched by a quick sense of humor and even by a playfulness which often gave to this tall, slender New Englander, seemingly one of the gravest men in the world, an accent of gayety. I came to love it peculiarly when we foregathered in Rome, many years ago. We wandered constantly amongst the historic monuments and Kendall was an ideal guide to them, an insatiable devotee of the grand style, of which he was to become in due course himself a notable exponent. But though he could be, and was, serious and scholarly in our explorations, he could also be merry and as I remember him then I remember, too, his frequent laughter. He was, in a word, a man of whom to think pleasantly, cheerfully, and it is as such that I would recall him.

There went with his buoyant vivacity a strong inclination toward discipline in the arts, a strong feeling for the fundamental admonitions of the great masters. Born at Jamaica Plain, Mass., in 1856, he went early to Harvard and there fell delightedly under the influence of Charles Eliot Norton. Directly after his graduation from the university in 1876, he passed through two years of severe training at the Massachusetts Institute of Technology. Then followed several years of European travel and in 1882 his entrance, well fitted for an architectural life, into the office of McKim, Mead and White. He fell into perfect harmony with McKim's austere genius. He continued with the firm until the end, finally becoming its senior partner. But it is of his spirit in architecture rather than of his official status, so to say, that I would prefer to speak. All his professional life he was in close communion with that grand style to which I have alluded in touching upon our Roman days together. He had an instinct for it, for heroic nobility in mass and for refinement in detail. He knew how to impart stateliness to a design and he could fashion a good moulding, one of the prime tests of an architect's ability. Laboring with the same enthusiasm upon a majestic pile like the New York Post Office or such a little masterpiece as the Morgan Library, he exercised a gift for the simplicity that is never bald, the measured restraint that is never cold.

WILLIAM MITCHELL KENDALL

And he could be versatile, as he showed when he designed the New York Post Office, and the New York Municipal Building. I must cite likewise, as a manifestation of his range, the lovely Arlington Bridge at Washington, which, I may add, was a work done in his later years in which he took particular pride. It is a monumental structure and it is, besides, an illustration of the grace that was within his scope. In all that he did there is expressed something of the magic of Rome, the ancient city and the city of the Renaissance. Rome was, indeed, his spiritual home, though he knew Greece and loved its temples and knew, to be sure, much of Europe. It was by a kind of predestination that he became a Charter Member of the American Academy in Rome, long served as a Trustee and on various of its committees. For the last twelve years of his life he acted as its Second Vice President. It was Kendall who designed the Roman habitation of the Academy. If all this testifies to his affection for the institution founded by his mentor and associate, Charles F. McKim, the founder of the Academy, it testifies as clearly to his unshakable fidelity to the Roman tradition. Kendall was a shining exemplar of that recognition of what is salutary in the lessons of the past which marks the healthily conservative architect.

He studied the past with unremitting zeal, but he lived also, and joyously, in the present. He was an exacting gourmet and he was a discriminating lover of music, especially operatic music. He travelled widely and he was a tireless reader. A finished man of the world, he had stored within himself many of the secrets of the art of living. Best of all, to end as I began, he had the unconscious art of making friends. He left a mark upon the architecture of his time and he left one upon the hearts of those who knew him. Elected to this Academy in 1929, he was one of its most significant members and his memory will be cherished here.

CHARLES DOWNER HAZEN

BY WILLIAM LYON PHELPS

IN THE BRIGHT AGES of the nineteenth century, when I was a sophomore at Yale, we had an instructor in Latin, Mr. Ambrose Tighe, who made his subject so interesting that the Faculty refused to reappoint him. I remember many of his *obiter dicta*. He said there were two qualities in a literary style that, when united, produced masterpieces. These two qualities were Sincerity and Luminosity. Caesar's Commentaries on the Gallic and on the Civil Wars had more sincerity than luminosity, and Cicero's orations had more luminosity than sincerity. At about that time, for my own pleasure, which is the best reason for reading anything, I was reading late at night Mommsen's *History of Rome*. And I found that Mommsen made a somewhat similar comparison between the *oratory* of Caesar and that of Cicero. He said that Cicero's speeches had the eloquence of rounded periods, whereas those of Curio, the brilliant lieutenant of Caesar, had, like those of his master, the eloquence of deeply felt thought. I have ever since applied those two tests to written and oral work.

Charles Downer Hazen was born in Vermont on the 17th of March, 1868, and died on the 18th of September, 1941. He took his bachelor's degree at Dartmouth, and pursued advance studies, frequently catching up with them, at Johns Hopkins, Göttingen, Berlin and Paris. He was professor of History at Smith College for ten years, and in 1916 became professor of History at Columbia University. In 1920-21, he was professor of History at Strasbourg, which then was a city in France. He was a member of many learned societies in Europe and in America, was elected to our National Institute of Arts and Letters in 1918, and to the American Academy in 1924. To enumerate his honorary degrees and decorations would take too much of those realities, space and time; but it should be remembered that no American was more beloved in France. He was a member of the *Société d'Histoire Moderne*

431

(in Paris), of the *Institut International d'Histoire de la Révolution Française* and was *Chevalier Légion d'Honneur*.

The subject to which he devoted the most of his time as a scholar appears in his first published work in 1897, *Contemporary American Opinion of the French Revolution*, although he never forgot his own native New England, as is shown by his next book, *Old Northampton*. His publications were numerous and important and gave him a well-earned international reputation: *Europe Since 1815*, *The French Revolution, Alsace-Lorraine under German Rule, Fifty Years of Europe*, etc. In addition to many papers showing special research, two of his books were studied by many thousands of American undergraduates, *Modern European History* and *Modern Europe*.

Much of his writing not only shows literary distinction united to scrupulous research; it exhibits those qualities recommended to me by my teacher and by the great German historian; Dr. Hazen did succeed in combining luminosity and sincerity, and his stirring pages often reveal the eloquence of deeply felt thought.

Apart from natural gifts increased by faithful and devoted application, there is a reason for the excellence of his style. It was an emanation of a beautiful personality. I do not hesitate to describe his character by this adjective. I had the honor of knowing Dr. Hazen very well. No one could come into contact with him without feeling the beauty of his mind and heart. He had a masculine modesty, a kindness of temper, a consideration for others, a gentleness of temperament. These qualities not only gave a radiance to his conversation, they illuminated his books.

No wonder the French scholars and men of letters, who understand and recognize the finest shades of art and of character, respected him and loved him. He was equally at home in Vermont and Paris; because he was always the same man.

He was extremely fortunate in his marriage to Sara Sefton Duryea in 1901. Her grace and charm are felt by all who meet her.

432